P9-CFG-269

America's
TEST KITCHEN

ALSO BY THE EDITORS AT AMERICA'S TEST KITCHEN

The America's Test Kitchen
Healthy Family Cookbook

The America's Test Kitchen
Family Baking Book

The America's Test Kitchen
Family Cookbook

The Best Simple Recipes

AMERICA'S TEST KITCHEN ANNUALS:

The Best of America's Test Kitchen
(2007-2011 Editions)

Cooking for Two (2009 and 2010 Editions)

Light & Healthy (2010 and 2011 Editions)

THE COOK'S COUNTRY SERIES:

Cook's Country Blue Ribbon Desserts

Cook's Country Best Potluck Recipes

Cook's Country Best Lost Suppers

Cook's Country Best Grilling Recipes

The Cook's Country Cookbook

America's Best Lost Recipes

THE TV COMPANION SERIES:

America's Test Kitchen: The TV Companion
Cookbook 2011

The Complete America's Test Kitchen
TV Show Cookbook

America's Test Kitchen TV
Companion Book 2009

Behind the Scenes with
America's Test Kitchen

Test Kitchen Favorites

Cooking at Home with
America's Test Kitchen

America's Test Kitchen Live!

Inside America's Test Kitchen

Here in America's Test Kitchen

The America's Test Kitchen Cookbook

THE BEST RECIPE SERIES:

The Best One-Dish Suppers

Soups, Stews & Chilis

More Best Recipes

The New Best Recipe

The Best Skillet Recipes

The Best Slow & Easy Recipes

The Best Chicken Recipes

The Best International Recipe

The Best Make-Ahead Recipe

The Best 30-Minute Recipe

The Best Light Recipe

The Cook's Illustrated Guide
to Grilling and Barbecue

Best American Side Dishes

Cover & Bake

Steaks, Chops, Roasts, and Ribs

Baking Illustrated

Restaurant Favorites at Home

Perfect Vegetables

Italian Classics

American Classics

**FOR A FULL LISTING OF ALL OUR BOOKS
OR TO ORDER TITLES:**

http://www.cooksillustrated.com

http://www.americastestkitchen.com

or call 800-611-0759

PRAISE FOR OTHER AMERICA'S TEST KITCHEN TITLES

"Forget about marketing hype, designer labels and pretentious entrées: This is an unblinking, unbedazzled guide to the Beardian good-cooking ideal."
THE WALL STREET JOURNAL ON
THE BEST OF AMERICA'S TEST KITCHEN 2009

"Expert bakers and novices scared of baking's requisite exactitude can all learn something from this hefty, all-purpose home baking volume."
PUBLISHERS WEEKLY ON
THE AMERICA'S TEST KITCHEN FAMILY BAKING BOOK

"Scrupulously tested regional and heirloom recipes."
NEW YORK TIMES ON
THE COOK'S COUNTRY COOKBOOK

"If you're hankering for old-fashioned pleasures, look no further."
PEOPLE MAGAZINE ON
AMERICA'S BEST LOST RECIPES

"This tome definitely raises the bar for all-in-one, basic, must-have cookbooks. . . . Kimball and his company have scored another hit."
PORTLAND OREGONIAN ON
THE AMERICA'S TEST KITCHEN FAMILY COOKBOOK

"A foolproof, go-to resource for everyday cooking."
PUBLISHERS WEEKLY ON
THE AMERICA'S TEST KITCHEN FAMILY COOKBOOK

"The strength of the Best Recipe series lies in the sheer thoughtfulness and details of the recipes."
PUBLISHERS WEEKLY ON
THE BEST RECIPE SERIES

"These dishes taste as luxurious as their full-fat siblings. Even desserts are terrific."
PUBLISHERS WEEKLY ON
THE BEST LIGHT RECIPE

"Further proof that practice makes perfect, if not transcendent. . . . If an intermediate cook follows the directions exactly, the results will be better than takeout or Mom's."
NEW YORK TIMES ON
THE NEW BEST RECIPE

"Like a mini-cooking school, the detailed instructions and illustrations ensure that even the most inexperienced cook can follow these recipes with success."
PUBLISHERS WEEKLY ON
BEST AMERICAN SIDE DISHES

"Makes one-dish dinners a reality for average cooks, with honest ingredients and detailed make-ahead instructions."
NEW YORK TIMES ON
COVER & BAKE

"Sturdy, stick-to-your-ribs fare that deserves a place at the table."
PORTLAND OREGONIAN ON
COOK'S COUNTRY BEST LOST SUPPERS

"The best instructional book on baking this reviewer has seen."
LIBRARY JOURNAL (STARRED REVIEW) ON
BAKING ILLUSTRATED

"A must-have for anyone into our nation's cooking traditions—and a good reference, too."
LOS ANGELES DAILY NEWS ON
AMERICAN CLASSICS

"If you've always wanted to make real Italian dishes as close to the Italian way as we can make them in America, here's a cookbook that shows you how."
PITTSBURGH POST-GAZETTE ON
ITALIAN CLASSICS

*Slow*Cooker
REVOLUTION

ONE TEST KITCHEN. 30 SLOW COOKERS.
200 AMAZING RECIPES.

BY THE EDITORS AT
America's Test Kitchen

PHOTOGRAPHY BY
Keller + Keller

ADDITIONAL PHOTOGRAPHY BY
Daniel J. van Ackere
Carl Tremblay

Copyright © 2011
by the Editors at America's Test Kitchen

AMERICA'S TEST KITCHEN
17 Station Street, Brookline, MA 02445
Library of Congress
Cataloging-in-Publication Data
The Editors at America's Test Kitchen

AMERICA'S TEST KITCHEN
SLOW COOKER REVOLUTION:
One Test Kitchen. 30 Slow Cookers.
200 Amazing Recipes.

1st Edition
Paperback: $26.95 US
ISBN-13: 978-1-933615-69-1
ISBN-10: 1-933615-69-9

1. Cooking. 1. Title
2. 2011

Manufactured in the United States

10 9 8 7 6 5 4 3

DISTRIBUTED BY
America's Test Kitchen
17 Station Street, Brookline, MA 02445

EDITORIAL DIRECTOR: Jack Bishop
EXECUTIVE EDITOR: Elizabeth Carduff
EXECUTIVE FOOD EDITOR: Julia Collin Davison
ASSOCIATE EDITOR: Dan Zuccarello
TEST COOKS: Chris O'Connor, Jennifer Lalime, Kate Williams
EDITORIAL ASSISTANT: Alyssa King
DESIGN DIRECTOR: Amy Klee
ART DIRECTOR: Greg Galvan
DESIGNER: Beverly Hsu
PHOTOGRAPHY: Keller + Keller and Carl Tremblay
STAFF PHOTOGRAPHER: Daniel J. van Ackere
FOOD STYLING: Mary Jane Sawyer, Marie Piraino
PRODUCTION DIRECTOR: Guy Rochford
SENIOR PRODUCTION MANAGER: Jessica Quirk
SENIOR PROJECT MANAGER: Alice Carpenter
PRODUCTION AND TRAFFIC COORDINATOR: Kate Hux
WORKFLOW AND IMAGING MANAGER: Andrew Mannone
PRODUCTION AND IMAGING SPECIALISTS: Judy Blomquist,
Heather Dube, Lauren Pettapiece
COPYEDITOR: Cheryl Redmond
PROOFREADER: Debra Hudak
INDEXER: Elizabeth Parson

PICTURED ON FRONT COVER: Sausage Lasagna (page 234)
PICTURED OPPOSITE TITLE PAGE: Santa Fe Meatloaf (page 192)
PICTURED ON BACK OF JACKET: Pork Loin with Cranberries and Orange
(page 115), Easy Barbecued Ribs (page 148), Bachelor Beef Stew
(page 56), French Toast Casserole (page 282)

Contents

Preface

The promise of the microwave was universal in its application. One could use it for reheating leftovers, to be sure, but one was told that it was also a lovely timesaving way to make gourmet meals including meat, poultry, fish, vegetables, and desserts. And then there was a raft of pressure cooker cookbooks that offered similar promises—I know since I actually cooked a cheesecake in one! (Very hard to get it out as you can imagine.) And, of course, bread machines became all the rage and the instruction books came with all sorts of other recipes for jams, jellies, and the like. As one of my Vermont neighbors said about a bagel recipe using a bread machine, "That's going to make one really BIG bagel!"

So here we are again, poised to offer you the same line about the slow cooker. After all, we call this work *Slow Cooker Revolution,* a title that promises a great deal from a test kitchen that we hope you trust. So, let's get to the bottom line: Do we deliver?

Let's start at the beginning. To do the testing, we had to purchase two dozen slow cookers and had to get one entire wall of the test kitchen rewired to accommodate them. And this was by far our most complicated project to date since testing one version of one recipe lasted all day or overnight. But, in the end, we completely rethought this modest home appliance and transformed it from an appliance of convenience to one of almost magical transformation.

The first lesson was that most slow-cooker recipes are mediocre at best because, most of the time, one cannot simply dump a bunch of ingredients into a slow cooker and walk away. One needs to develop flavor using a host of mostly new and interesting techniques contained in this book. Aromatics (onions, garlic, and the like) were often microwaved first with spices and tomato paste to add flavor. The microwave was also helpful to par-cook many hearty vegetables that would otherwise not have become tender. A quick run under a broiler to finish a slow-cooker dish was well worth the additional effort to produce a perfect finishing touch, a glaze on a meatloaf, for example. Soy sauce and tomato paste were secret weapons for building flavor in many of the recipes in this book. Often, it was best to brown meat before putting it in the slow cooker but we did find that many recipes could do without, as with our Hearty Beef Stew.

In addition, we found that the cut of meat made a big difference, either by reducing the amount of prep work or by adding additional flavor. Foil packets were a huge discovery, used to ensure that vegetables did not turn to mush during the long cooking times or to slow down the cooking of chicken. Foil slings made getting dishes like meatloaf or lasagna out of the slow cooker a whole lot easier. (Yes, the lasagna on the front cover of this book was really made in a slow cooker.) When using ground meat, we found that a panade (bread mashed with milk) was essential to keep the meat tender during cooking.

Hundreds of hours of testing proved that chicken should never be cooked on high or for more than six hours on low. Pasta, other than lasagna, should be added raw to the slow cooker and cooked on high. Certain convenience products made the cut, including frozen onions, garlic powder, condensed cheese soup, frozen potato wedges, and store-bought pesto, to name a few.

We even came up with a table of contents that goes way beyond soups and stews. We also offer braises, barbecue, eggs and brunch, casseroles, desserts, and basics. One chapter is even titled Enchiladas, Tacos, and More and includes recipes for burritos, tostadas, and Mexican lasagna. (Easy slow-cooker fillings make these recipes a snap to make.)

We also figured out how to make risotto, polenta, poultry stuffing, mashed potatoes, gravy, and lots of other side dishes. We even invented a recipe that cooks a 7-pound turkey breast in the slow cooker with its own rich gravy. Or try Old-Fashioned Chicken and Dumplings, Maple-Glazed Pork Loin, Tex-Mex Stuffed Bell Peppers (the meat goes in raw), and Easy Barbecued Ribs. Some of my other favorite recipes include Ultimate Lentil Soup, Texas Chili, Fire-Roasted Tomato Sauce, Chicken in a Pot (using a whole chicken), Classic Breakfast Strata with Sausage, and Easy Pesto Meatballs.

Now I don't need 15 new things to do with my food processor, stand mixer, or ice cream machine. I don't need a tomato slicer, an electric pizza oven, or an electric corkscrew (I admit to having a short fling with one of the latter). I've even given up on my pressure cooker, although it does many things very well indeed. I do love my slow cooker because it does so many things well (okay, you need to purchase this book and use it to find out how!) but most of all, it means that dinner is done ahead of time, before I go to work or head outside for the day in the summer. I love that it makes me think ahead so when evening comes I have little to do but enjoy a glass of wine and good company.

With *Slow Cooker Revolution*, I can look forward to better and more interesting meals as well. We are not promising the world but we do promise that these recipes work and that they are a lot tastier than other slow-cooker recipes you may have come across. This may be a small revolution, but a revolution nonetheless. Now you can go out and storm the Bastille and still have dinner waiting when you get home!

CHRISTOPHER KIMBALL
Founder and Editor,
Cook's Illustrated and *Cook's Country*
Host, *America's Test Kitchen* and
Cook's Country from America's Test Kitchen

THE WALL OF SLOW COOKERS IN THE TEST KITCHEN

Slow Cooker 101

Introduction

Slow cookers may be the only modern kitchen appliance that saves the cook time by using more of it rather than less. The appeal, of course, is that with a relatively modest investment of up-front prep time, you can put the ingredients for dinner (or a side dish or dessert) into the slow cooker, turn it on, and walk away for a few hours or a whole day.

As the test kitchen tackled this, our first book of slow-cooker recipes, we had enough experience under our belts to know that creating slow-cooker recipes that were actually as flavorful as traditional recipes would be challenging. (The closed cooking environment doesn't permit much browning or reduction, the keys to flavor development for most cooking methods.) But we set out with some ambitious goals. First and foremost, the recipes would have to taste as good as food prepared on the stovetop or in the oven. Second, the recipes couldn't require an hour of prep time or an arsenal of pots and pans. Recognizing that anyone using a slow cooker is likely a time-pressed home cook, we were determined to include lots of recipes that were essentially easy prep. (Look for the Easy Prep icon throughout the book—these recipes take a minimal amount of prep time, and sometimes none). Finally, we wanted to expand beyond the obvious slow-cooker recipes (such as soups and stews) and develop satisfying casseroles, meatloaves, side dishes, desserts, and a variety of everyday basics that are handy to have around.

With our wish list of recipes and our goals in hand, our team of test cooks, most of whom had never used a slow cooker before this project, faced the harsh realities of slow-cooker recipe development. First, where in our busy test kitchen would more than two dozen slow cookers live? Turns out we had to devote an entire wall of the test kitchen to this endeavor, assemble racks against it to hold the slow cookers, and hire an electrician to upgrade the wiring; we had visions of blown fuses and frustrated test cooks without this dedicated testing area. Next up was how to orchestrate the recipe testing. Just how many recipes could one test cook make in a day? Turns out, about four. And we tested them on high, on low, and for multiple different time ranges. Some days, the team had up to 15 tastings at the very end of the day. But after six months of testing, 1,500 recipes, and more than $20,000 spent on groceries, we had learned a thing or two about using a slow cooker, such as how to build flavor, which shortcuts work, and why some recipes require that you get out a skillet first and others don't. In this section you will find an overview of what we learned while developing the recipes for this book.

Getting Started

CHOOSE THE RIGHT SLOW COOKER

Gone are the days of merely picking out a slow cooker based on size. We found dozens of models, varying not only in size but also in price—from $20 up to a staggering $200. We tested seven slow cookers to find out which one was best (and if we really had to shell out $200). We limited our lineup mainly to oval slow cookers, which can fit a large roast, with capacities of 6 quarts or more, so we could feed a crowd.

Six of the seven models had programmable timers and warming modes, features we like. Clear glass lids are also helpful, as they allow the cook to see through to assess the food as it cooks. Inserts that have handles, which make it easy to remove the insert from the slow cooker, and that can be washed in the dishwasher earned extra points.

To test performance, we made pot roast, meaty tomato sauce, and French onion soup. Ideally, a slow cooker should produce perfect results on all settings. Unfortunately, few of our models did just that. In our testing, we realized that some just didn't get hot enough, while others reached the boiling point. That's the reason some of the models variously gave us pot roast with dry, tough meat or juicy, sliceable meat; we also encountered extra-thick meaty tomato sauces and watery ones; moist, fork-tender ribs and beef as well as shrunken, tough meat. However, a few models did produce good food consistently. Our winner, the affordable **Crock-Pot Touchscreen Slow Cooker** ($129.99), cooked our dinner perfectly. It also had the best control panel (with a timer that counted up to 20 hours even on high); it was simple to set and clearly indicated that the cooker was programmed.

GET TO KNOW YOUR SLOW COOKER

If you already own a slow cooker, you probably think it works like other models. Not so. While ovens are all designed to maintain the same temperature when set to 350 degrees, slow cookers are more like your stovetop—"medium" on your stove is nothing like "medium" on your neighbor's stove. After working with dozens of slow cookers over the years, we've learned that some slow cookers run hot (and fast) while others run cool (and slow). And since slow-cooker recipes come with a time range, knowing how your individual slow cooker runs will be helpful in determining which end of the range will likely yield the best results.

We have done all of our testing using our winning slow cooker, but if you are using a different brand you might find that you need slightly altered cooking times. One quick way to determine how hot or cool your cooker runs is to perform a simple water test. Place 4 quarts of room temperature water in your slow cooker, cover it, and cook on either high or low for six hours, then measure the temperature of the water. Ideally, the water should register between 195 and 205 degrees on an instant-read thermometer. If your cooker runs hotter or cooler, be ready to check the food for doneness either earlier or later than our recipes indicate. Also, we've found that some cookers run hot or cool on just one of the settings (either low or high), so consider checking both if you find you are having problems.

Keys to Slow Cooker Success

PREP YOUR SLOW COOKER

Vegetable oil spray and aluminum foil are used in many recipes where sticking and burning were problematic. We found that for sweet or custardy dishes, sticking and burning were real issues, in part because the side of the slow cooker that faces the heating element (opposite the controls) gets noticeably hotter. See page 225 for information on the foil collar we used to protect many casseroles and the foil sling that allowed us to lift meatloaves, lasagnas, and other dishes out of the insert in one piece for easy serving and more attractive portions.

USE YOUR MICROWAVE

We used the microwave in several ways throughout this book. To save time, we microwaved aromatics (like onion and garlic) and spices to bloom their flavors. This takes just 5 minutes and is much easier than getting out a skillet to cook these ingredients. We also used the microwave to parcook hearty vegetables so they'd emerge from the slow cooker cooked through. We jump-started the cooking of some key ingredients and released excess moisture or fat (we microwaved potatoes, cabbage, and more), and we cooked more delicate vegetables so they could be added to the slow cooker at the end of the cooking time—still colorful and crisp-tender. For more details about how we used the microwave, see page 71.

SOMETIMES THE OVEN COMES IN HANDY

Yes, we know you are using your slow cooker to avoid using your oven, but there are times when it offers a convenient way to get a recipe ready for the slow cooker or finish it properly at the end. For instance, we used it to jump-start the cooking of our Sweet and Sour Cocktail Meatballs (page 187) and render off excess fat before adding them to the slow cooker; Since this recipe makes 60 meatballs, the oven was a more practical way to get the job done than microwaving multiple batches of meatballs. To infuse our Shredded Tomatillo-Chicken Filling (page 204) with the tart essence of tomatillos and lots of smoky flavor, we broiled them and the aromatics first. And for a sticky, glazy finish for meatloaves, ribs, and more, the broiler was the easy solution.

COOK ON LOW WHEN POSSIBLE

We understand that you want options when it comes to using a slow cooker; sometimes it is useful to cook a recipe all day while you're at work, while other times you want it done in just a few hours. So when possible, we've given you two options—one time range for using the high setting and one for the low setting. That said, given a choice, we prefer to use the slow cooker on the low setting, as we've found that recipes cooked on low emerge more moist and tender at the end of the long cooking time than recipes cooked on high.

COOK CHICKEN ON LOW FOR UP TO 6 HOURS

Although many recipes cook chicken all day, we found that led to dry, stringy chicken that no one would really want to eat. For tender, flavorful chicken every time, keep the heat level on low and mind our time ranges. For more information about chicken in the slow cooker, see page 85.

BROWN YOUR MEAT—SOMETIMES

There is no hard-and-fast rule about browning meat before placing it in the slow cooker. In many of our recipes, usually ones that used a lot of spicy or aromatic ingredients, we found that we could get away with not browning. But there were instances where for a deep flavor base, we needed to get out the skillet and brown the meat. When it comes to ground beef or turkey, with few exceptions we found that browning was important for meat that was tender and not grainy at the end of the long cooking time.

KEEP GROUND MEAT TENDER

Through extensive testing, we learned that the ground meat in chilis and pasta sauces turned tough and sandy by the end of the long cooking time. The solution to this problem was twofold. First, we found that in addition to browning the meat, it was important to add a panade, a mixture of bread and dairy, for tenderness. We simply mixed together the panade until soft and uniform and then gently combined it with the ground meat before browning it. These simple steps made all the difference.

MAKE A FOIL PACKET

Depending on the recipe, the cooking time, and how the vegetables are cut, it is sometimes necessary to wrap vegetables in an aluminum foil packet to keep them from overcooking. The packet helps keep them out of the cooking liquid and slows down their cooking, protecting their flavors from fading. Sometimes we also found it necessary to wrap chicken in a foil packet—for instance in Cassoulet (page 106), the foil packet kept the chicken thighs from drying out during the extra time needed to cook the beans and the pork ribs. For more information about making a foil packet, see page 60.

ADD SOY SAUCE AND TOMATO PASTE FOR MEATY FLAVOR

Soy sauce in beef stew? Tomato paste in chicken soup? We found that microwaving tomato paste with aromatics could mimic the meaty flavor usually achieved only by browning meat; also, when added to some of our chicken stews, it added meaty richness. Soy sauce appears throughout the book as well—just a small amount added to many soups, stews, or braises added surprising depth of flavor without calling attention to itself.

DON'T SKIMP ON AROMATICS

You'll see a hefty amount of onions, garlic, herbs, and other flavorful ingredients in our recipes. This is because the moist heat environment and long cooking times that come with the slow cooker tend to mute flavors. So chop those onions. Also, many recipes need a flavor boost at the end of the cooking time, which is why we often finish with fresh herbs, lemon juice, extra chipotle chiles, or other flavorful ingredients.

USE THE RIGHT THICKENER

Since there is no opportunity for sauces and stews to thicken naturally in the moist environment of the slow cooker, thickeners are necessary for many soups, stews, braises, and sauces. After years of testing flour, cornstarch, and tapioca, we found that for lightly thickened sauces, tapioca was the easiest solution and could be added right at the start. But if any more than ¼ cup was used, the tapioca pearls were too noticeable in the final dish. For very thick stews and gravies, you need to go a more traditional route and build a roux-based sauce in a skillet using flour and butter.

FRENCH ONION SOUP

Soups

Old-Fashioned Chicken Noodle Soup

Serves 6 to 8   **Cooking Time** 4 to 6 hours on Low

✔ **WHY THIS RECIPE WORKS:** Making chicken noodle soup with a deep, satisfying flavor requires a few tricks when using a slow cooker. First, we used a combination of bone-in chicken thighs and breasts. The cooked and shredded breast meat tasted nice in the final soup, but the bone-in thighs really gave the broth its flavor during the long cooking time. And for maximum flavor, we found it necessary to brown the chicken thighs (and remove the skin) before adding them to the slow cooker. To prevent the breast meat from overcooking (which happens when there is a lot of liquid in the slow cooker), we wrapped the chicken breast inside a foil packet. Do not try to cook the noodles in the slow cooker or they will turn out mushy and taste raw.

1½ pounds bone-in, skin-on chicken thighs, trimmed
    Salt and pepper
1   tablespoon vegetable oil
3   carrots, peeled and chopped medium
2   celery ribs, chopped medium
1   onion, minced
3   garlic cloves, minced
1   tablespoon tomato paste
2   teaspoons minced fresh thyme or ½ teaspoon dried
⅛   teaspoon red pepper flakes
8   cups low-sodium chicken broth
2   bay leaves
1   (12-ounce) bone-in, skin-on split chicken breast, trimmed
1½ ounces wide egg noodles (about 1 cup)
½   cup frozen peas
2   tablespoons minced fresh parsley

1. Dry chicken thighs with paper towels and season with salt and pepper. Heat oil in 12-inch skillet over medium-high heat until just smoking. Brown chicken thighs well on both sides, 6 to 8 minutes. Transfer to plate, let cool slightly, and discard skin.

2. Pour off all but 1 tablespoon fat left in pan. Add carrots, celery, and onion and cook over medium heat until vegetables are softened, 7 to 10 minutes. Stir in garlic, tomato paste, thyme, and red pepper flakes and cook until fragrant, about 30 seconds. Stir in 1 cup chicken broth, scraping up any browned bits; transfer to slow cooker.

3. Stir remaining 7 cups broth and bay leaves into slow cooker. Nestle browned chicken with any accumulated juice into slow cooker. Season chicken breast with salt and pepper, wrap in foil packet (see page 60), and lay on top of soup. Cover and cook until chicken is tender, 4 to 6 hours on low.

4. Remove foil packet, open it carefully (watch for steam), and transfer chicken breast to cutting board. Transfer chicken thighs to cutting board. Let all chicken cool slightly, then shred into bite-size pieces (see page 21), discarding skin and bones. Let soup settle for 5 minutes, then remove fat from surface using large spoon. Discard bay leaves.

5. Cook egg noodles in boiling salted water until tender, then drain. Stir cooked noodles, shredded chicken, and peas into soup and let sit until heated through, about 5 minutes. Stir in parsley, season with salt and pepper to taste, and serve.

Farmhouse Chicken and Corn Chowder

Serves 6 to 8   **Cooking Time** 4 to 6 hours on Low

✔ **WHY THIS RECIPE WORKS:** Creating a creamy and rich but fresh-flavored chowder in a slow cooker takes a few tricks. Our version of this chowder uses bacon, red potatoes, and cream for a chowder-y background, while chicken, corn, and bell peppers take center stage. We added meaty, boneless chicken thighs directly to the chowder (no browning required) and then shredded them when they were cooked through. To get good corn flavor into the broth, we found a can of creamed corn did wonders and required zero prep other than microwaving it and adding it at the end. Stirring freshly steamed bell peppers (we used the microwave again) into the soup before serving ensured that they stayed crisp-tender and colorful. Don't omit the chipotle chile or fresh herbs; they add valuable flavor to the broth.

2	slices bacon, minced
4	teaspoons vegetable oil
2	onions, minced
6	garlic cloves, minced
1	tablespoon tomato paste
2	teaspoons minced fresh thyme or ½ teaspoon dried
¼	cup all-purpose flour
5	cups low-sodium chicken broth
1	pound red potatoes (about 3 medium), scrubbed and cut into ½-inch chunks
1	carrot, peeled and sliced ¼ inch thick
2	bay leaves
1½	pounds boneless, skinless chicken thighs, trimmed Salt and pepper
1	red bell pepper, stemmed, seeded, and cut into ½-inch pieces (see page 91)
1	(15-ounce) can creamed corn
½	cup heavy cream
2	teaspoons minced canned chipotle chile in adobo
3	tablespoons minced fresh basil or cilantro

1. Cook bacon in 12-inch skillet over medium heat until crisp, 5 to 7 minutes. Stir in 1 tablespoon oil and onions and cook until softened, 5 to 7 minutes. Stir in garlic, tomato paste, and thyme and cook until fragrant, about 30 seconds. Stir in flour and cook for 1 minute. Whisk in 2 cups broth, scraping up any browned bits; transfer to slow cooker.

2. Stir remaining 3 cups broth, potatoes, carrot, and bay leaves into slow cooker. Season chicken with salt and pepper and nestle into slow cooker. Cover and cook until chicken is tender, 4 to 6 hours on low.

3. Transfer chicken to cutting board, let cool slightly, then shred into bite-size pieces (see page 21). Let soup settle for 5 minutes, then remove fat from surface using large spoon. Discard bay leaves.

4. Microwave bell pepper with remaining teaspoon oil in bowl, stirring occasionally, until softened, about 3 minutes. In separate bowl, microwave creamed corn until hot, about 3 minutes.

5. Stir softened peppers, hot creamed corn, shredded chicken, cream, and chipotles into soup and let sit until heated through, about 5 minutes. Stir in basil, season with salt and pepper to taste, and serve.

Tortilla Soup

Serves 6 to 8   **Cooking Time** 4 to 6 hours on Low

✔ **WHY THIS RECIPE WORKS:** This turbocharged, south-of-the-border chicken soup features a spicy, tomatoey broth overflowing with garnishes and tender shredded chicken. To replicate the traditionally deep, smoky roasted flavor of the broth in a slow cooker, typically achieved by charring the vegetables, we browned some of the vegetables in a skillet before adding them to the slow cooker. Using chipotle chiles in adobo sauce (which are dried, smoked jalapeños in a spicy chile sauce) also adds some smokiness along with a spicy kick. For even more heat, include the jalapeño seeds. Don't omit the garnishes; the flavor of the soup depends heavily on them.

1	tablespoon vegetable oil
2	tomatoes (about 12 ounces), cored and chopped medium
1	onion, minced
2	jalapeño chiles, stemmed, seeded, and minced
6	garlic cloves, minced
4	teaspoons minced canned chipotle chile in adobo
1	tablespoon tomato paste
8	cups low-sodium chicken broth
10	cilantro stems, tied together with twine
1½	pounds boneless, skinless chicken thighs, trimmed
	Salt and pepper

GARNISHES

4	cups crushed tortilla chips
2	cups crumbled Cotija cheese or shredded Monterey Jack cheese (about 8 ounces)
1	ripe avocado, pitted and cut into ½-inch pieces (see page 132)
½	cup sour cream
½	cup minced fresh cilantro
	Lime wedges, for serving

1. Heat oil in 12-inch skillet over medium-high heat until shimmering. Add tomatoes, onion, and half of jalapeños and cook until onion is softened and browned, 8 to 10 minutes. Stir in garlic, 1 tablespoon chipotles, and tomato paste and cook until fragrant, about 30 seconds. Stir in 1 cup broth, scraping up any browned bits; transfer to slow cooker.

2. Stir remaining 7 cups broth and cilantro stems into slow cooker. Season chicken with salt and pepper and nestle into slow cooker. Cover and cook until chicken is tender, 4 to 6 hours on low.

3. Transfer chicken to cutting board, let cool slightly, then shred into bite-size pieces (see page 21). Let soup settle for 5 minutes, then remove fat from surface using large spoon. Discard cilantro stems.

4. Stir in shredded chicken, remaining jalapeños, and remaining teaspoon chipotles and let sit until heated through, about 5 minutes. Season with salt and pepper to taste. Place tortilla chips in serving bowls, ladle soup over top, and serve with cheese, avocado, sour cream, cilantro, and lime wedges.

SMART SHOPPING TORTILLA CHIPS
Our recent taste test of nine brands of tortilla chips confirmed that some are definitely better than others. Offering a range of textures from thick and coarse (made with stone-ground cornmeal) to thin and crisp (made with corn flour), the chips were also rated on their freshness, salt levels, and of course, their flavor. In the end, **Santitas Authentic Mexican Style White Corn Tortilla Chips** won us over with a mild, pleasantly salty flavor and sturdy yet crisp texture.

Thai-Style Chicken Soup

Serves 6 to 8   **Cooking Time** 4 to 6 hours on Low

WHY THIS RECIPE WORKS: Thai-style chicken soup (aka *tom kha gai*) is famous for its exotic balance of sweet, spicy, and sour flavors. Though recipes for this soup usually call for foreign ingredients like galangal, kaffir lime leaves, and bird's eye chiles, we swapped them out for supermarket staples like ginger, jalapeños, limes, and Thai red curry paste. Adding some of the coconut milk to the soup just before serving (warmed, so it doesn't cool off the soup) helps deepen the sweet coconut flavor, which otherwise can taste washed out after several hours in the slow cooker.

2	onions, minced
6	garlic cloves, minced
2	tablespoons minced or grated fresh ginger
1	tablespoon vegetable oil
4	cups low-sodium chicken broth
2	(14-ounce) cans coconut milk
2	stalks lemon grass, bottom 5 inches only, bruised (see page 20)
2	carrots, peeled and sliced ¼ inch thick
3	tablespoons fish sauce
10	cilantro stems, tied together with twine
1½	pounds boneless, skinless chicken thighs, trimmed Salt and pepper
8	ounces white mushrooms, trimmed and sliced thin
3	tablespoons fresh lime juice from 2 limes
1	tablespoon sugar
2	teaspoons Thai red curry paste

GARNISHES

½	cup fresh cilantro leaves
2	fresh Thai, serrano, or jalapeño chiles, stemmed, seeded and sliced thin
2	scallions, sliced thin Lime wedges, for serving

1. Microwave onions, garlic, ginger, and oil in bowl, stirring occasionally, until onions are softened, about 5 minutes; transfer to slow cooker.

2. Stir broth, 1 can coconut milk, lemon grass, carrots, 1 tablespoon fish sauce, and cilantro stems into slow cooker. Season chicken with salt and pepper and nestle into slow cooker. Cover and cook until chicken is tender, 4 to 6 hours on low.

3. Transfer chicken to cutting board, let cool slightly, then shred into bite-size pieces (see page 21). Let soup settle for 5 minutes, then remove fat from surface using large spoon. Discard lemon grass and cilantro stems.

4. Stir in mushrooms, cover, and cook on high until mushrooms are tender, 5 to 15 minutes. Microwave remaining can coconut milk in bowl until hot, about 3 minutes, then whisk in remaining 2 tablespoons fish sauce, lime juice, sugar, and curry paste to dissolve.

5. Stir hot coconut milk mixture and shredded chicken into soup and let sit until heated through, about 5 minutes. Season with salt and pepper to taste and serve with garnishes.

SMART SHOPPING CURRY PASTE

Curry pastes, which can be either green or red, are a key ingredient for adding deep, well-rounded flavor to Thai curries. They are made from a mix of lemon grass, kaffir lime leaves, shrimp paste, ginger, garlic, chiles (fresh green Thai chiles for green curry paste and dried red Thai chiles for red curry paste), and other spices. So it's not surprising that making curry paste at home can be quite a chore. We have found that the store-bought variety does a fine job and saves significant time in terms of both shopping and prep. It is usually sold in small jars next to other Thai ingredients at the supermarket. Be aware that these pastes can vary in spiciness depending on the brand, so use more or less as desired.

Turkey and Wild Rice Soup

Serves 8   **Cooking Time** 6 to 8 on Low or 5 to 7 on High

WHY THIS RECIPE WORKS: Turkey soup is a dish perfectly suited for a slow cooker. The hearty flavor of turkey translates easily into a full-flavored soup without requiring any tricks, and turkey thighs (which we prefer for soup) seem to have been designed for the slow cooker's low and steady cooking environment. Turkey thighs, which are made up entirely of dark meat, are quite big and thick, which means they are nearly impossible to overcook and have lots of flavor to spare. (As a bonus, they're cheap, too!) Do not substitute a turkey breast for the thighs; the breast will not cook at the same rate as the thighs and will produce too much meat for the soup. We like the flavor of a wild and white rice blend in this soup; however, you can substitute 1 cup of long-grain white rice.

- 2 **onions, minced**
- 4 **garlic cloves, minced**
- 1 **tablespoon tomato paste**
- 1 **tablespoon vegetable oil**
- 2 **teaspoons minced fresh thyme or ½ teaspoon dried**
- 8 **cups low-sodium chicken broth**
- 3 **carrots, peeled and sliced ¼ inch thick**
- 2 **celery ribs, sliced ¼ inch thick**
- 2 **bay leaves**
- 2 **bone-in turkey thighs (about 2 pounds), skin removed, trimmed**
  Salt and pepper
- 1 **cup long-grain and wild rice blend**
- 2 **tablespoons minced fresh parsley**

1. Microwave onions, garlic, tomato paste, oil, and thyme in bowl, stirring occasionally, until onions are softened, about 5 minutes; transfer to slow cooker.

2. Stir broth, carrots, celery, and bay leaves into slow cooker. Season turkey with salt and pepper and nestle into slow cooker. Cover and cook until turkey is tender, 6 to 8 hours on low or 5 to 7 hours on high.

3. Transfer turkey to cutting board, let cool slightly, then shred into bite-size pieces (see page 21), discarding bones. Let soup settle for 5 minutes, then remove fat from surface using large spoon. Discard bay leaves. Stir in rice, cover, and cook on high until rice is tender, 30 to 40 minutes.

4. Stir in shredded turkey and let sit until heated through, about 5 minutes. Stir in parsley, season with salt and pepper to taste, and serve.

SMART SHOPPING LADLES
After we dunked eight stainless steel ladles (plastic stains and can melt on the stovetop) into pots of soup and stew, puddles on the test kitchen countertop made it clear that not all ladles are ergonomically equal. Ladles with handles shorter than 9 inches simply sank in deep pots, while more than 10 inches of grip proved cumbersome to maneuver. Ladles with small bowls are better suited to sauces than soups, and an offset handle is a must—without some slight bend in the handle, cleanly transferring a ladle's contents into a bowl is nearly impossible. **The Rösle Ladle with Pouring Rim** ($29.95) had everything we were looking for including a hook handle and a drip-prevention pouring rim.

Beef and Barley Soup

Serves 6 to 8   **Cooking Time** 9 to 11 hours on Low or 5 to 7 hours on High

✔ **WHY THIS RECIPE WORKS:** To build a flavorful base for this simple but comforting soup in a slow cooker, we needed to get out our skillet to sauté a hefty amount of onions with tomato paste and thyme and then deglaze the pan with wine, scraping up the flavorful brown bits left behind. This simple step made a world of difference in the soup's flavor and allowed us to skip the tedious process of browning the meat. To further simplify things we used trimmed beef blade steak, which we shredded after it had become meltingly tender in the slow cooker—no need to cut the meat into pieces to start. A mix of equal parts beef and chicken broth balanced this soup perfectly and, as with all our slow cooker beef soups and stews, soy sauce added a surprising amount of flavor. Since pearl barley can absorb two to three times its volume of cooking liquid, we needed to be judicious in the quantity we added to the soup. A modest ¼ cup was all that was needed to lend a pleasing velvety texture without overfilling the slow cooker with swollen grains.

2	tablespoons vegetable oil
3	onions, minced
¼	cup tomato paste
1	tablespoon minced fresh thyme or ¾ teaspoon dried
½	cup dry red wine
1	(28-ounce) can crushed tomatoes
2	cups beef broth
2	cups low-sodium chicken broth
2	carrots, peeled and chopped medium
⅓	cup soy sauce
¼	cup pearl barley
2	pounds beef blade steak, trimmed (see page 16)
	Salt and pepper
¼	cup minced fresh parsley

1. Heat oil in 12-inch skillet over medium-high heat until shimmering. Add onions, tomato paste, and thyme and cook until onions are softened and lightly browned, 8 to 10 minutes. Stir in wine, scraping up any browned bits; transfer to slow cooker.

2. Stir tomatoes, beef broth, chicken broth, carrots, soy sauce, and barley into slow cooker. Season beef with salt and pepper and nestle into slow cooker. Cover and cook until beef is tender, 9 to 11 hours on low or 5 to 7 hours on high.

3. Transfer beef to cutting board, let cool slightly, then shred into bite-size pieces (see page 21). Let soup settle for 5 minutes, then remove fat from surface using large spoon.

4. Stir in shredded beef and let sit until heated through, about 5 minutes. Stir in parsley, season with salt and pepper, and serve.

SMART SHOPPING PEARL BARLEY
There are three types of barley to choose from when shopping: hulled barley, pearl barley, and instant barley. Instant barley (sold as kernels and flakes) has been processed so that it cooks through in a snap, making it a terrible choice for the slow cooker. Hulled barley is primarily sold in natural foods stores, and although it requires hours of simmering time to cook through, we didn't like its chewy texture and strong earthy flavor in this soup. Pearl barley is our favorite because it is widely available, works well in a slow cooker, and has a mild, pleasantly nutty flavor and tender but toothsome texture.

Old-Fashioned Beef and Noodle Soup

Serves 6 to 8   **Cooking Time** 9 to 11 hours on Low or 5 to 7 hours on High

WHY THIS RECIPE WORKS: Beef soups are a natural for the slow cooker because the meat becomes meltingly tender in its moist heat environment, and this old-fashioned soup is no exception. We used blade steaks, which contributed rich, beefy flavor and were easily shredded at the end of cooking. We found that cremini mushrooms gave this soup a rich dimension and their intense mushroom flavor held up even in the slow cooker. A traditional mirepoix, jump-started in the microwave with a little oil and tomato paste, formed the base of the soup while store-bought beef broth, enhanced with soy sauce, imparted deep flavor. Don't try to cook the noodles directly in the soup or they will be mushy.

2	onions, minced
4	garlic cloves, minced
1	tablespoon tomato paste
1	tablespoon vegetable oil
2	teaspoons minced fresh thyme or ½ teaspoon dried
6	cups beef broth
1	pound cremini mushrooms, trimmed and sliced ½ inch thick
3	carrots, peeled and chopped medium
2	celery ribs, chopped medium
2	tablespoons soy sauce
2	bay leaves
1½	pounds beef blade steak, trimmed
	Salt and pepper
3	ounces wide egg noodles (about 2 cups)
2	tablespoons minced fresh parsley

1. Microwave onions, garlic, tomato paste, oil, and thyme in bowl, stirring occasionally until onions are softened, about 5 minutes; transfer to slow cooker.

2. Stir broth, mushrooms, carrots, celery, soy sauce, and bay leaves into slow cooker. Season beef with salt and pepper and nestle into slow cooker. Cover and cook until beef is tender, 9 to 11 hours on low or 5 to 7 hours on high.

3. Transfer beef to cutting board, let cool slightly, then shred into bite-size pieces (see page 21). Let soup settle for 5 minutes, then remove fat from surface using large spoon. Discard bay leaves.

4. Cook egg noodles in boiling salted water until tender, then drain. Stir cooked noodles and shredded beef into soup and let sit until heated through, about 5 minutes. Stir in parsley, season with salt and pepper to taste, and serve.

QUICK PREP TIP **TRIMMING BLADE STEAK**
Blade steaks have a thin line of gristle running through their center that needs to be removed before cooking. To do this, simply cut the steak in half lengthwise to expose the gristle completely, then carefully trim it away from the meat.

Italian Meatball Soup

Serves 6 to 8   **Cooking Time** 4 to 6 hours on Low

✔ WHY THIS RECIPE WORKS: The key to making this brothy soup slow cooker friendly was to find a way to avoid the tedious step of browning the meatballs but still end up with meatballs that held together. To make flavorful and firm meatballs (that wouldn't disintegrate in the slow cooker), we added a panade (a paste of bread and milk) along with Parmesan, parsley, garlic, and oregano to meatloaf mix. And we found that if we microwaved the meatballs before adding them to the slow cooker they remained firm (plus this kept the finished soup from being greasy). Kale and orzo, added to the slow cooker for the last 20 to 30 minutes, cooked through perfectly.

2	slices high-quality white sandwich bread, torn into quarters
½	cup whole milk
1	pound meatloaf mix
½	cup grated Parmesan cheese (about 1 ounce), plus extra for serving
3	tablespoons minced fresh parsley
1	large egg yolk
6	garlic cloves, minced
1½	teaspoons minced fresh oregano or ½ teaspoon dried
	Salt and pepper
1	onion, minced
1	tablespoon extra-virgin olive oil, plus extra for serving
¼	teaspoon red pepper flakes
8	cups low-sodium chicken broth
8	ounces kale, stemmed and leaves sliced ¼ inch thick (see page 33)
6	ounces orzo (about 1 cup)

1. Mash bread and milk into paste in large bowl using fork. Mix in meatloaf mix, Parmesan, parsley, egg yolk, 3 garlic cloves, oregano, ¾ teaspoon salt, and ½ teaspoon pepper using hands. Pinch off and roll mixture into tablespoon-size meatballs (30 to 35 meatballs total). Microwave meatballs on large plate until fat renders and meatballs are firm, 3 to 5 minutes. Pour off fat and transfer meatballs to slow cooker.

2. Microwave onion, remaining 3 garlic cloves, oil, and red pepper flakes in bowl, stirring occasionally, until softened, about 5 minutes; transfer to slow cooker.

3. Add broth to slow cooker. Cover and cook until meatballs are tender, 4 to 6 hours on low.

4. Let soup settle for 5 minutes, then remove fat from surface using large spoon. Stir in kale and orzo, cover, and cook on high until kale and orzo are tender, 20 to 30 minutes. Season with salt and pepper to taste and serve with additional Parmesan and olive oil.

ALL ABOUT Broths

Our homemade slow-cooker broths (see pages 310-312) are a snap to make and great to make ahead and freeze, but certainly good store-bought broths are handy to have on hand for the recipes in this book (and for all your cooking needs). For some soups and stews in this book you will need extra broth (usually chicken) on hand to add at the end of cooking to adjust the final consistency.

Chicken Broth

We prefer chicken broth to both beef and vegetable broth, though all have their place in our recipes and we often use them in combination in our slow-cooker recipes. And while we love homemade chicken broth, we know that few have time to make it from scratch (though our slow-cooker recipe is very easy). While searching for the best commercial broth, we discovered a few critical characteristics. First, look for a lower sodium content—less than 700 milligrams per serving—especially since we use a fair amount of broth in many of our slow-cooker recipes and they can easily turn out overly salty (especially when combined with other salty ingredients such as canned beans and tomatoes, soy sauce, and ham hocks). Also, pick a mass-produced broth. We tasted several broths with rancid off-flavors, which are caused by fat oxidation, and the worst offenders were those made by smaller companies. Lastly, look for a short ingredient list that includes vegetables like carrots, celery, and onions. Our pick? **Swanson Certified Organic Free Range Chicken Broth**. If you can't find it, Swanson's "Natural Goodness" Chicken Broth rated almost as highly in our tasting.

Beef Broth

Historically, we've found beef broth to be light on beefy flavor, but that said, sometimes it adds a much needed kick. Wanting to find out if supermarket offerings had improved, we gathered 13 top-selling beef broths, stocks, and bases and rated them on beef flavor, aroma, saltiness, and overall appeal. The top eight brands were then tasted in gravy and French onion soup (five were eliminated). Ultimately, our top two broths delivered on rich, beefy flavor—but using very different ingredients. The runner-up, College Inn, relies on beef, beef derivatives, and glutamate-rich additives (such as yeast extract and tomato paste) for flavor, and other additives for body. The winning brand, **Rachael Ray Stock-in-a-Box All-Natural Beef Flavored Stock** (made by Colavita), has a shorter but less foreign ingredient list that starts with concentrated beef stock, which means this stock has more fresh, real meat than the other samples. Also, this broth contained no processed additives except for yeast extract, but it still tasted really beefy. Tasters called it "steak-y" and "rich" with "thick, gelatin-like body."

Vegetable Broth

We turn to vegetable broth for vegetarian dishes and for lighter soups or vegetable dishes that might be overwhelmed by the flavor of chicken broth. Often we use a mix of chicken and vegetable broths since vegetable broth can be too sweet used alone. In our search for the best vegetable broth, we tested 10 brands, finding that a hefty amount of salt and the presence of enough vegetable content to be listed on the ingredient list were key. Our favorite? **Swanson Vegetarian Vegetable Broth**.

Clam Juice

When we need clam juice for a slow-cooker shellfish stew or chowder it's just not practical to shuck fresh clams—after all, we're using the slow cooker because we are busy. To find the best storebought clam juice, we tested three brands, and only one tasted "too strong" and "too clammy," perhaps because its sodium was more than double that of the other two. Our winner, **Bar Harbor**, hails from the shores of clam country in Maine and is available nationwide. It brings a "bright" and "mineral-y" flavor to seafood dishes.

Vietnamese-Style Beef and Noodle Soup

Serves 8 **Cooking Time** 9 to 11 hours on Low or 5 to 7 hours on High

✔ **WHY THIS RECIPE WORKS:** With its richly perfumed broth and mix of raw and cooked, hot and cold ingredients, this traditional Southeast Asian soup (called *pho*) seemed like a long shot for the slow cooker. But actually, it turned out to be one of our easiest soups. Fish sauce and soy sauce punched up store-bought broth, which we further enhanced with bruised lemon grass, star anise, and cloves. And blade steak was a great and easy choice for this soup since it is so full of rich beefy flavor. Finicky rice noodles, as it turns out, work perfectly in a slow cooker; since the liquid doesn't come to a full boil, the noodles cook gently and do not break apart or turn mushy. Finishing with the requisite garnishes created a perfectly balanced soup.

2 **onions, minced**
6 **garlic cloves, minced**
1 **tablespoon vegetable oil**
4 **cups low-sodium chicken broth**
4 **cups beef broth**
2 **cups water**
¼ **cup fish sauce**
2 **tablespoons soy sauce**
2 **tablespoons sugar**
1 **stalk lemon grass, bottom
   5 inches only, bruised**
4 **star anise pods**
4 **whole cloves**
2 **pounds beef blade steak,
   trimmed (see page 16)
   Salt and pepper**
8 **ounces thick rice noodles**

GARNISHES
2 **cups bean sprouts**
1 **cup fresh Thai basil or regular
   basil leaves**
1 **cup fresh cilantro leaves**
2 **scallions, sliced thin**
1 **fresh Thai, serrano, or jalapeño
   chile, stemmed, and sliced thin
   Lime wedges, for serving**

1. Microwave onions, garlic, and oil in bowl, stirring occasionally, until onions are softened, about 5 minutes; transfer to slow cooker.

2. Stir chicken broth, beef broth, water, fish sauce, soy sauce, sugar, and lemon grass into slow cooker. Secure star anise and cloves in small cheesecloth pouch or tea bag and add to slow cooker. Season beef with salt and pepper and nestle into slow cooker. Cover and cook until beef is tender, 9 to 11 hours on low or 5 to 7 hours on high.

3. Transfer beef to cutting board, let cool slightly, then shred into bite-size pieces (see page 21). Let soup settle for 5 minutes, then remove fat from surface using large spoon. Discard lemon grass and spice pouch.

4. Stir in noodles, cover, and cook on high until noodles are tender, 10 to 20 minutes. Stir in shredded beef and let sit until heated through, about 5 minutes. Serve with garnishes.

QUICK PREP TIP BRUISING LEMON GRASS
To release the flavor from a stalk of lemon grass, trim and discard all but the bottom 5 inches of the stalk. Peel off the discolored outer layer, then lightly smash the stalk with the back of a chef's knife.

Chinese Chicken and Ramen Soup

Serves 8   **Cooking Time** 4 to 6 hours on Low

✔ **WHY THIS RECIPE WORKS:** This easy soup relies on chicken broth infused with aromatics (including a hefty dose of fresh ginger), soy sauce, and star anise. We also included tomato paste, an unusual ingredient for ramen soup but one that adds body and a rich flavor that deepens at it cooks; and we used meaty chicken thighs to add to the broth's richness. To keep things fresh (and simple), we added quick-cooking instant ramen noodles at the end of cooking along with shredded napa cabbage—both ingredients cook through in the same amount of time right in the slow cooker. And since several hours in a slow cooker can mute the punch of aromatics, we stirred in a tablespoon of grated fresh ginger at the end to give the soup a burst of flavor. We like to serve this soup with extra soy sauce to taste.

2   **onions, minced**

6   **garlic cloves, minced**

2   **tablespoons minced or grated fresh ginger**

1   **tablespoon tomato paste**

1   **tablespoon vegetable oil**

⅛   **teaspoon red pepper flakes**

8   **cups low-sodium chicken broth**

2   **carrots, peeled and sliced ¼ inch thick**

3   **tablespoons soy sauce, plus extra for serving**

2   **tablespoons sugar**

2   **star anise pods**

2   **bay leaves**

1½   **pounds boneless, skinless chicken thighs, trimmed Salt and pepper**

2   **(3-ounce) packages ramen noodles, flavoring packets discarded**

½   **medium head napa cabbage, shredded**

2   **scallions, sliced thin**

1. Microwave onions, garlic, 1 tablespoon ginger, tomato paste, oil, and red pepper flakes in bowl, stirring occasionally, until onions are softened, about 5 minutes; transfer to slow cooker.

2. Stir broth, carrots, soy sauce, sugar, star anise, and bay leaves into slow cooker. Season chicken with salt and pepper and nestle into slow cooker. Cover and cook until chicken is tender, 4 to 6 hours on low.

3. Transfer chicken to cutting board, let cool slightly, then shred into bite-size pieces. Let soup settle for 5 minutes, then remove fat from surface using large spoon. Discard star anise and bay leaves.

4. Stir in ramen and cabbage, cover, and cook on high until noodles are tender, 3 to 8 minutes. Stir in shredded chicken and remaining tablespoon ginger and let sit until heated through, about 5 minutes. Stir in scallions, season with salt and pepper to taste, and serve with additional soy sauce.

QUICK PREP TIP **SHREDDING MEAT**

To shred poultry and beef into bite-size pieces that fit easily onto a soupspoon, simply hold a fork in each hand (tines facing down), insert the forks into the cooked meat, and gently pull the meat apart.

Japanese Pork and Ramen Soup

Serves 8   **Cooking Time** 6 to 8 hours on Low or 5 to 7 hours on High

WHY THIS RECIPE WORKS: A great ramen soup requires a great broth and to accomplish this in a slow cooker we enhanced store-bought chicken broth with onions, garlic, and ginger at the beginning of cooking, then stirred in white miso (fermented soybean paste), soy sauce, mirin (Japanese rice wine), and sesame oil at the end. The combination of slow-cooking boneless country-style pork ribs, which are easy to shred after cooking, and hearty shiitakes imparted an intense, meaty flavor to the finished soup. Fresh spinach, stirred in at the end, added an earthy flavor, and supermarket ramen noodles cooked perfectly in the same amount of time.

2   onions, minced

6   garlic cloves, minced

2   tablespoons minced or grated fresh ginger

1   tablespoon vegetable oil

8   cups low-sodium chicken broth

12   ounces shiitake mushrooms, stemmed and sliced thin

1½   pounds boneless country-style pork ribs, trimmed
      Salt and pepper

2   (3-ounce) packages ramen noodles, flavoring packets discarded

6   ounces baby spinach (about 6 cups)

2   tablespoons white miso, plus extra for serving

2   tablespoons low-sodium soy sauce, plus extra for serving

1   tablespoon mirin

1   teaspoon toasted sesame oil

2   scallions, sliced thin

1   tablespoon sesame seeds, toasted (see page 87)

1. Microwave onions, garlic, ginger, and oil in bowl, stirring occasionally, until onions are softened, about 5 minutes; transfer to slow cooker.

2. Stir broth and shiitakes into slow cooker. Season pork with salt and pepper and nestle into slow cooker. Cover and cook until pork is tender, 6 to 8 hours on low or 5 to 7 hours on high.

3. Transfer pork to cutting board, let cool slightly, then shred into bite-size pieces (see page 21). Let soup settle for 5 minutes, then remove fat from surface using large spoon. Stir in noodles and spinach, cover, and cook on high until noodles are tender, 3 to 8 minutes.

4. Stir in shredded pork, miso, soy sauce, mirin, and sesame oil, and let sit until heated through, about 5 minutes. Season with additional miso and additional soy sauce to taste. Serve with scallions and sesame seeds.

SMART SHOPPING MISO

Made from a fermented mixture of soy beans and rice, barley, or rye, miso is incredibly versatile, suitable for use in soups, braises, dressings, and sauces as well as for topping grilled foods. This salty, deep-flavored paste ranges in strength and color from mild, pale yellow (referred to as white) to stronger-flavored red or brownish black, depending on the fermentation method and ingredients.

Butternut Squash Chowder

Serves 6 to 8   **Cooking Time** 4 to 6 hours on Low

✓ **WHY THIS RECIPE WORKS:** For this rustic chowder, we developed a flavorful, smoky base by cooking minced bacon (and then the aromatics) on the stovetop. We included half the squash in the soup base to flavor it and then wrapped the remaining squash in a foil packet to ensure that the chowder included tender but distinct (and not mushy) pieces of squash. Hearty kale leaves, added during the last 20 to 30 minutes of cooking, added both color and an earthy flavor.

4	ounces bacon (about 4 slices), minced
1	onion, minced
3	garlic cloves, minced
1½	teaspoons minced fresh thyme or ½ teaspoon dried
⅛	teaspoon ground nutmeg, plus extra as needed
⅓	cup all-purpose flour
4	cups low-sodium chicken broth
3	cups vegetable broth
3	pounds butternut squash, peeled, seeded, and cut into ½-inch pieces
2	bay leaves
1	tablespoon vegetable oil
	Salt and pepper
8	ounces kale, stemmed and leaves sliced ¼ inch thick (see page 33)
½	cup heavy cream
1	tablespoon minced fresh sage
1	teaspoon brown sugar
	Grated Parmesan cheese, for serving

1. Cook bacon in 12-inch skillet over medium-high heat until crisp, about 5 minutes. Stir in onion, garlic, thyme, and nutmeg and cook until onion is softened and lightly browned, 8 to 10 minutes. Stir in flour and cook for 1 minute. Slowly whisk in 2 cups chicken broth, scraping up any browned bits; transfer to slow cooker.

2. Stir remaining 2 cups chicken broth, vegetable broth, half of squash, and bay leaves into slow cooker. Toss remaining squash with oil, season with salt and pepper, and wrap in foil packet (see page 60). Lay foil packet on top of soup. Cover and cook until squash is tender, 4 to 6 hours on low.

3. Transfer foil packet to plate. Discard bay leaves. Stir in kale, cover, and cook on high until kale is tender, 20 to 30 minutes.

4. Carefully open foil packet (watch for steam) and stir squash with accumulated juice into soup. Stir in cream, sage, and sugar, and let sit until heated through, about 5 minutes. Season with salt, pepper, and additional nutmeg to taste and serve with Parmesan.

QUICK PREP TIP CUTTING UP BUTTERNUT SQUASH
Peel away the tough outer skin using a peeler, then trim off the top and bottom of the squash. Using a chef's knife, slice the squash in half widthwise, separating the solid, narrow neck piece from the hollow, rounded bottom. Slice the solid neck piece crosswise into rounds, then cut into pieces as directed. Slice the bottom piece in half, remove seeds from the hollow end with a spoon, then cut into pieces as directed in the recipe.

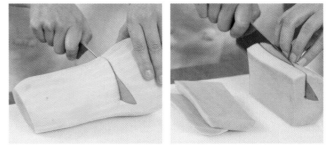

Portuguese-Style Potato and Kale Soup

Serves 6 to 8　　**Cooking Time** 4 to 6 hours on Low

✔ WHY THIS RECIPE WORKS: Most recipes for this classic Portuguese soup use spicy chorizo sausage. While this sausage imparted great flavor, it turned extremely dry while in the slow cooker. Looking for a better option, we found that kielbasa fit the bill—it retained its moisture and good texture in the slow cooker and lent a rich meaty flavor to the soup. To compensate for some of the spices that are in chorizo, we added chili powder, oregano, and minced chipotle chile. And microwaving them with the aromatics bloomed their flavors further. Stirring in kale at the end prevented it from tasting washed out and ensured the hearty greens would be perfectly tender.

1　**onion, minced**

4　**garlic cloves, minced**

1　**tablespoon extra-virgin olive oil, plus extra for serving**

1　**tablespoon chili powder**

1½　**teaspoons fresh minced oregano or ½ teaspoon dried**

½　**teaspoon minced canned chipotle chile in adobo, plus extra as needed**

6　**cups low-sodium chicken broth**

1　**pound red potatoes (about 3 medium), scrubbed and cut into ½-inch pieces**

8　**ounces kielbasa sausage, halved lengthwise and sliced ½ inch thick**

8　**ounces kale, stemmed and leaves sliced ¼ inch thick (see page 33)**

　　Salt and pepper

　　Grated Parmesan cheese, for serving

1. Microwave onion, garlic, oil, chili powder, oregano, and chipotles in bowl, stirring occasionally, until onion is softened, about 5 minutes; transfer to slow cooker.

2. Stir broth, potatoes, and kielbasa into slow cooker. Cover and cook until potatoes are tender, 4 to 6 hours on low.

3. Stir in kale, cover, and cook on high until tender, 20 to 30 minutes. Season with salt, pepper, and additional chipotles to taste. Serve with Parmesan, Garlic Toasts, and additional olive oil.

ON THE SIDE GARLIC TOASTS
Adjust oven rack to middle position and heat oven to 400 degrees. Arrange twelve ½-inch-thick slices baguette on baking sheet. Bake until bread is dry and crisp, about 10 minutes, flipping slices halfway through baking time. Rub one side of each toast with peeled garlic clove, then drizzle toasts with extra-virgin olive oil. Season with salt and pepper. Makes 12 toasts.

French Onion Soup

Serves 6 to 8   **Cooking Time** 8 to 12 hours on High

✓ **WHY THIS RECIPE WORKS:** This soup is so rich and flavorful and so packed with darkly caramelized onions that no one would ever imagine it was made in a slow cooker. The secret? For the roasted beefy flavor that usually only comes with homemade beef broth, we microwaved beef bones before tucking them into the slow cooker around the onions. As for the onions, we had to be inventive given the moist heat of the slow cooker; through trial and error, we found that a mix of apple butter and soy sauce gave the onions a silken texture and deep color that made them taste like they took hours of stovetop browning. This recipe has a wide range for the cooking time because we learned that onions can go from caramelized to burnt very quickly if left too long in a slow cooker; be sure to keep an eye on the onions starting at 8 hours the first time you make this soup to be sure they don't burn. Look for beef bones in the freezer section of your grocery store; if using frozen beef bones, be sure to thaw them completely before using.

2	pounds beef bones
6	onions, halved and sliced ¼ inch thick
4	tablespoons (½ stick) unsalted butter, melted
	Salt and pepper
1	tablespoon brown sugar
1	teaspoon minced fresh thyme or ¼ teaspoon dried
5	tablespoons all-purpose flour
¾	cup apple butter
¾	cup dry sherry
¼	cup soy sauce
2	cups low-sodium chicken broth
2	cups beef broth
1	(24-inch) loaf French baguette, cut into ½-inch slices
2½	cups shredded Gruyère cheese (about 10 ounces)

1. Arrange beef bones on paper towel–lined plate and microwave (in batches, if microwave is small) until well browned, 8 to 10 minutes.

2. Add onions, butter, 1 teaspoon salt, 1 teaspoon pepper, sugar, and thyme to slow cooker. Whisk flour, apple butter, sherry, and soy sauce together in bowl until smooth, then stir into slow cooker. Nestle microwaved bones into slow cooker. Cover and cook until onions are softened and deep golden brown, 8 to 12 hours on high.

3. Discard beef bones. Bring chicken broth and beef broth to boil in covered saucepan over high heat, then stir into slow cooker. Let soup sit until heated through, about 5 minutes. Season with salt and pepper to taste.

4. Just before serving, position oven rack 6 inches from broiler element and heat broiler. Lay bread on baking sheet and broil until golden on both sides, about 2 minutes per side. Sprinkle cheese over one side of bread and continue to broil until melted and bubbly, 3 to 5 minutes. Ladle soup into serving bowls and top with broiled cheese bread.

QUICK PREP TIP **NO-TEARS ONION SLICING**

When an onion is cut, the cells that are damaged in the process release sulfuric compounds as well as various enzymes that mix to form a new compound that evaporates in the air and irritates the eyes, causing us to cry. Of all the suggested ways to lessen this teary effect, we've found the best options are to protect the eyes by covering them with goggles or contact lenses, or to introduce a flame (from a candle or gas burner) near the cut onions. The flame changes the activity of the compound that causes the tearing, while contact lenses and goggles simply form a physical barrier that the compound cannot penetrate. So if you want to keep tears at bay when handling onions, light a candle or gas burner or put on some ski goggles.

Loaded Baked Potato Soup

Serves 6 to 8   **Cooking Time** 4 to 6 hours on Low

☑ **WHY THIS RECIPE WORKS:** As satisfying and irresistible as a baked potato with all the fixings, this creamy soup is easy to make in a slow cooker. A hefty amount of chopped bacon is the key, and after cooking it, we reserved it for topping the soup when serving to ensure it would be crunchy and flavorful. Cooking the aromatics in some of the rendered bacon fat also helped infuse the soup with flavor. As for the potatoes themselves, we found that just cooking the potatoes in the broth resulted in a soup that was thin on potato flavor. To solve this, we mashed some of the cooked potato pieces and then stirred them back into the soup.

8	ounces bacon (about 8 slices), chopped
1	onion, minced
2	garlic cloves, minced
1½	teaspoons minced fresh thyme or ½ teaspoon dried
2	tablespoons all-purpose flour
4	cups low-sodium chicken broth
3	pounds russet potatoes (about 6 medium), peeled and cut into ½-inch pieces
2	cups shredded cheddar cheese (about 8 ounces), plus extra for serving
½	cup heavy cream
	Salt and pepper
3	scallions, sliced thin

1. Cook bacon in 12-inch skillet over medium heat until crisp, 5 to 7 minutes. Transfer bacon to paper towel–lined plate and refrigerate until serving. Pour off all but 2 tablespoons bacon fat left in skillet.

2. Add onion, garlic, and thyme to fat in skillet and cook over medium-high heat until onion is softened and lightly browned, 8 to 10 minutes. Stir in flour and cook for 1 minute. Slowly whisk in 1 cup broth, scraping up any browned bits; transfer to slow cooker.

3. Stir remaining 3 cups broth and potatoes into slow cooker. Cover and cook until potatoes are tender, 4 to 6 hours on low.

4. Transfer 2 cups cooked potatoes to bowl and mash smooth with potato masher. Stir cheddar into soup until evenly melted, then stir in mashed potatoes and cream. Let soup sit until heated through, about 5 minutes.

5. Microwave bacon on paper towel–lined plate until hot and crisp, about 30 seconds. Season soup with salt and pepper to taste and serve with scallions, crisp bacon, and additional cheddar.

QUICK PREP TIP **WHEN POTATOES TURN GREEN**
When potatoes are left on the counter for more than a few days, they sometimes turn slightly green under the skin. It turns out that when potatoes are exposed to light for prolonged periods of time, they begin to produce chlorophyll in the form of a green ring under their skin. While the chlorophyll itself is tasteless and harmless, it does mark the potential presence of solanine, a toxin that can cause gastrointestinal distress. Since solanine develops on the skin of the potato (or just below), discarding the peel greatly reduces the risk of becoming ill from a slightly green spud. We've found that potatoes stored in a well-ventilated, dark, dry, cool place will stay solanine-free for up to a month, while potatoes left on the counter will begin to exhibit signs of solanine in as little as a week.

Rustic Potato and Leek Soup

Serves 6 to 8   **Cooking Time** 4 to 6 hours on Low

✔ **WHY THIS RECIPE WORKS:** When we tried making this classic French-style soup by simply adding the ingredients to the slow cooker from the start, the resulting soup was bland and somewhat bitter from the long-cooked leeks. The key, it turned out, was to mellow the leeks first by cooking them in butter until they started to brown and become deeply sweet and caramelized. Adding an onion complemented the sweetness of the leeks and deepened the overall flavor of the soup without adding any bitterness. Be sure to wash the leeks well to remove any grit or dirt.

2	tablespoons unsalted butter
2	leeks, white and light green parts only, halved lengthwise, sliced thin, and washed thoroughly
1	onion, minced
1	garlic clove, minced
1½	teaspoons minced fresh thyme or ½ teaspoon dried
6	cups low-sodium chicken broth
1½	pounds red potatoes (about 4 medium), scrubbed and cut into ½-inch pieces
3	carrots, peeled and cut into ½-inch pieces
2	bay leaves
½	cup heavy cream
2	tablespoons minced fresh dill
	Salt and pepper

1. Melt butter in 12-inch skillet over medium-high heat. Add leeks, onion, garlic, and thyme and cook until onion is softened and lightly browned, 10 to 12 minutes. Stir in 1 cup broth, scraping up any browned bits; transfer to slow cooker.

2. Stir remaining 5 cups broth, potatoes, carrots, and bay leaves into slow cooker. Cover and cook until vegetables are tender, 4 to 6 hours on low.

3. Discard bay leaves. Stir in cream and let sit until heated through, about 5 minutes. Stir in dill, season with salt and pepper to taste, and serve.

QUICK PREP TIP PREPARING LEEKS

Trim and discard the root and dark green leaves. Cut the trimmed leek in half lengthwise, then slice it crosswise into ½-inch-thick pieces. Rinse the cut leeks thoroughly to remove all dirt and sand using either a salad spinner or a bowl of water.

Garden Minestrone

Serves 8   **Cooking Time** 9 to 11 hours on Low or 5 to 7 hours on High

✔ **WHY THIS RECIPE WORKS:** Creating anything garden-fresh in a slow cooker is a tall order, but we were willing to try to beat the odds and develop a recipe for a bright, lively-tasting minestrone that married a flavorful tomato broth with fresh vegetables, beans, and pasta. The base of our soup would be our broth, and after microwaving the aromatics, we added broth and canned tomato sauce along with carrots and dried beans—both of which could sustain a long stay in a slow cooker. Sliced zucchini and chopped chard were simply added during the last 30 minutes of cooking along with the pasta. Be sure to finish this soup with additional olive oil and freshly grated Parmesan for a final burst of flavor.

1   onion, minced

4   garlic cloves, minced

1   tablespoon extra-virgin olive oil, plus extra for serving

1½   teaspoons minced fresh oregano or ½ teaspoon dried

⅛   teaspoon red pepper flakes

6   cups low-sodium chicken broth

1   (15-ounce) can tomato sauce

1   cup dried great Northern or cannellini beans (6½ ounces), picked over, salt-soaked (see page 35), and rinsed

2   carrots, peeled and cut into ½-inch pieces

1   zucchini (about 8 ounces), quartered lengthwise and sliced ¼ inch thick

8   ounces Swiss chard, stemmed and leaves sliced ½ inch thick

½   cup small pasta, such as ditalini, tubettini, or mini elbows

½   cup minced fresh basil

   Salt and pepper

   Grated Parmesan cheese, for serving

1. Microwave onion, garlic, oil, oregano, and red pepper flakes in bowl, stirring occasionally, until onion is softened, about 5 minutes; transfer to slow cooker.

2. Stir broth, tomato sauce, soaked beans, and carrots into slow cooker. Cover and cook until beans are tender, 9 to 11 hours on low or 5 to 7 hours on high.

3. Stir in zucchini, chard, and pasta, cover, and cook on high until vegetables and pasta are tender, 20 to 30 minutes. Stir in basil, season with salt and pepper to taste, and serve with Parmesan and additional olive oil.

QUICK PREP TIP **PREPARING HEARTY GREENS**
To prepare kale, Swiss chard, and collard greens, cut away the leafy green portion from either side of the stalk or stem using a chef's knife. Stack several leaves on top of one another, and either slice the leaves crosswise or chop them into pieces (as directed in the recipe). Wash and dry the leaves after they are cut, using a salad spinner.

Tuscan White Bean Soup

Serves 6 to 8   **Cooking Time** 9 to 11 hours on Low or 5 to 7 hours on High

✔ **WHY THIS RECIPE WORKS:** With few ingredients to distract from flaws like mushy beans and a thin broth, Tuscan White Bean Soup is rarely well prepared in a slow cooker. To create a richly perfumed base for our soup, we sautéed a hefty amount of flavorful pancetta along with a lot of minced onion and garlic. And since dried beans rarely cook properly if added directly to the slow cooker, salt-soaking them overnight was critical and allowed them to cook through evenly without bursting. Rosemary is traditional in this soup but after several hours, it gave the broth a bitter, medicinal taste. Placing a sprig of rosemary in the soup to steep for a few minutes at the end of cooking allowed us to achieve just the right amount of fresh rosemary flavor. Serve with Garlic Toasts (page 28).

2	tablespoons extra-virgin olive oil, plus extra for serving
6	ounces pancetta, minced
3	onions, minced
8	garlic cloves, minced
¼	teaspoon red pepper flakes
3	cups low-sodium chicken broth
3	cups water
1	pound great Northern or cannellini beans (2½ cups), picked over, salt-soaked, and rinsed
1	Parmesan cheese rind (optional)
2	bay leaves
1	fresh rosemary sprig
	Salt and pepper
	Grated Parmesan cheese, for serving

1. Heat oil in a 12-inch skillet over medium-high heat until shimmering. Add pancetta and cook until lightly browned and crisp, about 8 minutes. Stir in onions, garlic, and red pepper flakes and cook until onions are softened and lightly browned, 8 to 10 minutes. Stir in 1 cup broth, scraping up any browned bits; transfer to slow cooker.

2. Stir remaining 2 cups broth, water, soaked beans, Parmesan rind (if using), and bay leaves into slow cooker. Cover and cook until beans are tender, 9 to 11 hours on low or 5 to 7 hours on high.

3. Add rosemary sprig, cover, and cook on high until rosemary is fragrant, about 15 minutes. Discard rosemary, bay leaves, and Parmesan rind (if using). Season with salt and pepper to taste and serve with grated Parmesan and additional olive oil.

QUICK PREP TIP SALT-SOAKING BEANS

Here in the test kitchen, we've found that soaking dried beans in salt water, before cooking them, is a very good idea. The soaking evens out the cooking time, while the salt tenderizes the otherwise tough and chewy bean skins.

Overnight Salt-Soaking Method:

Pick through and rinse the beans. For every pound of beans, dissolve 2 tablespoons salt in 4 quarts cold water. Combine the beans and salt water in a large container and let the beans soak at room temperature for at least 8 hours or up to 24 hours. Drain the beans, discarding the soaking liquid, and rinse well before cooking.

Quick Salt-Soaking Method:

Pick through and rinse the beans. For every pound of beans, dissolve 3 tablespoons salt in 2 quarts boiling water. Combine the beans and hot salt water in a large pot and let the beans soak at room temperature for 1 hour. Drain the beans, discarding the soaking liquid, and rinse well before cooking.

Black Bean Soup

Serves 6 to 8   **Cooking Time** 9 to 11 hours on Low or 5 to 7 hours on High

WHY THIS RECIPE WORKS: To create an easy black bean soup that was robust even after hours in the slow cooker, we added chili powder to our microwaved aromatics, tossed in a smoked ham hock (which we later shredded), and included chopped celery and carrot. We did not salt-soak these beans since that would ensure that they remained fully intact and we actually wanted some of the beans to burst and thicken the soup. As for texture, we tried various thickeners such as flour, however they only muted the overall flavor of the soup. Mashing some of the cooked beans and stirring them back into the finished soup worked best, providing excellent body and intensifying flavors as well. To add a touch of brightness, we stirred in minced fresh cilantro. Serve this soup with minced red onion, sour cream, and hot sauce.

3	**onions, minced**
6	**garlic cloves, minced**
2	**tablespoons vegetable oil**
2	**tablespoons chili powder**
3	**cups low-sodium chicken broth**
3	**cups water**
1	**pound dried black beans (2½ cups), picked over and rinsed**
3	**celery ribs, cut into ½-inch pieces**
2	**carrots, peeled and cut into ½-inch pieces**
2	**bay leaves**
1	**smoked ham hock, rinsed**
2	**tablespoons minced fresh cilantro**
	Salt and pepper

1. Microwave onions, garlic, oil, and chili powder in bowl, stirring occasionally, until onions are softened, about 5 minutes; transfer to slow cooker.

2. Stir broth, water, beans, celery, carrots, and bay leaves into slow cooker. Nestle ham hock into slow cooker. Cover and cook until beans are tender, 9 to 11 hours on low or 5 to 7 hours on high.

3. Transfer ham hock to cutting board, let cool slightly, then shred into bite-size pieces (see page 21), discarding skin and bones. Let soup settle for 5 minutes, then remove fat from surface using large spoon. Discard bay leaves.

4. Transfer 1 cup cooked beans to bowl and mash smooth with potato masher. Stir shredded ham hock and mashed beans into soup and let sit until heated through, about 5 minutes. Stir in cilantro, season with salt and pepper to taste, and serve.

SMART SHOPPING SMOKED HAM HOCKS
Ham hocks add a deep, smoky, meaty flavor to our Black Bean Soup along with several other recipes in this book. Cut from the ankle joint of the hog's leg, hocks contain a great deal of bone, fat, and connective tissue, which lend a complex flavor and a rich, satiny texture to a soup or sauce. Though ham hocks can contain quite a bit of meat, they must be braised or slow-cooked for long periods of time to break down the connective tissue, making them perfect for the slow cooker. Once cooked, the ham hock meat can be easily removed from the bone, shredded, then returned to the dish. Ham hocks can be quite salty, however, so be sure to give them a rinse before cooking.

15-Bean Soup

Serves 6 to 8   **Cooking Time** 9 to 11 hours on Low or 5 to 7 hours on High

✔ WHY THIS RECIPE WORKS: With the ubiquitous 15-bean soup mix as our inspiration, we set out to make an easy bean soup with meaty undertones, a bright flavor, and an appealingly chunky texture. Our first step was to ditch the flavoring packets that come with these soup mixes since their dried seasonings and petrified bits of vegetables offered up zero flavor and made for a dusty and stale-tasting soup. To ensure that the mix of interesting beans cooked evenly we salt-soaked them. And to add a meaty flavor we did something unorthodox: we added uncooked slices of bacon directly to the slow cooker and then removed them before serving. This gave the soup a savory depth without the presence of bits of bacon and without the soup tasting overtly like bacon. A combination of fresh white mushrooms (for mild mushroom flavor) and dried porcini mushrooms (for intense mushroom flavor) rounded out the flavor of this simple, hearty soup. For a fresh, bright element, we added Swiss chard and allowed it to cook through for about 20 minutes.

1	onion, minced
6	garlic cloves, minced
1	tablespoon vegetable oil
2	teaspoons minced fresh thyme or ½ teaspoon dried
6	cups low-sodium chicken broth
12	ounces white mushrooms, quartered
8	ounces 15-bean soup mix (1¼ cups), flavoring packet discarded, picked over, salt-soaked (see page 35), and rinsed
4	ounces bacon (about 4 slices)
½	ounce dried porcini mushrooms, rinsed and minced
2	bay leaves
8	ounces Swiss chard, stemmed and leaves sliced ½ inch thick (see page 33)
1	(14.5-ounce) can whole tomatoes, drained and chopped medium
	Salt and pepper

1. Microwave onion, garlic, oil, and thyme in bowl, stirring occasionally, until onion is softened, about 5 minutes; transfer to slow cooker.

2. Stir broth, white mushrooms, soaked beans, bacon, porcini mushrooms, and bay leaves into slow cooker. Cover and cook until beans are tender, 9 to 11 hours on low or 5 to 7 hours on high.

3. Let soup settle for 5 minutes, then remove fat from surface using large spoon. Discard bacon and bay leaves.

4. Stir in chard and tomatoes, cover, and cook on high until chard is tender, 20 to 30 minutes. Season with salt and pepper to taste and serve.

QUICK PREP TIP MUSHROOMS: WASH OR BRUSH?
Culinary wisdom holds that raw mushrooms must never touch water, lest they soak up the liquid and become soggy. Many sources call for cleaning dirty mushrooms with a soft-bristled brush or a damp cloth. These fussy techniques may be worth the effort if you plan to eat the mushrooms raw, but we wondered whether mushrooms destined for the sauté pan could be simply rinsed and patted dry. To test this, we submerged 6 ounces of white mushrooms in a bowl of water for 5 minutes. We drained and weighed the mushrooms and found that they had soaked up only ¼ ounce (about 1½ teaspoons) of water, not nearly enough to affect their texture. So when we plan to cook mushrooms we don't bother with the brush. Instead, we place the mushrooms in a salad spinner, rinse the dirt and grit away with cold water, and spin to remove excess moisture.

Curried Chickpea Soup

Serves 6 to 8   **Cooking Time** 4 to 6 hours on Low

WHY THIS RECIPE WORKS: This bright and lively-tasting soup is packed with chickpeas and vegetables and requires only the microwaving of aromatics and spices in advance of cooking. Fortunately, chickpeas are one of the few varieties of canned beans that don't break down after hours in the slow cooker. For an Indian-inspired soup, we paired them with curry powder and fresh ginger. For a fresh finish to the soup, we added the zucchini and peas during the last 20 minutes of cooking, ensuring that they remained green and tender. A hefty dose of minced cilantro brightens up this soup just before serving.

2	onions, minced
2	tablespoons vegetable oil
2	tablespoons tomato paste
4	teaspoons curry powder
1	tablespoon minced or grated fresh ginger
2	garlic cloves, minced
6	cups low-sodium chicken broth
2	(15-ounce) cans chickpeas, drained and rinsed
2	carrots, peeled and cut into ½-inch pieces
1	zucchini, quartered lengthwise and sliced ¼ inch thick
1	cup frozen peas
¼	cup minced fresh cilantro
	Salt and pepper

1. Microwave onions, oil, tomato paste, curry powder, ginger, and garlic in bowl, stirring occasionally, until onions are softened, about 5 minutes. Transfer to slow cooker.

2. Stir broth, chickpeas, and carrots into slow cooker. Cover and cook until soup is flavorful, 4 to 6 hours on low.

3. Stir in zucchini and peas, cover, and cook on high until zucchini is tender, about 20 minutes. Stir in cilantro, season with salt and pepper to taste, and serve.

SMART SHOPPING CANNED CHICKPEAS
Think all brands of canned chickpeas taste the same? So did we until we tried six brands of them in a side-by-side taste test. Once we peeled back the can lids and drained and rinsed the beans, we found that many of them were incredibly bland or worse yet, had bitter and metallic flavors. Tasters preferred those that were well seasoned and had a creamy yet "al dente" texture. **Pastene Chickpeas** came out on top for their clean flavor and firm yet tender texture.

Ultimate Lentil Soup

Serves 8   **Cooking Time** 9 to 11 hours on Low or 5 to 7 hours on High

✔ **WHY THIS RECIPE WORKS:** Lentil soup is one of the easiest soups to make in a slow cooker yet all too often it turns into a hodgepodge of lentils, canned tomatoes, and whatever assortment of vegetables happen to be lingering in the crisper drawer. To create a fresh-tasting, healthy recipe in the slow cooker, we started by microwaving aromatics with a little tomato paste for deep, round flavor and minced dried porcini mushrooms, which we found added a surprising amount of richness to the soup. For smoky flavor we simply added whole bacon slices, since we didn't want bits of bacon in our finished soup, and then removed them at the end of cooking. Carrots added sweetness to the mix and portobello mushrooms an appealing texture. Searching for a hearty green to offer an earthy and colorful contrast to the brown lentils, we settled on Swiss chard, which can be added during the last 30 minutes of cooking.

2	onions, minced
4	garlic cloves, minced
2	tablespoons extra-virgin olive oil, plus extra for serving
1	tablespoon tomato paste
½	ounce dried porcini mushrooms, rinsed and minced
1½	teaspoons minced fresh thyme or 1 teaspoon dried
4	cups low-sodium chicken broth
4	cups vegetable broth
4	ounces bacon (about 4 slices)
3	carrots, peeled and cut into ½-inch pieces
12	ounces portobello caps (about 2 medium caps), gills removed and cut into ½-inch pieces
1	cup brown lentils (7 ounces), picked over and rinsed
2	bay leaves
8	ounces Swiss chard, stemmed and leaves sliced ½ inch thick (see page 33)
	Salt and pepper

1. Microwave onions, garlic, oil, tomato paste, porcini mushrooms, and thyme in bowl, stirring occasionally, until onions are softened, about 5 minutes; transfer to slow cooker.

2. Stir chicken broth, vegetable broth, bacon, carrots, portobello mushrooms, lentils, and bay leaves into slow cooker. Cover and cook until lentils are tender, 9 to 11 hours on low or 5 to 7 hours on high.

3. Stir in chard, cover, and cook on high until chard is tender, 20 to 30 minutes. Discard bacon and bay leaves. Season with salt and pepper to taste and serve with additional olive oil.

QUICK PREP TIP **REMOVING PORTOBELLO GILLS**

The black gills on the underside of a portobello mushroom cap can make a soup, stew, or sauce taste particularly muddy and look dark (especially if using lots of them). To avoid this, simply scrape the gills off the mushroom using a soupspoon before cooking.

Split Pea Soup

Serves 6 to 8   **Cooking Time** 9 to 11 hours on Low or 5 to 7 hours on High

WHY THIS RECIPE WORKS: To give our split pea soup a rich smoky flavor we added a ham hock to the mix from the start of the cooking time but for robust meatiness, making this recipe a meal in a bowl, we also cut up a ham steak and added it at the end to heat through. A handful of carrots add the traditional sweetness, color, and texture to this super-easy slow-cooker soup. Be sure to add the lemon juice at the end as it brightens the deep flavors of this rustic soup. Dried green peas can often contain small stones, so make sure to pick them over carefully.

2   onions, minced

3   garlic cloves, minced

1   tablespoon vegetable oil

1½ teaspoons minced fresh thyme
    or ½ teaspoon dried

⅛   teaspoon red pepper flakes

4   cups low-sodium chicken broth

3   cups water

1   pound green split peas (2 cups),
    picked over and rinsed

4   carrots, peeled and cut into
    ½-inch pieces

2   bay leaves

1   smoked ham hock, rinsed

8   ounces ham steak, cut into
    ½-inch pieces

1   tablespoon lemon juice
    Salt and pepper

1. Microwave onions, garlic, oil, thyme, and red pepper flakes in bowl, stirring occasionally, until onions are softened, about 5 minutes; transfer to slow cooker.

2. Stir broth, water, split peas, carrots, and bay leaves into slow cooker. Nestle ham hock into slow cooker. Cover and cook until peas are tender, 9 to 11 hours on low or 5 to 7 hours on high.

3. Remove ham hock, let cool slightly, then shred into bite-size pieces (see page 21), discarding skin and bones. Let soup settle for 5 minutes, then remove fat from surface using large spoon. Discard bay leaves.

4. Stir in ham steak and shredded ham hock, cover, and cook on high until heated through, about 15 minutes. Stir in lemon juice, season with salt and pepper to taste, and serve.

ON THE SIDE BUTTERY CROUTONS
Adjust oven rack to middle position and heat oven to 350 degrees. Toss 6 slices high-quality white sandwich bread, crusts removed and cut into ½-inch cubes (about 3 cups), with 3 tablespoons melted unsalted butter and season with salt and pepper. Spread croutons onto rimmed baking sheet and bake until golden brown and crisp, 20 to 25 minutes, tossing halfway through baking time. Let cool and serve. (Croutons can be stored in airtight container for up to 3 days.) Makes about 3 cups.

OLD-FASHIONED CHICKEN AND DUMPLINGS

Old-Fashioned Chicken and Dumplings

Serves 6 to 8   **Cooking Time** 4 to 6 hours on Low

✔ **WHY THIS RECIPE WORKS:** There's nothing more comforting than chicken and dumplings with its rich and velvety sauce topped by dense, buttery dumplings. The dumplings came together quickly with the help of the microwave, and after turning the slow cooker to high and bringing the stew to a simmer, the dumplings cooked through perfectly. If your slow cooker runs slow (or low—see our test on page 3), transfer the filling to a Dutch oven and add the dumplings after it has come to a simmer on the stovetop.

STEW

- 3 pounds boneless, skinless chicken thighs, trimmed
  Salt and pepper
- 3 tablespoons vegetable oil
- 2 onions, minced
- 2 celery ribs, sliced ¼ inch thick
- 6 garlic cloves, minced
- 1 tablespoon tomato paste
- 2 teaspoons minced fresh thyme or ½ teaspoon dried
- ⅓ cup all-purpose flour
- ¼ cup dry sherry
- 4½ cups low-sodium chicken broth, plus extra as needed
- 4 carrots, peeled and sliced ¼ inch thick
- 2 bay leaves
- 1 cup frozen peas
- 3 tablespoons minced fresh parsley

DUMPLINGS

- 2 cups all-purpose flour
- 1 tablespoon baking powder
- 1 teaspoon salt
- 1 cup whole milk
- 3 tablespoons unsalted butter

1. FOR THE STEW: Dry chicken with paper towels and season with salt and pepper. Heat 1 tablespoon oil in 12-inch skillet over medium-high heat until just smoking. Brown half of chicken lightly on both sides, 5 to 8 minutes; transfer to bowl. Repeat with 1 tablespoon more oil and remaining chicken; transfer to bowl.

2. Heat remaining tablespoon oil over medium-high heat until shimmering. Add onions, celery, garlic, tomato paste, and thyme, and cook until vegetables are softened and lightly browned, 8 to 10 minutes. Stir in flour and cook for 1 minute. Slowly whisk in sherry, scraping up any browned bits. Whisk in 1 cup broth, smoothing out any lumps; transfer to slow cooker.

3. Stir remaining 3½ cups broth, carrots, and bay leaves into slow cooker. Nestle browned chicken with any accumulated juice into slow cooker. Cover and cook until chicken is tender, 4 to 6 hours on low.

4. Transfer chicken to cutting board, let cool slightly, then shred into bite-size pieces (see page 21). Let stew settle for 5 minutes, then remove fat from surface using large spoon. Discard bay leaves.

5. Stir shredded chicken, peas, and parsley into stew, and season with salt and pepper to taste. (Adjust stew consistency with additional hot broth as needed.) Cover and cook on high until simmering (or transfer stew to Dutch oven and bring to simmer over medium heat).

6. FOR THE DUMPLINGS: Whisk flour, baking powder, and salt together in large bowl. Microwave milk and butter together until warm (do not overheat), about 1 minute, then whisk to melt butter. Stir milk mixture into flour mixture until just incorporated and smooth.

7. Drop golf ball–size dumplings on top of simmering stew, leaving about ¼ inch between each dumpling (you should have about 18 dumplings). Cover and cook until dumplings have doubled in size, 25 to 35 minutes. Serve.

Moroccan Chicken Stew

Serves 6 to 8   **Cooking Time** 4 to 6 hours on Low

✓ **WHY THIS RECIPE WORKS:** We were able to create an authentic and "exotic" Moroccan chicken stew in a slow cooker with minimal prep and using supermarket staples. Onions and garlic provided the backbone of flavor, while tomato paste added depth to our slow-simmered sauce. A few dried spices from the pantry—paprika, cardamom, and cayenne—as well as bay leaves and a cinnamon stick rounded out the base of flavor in this dish. Chickpeas, with their slightly nutty flavor and creamy texture, complemented the chicken perfectly. Adding the apricots twice, at the beginning of cooking and at the end of cooking, ensured that their flavor permeated the sauce and that some pieces retained their texture in the finished stew. Serve with Easy White Rice (page 134) or Toasted Couscous (page 70).

2	onions, minced
3	garlic cloves, minced
1	tablespoon tomato paste
1	tablespoon vegetable oil
1½	teaspoons sweet paprika
½	teaspoon ground cardamom
¼	teaspoon cayenne pepper
4	cups low-sodium chicken broth, plus extra as needed
½	cup dry white wine
2	(15-ounce) cans chickpeas, drained and rinsed
1	cup dried apricots, chopped medium
3	tablespoons Minute tapioca
2	bay leaves
1	cinnamon stick
3	pounds boneless, skinless chicken thighs, trimmed
	Salt and pepper
2	tablespoons minced fresh cilantro
	Light brown sugar
	Lemon wedges, for serving

1. Microwave onions, garlic, tomato paste, oil, paprika, cardamom, and cayenne in bowl, stirring occasionally, until onions are softened, about 5 minutes; transfer to slow cooker.

2. Stir broth, wine, chickpeas, half of apricots, tapioca, bay leaves, and cinnamon stick into slow cooker. Season chicken with salt and pepper and nestle into slow cooker. Cover and cook until chicken is tender, 4 to 6 hours on low.

3. Transfer chicken to cutting board, let cool slightly, then shred into bite-size pieces (see page 21). Let stew settle for 5 minutes, then remove fat from surface using large spoon. Discard bay leaves and cinnamon stick.

4. Stir in remaining apricots, cover, and cook on high until softened, 5 to 10 minutes. Stir in shredded chicken and let sit until heated through, about 5 minutes. (Adjust stew consistency with additional hot broth as needed.) Stir in cilantro, season with salt, pepper, and sugar to taste, and serve with lemon wedges.

QUICK PREP TIP **CHOPPING DRIED FRUIT**

Dried fruit, especially apricots (or dates), very often stick to the knife when you try to chop them. To avoid this problem, coat the blade with a thin film of vegetable cooking spray just before you begin chopping any dried fruit. The chopped fruit won't cling to the blade, and the knife will stay relatively clean.

Chicken Bouillabaisse

Serves 6 to 8   **Cooking Time** 4 to 6 hours on Low

✔ **WHY THIS RECIPE WORKS:** We adapted the flavors of France's most famous fish stew, bouillabaisse, rich with garlic, fennel, orange, and saffron, to the slow cooker using chicken instead of fish. The ingredients that give bouillabaisse its robust traditional flavor could withstand hours in the slow cooker, making for an intensely flavorful broth at the end of cooking. The flavors were so deep that we didn't even need to brown the chicken to boost its mild flavor, just the aromatics. A small amount of licorice-flavored liqueur (we prefer pastis) intensified the traditional anise backbone of this stew, while canned tomatoes lent welcome acidity and brightness.

3   **tablespoons olive oil**

1   **large leek, white and light green parts only, halved lengthwise, sliced thin, and washed thoroughly (see page 32)**

1   **small fennel bulb (about 8 ounces), tops discarded, halved, cored, and sliced thin (see page 66)**

4   **garlic cloves, minced**

1   **tablespoon tomato paste**

¼   **teaspoon saffron threads, crumbled**

⅛   **teaspoon cayenne pepper**

¼   **cup all-purpose flour**

¼   **cup pastis, Pernod, or ouzo**

½   **cup dry white wine**

4   **cups low-sodium chicken broth, plus extra as needed**

12   **ounces Yukon Gold potatoes (about 1 large), peeled and cut into ½-inch pieces**

1   **(14.5-ounce) can diced tomatoes, drained**

1   **(3-inch-long) strip orange zest, trimmed of white pith (see page 150)**

3   **pounds boneless, skinless chicken thighs, trimmed Salt and pepper**

1   **tablespoon minced fresh tarragon or parsley**

1   **recipe Garlic Toasts (page 28)**

1   **recipe Saffron Rouille**

1. Heat 2 tablespoons oil in 12-inch skillet over medium-high heat until shimmering. Add leek, fennel, garlic, tomato paste, saffron, and cayenne and cook until vegetables are softened and lightly browned, 8 to 10 minutes. Stir in flour and cook for 1 minute. Slowly whisk in pastis and wine, scraping up any browned bits. Whisk in 1 cup broth, smoothing out any lumps; transfer to slow cooker.

2. Microwave potatoes with remaining tablespoon oil in covered bowl, stirring occasionally, until nearly tender, about 3 minutes; transfer to slow cooker. Stir remaining 3 cups broth, tomatoes, and orange zest into slow cooker. Season chicken with salt and pepper and nestle into slow cooker. Cover and cook until chicken is tender, 4 to 6 hours on low.

3. Transfer chicken to cutting board, let cool slightly, then shred into bite-size pieces (see page 21). Let stew settle for 5 minutes, then remove fat from surface using large spoon. Discard orange zest.

4. Stir in shredded chicken and let sit until heated through, about 5 minutes. (Adjust stew consistency with additional hot broth as needed.) Stir in tarragon, season with salt and pepper to taste, and serve with Garlic Toasts and Saffron Rouille.

ON THE SIDE SAFFRON ROUILLE
Microwave 4½ teaspoons water and ⅛ teaspoon crumbled saffron threads together in medium bowl until steaming, about 10 seconds, then let steep for 5 minutes. Stir in 1 crustless slice white sandwich bread, torn into pieces, and 2 teaspoons lemon juice; let bread soften, about 5 minutes, then mash to smooth paste. Whisk in 1 large egg yolk, 1 teaspoon Dijon mustard, 1 small minced garlic clove, and pinch cayenne until smooth. Whisking constantly, slowly drizzle in ¼ cup vegetable oil and ¼ cup extra-virgin olive oil until mixture resembles smooth mayonnaise. Season with salt and pepper to taste and serve. (Rouille can be refrigerated in airtight container for up to 2 days.) Makes about ¾ cup.

Tex-Mex Chicken Stew

Serves 6 to 8   **Cooking Time** 4 to 6 hours on Low

WHY THIS RECIPE WORKS: This recipe is not only hearty and satisfying but it also comes together quickly thanks to canned tomatoes and beans and frozen corn. The flavors of this stew are so robust that we didn't even need to brown the aromatics or chicken. Instead of reaching for multiple jars of dried spices from the pantry, we opted for chili powder here, a blend of ground chiles, garlic powder, onion powder, oregano, ground cumin, and salt, which lent just the complexity we were seeking. For moderate heat we cooked a couple of jalapeño chiles with the chicken, which imparted subtle warmth to the finished stew. (To make this dish spicier, add the chile seeds.) For an added kick at the end of cooking as well as a boost of smoky flavor, we stirred in canned chipotles just before serving. Serve with Easy White Rice (page 134).

2	onions, minced
2	jalapeño chiles, stemmed, seeded, and minced
6	garlic cloves, minced
1	tablespoon tomato paste
1	tablespoon vegetable oil
1	tablespoon chili powder
4	cups low-sodium chicken broth, plus extra as needed
1	(14.5-ounce) can diced tomatoes, drained
¼	cup Minute tapioca
1	tablespoon light brown sugar
3	pounds boneless, skinless chicken thighs, trimmed
	Salt and pepper
2	cups frozen corn
1	(15-ounce) can black beans, drained and rinsed
	Minced canned chipotle chile in adobo sauce
¼	cup minced fresh cilantro

1. Microwave onions, jalapeños, garlic, tomato paste, oil, and chili powder in bowl, stirring occasionally, until onions are softened, about 5 minutes; transfer to slow cooker.

2. Stir broth, tomatoes, tapioca, and sugar into slow cooker. Season chicken with salt and pepper and nestle into slow cooker. Cover and cook until chicken is tender, 4 to 6 hours on low.

3. Transfer chicken to cutting board, let cool slightly, then shred into bite-size pieces (see page 21). Let stew settle for 5 minutes, then remove fat from surface using large spoon.

4. Stir in corn and beans, cover, and cook on high until heated through, about 10 minutes. Stir in shredded chicken, chipotles to taste, and let sit until heated through, about 5 minutes. (Adjust stew consistency with additional hot broth as needed.) Stir in cilantro, season with salt and pepper to taste, and serve.

SMART SHOPPING CHIPOTLE CHILES IN ADOBO
Canned chipotle chiles are jalapeños that have been ripened until red and then smoked and dried. They are sold as is, ground to a powder, or packed in a tomato-based sauce. We prefer the latter since they are already reconstituted by the sauce, making them easier to use. Most recipes don't use an entire can, but these chiles will keep for 2 weeks in the refrigerator or they can be frozen. To freeze, puree the chiles and quick-freeze teaspoonfuls on a plastic wrap–covered plate. Once these "chipotle chips" are hard, peel them off the plastic and transfer them to a zipper-lock freezer bag. Then thaw what you need before use. They can be stored this way for up to 2 months.

Spicy Thai-Style Chicken Stew

Serves 6 to 8   Cooking Time 4 to 6 hours on Low

WHY THIS RECIPE WORKS: This recipe awakens all the senses with its characteristic Thai balance of hot, sweet, sour, and salty flavors amid varying textures and bright colors. Fresh lemon grass, garlic, and ginger perfume the slow-simmered sauce, while warmed coconut milk, stirred in at the end, ties everything together. To get the perfect texture for the snow peas we microwaved them until just tender before mixing them into the finished stew (adding them at the start resulted in washed out flavor, color, and texture). The addition of lime juice, fish sauce, brown sugar, and cilantro at the end of cooking imparted fresh and bright notes, while jarred Thai green curry paste deepened the flavor. Serve with Easy White Rice (page 134).

1   **pound carrots (about 6), peeled and sliced ¼ inch thick**
2   **onions, minced**
2   **fresh Thai or jalapeño chiles, stemmed, seeded, and minced**
6   **garlic cloves, minced**
2   **tablespoons minced or grated fresh ginger**
3   **tablespoons vegetable oil**
2   **cups low-sodium chicken broth, plus extra as needed**
1   **stalk lemon grass, bottom 5 inches only, bruised (see page 20)**
¼   **cup Minute tapioca**
3   **pounds boneless, skinless chicken thighs, trimmed Salt and pepper**
1   **(14-ounce) can coconut milk**
2   **tablespoons fresh lime juice**
1   **tablespoon fish sauce**
1   **tablespoon Thai green curry paste (see page 12)**
1   **tablespoon light brown sugar**
8   **ounces snow peas (about 4 cups), trimmed**
¼   **cup minced fresh cilantro or basil Lime wedges, for serving**

1. Microwave carrots, onions, chiles, garlic, ginger, and 2 tablespoons oil in bowl, stirring occasionally, until vegetables are softened, 8 to 10 minutes; transfer to slow cooker.

2. Stir broth, lemon grass, and tapioca into slow cooker. Season chicken with salt and pepper and nestle into slow cooker. Cover and cook until chicken is tender, 4 to 6 hours on low.

3. Transfer chicken to cutting board, let cool slightly, then shred into bite-size pieces (see page 21). Let stew settle for 5 minutes, then remove fat from surface using large spoon. Discard lemon grass.

4. Microwave coconut milk in bowl, stirring occasionally, until hot, about 3 minutes. Stir lime juice, fish sauce, curry paste, and sugar into hot coconut milk to dissolve, then stir mixture into stew.

5. Microwave snow peas with remaining tablespoon oil in bowl, stirring occasionally, until tender, about 5 minutes. Stir shredded chicken and snow peas into stew and let sit until heated through, about 5 minutes. (Adjust stew consistency with additional hot broth as needed.) Stir in cilantro, season with salt and pepper to taste, and serve with lime wedges.

Chicken Curry in a Hurry

Serves 6 to 8   **Cooking Time** 4 to 6 hours on Low

WHY THIS RECIPE WORKS: Curry is a stew that is especially well suited for a slow cooker. When the ingredients have the opportunity to cook for hours, the flavors meld and the result is a deeply flavorful and complex dish. To pack the most flavor into our curry, we focused on the essentials: curry powder, garlic, ginger, chiles, and garam masala, and we bloomed them in oil in the microwave before adding them to the slow cooker. Coconut milk tempered the heat of this stew and married the flavors of the dish, while the sweetness of plump golden raisins added another necessary flavor dimension. For thickening, we added tapioca directly to the slow cooker. Plum tomatoes, peas, and cilantro lent brightness as well as touches of color to the finished dish. Creamy, slightly nutty canned chickpeas worked well with the flavors of the curry and accented the mild flavor of the chicken. Serve with Easy White Rice (page 134) or Toasted Couscous (page 70).

2	onions, minced
2	jalapeño chiles, stemmed, seeded, and minced
3	tablespoons vegetable oil
6	garlic cloves, minced
2	tablespoons minced or grated fresh ginger
2	tablespoons curry powder
1	tablespoon tomato paste
1	teaspoon garam masala (see page 74)
2	(15-ounce) cans chickpeas, drained and rinsed
2	cups water, plus extra as needed
1	(14-ounce) can coconut milk
3	tablespoons Minute tapioca
3	pounds boneless, skinless chicken thighs, trimmed
	Salt and pepper
12	ounces plum tomatoes (3 to 4), cored and chopped fine
½	cup golden raisins
1	cup frozen peas
¼	cup minced fresh cilantro
	Lime wedges, for serving

1. Microwave onions, jalapeños, oil, garlic, ginger, curry, tomato paste, and garam masala in bowl, stirring occasionally, until onions are softened, about 5 minutes; transfer to slow cooker.

2. Stir chickpeas, water, coconut milk, and tapioca into slow cooker. Season chicken with salt and pepper and nestle into slow cooker. Cover and cook until chicken is tender, 4 to 6 hours on low.

3. Transfer chicken to cutting board, let cool slightly, then shred into bite-size pieces (see page 21). Let stew settle for 5 minutes, then remove fat from surface using large spoon.

4. Stir in tomatoes and raisins, cover, and cook on high until heated through, about 10 minutes. Stir in shredded chicken and peas and let sit until heated through, about 5 minutes. (Adjust stew consistency with additional hot broth as needed.) Stir in cilantro, season with salt and pepper to taste, and serve with lime wedges.

SMART SHOPPING CURRY POWDER
Though blends can vary dramatically, curry powders come in two basic styles: mild or sweet and a hotter version called Madras. The former combines as many as 20 different ground spices, herbs, and seeds. We tasted six curry powders, mixed into a simple rice pilaf and in a plain vegetable curry. Our favorite was **Penzeys Sweet Curry Powder**, though Durkee Curry Powder came in a close second.

Chicken Gumbo

Serves 6 to 8   **Cooking Time** 4 to 6 hours on Low

✓ **WHY THIS RECIPE WORKS:** To make a flavorful gumbo in a slow cooker we started by making a traditional dark roux (be sure to use a deep pot). Because the roux and sautéed vegetables and cayenne add deep flavor to the mix, we were able to skip browning the chicken and sausage, instead simply nestling them into the broth along with the okra and bay leaves after adding the fragrant broth mixture to the slow cooker. Serve with Easy White Rice (page 134).

½ cup all-purpose flour
½ cup vegetable oil
2 onions, minced
1 red bell pepper, stemmed, seeded, and chopped fine (see page 91)
1 green bell pepper, stemmed, seeded, and chopped fine (see page 91)
1 celery rib, minced
6 garlic cloves, minced
2 teaspoons minced fresh thyme or ½ teaspoon dried
¼ teaspoon cayenne pepper
3½ cups low-sodium chicken broth, plus extra as needed
1 pound andouille sausage, sliced ½ inch thick
12 ounces fresh okra, sliced ½ inch thick, or frozen cut okra, thawed and thoroughly patted dry
2 bay leaves
2 pounds boneless, skinless chicken thighs, trimmed
Salt and pepper
4 scallions, sliced thin
2 tablespoons minced fresh parsley

1. Adjust oven rack to lowest position and heat oven to 350 degrees. Toast flour in large Dutch oven over medium heat, stirring constantly, until it begins to brown, about 5 minutes. Off heat, whisk in oil until smooth. Cover pot, transfer to oven, and cook until roux is deep brown and fragrant, about 45 minutes.

2. Remove pot from oven and whisk roux to combine.

3. Stir onions, bell peppers, celery, garlic, thyme, and cayenne into hot roux and cook over medium heat, stirring often, until vegetables are softened, 10 to 12 minutes. Slowly whisk in chicken broth, scraping up any browned bits and smoothing out any lumps. Increase heat to medium-high, bring to simmer; carefully transfer to slow cooker.

4. Stir sausage, okra, and bay leaves into slow cooker. Season chicken with salt and pepper and nestle into slow cooker. Cover and cook until chicken is tender, 4 to 6 hours on low.

5. Transfer chicken to cutting board, let cool slightly, then shred into bite-size pieces (see page 21). Let stew settle for 5 minutes, then remove fat from surface using large spoon. Discard bay leaves. Stir in shredded chicken and let sit until heated through, about 5 minutes. (Adjust stew consistency with additional hot broth as needed.) Stir in scallions and parsley, season with salt and pepper to taste, and serve.

QUICK PREP TIP EASIEST-EVER ROUX
The dark roux is what gives gumbo its toasty depth of flavor, but it can takes upwards of an hour to cook, and can be quite dangerous on the stovetop because it is incredibly hot and requires constant stirring. We developed a quicker and safer alternative by pretoasting the flour and cooking the roux in the oven. The even heat of the oven allows the roux to brown evenly, so less stirring is required, and it keeps the scalding pot out of harm's way. A fully cooked roux should look dark and glossy, and be the color of an old copper penny.

Chicken Stew with Sausage and White Beans

Serves 6 to 8   **Cooking Time** 4 to 6 hours on Low

✔ **WHY THIS RECIPE WORKS:** This hearty stew takes its inspiration from classic Tuscan white bean stew; only here, we combined meaty chicken thighs with sausage. For convenience we used canned white beans, adding them to the slow cooker to heat through at the end of the cooking time. We found it was worth getting out the skillet to brown the chicken and sausage and sauté the aromatics and fennel; this step added a richer, deeper flavor. The sliced fennel, thyme, and red pepper flakes complemented the flavors of the Italian sausage and worked nicely with the mellow flavor and creamy texture of the beans. The spinach may seem like a lot at first, but it wilts down substantially. A sprinkling of grated Parmesan cheese is a must here—its nutty and salty flavor enhances the other flavors in the stew. Serve with Garlic Toasts (page 28).

2	pounds boneless, skinless chicken thighs, trimmed
	Salt and pepper
3	tablespoons vegetable oil
1	pound Italian sausage links, sliced ½ inch thick
2	onions, minced
1	fennel bulb (about 12 ounces), tops discarded, halved, cored, and sliced thin (see page 66)
6	garlic cloves, minced
1	tablespoon tomato paste
2	teaspoons minced fresh thyme or ½ teaspoon dried
⅛	teaspoon red pepper flakes
⅓	cup all-purpose flour
½	cup dry white wine
4	cups low-sodium chicken broth, plus extra as needed
2	bay leaves
2	(15-ounce) cans cannellini beans, drained and rinsed
6	ounces baby spinach (about 6 cups)
	Grated Parmesan cheese, for serving

1. Dry chicken with paper towels and season with salt and pepper. Heat 1 tablespoon oil in 12-inch skillet over medium-high heat until just smoking. Brown half of chicken lightly on both sides, 5 to 8 minutes; transfer to bowl. Repeat with 1 tablespoon more oil and remaining chicken; transfer to bowl.

2. Heat remaining tablespoon oil over medium-high heat until just smoking. Brown sausage well, about 3 minutes; transfer to bowl with chicken. Pour off all but 1 tablespoon fat left in pan, add onions, fennel, garlic, tomato paste, thyme, and red pepper flakes and cook over medium-high heat until vegetables are softened and lightly browned, 8 to 10 minutes.

3. Stir in flour and cook for 1 minute. Slowly whisk in wine, scraping up any browned bits. Whisk in 1 cup broth, smoothing out any lumps; transfer to slow cooker. Stir remaining 3 cups broth and bay leaves into slow cooker. Nestle browned chicken with any accumulated juice into slow cooker. Cover and cook until chicken is tender, 4 to 6 hours on low.

4. Transfer chicken to cutting board, let cool slightly, then shred into bite-size pieces (see page 21). Let stew settle for 5 minutes, then remove fat from surface using large spoon. Discard bay leaves.

5. Stir in beans and spinach, cover, and cook on high until heated through, about 10 minutes. Stir in shredded chicken and let sit until heated through, about 5 minutes. (Adjust stew consistency with additional hot broth as needed.) Season with salt and pepper to taste and serve with Parmesan.

Bachelor Beef Stew

Serves 6   **Cooking Time** 9 to 11 hours on Low or 5 to 7 hours on High

WHY THIS RECIPE WORKS: You won't even need to dirty a knife to make this super-streamlined but surprisingly flavorful beef stew. To start, we chose whole steak tips over our traditional choice—cubes of chuck—alleviating the need to cut any raw meat (we shredded it into bite-sized pieces once it was cooked and tender). As for the aromatics and accompanying vegetables, we further simplified things by choosing frozen onions, baby carrots, and frozen roasted potatoes (which we microwaved and added to the stew at the end of the cooking time). A little tomato paste and soy sauce add meaty flavor and richness to this stew.

2 **cups frozen chopped onions (or 2 onions, minced)**
3 **tablespoons tomato paste**
2 **tablespoons vegetable oil**
1½ **teaspoons garlic powder (or 6 garlic cloves, minced)**
2 **teaspoons minced fresh thyme or ½ teaspoon dried**
1 **cup low-sodium chicken broth, plus extra as needed**
1 **cup beef broth**
8 **ounces baby carrots**
¼ **cup soy sauce**
2 **tablespoons Minute tapioca**
2 **bay leaves**
3 **pounds beef steak tips**
	Salt and pepper
1 **pound frozen roasted potatoes, steak fries, or French fries**
1 **cup frozen peas**

1. Microwave onions, tomato paste, 1 tablespoon oil, garlic powder, and thyme in bowl, stirring occasionally, until onions are softened, about 5 minutes; transfer to slow cooker.

2. Stir chicken broth, beef broth, carrots, soy sauce, tapioca, and bay leaves into slow cooker. Season beef with salt and pepper and nestle into slow cooker. Cover and cook until beef is tender, 9 to 11 hours on low or 5 to 7 hours on high.

3. Transfer beef to cutting board, let cool slightly, then shred into bite-size pieces (see page 21). Let stew settle for 5 minutes, then remove fat from surface using large spoon. Discard bay leaves.

4. Microwave potatoes with remaining tablespoon oil in bowl, stirring occasionally, until thawed and warm, 5 to 7 minutes. Stir warm potatoes, shredded beef, and peas into stew and let sit until heated through, about 5 minutes. (Adjust stew consistency with additional hot broth as needed.) Season with salt and pepper to taste and serve.

SMART SHOPPING FROZEN CHOPPED ONIONS

Frozen chopped onions can be a convenient way to save a few minutes of prep time (as well as a few tears). Though we would never recommend them for salads or for recipes in which the onion flavor is important (such as French onion soup), we think they work just fine in hearty dishes such as stew and are well suited to the slow cooker. You can swap one packed cup of frozen chopped onions for one medium minced onion. Just be sure to cook (sauté or microwave) the frozen onions as directed before adding them to the slow cooker.

Easy Asian-Style Beef Stew

Serves 6   **Cooking Time** 9 to 11 hours on Low or 5 to 7 hours on High

WHY THIS RECIPE WORKS: Inspired by our success with our no-prep Bachelor Beef Stew (page 56) we decided to give it an Asian spin with the help of ingredients like ginger and dry sherry. We minimized the preparation of vegetables by incorporating baby carrots at the outset of cooking, then stirred in snow peas and water chestnuts at the end, microwaving the snow peas just before adding them to ensure their bright flavor and crisp texture. Finishing the stew with a little brown sugar helped balance the flavors while a few sliced scallions added a burst of fresh flavor. We like to serve this stew with extra soy sauce to taste. Serve with Easy White Rice (page 134).

2	**cups frozen chopped onions (or 2 onions, minced)**
3	**tablespoons tomato paste**
2	**tablespoons vegetable oil**
1	**tablespoon ground ginger (or 2 tablespoons minced or grated fresh ginger)**
1 ½	**teaspoons garlic powder (or 6 garlic cloves, minced)**
1	**cup beef broth**
¾	**cup chicken broth, plus extra as needed**
8	**ounces baby carrots**
¼	**cup soy sauce, plus extra for serving**
¼	**cup dry sherry**
2	**tablespoons Minute tapioca**
2	**bay leaves**
3	**pounds beef steak tips**
	Salt and pepper
6	**ounces snow peas (about 3 cups), trimmed**
1	**(8-ounce) can sliced water chestnuts, drained and patted dry**
4	**scallions, sliced thin**
1	**tablespoon brown sugar**

1. Microwave onions, tomato paste, 1 tablespoon oil, ginger, and garlic powder in bowl, stirring occasionally, until onions are softened, about 5 minutes; transfer to slow cooker

2. Stir beef broth, chicken broth, carrots, soy sauce, sherry, tapioca, and bay leaves into slow cooker. Season beef with salt and pepper and nestle into slow cooker. Cover and cook until beef is tender, 9 to 11 hours on low or 5 to 7 hours on high.

3. Transfer beef to cutting board, let cool slightly, then shred into bite-size pieces (see page 21). Let stew settle for 5 minutes, then remove fat from surface using large spoon. Discard bay leaves.

4. Microwave snow peas with remaining tablespoon oil in bowl, stirring occasionally, until tender, about 5 minutes. Stir shredded beef, peas, and water chestnuts into stew and let sit until heated through, about 5 minutes. (Adjust stew consistency with additional hot broth as needed.) Stir in scallions and brown sugar, season with salt and pepper to taste, and serve with additional soy sauce.

ON THE SIDE SPINACH SALAD WITH CARROT AND SESAME
Whisk 7 teaspoons rice vinegar, 1 tablespoon minced shallot, 1 tablespoon toasted sesame seeds, 1 teaspoon Dijon mustard, ¾ teaspoon mayonnaise, and ½ teaspoon grated orange zest together in bowl. Slowly whisk in 3 tablespoons vegetable oil and 1½ tablespoons toasted sesame oil. In large bowl gently toss 6 ounces baby spinach and 2 peeled, thinly sliced carrots with dressing. Serves 6.

Hearty Beef Stew

Serves 6 to 8   **Cooking Time** 9 to 11 hours on Low or 5 to 7 hours on High

WHY THIS RECIPE WORKS: Achieving big, bold, beefy flavor in a beef stew typically starts with browning the meat, but we wanted maximum flavor without all the labor. To avoid browning the meat and still achieve a blue-ribbon beef stew, we enlisted the help of tomato paste—which we browned with the other aromatics—to help create a rich, complex base. A combination of chicken and beef broths also helped pump up the meaty notes, though it was the unlikely addition of soy sauce that finally took this stew to the next level. We kept the potatoes and carrots tender but distinct during the long cooking time by placing them in a foil packet on top of the stew.

3	tablespoons vegetable oil
3	onions, minced
¼	cup tomato paste
6	garlic cloves, minced
1	tablespoon minced fresh thyme or 1 teaspoon dried
⅓	cup all-purpose flour
1½	cups low-sodium chicken broth, plus extra as needed
1½	cups beef broth
⅓	cup soy sauce
2	bay leaves
1	(4-pound) boneless beef chuck roast, trimmed and cut into 1½-inch chunks
	Salt and pepper
1½	pounds red potatoes (4 to 5 medium), scrubbed and cut into 1-inch chunks
1	pound carrots (about 6), peeled, halved lengthwise, and sliced 1 inch thick
2	cups frozen peas

1. Heat 2 tablespoons oil in 12-inch skillet over medium-high heat until shimmering. Add onions, tomato paste, garlic, and thyme and cook until onions are softened and lightly browned, 8 to 10 minutes. Stir in flour and cook for 1 minute. Slowly whisk in chicken broth, scraping up any browned bits and smoothing out any lumps; transfer to slow cooker.

2. Stir in beef broth, soy sauce, and bay leaves. Season beef with salt and pepper and nestle into slow cooker. Toss potatoes and carrots with remaining tablespoon oil, season with salt and pepper, and wrap in foil packet (see page 60). Lay foil packet on top of stew. Cover and cook until beef is tender, 9 to 11 hours on low or 5 to 7 hours on high.

3. Transfer foil packet to plate. Let stew settle for 5 minutes, then remove fat using large spoon. Discard bay leaves.

4. Carefully open foil packet (watch for steam), and stir vegetables with any accumulated juice into stew. Stir in peas and let sit until heated through, about 5 minutes. (Adjust stew consistency with additional hot broth as needed.) Season with salt and pepper to taste and serve.

QUICK PREP TIP CUTTING STEW MEAT
Pull apart the roast at its major seams (delineated by lines of fat and silver skin). Use a knife as necessary. Then trim off the excess fat and silver skin. Cut the meat into chunks as specified by the recipe.

Super-Veggie Beef Stew

Serves 6 to 8   **Cooking Time** 9 to 11 hours on Low or 5 to 7 hours on High

WHY THIS RECIPE WORKS: Here we added parsnips, portobello mushroom caps, and earthy kale to the usual carrots and potatoes. We were able to avoid browning the meat by sautéing aromatics with tomato paste, which, when browned, created a fond in the bottom of the pan similar to that left behind by browning meat. A little flour, cooked in this mixture, thickened the stew and deglazing the pan with chicken broth helped give our stew a flavorful foundation.

3	tablespoons vegetable oil
3	onions, minced
¼	cup tomato paste
6	garlic cloves, minced
1	tablespoon minced fresh thyme or 1 teaspoon dried
⅓	cup all-purpose flour
1½	cups low-sodium chicken broth, plus extra as needed
1½	cups beef broth
8	ounces portobello caps (about 2 medium caps), gills removed (see page 40), cut into ½-inch pieces
⅓	cup soy sauce
2	bay leaves
1	(4-pound) boneless beef chuck roast, trimmed and cut into 1½-inch chunks (see page 59) Salt and pepper
12	ounces red potatoes (2 to 3 medium), scrubbed and cut into 1-inch chunks
4	carrots, peeled, halved lengthwise, and sliced 1 inch thick
3	parsnips, peeled, halved lengthwise, and sliced 1 inch thick
8	ounces kale, stemmed and leaves sliced ¼ inch thick (see page 33)

1. Heat 2 tablespoons oil in 12-inch skillet over medium-high heat until shimmering. Add onions, tomato paste, garlic, and thyme and cook until onions are softened and lightly browned, 8 to 10 minutes. Stir in flour and cook for 1 minute. Slowly whisk in chicken broth, scraping up any browned bits and smoothing out any lumps; transfer to slow cooker.

2. Stir beef broth, portobellos, soy sauce, and bay leaves into slow cooker. Season beef with salt and pepper and nestle into slow cooker. Toss potatoes, carrots, and parsnips with remaining tablespoon oil, season with salt and pepper, and wrap in foil packet. Lay foil packet on top of stew. Cover and cook until beef is tender, 9 to 11 hours on low or 5 to 7 hours on high.

3. Transfer foil packet to plate. Let stew settle for 5 minutes, then remove fat from surface using large spoon. Discard bay leaves. Stir in kale, cover, and cook on high until tender, 20 to 30 minutes.

4. Carefully open foil packet (watch for steam), stir vegetables with any accumulated juice into stew, and let sit until heated through, about 5 minutes. (Adjust stew consistency with additional hot broth as needed.) Season with salt and pepper to taste and serve.

QUICK PREP TIP MAKING A FOIL PACKET
Place vegetables (or chicken) on one side of a large piece of foil. Fold the foil over and crimp to seal the edges. Place the packet on top of the soup or stew, pressing gently as needed.

ALL ABOUT Beef

The slow cooker, with its moist heat environment, is a great vehicle for braising meat. So this means choosing cuts that will benefit from braising, namely the tougher, fattier cuts, mostly from the shoulder, cuts that turn meltingly tender after hours of cooking (when the collagen in the meat has broken down). Don't even think about using a premium cut like filet mignon or strip steak in a slow cooker—it would be a waste of money. Save them for the grill or the stovetop. Here's a list of the meat we've chosen to use in the slow cooker and why.

Chuck-Eye Roast

One of our favorite cuts of meat for the slow cooker, this roast is cut from the center of the first five ribs and, because of its relatively high and even distribution of fat, it will taste succulent when braised. It's our favorite choice for pot roast (in the slow cooker or in the oven), and makes great stew meat. We use it in many of our hearty slow-cooker beef stews, meaty chilis, and enchilada fillings.

Blade Steaks

Cut from the shoulder of the cow, top blade steaks are tender, but each has a line of gristle running down the center so they need to be trimmed before they are placed in the slow cooker (see page 16). When braised, blade steaks yield tender, easy-to-shred meat with big, beefy flavor. We use them in several recipes including Beef and Barley Soup (page 15) and Old-Fashioned Beef and Noodle Soup (page 16).

Flank Steak

Flank steak is a large, thin, flat steak. Although it might not seem like an obvious choice for the slow cooker because it is so lean, we found that it did become tender and shreddable in the slow cooker and its big beefy flavor was an asset in our Italian Sunday Gravy (page 172).

Brisket

Brisket is a great cut of meat for the slow cooker despite the fact that it is not marbled throughout like a chuck roast. It is sold as either first (flat) cut, pictured here, or second (point) cut. Either cut will work fine in the slow cooker, but if you can find a point cut brisket, it is ideal because it is fattier and will be even more tender after slow cooking. Since the fat on a brisket renders into the sauce rather than basting the interior of the meat, it takes a few tricks to ensure flavorful meat and a richly flavored sauce.

Steak Tips

Steak tips can come from two areas of the cow. One kind comes from tender, expensive cuts in the middle of the cow, such as the tenderloin. If the steak tips at your market cost $8 to $10 a pound, they most likely came from the tenderloin. True steak tips come from various muscles in the sirloin and round and cost about $5 per pound. We used these inexpensive steak tips in our Bachelor Beef Stew (page 56) because they required no prep (we added them whole to the slow cooker) and they were easy to shred before serving.

Short Ribs

Cut from any part along the length of the cow's ribs, short ribs require a long, slow braise to achieve fork-tender perfection. They can be cut English or flanken style; we use the more affordable and more widely available English-style ribs, which contain one long flat rib bone to which a rectangular piece of fatty meat is attached; flanken-style ribs feature a long, continuous piece of meat that has been cut across the grain and contains two or three small rib bone segments. Short ribs ooze fat into the sauce making it essential to degrease before serving.

Beef Burgundy

Serves 8   **Cooking Time** 9 to 11 hours on Low or 5 to 7 hours on High

✔ **WHY THIS RECIPE WORKS:** To ensure a rich-tasting, company-worthy beef burgundy, we decided it was worth a little extra prep time. So to start, we browned half the meat (the other half can be added raw to the slow cooker). Then we boosted the base of the stew by sautéing bacon with a hefty amount of garlic and thyme and adding tomato paste for sweetness and soy sauce for extra meatiness. To keep the flavor of the wine in balance, we added half of it at the outset and then reduced the remaining half to mellow its sharpness before adding it to the stew at the end. Frozen pearl onions made things easy; we simply cooked them through and browned them in a skillet before adding them and browned mushrooms to the finished stew. Serve with Easy Mashed Potatoes (page 96) or Buttered Egg Noodles (page 64).

1 **(5-pound) boneless beef chuck roast, trimmed and cut into 1½-inch chunks (see page 59)**
Salt and pepper
1 **tablespoon vegetable oil**
4 **ounces bacon (about 4 slices), minced**
3 **onions, minced**
1 **carrot, peeled and minced**
¼ **cup tomato paste**
6 **garlic cloves, minced**
1 **tablespoon minced fresh thyme or 1 teaspoon dried**
⅓ **cup all-purpose flour**
2½ **cups Pinot Noir**
1½ **cups low-sodium chicken broth, plus extra as needed**
⅓ **cup soy sauce**
2 **bay leaves**
2 **cups frozen pearl onions**
½ **cup water**
3 **tablespoons unsalted butter**
2 **teaspoons sugar**
1 **pound cremini mushrooms, trimmed and halved if small or quartered if large**

1. Dry beef with paper towels and season with salt and pepper. Place half of beef in slow cooker. Heat oil in 12-inch skillet over medium-high heat until just smoking. Brown remaining beef well on all sides, 7 to 10 minutes; transfer to slow cooker.

2. Cook bacon in skillet over medium-high heat until crisp, about 5 minutes. Stir in onions, carrot, tomato paste, garlic, and thyme and cook until onions are softened and lightly browned, 8 to 10 minutes. Stir in flour and cook for 1 minute. Slowly whisk in 1¼ cups wine, scraping up any browned bits and smoothing out any lumps; transfer to slow cooker.

3. Stir broth, soy sauce, and bay leaves into slow cooker. Cover and cook until beef is tender, 9 to 11 hours on low or 5 to 7 hours on high.

4. About 20 minutes before serving, bring frozen pearl onions, water, butter, and sugar to boil in 12-inch skillet. Reduce to simmer, cover, and cook until onions are fully thawed and tender, 5 to 8 minutes. Uncover, bring to a boil, and cook until all liquid evaporates, 3 to 4 minutes. Stir in mushrooms and cook until vegetables are browned and glazed, 8 to 12 minutes; transfer to slow cooker.

5. Add remaining 1¼ cups wine to skillet and simmer until it has reduced by half, 6 to 8 minutes; transfer to slow cooker. Let stew settle for 5 minutes, then remove fat from surface using large spoon. Discard bay leaves. (Adjust stew consistency with additional hot broth as needed.) Season with salt and pepper to taste and serve.

Beef Stroganoff

Serves 6 to 8   **Cooking Time** 9 to 11 hours on Low or 5 to 7 hours on High

✔ **WHY THIS RECIPE WORKS:** To make sure our slow-cooker version of beef stroganoff delivered tender beef in a meaty mushroom sauce, we started by getting out our skillet and browning the mushrooms to concentrate their flavor, augmenting them with dried porcini mushrooms for an even deeper mushroom flavor that wouldn't be muted by hours in a slow cooker. Then, since we had our skillet out to brown the mushrooms, we sautéed the aromatics and created a flour-thickened base for the stew to produce the proper consistency. With such a flavorful base, we didn't need to brown the meat but could add it directly to the slow cooker—a real timesaver. Serve with Buttered Egg Noodles.

3	tablespoons vegetable oil
1½	pounds white mushrooms, trimmed and halved if small or quartered if large
	Salt and pepper
3	onions, minced
¼	cup tomato paste
6	garlic cloves, minced
½	ounce dried porcini mushrooms, rinsed and minced
1	tablespoon minced fresh thyme or 1 teaspoon dried
⅓	cup all-purpose flour
1½	cups low-sodium chicken broth, plus extra as needed
½	cup dry white wine
⅓	cup soy sauce
2	bay leaves
1	(4-pound) boneless beef chuck roast, trimmed and cut into 1½-inch chunks (see page 59)
⅓	cup sour cream
2	teaspoons Dijon mustard
2	tablespoons minced fresh dill

1. Heat 1 tablespoon oil in 12-inch skillet over medium heat until shimmering. Add mushrooms and ¼ teaspoon salt, cover, and cook until mushrooms are softened, about 5 minutes. Uncover and continue to cook until mushrooms are dry and browned, 5 to 10 minutes longer; transfer to slow cooker.

2. Heat remaining 2 tablespoons oil in skillet over medium-high heat until shimmering. Add onions, tomato paste, garlic, porcini, and thyme and cook until onions are softened and lightly browned, 8 to 10 minutes. Stir in flour and cook for 1 minute. Slowly whisk in broth, scraping up any browned bits and smoothing out any lumps; transfer to slow cooker.

3. Stir wine, soy sauce, and bay leaves into slow cooker. Season beef with salt and pepper and nestle into slow cooker. Cover and cook until beef is tender, 9 to 11 hours on low or 5 to 7 hours on high.

4. Let stew settle for 5 minutes, then remove fat from surface using large spoon. Discard bay leaves. In bowl, combine 1 cup hot stew liquid with sour cream and Dijon (to temper), then stir mixture into stew. (Adjust stew consistency with additional hot broth as needed.) Stir in dill, season with salt and pepper to taste, and serve.

ON THE SIDE BUTTERED EGG NOODLES
Cook 1 pound egg noodles in salted boiling water, drain, and toss with 2 tablespoons butter. Season with salt and pepper to taste. Serves 6 to 8.

Beef Goulash

Serves 6 to 8   **Cooking Time** 9 to 11 hours on Low or 5 to 7 hours on High

✔ **WHY THIS RECIPE WORKS:** A great beef goulash contains chunks of tender meat in a fragrant and creamy paprika-flavored sauce. But when made in a slow cooker, the delicate flavors of this dish often turn muddy and the paprika is nearly impossible to detect. In order to maintain the vibrant flavors of the dish, we used a hefty amount of paprika along with some caraway seeds, which we bloomed with the other aromatics in the microwave to help their flavors permeate the stew. Tempering the sour cream with a little of the hot stewing liquid at the end helped prevent it from curdling once added to the goulash. Serve with Buttered Egg Noodles (page 64).

3	onions, minced
¼	cup sweet paprika
¼	cup tomato paste
3	tablespoons vegetable oil
6	garlic cloves, minced
1	teaspoon caraway seeds
2	cups low-sodium chicken broth, plus extra as needed
⅓	cup soy sauce
¼	cup Minute tapioca
2	bay leaves
1	(4-pound) boneless beef chuck roast, trimmed and cut into 1½-inch chunks (see page 59)
	Salt and pepper
⅓	cup sour cream
2	tablespoons minced fresh parsley

1. Microwave onions, paprika, tomato paste, oil, garlic, and caraway seeds in bowl, stirring occasionally, until onions are softened, about 5 minutes; transfer to slow cooker.

2. Stir broth, soy sauce, tapioca, and bay leaves into slow cooker. Season beef with salt and pepper and nestle into slow cooker. Cover and cook until beef is tender, 9 to 11 hours on low or 5 to 7 hours on high.

3. Let stew settle for 5 minutes, then remove fat from surface using large spoon. Discard bay leaves. In bowl, combine 1 cup hot stew liquid with sour cream (to temper), then stir mixture into stew. (Adjust stew consistency with additional hot broth as needed.) Stir in parsley, season with salt and pepper to taste, and serve.

SMART SHOPPING PAPRIKA
"Paprika" is a generic term for a spice made from ground dried red peppers and is available in several forms. Sweet paprika (or "Hungarian paprika," or simply "paprika") is the most common. Typically made from a combination of mild red peppers, it is prized more for its deep scarlet hue than for its very subtle flavor. Smoked paprika, a Spanish favorite, is produced by drying sweet or hot peppers over smoldering oak embers. We don't recommend using this variety for all paprika applications; it is best for seasoning grilled meats or adding a smoky aroma to boldly flavored dishes. Hot paprika, most often used in chilis, curries, and stews, can range from slightly spicy to punishingly assertive. Although hot paprika shouldn't be substituted for sweet paprika in cooking, sweet paprika can be substituted for hot by adding cayenne pepper.

Fancy Pork Stew with Fennel and Prunes

Serves 6 to 8   **Cooking Time** 9 to 11 hours on Low or 5 to 7 hours on High

✔ **WHY THIS RECIPE WORKS:** This French-inspired dish with fall-apart tender chunks of pork, fennel, carrots, and prunes in a rich and creamy sauce will have friends and family thinking you slaved for hours over a hot stovetop. We microwaved leeks and garlic with oil to get a flavorful base underway and to keep the vegetables tender, we placed them in a foil pouch on top of the stew. The prunes are added at the end to preserve their flavor, and a hefty dose of tarragon and fresh lemon juice brighten the flavors of the stew just before serving. Serve with Buttered Egg Noodles (page 64) or Easy Mashed Potatoes (page 96).

1	pound leeks, white and light green parts only, halved lengthwise, sliced ½ inch thick, and washed thoroughly (see page 32)
3	garlic cloves, minced
2	tablespoons vegetable oil
2½	cups low-sodium chicken broth, plus extra as needed
½	cup brandy
3	tablespoons Minute tapioca
2	bay leaves
1	(4-pound) boneless pork butt roast, trimmed and cut into 1½-inch chunks (see page 59) Salt and pepper
1	pound carrots (about 6), peeled, halved lengthwise, and sliced 1 inch thick
1	fennel bulb (about 12 ounces), tops discarded, halved, cored, and sliced ½ inch thick
1½	cups prunes, quartered
1	cup heavy cream
2	tablespoons minced fresh tarragon
1	tablespoon fresh lemon juice

1. Microwave leeks, garlic, and 1 tablespoon oil in bowl, stirring occasionally, until leeks are softened, about 5 minutes; transfer to slow cooker.

2. Stir broth, brandy, tapioca, and bay leaves into slow cooker. Season pork with salt and pepper and nestle into slow cooker. Toss carrots and fennel with remaining tablespoon oil, season with salt and pepper, and wrap in foil packet (see page 60). Lay foil packet on top of stew. Cover and cook until pork is tender, 9 to 11 hours on low or 5 to 7 hours on high.

3. Transfer foil packet to plate. Let stew settle for 5 minutes, then remove fat from surface using large spoon. Discard bay leaves.

4. Carefully open foil packet (watch for steam) and stir vegetables with any accumulated juice into stew. Stir in prunes and cream and let sit until heated through, about 5 minutes. (Adjust stew consistency with additional hot broth as needed.) Stir in tarragon and lemon juice, season with salt and pepper to taste, and serve.

QUICK PREP TIP TRIMMING AND SLICING FENNEL
After cutting off the stems, feathery fronds, and a thin slice from the base of the fennel bulb, remove any tough or blemished layers and cut the bulb in half vertically through the base. Use a small knife to remove the pyramid-shaped core, and then slice each half into thin strips.

Mexican-Style Pork and Hominy Stew

Serves 6 to 8   **Cooking Time** 9 to 11 hours on Low or 5 to 7 hours on High

WHY THIS RECIPE WORKS: Known as *pozole*, this fragrant and spicy stew is all about the combination of hominy, spices, and tender chunks of pork. To thicken this stew we pureed a can of hominy at the outset with chicken broth—this also added a nice base of corn flavor. A hefty amount of onions microwaved with an equally generous amount of aromatics and spices ensured that this was one flavorful stew. Soy sauce deepened the meaty flavor of the stew without calling any attention to itself. Serve with Easy White Rice (page 134).

3   **(15-ounce) cans white or yellow hominy, drained and rinsed**
3   **cups low-sodium chicken broth, plus extra as needed**
3   **onions, minced**
¼   **cup tomato paste**
¼   **cup vegetable oil**
6   **garlic cloves, minced**
2   **tablespoons chili powder**
2   **tablespoons minced fresh oregano or 2 teaspoons dried**
1   **(14.5-ounce) can diced tomatoes**
⅓   **cup soy sauce**
1   **(4-pound) boneless pork butt roast, trimmed and cut into 1½-inch chunks (see page 59) Salt and pepper**
1   **pound carrots (about 6), peeled, halved lengthwise, and sliced 1 inch thick**
¼   **cup minced fresh cilantro**
1   **tablespoon fresh lime juice**

1. Puree 1 can hominy and 2 cups broth in blender until smooth, about 1 minute; transfer to slow cooker.

2. Microwave onions, tomato paste, 3 tablespoons oil, garlic, chili powder, and oregano, stirring occasionally, until onions are softened, about 5 minutes; transfer to slow cooker.

3. Stir remaining 2 cans hominy, remaining cup broth, tomatoes with juice, and soy sauce into slow cooker. Season pork with salt and pepper and nestle into slow cooker. Toss carrots with remaining tablespoon oil, season with salt and pepper, and wrap in foil packet (see page 60). Lay foil packet on top of stew. Cover and cook until pork is tender, 9 to 11 hours on low or 5 to 7 hours on high.

4. Transfer foil packet to plate. Let stew settle for 5 minutes, then remove fat from surface using large spoon. Carefully open foil packet (watch for steam), stir carrots with accumulated juice into stew, and let sit until heated through, about 5 minutes. (Adjust stew consistency with additional hot broth as needed.) Stir in cilantro and lime juice, season with salt and pepper to taste, and serve.

SMART SHOPPING HOMINY
Hominy is made from dried corn kernels that have been soaked (or cooked) in an alkaline solution (commonly lime-water or calcium hydroxide) to remove the germ and hull. It has a slightly chewy texture and toasted corn flavor, and is widely used in soups, stews, and chilis throughout the Southern U.S. and South America. Given its sturdy texture, hominy can easily withstand hours of simmering and is perfectly suited for the slow cooker. It is sold both dried and canned; however, we prefer the convenience of canned hominy, which only requires a quick rinse before using.

Brazilian Black Bean and Pork Stew

Serves 6 to 8   **Cooking Time** 9 to 11 hours on Low or 5 to 7 hours on High

WHY THIS RECIPE WORKS: Inspired by the meaty Brazilian stew known as *feijoada*, this slow-cooker recipe is packed with creamy black beans and tender, juicy chunks of pork with an intense smoky flavor. To start, we relied on sautéing bacon with onions, garlic, tomato paste, and a trio of spices—chili powder, cumin, and coriander—to build a strong foundation. Since the black beans didn't require soaking, we simply added them next along with the pork and broth and allowed everything to cook until tender. The addition of a little kielbasa sausage to the mix was untraditional, but added even more smoky, meaty flavor. Be sure to serve this stew with the traditional salsalike Brazilian Hot Sauce, as it adds the perfect tangy background for the rich flavors of the dish. Serve with Easy White Rice (page 134).

6	ounces bacon (about 6 slices), minced
3	onions, minced
¼	cup tomato paste
6	garlic cloves, minced
2	tablespoons chili powder
2	teaspoons ground cumin
1	teaspoons ground coriander
1	cup water
4	cups low-sodium chicken broth, plus extra as needed
1	pound dried black beans (2½ cups), picked over and rinsed
1	pound kielbasa sausage, halved lengthwise and sliced ½ inch thick
2	bay leaves
1	(3-pound) boneless pork butt roast, trimmed and cut into 1½-inch chunks (see page 59) Salt and pepper

1. Cook bacon in 12-inch skillet over medium-high heat until crisp, about 5 minutes. Stir in onions, tomato paste, garlic, chili powder, cumin, and coriander and cook until onions are softened and lightly browned, 8 to 10 minutes. Stir in water, scraping up any browned bits; transfer to slow cooker.

2. Stir broth, beans, kielbasa, and bay leaves into slow cooker. Season pork with salt and pepper and nestle into slow cooker. Cover and cook until pork is tender, 9 to 11 hours on low or 5 to 7 hours on high.

3. Let stew settle for 5 minutes, then remove fat from surface using large spoon. Discard bay leaves. (Adjust stew consistency with additional hot broth as needed.) Season with salt and pepper to taste and serve with Brazilian Hot Sauce.

ON THE SIDE BRAZILIAN HOT SAUCE (*MOLHO APIMENTADO*)
Combine 2 large finely chopped tomatoes, 1 minced onion, 1 minced green bell pepper, 1 minced jalapeño chile, ⅓ cup white wine vinegar, 3 tablespoons extra-virgin olive oil, 1 tablespoon minced fresh cilantro, and ½ teaspoon salt in a bowl. Let sauce stand at room temperature until flavors meld, about 30 minutes. (Hot sauce can be refrigerated in an airtight container for up to 2 days.) Makes about 3 cups.

Lamb Vindaloo

Serves 6 to 8   **Cooking Time** 9 to 11 hours on Low or 5 to 7 hours on High

WHY THIS RECIPE WORKS: With roots in India, this classic dish is a natural for the slow cooker, combining slowly simmered lamb with a rich tomato-based sauce perfumed with paprika, cumin, cardamom, and cayenne. We chose a hearty boneless lamb shoulder roast for this recipe, and it remained tender and juicy during the extended cooking time. A hefty amount of spices is key in this dish, but too much produced a chalky texture. Instead, we bloomed the spices with the aromatics so we could use a more moderate amount. Some sugar and red wine vinegar also enhanced the flavors of the dish. Serve with Easy White Rice (page 134) or Toasted Couscous.

3	onions, minced
3	tablespoons vegetable oil
3	tablespoons sweet paprika
8	garlic cloves, minced
2	tablespoons tomato paste
4	teaspoons ground cumin
½	teaspoon ground cardamom
¼	teaspoon cayenne pepper
1	(14.5-ounce) can diced tomatoes
1	cup low-sodium chicken broth, plus extra as needed
3	tablespoons Minute tapioca
2	tablespoons red wine vinegar
2	bay leaves
1	teaspoon sugar
1	(4-pound) boneless lamb shoulder roast, trimmed and cut into 1½-inch chunks (see page 59)
	Salt and pepper
¼	cup minced fresh cilantro

1. Microwave onions, oil, paprika, garlic, tomato paste, cumin, cardamom, and cayenne in a bowl, stirring occasionally, until onions are softened, about 5 minutes; transfer to slow cooker.

2. Stir in tomatoes with juice, broth, tapioca, vinegar, bay leaves, and sugar. Season lamb with salt and pepper and nestle into slow cooker. Cover and cook until lamb is tender, 9 to 11 hours on low or 5 to 7 hours on high.

3. Let stew settle for 5 minutes, then remove fat from surface using large spoon. Discard bay leaves. (Adjust stew consistency with additional hot broth as needed.) Stir in cilantro, season with salt and pepper to taste, and serve.

ON THE SIDE TOASTED COUSCOUS
Toast couscous with olive oil (see chart for amounts and serving sizes) in skillet over medium heat, stirring occasionally, until lightly browned, 3 to 5 minutes; transfer to medium bowl. Stir in ½ teaspoon salt and boiling water, cover, and let sit until couscous is tender, about 12 minutes. Fluff with fork and season with salt and pepper.

Serves	Couscous	Boiling Water	Olive Oil
4	1½ cups	2 cups	2 tablespoons
6	2¼ cups	3 cups	2 tablespoons
8	3 cups	4 cups	3 tablespoons
10	3¾ cups	5 cups	4 tablespoons

ALL ABOUT Using the Microwave and the Slow Cooker

Oddly enough, the fastest appliance in your kitchen, your microwave, can come in especially handy when using the slowest appliance in your kitchen, your slow cooker. We put it to use in our recipes in many different ways that will save you time (and avoid dirty skillets) and also result in dishes that are fresher tasting, with vegetables that are cooked to perfection. Here are some of the key ways we put the microwave to use.

Microwave Aromatics and Bloom Spices

It's not always necessary to brown meat, render bacon, or sauté mushrooms or other vegetables when making a slow-cooker recipe. But you can never add raw onions to the slow cooker because they just don't get soft. So if we didn't need to use our skillet to brown meat (or anything else), it seemed like a hassle to pull out a skillet just to sauté them (along with other aromatics) to build a flavorful base. Looking for an alternative, we gave the microwave a try and it worked perfectly. Sometimes we take things a step further and bloom spices like chili powder or paprika at the same time to increase their flavor. For meaty undertones without browning, we often add a small amount of tomato paste to the mix of aromatics as well.

Place the aromatics (such as onions, garlic, celery, and ginger) and any spices along with vegetable oil in a bowl and microwave, stirring occasionally until softened, about 5 minutes.

Heat Up Last-Minute Additions

Slow cookers are not a good vehicle for heating up liquids in a short amount of time, so when you need to even out the consistency of a stew with more than a little broth or add a fair amount of something just before serving—like a can of creamed corn (which we add to our Farmhouse Chicken and Corn Chowder on page 10) or a can of coconut milk (see Thai-Style Chicken Soup on page 12)—it's best to microwave it first. Sometimes, too, this step allows you to incorporate other flavorful last-minute ingredients into the hot liquid so that they disperse more easily throughout the finished dish for the best overall flavor.

Parcook Root Vegetables

There are a few problems with vegetables in the slow cooker, chief among them vegetables that remain crunchy and vegetables that are so overcooked that they are mushy, colorless, and flavorless. For soups, stews, and braises designed for a short stay in the slow cooker (4 to 6 hours on low), sometimes sturdier vegetables like potatoes and carrots, depending on how large they are cut, just cannot cook through properly. In these instances, as in our Homey Chicken Stew (page 44), we microwave them briefly before adding them to the slow cooker.

"Steam" Delicate Vegetables

All too often, delicate vegetables are simply dumped into a slow cooker only to emerge brown or army green and mushy after hours of cooking—virtually ruining the fresh flavor they were meant to add. To keep vegetables like snow peas, pea pods, and bell peppers crisp-tender and colorful in the final dish, we cook them in the microwave and add them to the slow cooker at the last minute.

To steam delicate vegetables in the slow cooker, place them in a bowl with 1 tablespoon oil and microwave until tender about 5 minutes.

Cook Toppings for Casseroles

The microwave came in handy for some of our casseroles (see Old-Fashioned Tamale Pie, page 222, and Shepherd's Pie, page 231) where we minimized stovetop prep for our polenta and mashed potato toppings.

Italian Vegetable Stew

Serves 6   **Cooking Time** 4 to 6 hours on Low

✔ **WHY THIS RECIPE WORKS:** Creating any vegetable stew in the slow cooker so that the vegetables remain bright and flavorful requires just a few tricks. For this Italian-inspired stew we found that we needed to brown the eggplant first or else it was soggy and wan-tasting in the final stew. Since we had our skillet out already we added more oil to it and browned the chopped tomatoes, which gave them a deeper flavor, along with a little tomato paste and the aromatics and oregano. The potatoes cooked perfectly in this stew without a foil packet given the short cooking time, but we needed to add the zucchini at the end to ensure that it remained green and crisp-tender. Serve with Garlic Toasts (page 28), Quick Polenta (page 98), or focaccia.

¼ cup extra-virgin olive oil, plus extra for serving

1 eggplant (about 1 pound), cut into 1-inch chunks

1 (28-ounce) can whole tomatoes, drained, tomatoes chopped medium, and juice reserved

1 onion, minced

1 red bell pepper, stemmed, seeded, and cut into 1-inch chunks (see page 91)

4 garlic cloves, minced

1 tablespoon tomato paste

1 tablespoon minced fresh oregano or 1 teaspoon dried

3 cups vegetable broth, plus extra as needed

1 pound Yukon Gold potatoes (about 2 medium), peeled and cut into ½-inch pieces

2 zucchini (about 1 pound), quartered lengthwise and sliced 1 inch thick

2 tablespoons chopped fresh basil
Salt and pepper
Grated Parmesan cheese, for serving

1. Heat 2 tablespoons oil in 12-inch skillet over medium-high heat until shimmering. Brown eggplant lightly on all sides, 5 to 7 minutes; transfer to slow cooker.

2. Heat remaining 2 tablespoons oil in skillet over medium-high heat until shimmering. Add tomatoes, onion, bell pepper, garlic, tomato paste, and oregano and cook until dry and beginning to brown, 8 to 10 minutes. Stir in 1 cup broth, scraping up any browned bits; transfer to slow cooker.

3. Stir reserved tomato juice, remaining 2 cups broth, and potatoes into slow cooker. Cover and cook until vegetables are tender, 4 to 6 hours on low.

4. Stir in zucchini, cover, and cook on high until tender, 20 to 30 minutes. (Adjust stew consistency with additional hot broth as needed.) Stir in basil, season with salt and pepper to taste, and serve with Parmesan and additional olive oil.

ON THE SIDE ROSEMARY-OLIVE FOCACCIA
Adjust oven rack to middle position and heat oven to 400 degrees. Press 1 pound pizza dough into well-oiled 13 by 9-inch baking dish or 10-inch pie plate and dimple surface with your fingers. Brush dough liberally with extra-virgin olive oil and sprinkle with ¼ cup chopped olives, ½ teaspoon minced fresh rosemary, ½ teaspoon kosher salt, and ½ teaspoon pepper. Bake until golden brown, about 30 minutes. Cool on wire rack and serve warm. Serves 6 to 8.

Chickpea Tagine

Serves 6   **Cooking Time** 9 to 11 hours on Low or 5 to 7 hours on High

WHY THIS RECIPE WORKS: This tagine (aka Moroccan-style stew) gets its complex flavor from a combination of sweet paprika and garam masala (a blend of warm spices), along with onions, garlic, and lemon zest, all of which perfume the sauce. Since many vegetables would be obliterated after hours in a slow cooker we opted to stir in softened bell peppers and thawed frozen artichokes at the end, cooking them just enough to heat through. (Frozen artichokes are generally packaged already quartered; if yours are not, cut the artichoke hearts into quarters before using.) To continue with the Mediterranean flavor profile we added chopped kalamata olives and Greek-style yogurt to the stew. Golden raisins and honey added a touch of sweetness, while fresh cilantro and grated lemon zest brightened up the dish before serving. Serve with Easy White Rice (page 134) or Toasted Couscous (page 70).

2 **onions, minced**
8 **garlic cloves, minced**
3 **tablespoons extra-virgin olive oil, plus extra for serving**
4 **teaspoons sweet paprika**
2 **teaspoons garam masala**
6 **cups low-sodium chicken broth, plus extra as needed**
1 **pound dried chickpeas (2½ cups), picked over, salt-soaked (see page 35), and rinsed**
4 **(3-inch-long) strips lemon zest, trimmed of white pith (see page 150)**
2 **red or yellow bell peppers, stemmed, seeded, and cut into matchsticks (see page 91)**
2 **(9-ounce) boxes frozen artichokes, thawed**
½ **cup pitted kalamata olives, chopped coarse**
½ **cup golden raisins**
½ **cup plain whole-milk Greek yogurt**
½ **cup minced fresh cilantro**
2 **tablespoons honey**
1 **teaspoon grated lemon zest**
Salt and pepper

1. Microwave onions, garlic, 2 tablespoons oil, paprika, and garam masala in bowl, stirring occasionally, until onions are softened, about 5 minutes; transfer to slow cooker.

2. Stir broth, chickpeas, and lemon zest into slow cooker. Cover and cook until chickpeas are tender, 9 to 11 hours on low or 5 to 7 hours on high.

3. Discard lemon zest. Microwave bell peppers with remaining tablespoon oil in bowl, stirring occasionally, until tender, about 5 minutes. Stir softened bell peppers, artichokes, olives, and raisins into stew, cover, and cook on high until heated through, about 10 minutes.

4. In bowl, combine ¼ cup hot stew liquid with yogurt (to temper), then stir mixture into stew. Stir in cilantro, honey, and grated lemon zest. (Adjust stew consistency with additional hot broth as needed.) Season with salt and pepper to taste and serve with extra-virgin olive oil.

SMART SHOPPING GARAM MASALA
This Indian spice blend, made from up to 12 spices, can be made at home from scratch, but doing so can add a great deal of prep time to a recipe. In search of a good-tasting commercial garam masala, we tested a handful of top brands. Tasters' favorite was **McCormick Gourmet Collection Garam Masala** for its ability to both blend into dishes and round out their acidic and sweet notes. Tasters also liked the subtle warmth of cardamom, cinnamon, and cloves. Widely available in supermarkets, the McCormick blend won praise from tasters for adding a mellow, well-balanced aroma to most dishes.

Red Beans and Rice Stew

Serves 6   **Cooking Time** 9 to 11 hours on Low or 5 to 7 hours on High

✔ **WHY THIS RECIPE WORKS:** When we think of New Orleans we long for a bowl of smoky, spicy red beans and rice, perhaps the region's most notable specialty. When done right, this dish elevates ordinary ingredients—onions, celery, green bell peppers, kidney beans, and rice—to extraordinary heights. With its tender rice, creamy beans, and robustly flavored slow-simmered sauce, this dish is well suited to the slow cooker. We found the classic Cajun trinity of onions, celery, and green peppers a must, and stirring in the peppers for the last half hour of cooking (along with the rice) preserved their texture and color. In addition to paprika and cayenne, spicy andouille sausage provided just the intensity we were seeking, though a milder andouille or kielbasa can be substituted. A splash of red vine vinegar and a sprinkling of scallions before serving provide welcome brightness and are a must.

2	onions, minced
1	celery rib, minced
6	garlic cloves, minced
1	tablespoon vegetable oil
2	teaspoons minced fresh thyme or ½ teaspoon dried
2	teaspoons sweet paprika
¼	teaspoon cayenne pepper
4	cups low-sodium chicken broth, plus extra as needed
3	cups water
1	pound dried red kidney beans (2½ cups), picked over, salt-soaked (see page 35), and rinsed
1	pound andouille sausage, sliced ½ inch thick
2	bay leaves
2	green bell peppers, stemmed, seeded, and chopped medium (see page 91)
½	cup long-grain white rice
	Salt and pepper
	Red wine vinegar
3	scallions, sliced thin

1. Microwave onions, celery, garlic, oil, thyme, paprika, and cayenne in bowl, stirring occasionally, until softened, about 5 minutes; transfer to slow cooker.

2. Stir broth, water, beans, sausage, and bay leaves into slow cooker. Cover and cook until beans are tender, 9 to 11 hours on low or 5 to 7 hours on high.

3. Let stew settle for 5 minutes, then remove fat from surface using large spoon. Discard bay leaves.

4. Stir bell peppers and rice into stew, cover, and cook on high until tender, 30 to 40 minutes. (Adjust stew consistency with additional hot broth as needed.) Season with salt, pepper, and vinegar to taste. Sprinkle with scallions and serve.

SMART SHOPPING ANDOUILLE
Traditional andouille (pronounced an-DOO-ee) sausage from Louisiana is made from ground pork, salt, and garlic and seasoned with plenty of black pepper, then slowly smoked over pecan wood and sugarcane for up to 14 hours. Used in a wide range of Louisiana dishes, such as gumbo, jambalaya, and red beans and rice, it bolsters any dish with intense smoky, spicy, earthy flavor. We tasted four brands, looking for the right combination of smokiness and heat with a traditionally chewy but dry texture. Not surprisingly, a sausage straight from Louisiana, **Jacob's World Famous Andouille**, won the contest with the smokiest and spiciest flavors in the lineup.

Red Lentil Stew

Serves 6   **Cooking Time** 6 to 8 hours on Low or 3 to 5 hours on High

✔ WHY THIS RECIPE WORKS: Deeply flavorful, exotically spiced *dal*—dishes made from lentils—are comforting, hearty Indian stews that have a porridgelike consistency when cooked. We like mild, slightly nutty-tasting red lentils, which fade to a light mustard hue during cooking, and set out to create a slow-cooked version of *masoor dal*. In order to capture the complex flavors of Indian cuisine we needed to use a handful of warm spices—coriander, cumin, cinnamon, turmeric, cardamom, and red pepper flakes—and were pleased to find these contributed vibrant flavor notes even after hours in the slow cooker. Coconut milk ensured the lentils had a creamy consistency and imparted a rich flavor, while tender carrots, peas, diced raw tomatoes, and cilantro accented the stew with colorful bursts of flavor. Though it is typically served as a side dish, we like to serve this striking, creamy dal over Easy White Rice (page 134) as a hearty, vegetarian main course. It's also nice served with dollops of yogurt.

2	**onions, minced**
6	**garlic cloves, minced**
2	**tablespoons vegetable oil**
1	**tablespoon minced or grated fresh ginger**
½	**teaspoon ground coriander**
½	**teaspoon ground cumin**
½	**teaspoon ground cinnamon**
½	**teaspoon ground turmeric**
⅛	**teaspoon ground cardamom**
⅛	**teaspoon red pepper flakes**
4	**cups water, plus extra as needed**
1	**(14-ounce) can coconut milk**
1	**pound red lentils (2¼ cups), picked over and rinsed**
1	**pound carrots (about 6), peeled and chopped medium**
1	**pound plum tomatoes (4 to 6), cored and chopped medium**
1	**cup frozen peas**
	Salt and pepper
¼	**cup minced fresh cilantro**

1. Microwave onions, garlic, oil, ginger, coriander, cumin, cinnamon, turmeric, cardamom, and red pepper flakes in bowl, stirring occasionally, until onions are softened, about 5 minutes; transfer to slow cooker.

2. Stir water, coconut milk, lentils, and carrots into slow cooker. Cover and cook until lentils are tender, 6 to 8 hours on low or 3 to 5 hours on high.

3. Stir in tomatoes, cover, and cook on high until heated through, about 10 minutes. Stir in peas and let sit until heated through, about 5 minutes. (Adjust stew consistency with additional hot broth as needed.) Stir in cilantro, season with salt and pepper to taste, and serve.

SMART SHOPPING COCONUT MILK

Coconut milk is not the thin liquid found inside the coconut itself; that is called coconut water. Coconut milk is a product made by steeping equal parts shredded coconut meat and either warm milk or water. The meat is pressed or mashed to release as much liquid as possible, the mixture is strained, and the result is coconut milk. We tasted seven nationally available brands (five regular and two light) in coconut pudding, coconut rice, a Thai-style chicken soup, and chicken curry. In the soup and curry, tasters preferred **Chaokoh** because of its exceptionally low sugar content. Ka-Me brand coconut milk is best suited for sweet recipes. Of the two light brands tasted, we preferred the richer flavor of A Taste of Thai, though neither was nearly as creamy as the full-fat options.

CHICKEN VESUVIO

Braises

Chicken with White Wine, Tarragon, and Cream

Serves 6   **Cooking Time** 4 to 6 hours on Low

WHY THIS RECIPE WORKS: To get the richest and deepest chicken flavor for this creamy, company-worthy braised chicken, we opted to get out a skillet and brown bone-in chicken breasts. Since we had our skillet out, we also browned the mushrooms and aromatics and deglazed the pan with white wine, seriously elevating the overall flavor. We further boosted the flavor with an unusual ingredient, soy sauce, which brought an extra level of meatiness without taking over. We added cream at the end of the cooking time, along with a hefty dose of fresh tarragon for bright flavor.

6	(12-ounce) bone-in, skin-on split chicken breasts, trimmed
	Salt and pepper
¼	cup vegetable oil
1¼	pounds cremini mushrooms, trimmed and halved if small or quartered if large
2	onions, minced
2	teaspoons minced fresh thyme or ½ teaspoon dried
4	garlic cloves, minced
¼	cup all-purpose flour
¾	cup dry white wine
1	cup low-sodium chicken broth
1	pound carrots (about 6), peeled, halved lengthwise, and sliced ½ inch thick
2	tablespoons soy sauce
2	bay leaves
½	cup heavy cream
¼	cup minced fresh tarragon

1. Dry chicken with paper towels and season with salt and pepper. Heat 1 tablespoon oil in 12-inch skillet over medium-high heat until just smoking. Add half of chicken, skin side down, and brown lightly, about 5 minutes; transfer to plate. Repeat with 1 tablespoon more oil and remaining chicken; transfer to plate. Let chicken cool slightly and discard skin.

2. Add remaining 2 tablespoons oil, mushrooms, onions, thyme, and ¼ teaspoon salt to pan. Cover and cook over medium heat until mushrooms are softened, 5 to 10 minutes. Uncover and continue to cook until mushrooms are dry and browned, 5 to 10 minutes.

3. Stir in garlic and cook until fragrant, about 30 seconds. Stir in flour and cook for 1 minute. Slowly whisk in wine, scraping up any browned bits and smoothing out any lumps; transfer to slow cooker.

4. Stir broth, carrots, soy sauce, and bay leaves into slow cooker. Nestle browned chicken with any accumulated juice into slow cooker. Cover and cook until chicken is tender, 4 to 6 hours on low.

5. Transfer chicken and vegetables to serving platter and tent loosely with aluminum foil. Let braising liquid settle for 5 minutes, then remove fat from surface using large spoon. Discard bay leaves. Stir in cream and tarragon and season with salt and pepper to taste. Spoon 1 cup sauce over chicken and serve with remaining sauce.

Chicken with 40 Cloves of Garlic

Serves 6   **Cooking Time** 4 to 6 hours on Low

✔ **WHY THIS RECIPE WORKS:** To get the most garlic flavor possible into our slow-cooker version of this classic French dish, we found it necessary to spend a few minutes with a skillet. First we browned bone-in chicken breasts and then lightly browned the garlic and shallots. Giving the shallots and garlic time to brown added a subtle roasted taste and deepened their overall flavor, which became sweeter and mellower after hours in the slow cooker. Deglazing with a hefty dose of vermouth added herbaceous notes (which complemented the thyme and rosemary) and a slight sweetness to the braising liquid. If you don't have time to peel 40 cloves of garlic, prepeeled cloves available at supermarkets work just fine here.

6	**(12-ounce) bone-in, skin-on split chicken breasts, trimmed**
	Salt and pepper
2	**tablespoons extra-virgin olive oil**
40	**garlic cloves, peeled**
4	**shallots, peeled and quartered pole to pole**
¼	**cup all-purpose flour**
¾	**cup dry vermouth or dry white wine**
¾	**cup low-sodium chicken broth**
2	**teaspoons minced fresh thyme or ½ teaspoon dried**
½	**teaspoon minced fresh rosemary**
2	**bay leaves**
2	**tablespoons minced fresh parsley**

1. Dry chicken with paper towels and season with salt and pepper. Heat 1 tablespoon oil in 12-inch skillet over medium-high heat until just smoking. Add half of chicken, skin side down, and brown lightly, about 5 minutes; transfer to plate. Repeat with remaining tablespoon oil and remaining chicken; transfer to plate. Let chicken cool slightly and discard skin.

2. Add garlic and shallots to fat left in pan and cook over medium heat, stirring often, until garlic is fragrant and lightly browned, 8 to 10 minutes. Stir in flour and cook for 1 minute. Slowly whisk in vermouth, scraping up any browned bits and smoothing out any lumps; transfer to slow cooker.

3. Stir broth, thyme, rosemary, and bay leaves into slow cooker. Nestle browned chicken with any accumulated juice into slow cooker. Cover and cook until chicken is tender, 4 to 6 hours on low.

4. Transfer chicken, garlic, and shallots to serving platter and tent loosely with aluminum foil. Let braising liquid settle for 5 minutes, then remove fat from surface using large spoon. Discard bay leaves. Stir in parsley and season with salt and pepper to taste. Spoon 1 cup sauce over chicken and serve with remaining sauce.

SMART SHOPPING PREPEELED VS. FRESH GARLIC
Many supermarkets carry jars or deli containers of prepeeled garlic cloves, but how do they compare to fresh garlic bought by the head? We tasted both kinds of garlic in various recipes, both raw and cooked, and, in all cases, results were mixed. However, we did notice a difference in shelf life: A whole head of garlic stored in a cool, dry place will last for at least a few weeks, while prepeeled garlic in a jar (which must be kept refrigerated) lasts for only about two weeks before turning yellowish and developing an overly pungent aroma, even if kept unopened in its original packaging. (In fact, in several instances we found containers of garlic that had started to develop this odor and color on the supermarket shelf.) But if you go through a lot of garlic (or are making Chicken with 40 Cloves of Garlic), prepeeled cloves can be a fine alternative. Just make sure they look firm and white and have a matte finish when you purchase them.

Chicken Vesuvio

Serves 6   **Cooking Time** 4 to 6 hours on Low

✔ **WHY THIS RECIPE WORKS:** Chicken Vesuvio is a Chicago-inspired dish with bone-in chicken breasts and potatoes, smothered in a garlicky white wine sauce and garnished with peas. Getting this dish to work in a slow cooker required a few simple tricks: First, we browned the chicken breasts, followed by the aromatics. Second, we gave the potatoes a head start in the microwave so they would be tender when the chicken was cooked through.

6   **(12-ounce) bone-in, skin-on split chicken breasts, trimmed**
    Salt and pepper
3   **tablespoons extra-virgin olive oil**
2   **onions, minced**
4   **garlic cloves, minced to a paste**
1   **tablespoon minced fresh oregano or 1 teaspoon dried**
¼   **teaspoon red pepper flakes**
3   **tablespoons all-purpose flour**
½   **cup dry white wine**
1½   **pounds red potatoes (4 to 5 medium), scrubbed and cut into 1-inch chunks**
1   **cup low-sodium chicken broth**
1   **fresh rosemary sprig**
1   **cup frozen peas**
½   **teaspoon grated lemon zest plus 1 tablespoon fresh lemon juice**

1. Dry chicken with paper towels and season with salt and pepper. Heat 1 tablespoon oil in 12-inch skillet over medium-high heat until just smoking. Add half of chicken, skin side down, and brown lightly, about 5 minutes; transfer to plate. Repeat with 1 tablespoon more oil and remaining chicken; transfer to plate. Let chicken cool slightly and discard skin.

2. Add onions, half of garlic, oregano, and red pepper flakes to fat left in pan and cook over medium-high heat until onions are softened and lightly browned, 8 to 10 minutes. Stir in flour and cook for 1 minute. Slowly whisk in wine, scraping up any browned bits and smoothing out any lumps; transfer to slow cooker.

3. Microwave potatoes with remaining tablespoon oil in covered bowl, stirring occasionally, until nearly tender, about 5 minutes; transfer to slow cooker. Stir broth into slow cooker. Nestle browned chicken with any accumulated juice into slow cooker. Cover and cook until chicken is tender, 4 to 6 hours on low.

4. Add rosemary sprig, cover, and cook on high until rosemary is fragrant, about 15 minutes. Transfer chicken and potatoes to serving platter and tent loosely with aluminum foil. Let braising liquid settle for 5 minutes, then remove fat from surface using large spoon. Discard rosemary. Stir in peas and let sit until heated through, about 5 minutes. Stir in remaining garlic, lemon zest, and lemon juice and season with salt and pepper to taste. Spoon 1 cup sauce over chicken and serve with remaining sauce.

QUICK PREP TIP MINCING GARLIC TO A PASTE
Mashing garlic to a paste can be helpful when adding raw garlic to a dish. The flavor of the garlic mellows substantially, and it can be more easily incorporated. To make garlic paste, mince the garlic and then sprinkle it with a pinch of salt. Scrape the blade of a chef's knife across the garlic, mashing the garlic into the board. After a few scrapes, the garlic will turn into a sticky paste.

Gingery Chicken Breasts

Serves 6   **Cooking Time** 4 to 6 hours on Low

✔ **WHY THIS RECIPE WORKS:** This slow-cooker recipe for slightly sweet, Asian-inspired, gingery chicken breasts is built around a foundation of onion, garlic, soy sauce, sugar, and, of course, ginger. However, because of its simplicity, we needed an extra flavor boost that could only come from browning the chicken. Browning both the chicken breasts and the aromatics (onion, ginger, and garlic) gave much-needed depth and richness to the finished sauce. We have found that ingredients like ginger and garlic tend to mellow after hours in the slow cooker, so to achieve the bold ginger punch we were after required adding ginger a second time. We got the right amount of pungent and spicy ginger flavor by stirring in an additional tablespoon of grated ginger right before serving. Serve with Easy White Rice (page 134).

6	**(12-ounce) bone-in, skin-on split chicken breasts, trimmed**
	Salt and pepper
2	**tablespoons vegetable oil**
1	**onion, minced**
3	**tablespoons minced or grated fresh ginger**
6	**garlic cloves, minced**
¼	**cup all-purpose flour**
1	**cup low-sodium chicken broth**
3	**tablespoons soy sauce**
1	**tablespoon sugar**
2	**scallions, sliced thin**

1. Dry chicken with paper towels and season with salt and pepper. Heat 1 tablespoon oil in 12-inch skillet over medium-high heat until just smoking. Add half of chicken, skin side down, and brown lightly, about 5 minutes; transfer to plate. Repeat with remaining tablespoon oil and remaining chicken; transfer to plate. Let chicken cool slightly and discard skin.

2. Add onion, 2 tablespoons ginger, and garlic to fat left in pan and cook over medium-high heat until onion is softened and lightly browned, 8 to 10 minutes. Stir in flour and cook for 1 minute. Slowly whisk in broth, scraping up any browned bits and smoothing out any lumps; transfer to slow cooker.

3. Stir soy sauce and sugar into slow cooker. Nestle browned chicken with any accumulated juice into slow cooker. Cover and cook until chicken is tender, 4 to 6 hours on low.

4. Transfer chicken to serving platter and tent loosely with aluminum foil. Let braising liquid settle for 5 minutes, then remove fat from surface using large spoon. Stir in remaining tablespoon ginger and season with salt and pepper to taste. Spoon 1 cup sauce over chicken, sprinkle with scallions, and serve with remaining sauce.

QUICK PREP TIP **GRATING GINGER**
Although we love the floral pungency of fresh ginger, its fibrous texture can be distracting when coarsely grated or minced. What's the best way to avoid ginger's stringy texture? Although fancy kitchen stores sometimes carry porcelain "ginger graters" designed specifically for the job (at about $15 a pop), we prefer to use our trusty—and versatile—rasp-style grater. Its fine blades pulverize the ginger, releasing all of its flavorful juices without any stringy segments. Simply peel a small section of a large piece of ginger, then grate the peeled portion, using the rest of the ginger as a handle. Be sure to work with a large nub of ginger—and watch your knuckles.

ALL ABOUT Chicken in the Slow Cooker

It's hard enough to cook chicken properly on the stovetop or in the oven, when you have complete control, but in a slow cooker, it can be really tricky to ensure moist, flavorful chicken at the end of a long cooking time. We've seen stews and braises with dry, unappealing breast meat or bone-in thighs that have over-cooked to the point where the stew is full of floating bones and dry meat—not very appetizing. Here is what we learned about cooking chicken in a slow cooker.

Cook Chicken 4 to 6 Hours and Only on Low

Chicken parts cook through in the oven or on the stovetop in 30 to 45 minutes, so cooking them for hours in a slow cooker is a bit of a problem. We found that the only way to cook chicken in a slow cooker was on the low setting, which takes longer to get to the maximum heat level and allows the chicken time to gradually cook through without overcooking. Cooking chicken on high or longer than 4 to 6 hours on low leads to dry and unappealing chicken whether you are using a whole chicken, thighs, or breasts.

Brown Chicken Only When Necessary for Flavor

There is no hard and fast rule about when to brown chicken before adding it to the slow cooker. But if a recipe specifies browning, it is because this step adds an extra layer of chicken fla-vor that was deemed necessary for the most successful recipe. This is true, for instance, with our Old-Fashioned Chicken Noodle Soup (page 9) where we actu-ally use skin-on, bone-in thighs, brown them, then remove the skin to yield a chicken broth for this simple soup that really deliv-ers. In highly flavored recipes like our Tortilla Soup (page 11), there are so many aromatics and spices contributing flavor to the broth that the browning step is just not necessary.

Choose Meaty Chicken Thighs for Flavor

We are big fans of using chicken thighs in the slow cooker because they can withstand the longer cooking time more easily and still emerge meltingly tender and flavorful thanks to their fat and connective tissue. You will find a few elegantly flavored braises where we used bone-in breasts, like Chicken with White Wine, Tarragon, and Cream (page 80), because we thought the flavors were best suited to breasts and we know that some people prefer them to thighs. But in general, we use bone-in thighs for braises as they are the most flavorful, and we use boneless thighs for soups and stews because they can be easily shredded or cut into chunks when cooked—a great convenience.

Trimming Chicken Thighs

Trimming and removing excess fat from chicken thighs before adding them to the slow cooker reduces the amount of fat that can be rendered and helps to prevent the dish from becoming greasy. Holding one hand on top of the chicken thigh, trim off any excess fat with a sharp knife.

Removing Chicken Skin

Chicken skin is often slippery, making it a challenge to remove by hand, even when the chicken has been browned. To simplify the task, use a paper towel to provide extra grip while pulling.

Positioning a Whole Chicken in the Slow Cooker

When cooking a whole chicken in the slow cooker (see page 95), our testing revealed that placing the chicken breast side down yields a moister bird because the juices from the dark meat render down into the breast and the juice that collects on the bottom of the slow cooker also helps keep the breast meat moist.

Curried Chicken Breasts

Serves 6   **Cooking Time** 4 to 6 hours on Low

✓ **WHY THIS RECIPE WORKS:** Curries are well suited to the slow cooker because their strong and complex flavors hold up well even after hours of cooking. In our version, these strong flavors allowed us to forgo browning the chicken breasts or aromatics. Instead, we built the base of this quick and simple dish by microwaving curry powder with onions, garlic, ginger, and tomato paste before adding it to the slow cooker along with the chicken, some broth, and tapioca (for thickening). To complement the strong curry flavor we added full-fat plain yogurt to the finished sauce—this added a creamy, tangy richness that brought the dish together. A final addition of raisins, cilantro, and toasted almonds contributed the right amount of sweetness and further complexity to this simple dish. Serve with Easy White Rice (page 134).

2   **onions, minced**

6   **garlic cloves, minced**

2   **tablespoons minced or grated fresh ginger**

4   **teaspoons curry powder**

1   **tablespoon vegetable oil**

1   **tablespoon tomato paste**

1   **cup low-sodium chicken broth**

3   **tablespoons Minute tapioca**

6   **(12-ounce) bone-in split chicken breasts, skin removed, trimmed Salt and pepper**

½   **cup raisins**

½   **cup plain whole-milk yogurt**

2   **tablespoons minced fresh cilantro**

½   **cup sliced almonds, toasted**

1. Microwave onions, garlic, ginger, curry powder, oil, and tomato paste in bowl, stirring occasionally, until onions are softened, about 5 minutes; transfer to slow cooker.

2. Stir broth and tapioca into slow cooker. Season chicken with salt and pepper and nestle into slow cooker. Cover and cook until chicken is tender, 4 to 6 hours on low.

3. Gently stir in raisins and let sit until heated through, about 10 minutes. Transfer chicken to serving platter and tent loosely with aluminum foil. Let braising liquid settle for 5 minutes, then remove fat from surface using large spoon.

4. In bowl, combine ¼ cup hot braising liquid with yogurt (to temper), then stir mixture back into slow cooker. Stir in cilantro and season with salt and pepper to taste. Spoon 1 cup sauce over chicken, sprinkle with almonds, and serve with remaining sauce.

QUICK PREP TIP TOASTING NUTS AND SEEDS
Toasting nuts and seeds maximizes their flavor and takes only a few minutes. To toast a small amount (less than 1 cup) of nuts or seeds, put them in a dry skillet over medium heat. Shake the skillet occasionally to prevent scorching and toast until they are lightly browned and fragrant, 3 to 8 minutes. Watch the nuts closely because they can go from golden to burnt very quickly. To toast a large quantity of nuts, spread the nuts in a single layer on a rimmed baking sheet and toast in a 350-degree oven. To promote even toasting, shake the baking sheet every few minutes, and toast until the nuts are lightly browned and fragrant, 5 to 10 minutes.

Chicken Provençal

Serves 6 **Cooking Time** 4 to 6 hours on Low

✔ **WHY THIS RECIPE WORKS:** Chicken Provençal represents the best of French peasant cooking—chicken on the bone is slowly simmered with tomatoes, garlic, herbs, and olives—and translating it to a quick and easy slow-cooker dish was a snap. We preferred bone-in chicken thighs to breasts because their richness holds up to the strong garlicky tomato flavor of this classic dish. Once again, strong, bold flavors allowed us to eliminate any browning, simplifying the process. The long-stewed flavor is accented at the end with an addition of olives, parsley, and a dose of good-quality extra-virgin olive oil.

3 **onions, minced**

12 **garlic cloves, minced**

2 **tablespoons extra-virgin olive oil, plus extra for serving**

2 **tablespoons tomato paste**

2 **teaspoons minced fresh oregano or ½ teaspoon dried**

1 **(28-ounce) can crushed tomatoes**

½ **cup dry white wine**

2 **bay leaves**

12 **(6-ounce) bone-in chicken thighs, skin removed, trimmed**

Salt and pepper

½ **cup pitted niçoise olives, chopped coarse**

¼ **cup minced fresh parsley**

Lemon wedges, for serving

1. Microwave onions, garlic, oil, tomato paste, and oregano in bowl, stirring occasionally, until onions are softened, about 5 minutes; transfer to slow cooker.

2. Stir tomatoes, wine, and bay leaves into slow cooker. Season chicken with salt and pepper and nestle into slow cooker. Cover and cook until chicken is tender, 4 to 6 hours on low.

3. Transfer chicken to serving platter and tent loosely with aluminum foil. Let braising liquid settle for 5 minutes, then remove fat from surface using large spoon. Discard bay leaves. Stir in olives and parsley and season with salt and pepper to taste. Spoon 1 cup sauce over chicken and serve with additional olive oil, lemon wedges, and remaining sauce.

QUICK PREP TIP PITTING OLIVES

We prefer buying unpitted olives and pitting them ourselves since olives sold already pitted tend to be mushier and saltier and have less flavor than their unpitted counterparts. Buy olives from the refrigerated or salad bar section of the supermarket, rather than purchasing the jarred, shelf-stable variety. To pit them yourself, place the olives on a cutting board and hold the flat edge of a knife over an olive. Press the blade firmly with your hand to loosen the olive meat from the pit, then remove the pit with your fingers and repeat with the remaining olives.

Chicken Cacciatore

Serves 6   **Cooking Time** 4 to 6 hours on Low

✔ **WHY THIS RECIPE WORKS:** Chicken cacciatore is a classic Italian peasant dish of braised chicken thighs in a hearty and robust sauce of tomatoes and red wine highlighted by the flavor of earthy, woodsy mushrooms. With these robust flavors we were able to avoid browning. Instead we opted to use the microwave for our aromatics (a combination of onions, tomato paste, garlic, oregano, red pepper flakes, and porcini mushrooms), and we added the chicken thighs right into the slow cooker. The porcini proved to be crucial, providing complexity and depth of flavor that white mushrooms or cremini mushrooms alone would not provide.

2 **onions, minced**

¼ **cup tomato paste**

2 **tablespoons extra-virgin olive oil**

6 **garlic cloves, minced**

2 **tablespoons minced fresh oregano or 2 teaspoons dried**

¼ **ounce dried porcini mushrooms, rinsed and minced**

¼ **teaspoon red pepper flakes**

1 **pound cremini mushrooms, trimmed and halved if small or quartered if large**

1 **(14.5-ounce) can diced tomatoes, drained**

½ **cup low-sodium chicken broth**

½ **cup dry red wine**

2 **tablespoons Minute tapioca**

12 **(6-ounce) bone-in chicken thighs, skin removed, trimmed**

Salt and pepper

¼ **cup chopped fresh basil**

1. Microwave onions, tomato paste, oil, garlic, oregano, porcini, and red pepper flakes in bowl, stirring occasionally, until onions are softened, about 5 minutes; transfer to slow cooker.

2. Stir cremini, tomatoes, broth, wine, and tapioca into slow cooker. Season chicken with salt and pepper and nestle into slow cooker. Cover and cook until chicken is tender, 4 to 6 hours on low.

3. Transfer chicken to serving platter and tent loosely with aluminum foil. Let braising liquid settle for 5 minutes, then remove fat from surface using large spoon. Stir in basil and season with salt and pepper to taste. Spoon 1 cup sauce over chicken and serve with remaining sauce.

SMART SHOPPING DRIED PORCINI MUSHROOMS
Like fresh fruits and vegetables, the quality of dried porcini mushrooms can vary dramatically from package to package and brand to brand. Always inspect the mushrooms before you buy. Avoid those with small holes, which indicate that the mushroom was perhaps home to pinworms. Instead, look for large, smooth porcini, free of worm holes, dust, and grit.

Country Captain Chicken

Serves 6 **Cooking Time** 4 to 6 hours on Low

WHY THIS RECIPE WORKS: Legend has it that this curried chicken dish is named for a British sea captain who brought the recipe back from his travels in India. Now a Southern classic, it features chicken in a fragrant sauce of tomatoes, green pepper, onions, and curry powder, bolstered by garnishes of almonds and fruit. Our quick and easy slow-cooker version uses chicken thighs for their rich meaty flavor and tomato paste, garlic, paprika, and cayenne pepper for depth of flavor. To provide a bit of balance to this bold dish, we found that jarred mango chutney adds the right hint of sweetness. Serve with Easy White Rice (page 134).

2	onions, minced
1	green bell pepper, stemmed, seeded, and cut into ½-inch pieces
5	tablespoons tomato paste
2	tablespoons curry powder
4	garlic cloves, minced
1	tablespoon vegetable oil
1	tablespoon minced fresh thyme or 1 teaspoon dried
1½	teaspoons sweet paprika
¼	teaspoon cayenne pepper
1	(14.5-ounce) can diced tomatoes
1	cup mango chutney
¾	cup low-sodium chicken broth
12	(6-ounce) bone-in chicken thighs, skin removed, trimmed Salt and pepper
2	tablespoons minced fresh parsley
1	Granny Smith apple, cored and cut into ½-inch pieces
¼	cup sliced almonds, toasted (see page 87)

1. Microwave onions, pepper, tomato paste, curry powder, garlic, oil, thyme, paprika, and cayenne in bowl, stirring occasionally, until onions are softened, about 5 minutes; transfer to slow cooker.

2. Stir tomatoes with juice, chutney, and broth into slow cooker. Season chicken with salt and pepper and nestle into slow cooker. Cover and cook until chicken is tender, 4 to 6 hours on low.

3. Transfer chicken to serving platter and tent loosely with aluminum foil. Let braising liquid settle for 5 minutes, then remove fat from surface using large spoon. Stir in parsley and season with salt and pepper to taste. Spoon 1 cup sauce over chicken, sprinkle with apple and almonds, and serve with remaining sauce.

QUICK PREP TIP CUTTING BELL PEPPERS
Slice the top and bottom off the pepper, remove the core, then slice down through the side of the pepper. Lay the pepper flat on the cutting board, cut away any remaining ribs, then cut the pepper into pieces as directed in the recipe.

Balsamic-Braised Chicken with Swiss Chard

Serves 6   **Cooking Time** 4 to 6 hours on Low

✔ **WHY THIS RECIPE WORKS:** This Italian-inspired dish (consisting of chicken braised in red wine and balsamic vinegar with tomatoes and Swiss chard) translated to the slow cooker with relative ease, but required one crucial step: reducing the balsamic vinegar before adding it to the slow cooker. This simple step dramatically deepened its bright sweet-sour flavor. Since we had the skillet out for this step we opted to brown the aromatics prior to reducing the vinegar. To balance the flavor of the vinegar, a healthy dose of earthy-tasting Swiss chard served as the final addition. Serve with Quick Polenta (page 98).

1	tablespoon extra-virgin olive oil
1	onion, minced
5	teaspoons minced fresh thyme or 1½ teaspoons dried
1	tablespoon tomato paste
3	garlic cloves, minced
1	anchovy fillet, rinsed and minced
¼	teaspoon red pepper flakes
3	tablespoons all-purpose flour
½	cup balsamic vinegar
1	(14.5-ounce) can diced tomatoes, drained
½	cup low-sodium chicken broth
¼	cup dry red wine
2	bay leaves
12	(6-ounce) bone-in chicken thighs, skin removed, trimmed
	Salt and pepper
6	ounces Swiss chard, stemmed and leaves sliced ½ inch thick (see page 33)

1. Heat oil in 12-inch skillet over medium-high heat until shimmering. Add onion, thyme, tomato paste, garlic, anchovy, and red pepper flakes and cook until onion is softened and lightly browned, 8 to 10 minutes. Stir in flour and cook for 1 minute. Slowly whisk in vinegar, scraping up any browned bits and smoothing out any lumps; cook until slightly reduced, about 3 minutes, and transfer to slow cooker.

2. Stir tomatoes, broth, wine, and bay leaves into slow cooker. Season chicken with salt and pepper and nestle into slow cooker. Cover and cook until chicken is tender, 4 to 6 hours on low.

3. Gently stir in chard, cover, and cook on high until tender, 20 to 30 minutes. Transfer chicken to serving platter and tent loosely with aluminum foil. Let braising liquid settle for 5 minutes, then remove fat from surface using large spoon. Discard bay leaves. Season with salt and pepper to taste. Spoon 1 cup sauce over chicken and serve with remaining sauce.

SMART SHOPPING BALSAMIC VINEGAR
Curious about the difference between the various brands of balsamic vinegar found at the supermarket, we bought a bunch of them (ranging from $5 to $20) and pitted them against one another in a taste test. Right off the bat, we found that the sweetness and viscosity of the vinegars make a difference. A good balsamic vinegar must be sweet and thick, but it should also offer a bit of acidity. In the end, one supermarket vinegar—**Lucini Gran Riserva Balsamico**—impressed us with a nice compromise between sweet and tangy.

Kimchi-Braised Chicken Thighs

Serves 6   **Cooking Time** 4 to 6 hours on Low

WHY THIS RECIPE WORKS: This Korean-inspired dish comes together quickly and highlights the spicy flavor of kimchi (a fermented Korean condiment made from cabbage). The strong flavor of kimchi matches well with chicken thighs, which are fattier and meatier than breasts. We reinforced the Asian flavors by making a broth boosted by scallions, garlic, soy sauce, sugar, sesame oil, and fresh ginger. To get the most flavor from the kimchi and prevent it from tasting washed out, we added it at the end. Serve with Easy White Rice (page 134) and hot sauce.

1   **cup low-sodium chicken broth**
4   **scallions, white and green parts separated and sliced thin**
6   **garlic cloves, minced**
2   **tablespoons Minute tapioca**
1   **tablespoon soy sauce**
1   **tablespoon sugar**
1   **tablespoon toasted sesame oil**
1   **teaspoon minced or grated fresh ginger**
12   **(6-ounce) bone-in chicken thighs, skin removed, trimmed**
     Salt and pepper
2   **cups cabbage kimchi, drained**

1. Stir broth, scallion whites, garlic, tapioca, soy sauce, sugar, sesame oil, and ginger into slow cooker. Season chicken with salt and pepper and nestle into slow cooker. Cover and cook until chicken is tender, 4 to 6 hours on low.

2. Stir in kimchi, cover, and cook on high until tender, 20 to 30 minutes. Transfer chicken and cabbage to serving platter and tent loosely with aluminum foil. Let braising liquid settle for 5 minutes, then remove fat from surface using large spoon. Season with salt and pepper to taste. Spoon 1 cup sauce over chicken, sprinkle with scallion greens, and serve with remaining sauce.

SMART SHOPPING SESAME OIL
Raw sesame oil, which is very mild and light in color, is used mostly for cooking, while toasted sesame oil, which has a deep amber color, is primarily used for seasoning because of its intense, nutty flavor. For the biggest hit of sesame flavor, we prefer to use toasted sesame oil. Just a little of this oil (we use more than usual in slow-cooker recipes) will give dishes a deep, nutty flavor—but too much will be overpowering.

Chicken in a Pot

Serves 4   **Cooking Time** 4 to 6 hours on Low

✔ **WHY THIS RECIPE WORKS:** Getting a perfectly cooked, juicy whole bird with a richly flavored jus out of a slow cooker is much easier than it sounds. In our testing, we learned that placing the chicken in the slow-cooker insert upside down was the key to a moist chicken for two reasons: As the juice and fat render from the chicken, they travel over and through the breast meat (which can be notoriously dry) helping to maintain moistness. Additionally, as the juice pools in the bottom of the cooker, the breast becomes submerged and as a result retains more moisture. To boost the flavor of our jus, we did need to pull out the skillet to brown the aromatics, which we deglazed with a bit of wine. This step gave deep color and complex flavor to the juice released from the chicken during cooking.

1	tablespoon extra-virgin olive oil
2	onions, chopped medium
6	garlic cloves, peeled
1	teaspoon tomato paste
1	tablespoon all-purpose flour
¼	cup dry white wine
¼	cup low-sodium chicken broth
5	fresh thyme sprigs
2	bay leaves
1	(4½- to 5-pound) whole chicken, neck and giblets removed
	Salt and pepper

1. Heat oil in 12-inch skillet over medium-high heat until shimmering. Add onions, garlic, and tomato paste and cook until onions are softened and lightly browned, 8 to 10 minutes. Stir in flour and cook for 1 minute. Slowly whisk in wine and broth, scraping up any browned bits and smoothing out any lumps; transfer to slow cooker.

2. Add thyme sprigs and bay leaves to slow cooker. Season chicken with salt and pepper and place, breast side down, in slow cooker. Cover and cook until chicken is tender, 4 to 6 hours on low.

3. Transfer chicken to cutting board, tent loosely with aluminum foil, and let rest for 20 minutes. Let braising liquid settle for 5 minutes, then remove fat from surface using large spoon. Strain liquid, discarding any solids, and season with salt and pepper to taste. Carve chicken and serve with sauce.

QUICK PREP TIP CARVING A CHICKEN
Using a chef's knife, remove the legs. Cut the leg, through the joint, into the thigh and drumstick. Cut the breast meat away from the breast bone.

Turkey Breast and Gravy

Serves 6 to 8   **Cooking Time** 5 to 7 hours on Low

WHY THIS RECIPE WORKS: No one will ever guess that this Thanksgiving classic was turned out of a slow cooker when you serve up moist slices of turkey drizzled with a rich brown gravy. But it takes a little advance work (and a skillet) to get it right. We found that it was possible to skip the cumbersome step of browning the turkey breast, but to get a real gravy, we still needed the skillet to build a proper flavor base and make a roux. First we browned the onion, carrot, celery, and garlic. Then we added flour and cooked it until golden brown, deglazing the pan with wine. Added to the slow cooker with the turkey and some chicken stock, this base mingled with the juice released as the turkey cooked, resulting in a hearty gravy.

3	tablespoons unsalted butter
1	onion, chopped medium
1	carrot, peeled and chopped medium
1	celery rib, chopped medium
6	garlic cloves, peeled and crushed
⅓	cup all-purpose flour
2	cups low-sodium chicken broth
1	cup water
½	cup dry white wine
2	fresh thyme sprigs
2	bay leaves
1	(6- to 7-pound) whole bone-in, skin-on turkey breast, trimmed
	Salt and pepper

1. Melt butter in 12-inch skillet over medium-high heat. Add onion, carrot, celery, and garlic and cook until onion is softened and lightly browned, 8 to 10 minutes. Stir in flour and cook until golden brown, about 2 minutes. Stir in 1 cup broth, scraping up any browned bits and smoothing out any lumps; transfer to slow cooker.

2. Stir remaining cup broth, water, wine, thyme sprigs, and bay leaves into slow cooker. Season turkey with salt and pepper and place, skin side up, into slow cooker. Cover and cook until turkey reaches 165 degrees on instant-read thermometer, 5 to 7 hours on low.

3. Transfer turkey to cutting board, tent loosely with aluminum foil, and let rest for 20 minutes. Let braising liquid settle for 5 minutes, then remove fat from surface using large spoon. Strain braising liquid into saucepan, discarding solids, and simmer until thickened, about 15 minutes. Season with salt and pepper to taste. Carve turkey and serve with gravy.

ON THE SIDE **EASY MASHED POTATOES**
Cover 4 pounds russet potatoes, peeled, sliced ¾ inch thick, and rinsed well, with water in Dutch oven. Bring to boil, then reduce to simmer and cook until tender, 18 to 20 minutes. Drain potatoes, wipe pot dry, then return potatoes to pot. Mash potatoes thoroughly with potato masher. Fold in 12 tablespoons melted unsalted butter, then fold in 2 cups hot half-and-half, adding more as needed. Season with salt and pepper to taste. Serves 8. (This recipe can be halved to serve 4.)

Italian-Style Pot Roast

Serves 6 to 8   **Cooking Time** 9 to 11 hours on Low or 5 to 7 hours on High

✔ **WHY THIS RECIPE WORKS:** A slow cooker, with its slow, even, and moist heat, is the perfect environment for braising a pot roast until fork-tender. We put an Italian spin on this pot roast with the addition of red wine, oregano, tomatoes, red pepper flakes, and dried porcini mushrooms. To get loads of flavor into our pot roast we needed a skillet, not to brown the meat, but to cook some bacon, brown the aromatics, and deglaze and capture all the flavorful browned bits with wine. Boneless chuck-eye roast was our favorite cut for this dish, and we found that using two smaller roasts (2½ to 3 pounds each) yielded fork-tender meat more consistently than a single, larger roast. Serve with Quick Polenta.

8	ounces bacon (about 8 slices), chopped
2	onions, chopped medium
4	carrots, peeled and cut into 1-inch chunks
6	garlic cloves, minced
2	tablespoons minced fresh oregano or 2 teaspoons dried
2	tablespoons tomato paste
½	ounce dried porcini mushrooms, rinsed and minced
½	teaspoon red pepper flakes
½	cup dry red wine
1	(28-ounce) can crushed tomatoes
1	cup low-sodium chicken broth
2	bay leaves
2	(2½- to 3-pound) boneless beef chuck roasts, tied (see page 117)
	Salt and pepper
¼	cup minced fresh parsley

1. Cook bacon in 12-inch skillet over medium heat until crisp, 5 to 7 minutes; transfer to slow cooker. Pour off all but 2 tablespoons bacon fat left in skillet.

2. Add onions, carrots, garlic, oregano, tomato paste, porcini, and red pepper flakes to fat in skillet and cook over medium-high heat until vegetables are softened and lightly browned, 8 to 10 minutes. Stir in wine, scraping up any browned bits; transfer to slow cooker.

3. Stir tomatoes, broth, and bay leaves into slow cooker. Season roasts with salt and pepper and nestle into slow cooker. Cover and cook until beef is tender, 9 to 11 hours on low or 5 to 7 hours on high.

4. Transfer roasts to cutting board, tent loosely with aluminum foil, and let rest for 20 minutes. Let braising liquid settle for 5 minutes, then remove fat from surface using large spoon. Discard bay leaves. Stir in parsley and season with salt and pepper to taste.

5. Remove twine from roasts, slice into ½-inch-thick slices, and arrange on serving platter. Spoon 1 cup sauce over meat and serve with remaining sauce.

ON THE SIDE QUICK POLENTA
Bring 6 cups water and 1½ teaspoons salt to simmer in large saucepan over medium-high heat. Slowly pour 1½ cups instant polenta into water, stirring constantly. Reduce heat to low, cover, and cook, stirring occasionally, until soft and smooth, about 5 minutes. Stir in ½ cup grated Parmesan cheese and 2 tablespoons unsalted butter. Season with salt and pepper to taste. Serves 6 to 8.

Southwestern-Style Pot Roast

Serves 6 to 8   **Cooking Time** 9 to 11 hours on Low or 5 to 7 hours on High

EASY PREP

✔ **WHY THIS RECIPE WORKS:** Inspired by the success of our Italian-Style Pot Roast, we decided to put a Southwestern spin on pot roast as well. A blend of Tex-Mex spices, including chili powder, cumin, and oregano, were given a head start in the microwave along with onions, tomato paste, and garlic, all contributing Southwestern flair to this dish. An unusual ingredient, soy sauce, contributed meaty notes to the dish, while chipotle chiles in adobo sauce brought the right amount of smoky heat. We finished off the sauce with a healthy dose of fresh-tasting cilantro. To make this dish spicier, increase the chipotles to 4 teaspoons. Serve with Easy Mashed Potatoes (see page 96).

3	onions, minced
¼	cup tomato paste
3	tablespoons vegetable oil
8	garlic cloves, minced
2	tablespoons chili powder
1	tablespoon ground cumin
1	tablespoon minced fresh oregano or 1 teaspoon dried
1	(28-ounce) can crushed tomatoes
1½	cups low-sodium chicken broth
⅓	cup soy sauce
3	tablespoons Minute tapioca
2	teaspoons minced canned chipotle chile in adobo sauce
2	(2½- to 3-pound) boneless beef chuck roasts, tied (see page 117)
	Salt and pepper
3	tablespoons minced fresh cilantro

1. Microwave onions, tomato paste, oil, garlic, chili powder, cumin, and oregano in bowl, stirring occasionally, until onions are softened, about 5 minutes; transfer to slow cooker.

2. Stir tomatoes, broth, soy sauce, tapioca, and chipotles into slow cooker. Season roasts with salt and pepper and nestle into slow cooker. Cover and cook until beef is tender, 9 to 11 hours on low or 5 to 7 hours on high.

3. Transfer roasts to cutting board, tent loosely with aluminum foil, and let rest for 20 minutes. Let braising liquid settle for 5 minutes, then remove fat from surface using large spoon. Stir in cilantro and season with salt and pepper to taste.

4. Remove twine from roasts, slice into ½-inch-thick slices, and arrange on serving platter. Spoon 1 cup sauce over meat and serve with remaining sauce.

ON THE SIDE EASY DINNER ROLLS
Cut 1-pound pizza dough into 8 even pieces and roll into balls. Arrange on well-oiled baking sheet, brush lightly with olive oil, and sprinkle with salt and pepper. Bake in 400-degree oven until golden, about 20 minutes. Let cool for 5 minutes before serving. Serves 8.

Braised Brisket and Onions

Serves 8   **Cooking Time** 9 to 11 hours on Low or 5 to 7 hours on High

✔ **WHY THIS RECIPE WORKS:** Brisket is a tough cut of meat and needs prolonged cooking to make it tender, which, of course, is just what the slow cooker does best. In order to avoid browning the brisket and still achieve loads of flavor we opted to use a dry rub—consisting of paprika, onion powder, salt, garlic powder, and cayenne—on the brisket and let the flavors mingle for at least eight hours. To complement the spice rub, we sautéed onions with brown sugar, tomato paste, and garlic, achieving a deep, rich caramelized flavor. Thickened with a little flour and finished with a bit of vinegar, the slightly sweet onion gravy paired perfectly with the meltingly tender brisket.

1   tablespoon sweet paprika
2   teaspoons onion powder
     Salt and pepper
1   teaspoon garlic powder
⅛   teaspoon cayenne pepper
1   (5-pound) flat-cut beef brisket,
     trimmed
1   tablespoon vegetable oil
3   onions, halved and sliced
     ½ inch thick
1   tablespoon brown sugar
1   tablespoon tomato paste
3   garlic cloves, minced
3   tablespoons all-purpose flour
1   cup low-sodium chicken broth
2   tablespoons plus 1 teaspoon
     red wine vinegar
3   fresh thyme sprigs
3   bay leaves

1. Combine paprika, onion powder, 1 teaspoon salt, garlic powder, and cayenne in bowl. Using fork, prick brisket all over. Rub spice mixture over brisket, wrap tightly in plastic wrap, and refrigerate for 8 to 24 hours. Unwrap brisket and place in slow cooker.

2. Heat oil in 12-inch skillet over medium-high heat until shimmering. Add onions, sugar, tomato paste, and garlic and cook until onions are softened and lightly browned, 8 to 10 minutes. Stir in flour and cook for 1 minute. Slowly whisk in broth, scraping up any browned bits and smoothing out any lumps; transfer to slow cooker.

3. Stir 2 tablespoons vinegar, thyme sprigs, and bay leaves into slow cooker. Cover and cook until beef is tender, 9 to 11 hours on low or 5 to 7 hours on high.

4. Transfer brisket to cutting board, tent loosely with aluminum foil, and let rest for 20 minutes. Let braising liquid settle for 5 minutes, then remove fat from surface using large spoon. Discard thyme and bay leaves. Stir in remaining teaspoon vinegar and season with salt and pepper to taste.

5. Slice brisket ½ inch thick against grain and arrange on serving platter. Spoon 1 cup sauce over meat and serve with remaining sauce.

QUICK PREP TIP SERVING BEEF BRISKET
When serving, take care to slice the brisket across the grain of the meat. Slicing it with the grain will result in tough, stringy slices.

Swiss Steaks with Onions and Mushrooms

Serves 6   **Cooking Time** 9 to 11 hours on Low or 5 to 7 hours on High

✔ **WHY THIS RECIPE WORKS:** This dish promises meltingly tender blade steaks smothered in a sauce of sweet onions and earthy mushrooms, a combination that works perfectly in the slow cooker. To get the deep, robust flavor we were after we browned the onions (to bring out their natural sweetness) and the mushrooms (to deepen their inherent earthiness), added flour as a thickener, and a splash of sherry to deglaze the pan and complement the flavors of the onions and mushrooms. After hours in the slow cooker the steaks melded with the onions and mushrooms, turning fork-tender and rich-tasting. To finish the dish, we added a bit of cream to round out the flavors and some parsley for freshness.

3	tablespoons vegetable oil
1½	pounds white mushrooms, trimmed and sliced thin
	Salt and pepper
2	onions, halved and sliced thin
1	tablespoon minced fresh thyme or 1 teaspoon dried
1½	teaspoons sweet paprika
¼	cup all-purpose flour
¾	cup low-sodium chicken broth
¼	cup dry sherry
6	(6- to 8-ounce) beef blade steaks, ¾ to 1 inch thick
¼	cup heavy cream
2	tablespoons minced fresh parsley

1. Heat 1 tablespoon oil in 12-inch skillet over medium-high heat until shimmering. Add mushrooms and ¼ teaspoon salt, cover, and cook until softened, about 5 minutes. Uncover and continue to cook until mushrooms are dry and browned, 5 to 10 minutes longer; transfer to slow cooker.

2. Heat remaining 2 tablespoons oil in skillet over medium-high heat until shimmering. Add onions, thyme, and paprika and cook until onions are softened and lightly browned, 8 to 10 minutes. Stir in flour and cook for 1 minute. Slowly whisk in broth and sherry, scraping up any browned bits and smoothing out any lumps; transfer to slow cooker.

3. Season steaks with salt and pepper and nestle into slow cooker. Cover and cook until beef is tender, 9 to 11 hours on low or 5 to 7 hours on high.

4. Transfer steaks to serving platter and tent loosely with aluminum foil. Let braising liquid settle for 5 minutes, then remove fat from surface using large spoon. Stir in cream and parsley and season with salt and pepper to taste. Spoon 1 cup sauce over steaks and serve with remaining sauce.

SMART SHOPPING DRY SHERRY VERSUS CREAM SHERRY
Sherry is a fortified wine from southern Spain, and it comes in two distinct styles: dry sherry and cream sherry. Dry sherry is less sweet than cream sherry and is better suited for cooking. However, cream sherry (also called "sweet sherry") can be substituted in a pinch. To compensate for cream sherry's sweeter flavor, you may need to add a squirt of lemon juice to the dish before serving. Stay away from "cooking sherry" because it is loaded with salt and artificial caramel flavoring that will ruin the flavor of the food.

Korean Braised Short Ribs

Serves 4   **Cooking Time** 9 to 11 hours on Low or 5 to 7 hours on High

✔ **WHY THIS RECIPE WORKS:** For short ribs with a decidedly Korean spin, we made a thick, highly flavorful paste with common Asian ingredients, using a food processor to combine pear, garlic, ginger, soy sauce, rice vinegar, and scallions. With these bold ingredients driving the flavor of the dish, we did not need to pull out our skillet to brown the meat; we simply added the meat to the slow cooker along with the paste. But we did need to microwave the bones, which added a deeper roasted flavor to our braise.

5   **pounds bone-in English-style short ribs, meat and bones separated (see page 105)**
1   **pear, peeled, cored, and chopped coarse**
½   **cup soy sauce**
6   **garlic cloves, minced**
3   **scallions, sliced thin**
4   **teaspoons minced or grated fresh ginger**
1   **tablespoon rice vinegar**
1   **cup low-sodium chicken broth**
3   **tablespoons Minute tapioca Salt and pepper**
2   **tablespoons minced fresh cilantro**

1. Arrange beef bones in a dish and microwave (in batches, if microwave is small) until well browned, 10 to 15 minutes; transfer to slow cooker.

2. Process pear, soy sauce, garlic, scallions, ginger, and vinegar in food processor until smooth, about 1 minute; transfer to slow cooker. Stir broth and tapioca into slow cooker. Season short ribs with salt and pepper and nestle into slow cooker. Cover and cook until beef is tender, 9 to 11 hours on low or 5 to 7 hours on high.

3. Transfer short ribs to serving platter and tent loosely with aluminum foil. Let braising liquid settle for 5 minutes, then remove fat from surface using large spoon. Remove bones and season sauce with salt and pepper to taste. Stir in cilantro. Spoon 1 cup sauce over short ribs and serve with remaining sauce.

SMART SHOPPING BEEF SHORT RIBS
Short ribs are just that: fatty ribs (cut from any location along the length of the cow's ribs) that are shorter than the more common, larger beef ribs. Short ribs come in two styles: "English," which contain a single rib bone, and "flanken," which have several smaller bones. After cooking both, we found the two options to be equally tender and flavorful. However, the flanken-style ribs are more expensive, and you typically have to buy them from a butcher. We always opt for the cheaper and more readily available English-style ribs.

ENGLISH

FLANKEN

Red Wine–Braised Short Ribs

Serves 4   **Cooking Time** 9 to 11 hours on Low or 5 to 7 hours on High

✔ WHY THIS RECIPE WORKS: Short ribs are all about the meat and the sauce, so to get a deeply flavored sauce, we first focused on the bones, which we knew were one key to flavor. Not wanting to roast the bones in the oven, we turned to the microwave, which helped in two ways: It rendered out unwanted fat (and short ribs are notoriously greasy), and it gave the bones a roasted flavor which in turn deepened the sauce during the long cooking time. One taste of these long-cooked ribs with their dark glossy sauce and you'll be glad you put your microwave and skillet to work first. Serve with Easy Mashed Potatoes (page 96).

5 **pounds bone-in English-style short ribs, meat and bones separated**
   Salt and pepper
2 **tablespoons vegetable oil**
2 **onions, chopped medium**
1 **carrot, peeled and chopped medium**
1 **celery rib, chopped medium**
2 **tablespoons tomato paste**
1 **tablespoon minced fresh thyme or 1 teaspoon dried**
3 **tablespoons all-purpose flour**
2 **cups dry red wine**
2 **tablespoons balsamic vinegar**
2 **cups low-sodium chicken broth**
2 **bay leaves**
2 **tablespoons minced fresh parsley**

1. Arrange beef bones in a dish and microwave (in batches, if microwave is small) until well browned, 10 to 15 minutes; transfer to slow cooker.

2. Dry short ribs with paper towels and season with salt and pepper. Heat 1 tablespoon oil in 12-inch skillet over medium-high heat until just smoking. Brown half of short ribs well on all sides, 7 to 10 minutes; transfer to slow cooker. Repeat with remaining tablespoon oil and remaining short ribs; transfer to slow cooker.

3. Add onions, carrot, celery, tomato paste, and thyme to fat in skillet and cook over medium-high heat until onions are softened and lightly browned, 8 to 10 minutes. Stir in flour and cook for 1 minute. Slowly whisk in wine and vinegar, scraping up any browned bits and smoothing out any lumps. Bring to simmer and cook until reduced to 1 cup, about 5 minutes; transfer to slow cooker.

4. Stir broth and bay leaves into slow cooker. Cover and cook until beef is tender, 9 to 11 hours on low or 5 to 7 hours on high.

5. Transfer short ribs to serving platter and tent loosely with aluminum foil. Let braising liquid settle for 5 minutes, then remove fat from surface using large spoon. Strain braising liquid, discarding solids, and season with salt and pepper to taste. Stir in parsley. Spoon 1 cup sauce over short ribs and serve with remaining sauce.

QUICK PREP TIP MAKING SHORT RIBS
Separating the meat from the bones— and "roasting" the bones in a surprising way—yields the most flavorful dish. To remove the meat from the bones, insert a knife between the rib and meat, staying as close to the bone as possible, and saw the meat off the bone. Before adding the bones to the slow cooker, microwave them for 10 to 15 minutes.

Cassoulet

Serves 6 to 8   **Cooking Time** 6 to 8 hours on Low

✔ **WHY THIS RECIPE WORKS:** This simplified version of cassoulet, a classic French dish that features beans, duck confit, pork, garlic sausages, and tomatoes all topped with a crunchy bread-crumb crust, is tailor-made for the slow cooker where the long cooking and moist heat works its magic and easily melds all the flavors into a perfectly harmonious meal. Our new version gets its big meaty flavor from chunks of kielbasa, country-style pork ribs, and chicken thighs. To keep the chicken from drying out, we placed it in a foil packet to slow down the cooking time and keep it moist while the beans cook. We replicated the crunchy crust by processing sandwich bread into crumbs, toasting them in a skillet with butter, and sprinkling some on each portion just before serving.

2 **onions, minced**

2 **tablespoons vegetable oil**

6 **garlic cloves, minced**

1 **tablespoon minced fresh thyme or 1 teaspoon dried**

1 **tablespoon tomato paste**

3½ **cups low-sodium chicken broth**

1 **pound dried great Northern beans (2½ cups), picked over, salt-soaked (see page 35), and rinsed**

8 **ounces kielbasa sausage, sliced 1 inch thick**

1 **(14.5-ounce) can diced tomatoes, drained**

½ **cup dry white wine**

2 **bay leaves**

2 **pounds bone-in country-style pork ribs, trimmed**

2 **pounds bone-in chicken thighs, skin removed, trimmed Salt and pepper**

2 **slices high-quality white sandwich bread, torn into pieces**

2 **tablespoons unsalted butter, melted**

2 **tablespoons minced fresh parsley**

1. Microwave onions, oil, garlic, thyme, and tomato paste in bowl, stirring occasionally, until onions are softened, about 5 minutes; transfer to slow cooker.

2. Stir broth, beans, kielbasa, tomatoes, wine, and bay leaves into slow cooker. Season pork and chicken with salt and pepper and nestle pork into slow cooker. Wrap chicken in foil packet (see page 60) and lay on top of stew. Cover and cook until beans are tender, 6 to 8 hours on low.

3. Meanwhile, pulse bread, butter, ⅛ teaspoon salt, and ⅛ teaspoon pepper in food processor until coarsely ground, about 8 pulses. Transfer crumbs to 12-inch skillet and toast over medium-high heat, stirring often, until golden brown and dry, about 5 minutes; set aside.

4. Transfer foil packet to plate, open it carefully (watch for steam), and transfer chicken to cutting board. Let chicken cool slightly, then shred into bite-size pieces (see page 21), discarding skin and bones. Let braising liquid settle for 5 minutes, then remove fat from surface using large spoon. Discard bay leaves. Stir in shredded chicken and parsley, season with salt and pepper to taste, and serve with bread crumbs.

Braised Country-Style Ribs with Black-Eyed Peas

Serves 6 to 8   **Cooking Time** 9 to 11 hours on Low or 5 to 7 hours on High

✓ **WHY THIS RECIPE WORKS:** This Southern classic—creamy black-eyed peas and velvety collard greens paired with smoky, meaty pork—is a perfect slow-cooker meal. The slow and low heat of the slow cooker infuses the beans with all the flavor of the pork and renders the pork ribs fork-tender. Although most recipes include ham hocks, we turned to a combination of smoky bacon and country-style pork ribs, which delivered all the flavor we needed. After using a skillet to render the bacon, we built the backbone of this dish, sautéing red onion, celery, and garlic. To keep the greens fresh tasting, we added them to the braising liquid at the end to cook through. We like to serve this dish with pickled onions, which provide a bright acidic contrast to the meaty richness of the pork and beans.

4	ounces bacon (about 4 slices), chopped medium
1	red onion, chopped medium
1	celery rib, minced
6	garlic cloves, minced
3½	cups low-sodium chicken broth
1	pound dried black-eyed peas (2½ cups), picked over and rinsed
1	cup water
2	bay leaves
2	pounds bone-in country-style pork ribs, trimmed
	Salt and pepper
1	pound collard greens, stemmed and leaves sliced ¼ inch thick (see page 33)

1. Cook bacon in 12-inch skillet over medium heat until crisp, 5 to 7 minutes; transfer to slow cooker. Pour off all but 2 tablespoons bacon fat left in skillet.

2. Add onion, celery, and garlic to fat in skillet and cook over medium-high heat until onion is softened and lightly browned, 8 to 10 minutes. Stir in 1 cup broth, scraping up any browned bits; transfer to slow cooker.

3. Stir remaining 2½ cups broth, peas, water, and bay leaves into slow cooker. Season pork with salt and pepper and nestle into slow cooker. Cover and cook until peas are tender, 9 to 11 hours on low or 5 to 7 hours on high.

4. Let braising liquid settle for 5 minutes, then remove fat from surface using large spoon. Discard bay leaves. Stir in collard greens, cover, and cook on high until tender, 20 to 30 minutes. Season with salt and pepper to taste and serve.

ON THE SIDE PICKLED ONIONS
Bring ¾ cup red wine vinegar, 2 tablespoons sugar, ½ teaspoon salt, ¼ teaspoon red pepper flakes, and 2 bay leaves to boil over medium-high heat in small saucepan. Add 1 red onion, halved and sliced thin, and boil for 1 minute. Transfer to shallow bowl and refrigerate until cooled. Makes 1½ cups.

Smothered Pork Chops with Onions and Bacon

Serves 6   **Cooking Time** 6 to 8 hours on Low or 3 to 5 hours on High

✔ **WHY THIS RECIPE WORKS:** The best smothered pork chops are fall-off-the-bone tender, covered with caramelized onions, and enriched with a deeply flavored onion gravy. To get the tender chops we wanted, ¾-inch-thick blade-cut pork chops were crucial. They are cut from the shoulder end of the loin and contain a significant amount of fat and connective tissue, which can handle the hours of braising in the slow cooker without drying out. We built our gravy by first rendering bacon in a skillet, and in the leftover fat we browned up our onions (along with some brown sugar, garlic, and thyme). To further boost the gravy's flavor, we added some soy sauce (which added an extra bit of meatiness). We livened up the finished gravy with a splash of cider vinegar and a tablespoon of parsley.

4	ounces bacon (about 4 slices), chopped
3	onions, halved and sliced ½ inch thick
4	teaspoons brown sugar
3	garlic cloves, minced
1	tablespoon minced fresh thyme or 1 teaspoon dried
⅓	cup all-purpose flour
1	cup low-sodium chicken broth
¼	cup soy sauce
2	bay leaves
6	(7-ounce) bone-in blade-cut pork chops, about ¾ inch thick, sides slit to prevent curling (see page 110)
	Salt and pepper
1	tablespoon cider vinegar
1	tablespoon minced fresh parsley

1. Cook bacon in 12-inch skillet over medium heat until crisp, 5 to 7 minutes; transfer to slow cooker. Pour off all but 2 tablespoons bacon fat left in skillet.

2. Add onions, 1 teaspoon sugar, garlic, and thyme to fat in skillet and cook over medium-high heat until onions are softened and well browned, about 10 minutes. Stir in flour and cook for 1 minute. Slowly whisk in broth, scraping up any browned bits and smoothing out any lumps; transfer to slow cooker.

3. Stir remaining tablespoon sugar, soy sauce, and bay leaves into slow cooker. Season pork chops with salt and pepper and nestle into slow cooker. Cover and cook until pork is tender, 6 to 8 hours on low or 3 to 5 hours on high.

4. Transfer pork chops to serving platter, tent loosely with aluminum foil, and let rest for 10 minutes. Let braising liquid settle for 5 minutes, then remove fat from surface using large spoon. Discard bay leaves. Stir in vinegar and parsley and season with salt and pepper to taste. Spoon 1 cup sauce over chops and serve with remaining sauce.

SMART SHOPPING BACON
Premium bacon can cost double, even triple, the price of ordinary bacon. Is it worth it? To find out, we bought six artisanal mail-order bacons and two high-end grocery store bacons. The results? We were amazed that two of the four highest-rated bacons were not premium mail-order bacons, but supermarket brands. **Applegate Farms Uncured Sunday Bacon** (top) and **Farmland/Carando Apple Cider Cured Bacon, Applewood Smoked** (bottom) were a step up from the usual mass-produced bacon, straddling the gap between artisanal and more mainstream supermarket styles. Although these bacons didn't receive quite the raves of the two top-ranked premium bacons, tasters praised them both for good meaty flavor and mild smokiness.

Aloha Pork Chops

Serves 6   **Cooking Time** 6 to 8 hours on Low or 3 to 5 hours on High

WHY THIS RECIPE WORKS: Inspired by the success of our Smothered Pork Chops with Onions and Bacon (page 109), we decided to develop another pork chop dish, this time pairing the meatiness of pork with the sweetness of pineapple. To ensure that this recipe would be quick and easy, we opted to use canned pineapple in juice rather than fresh. Some cider vinegar, soy sauce, curry powder, ground ginger, and red pepper flakes balanced the pineapple's sweetness. To thicken the sauce at the end, we whisked in a slurry of cornstarch and water and let it simmer for a few minutes, which gave it an appealingly glazy texture.

1   **(20-ounce) can pineapple chunks in juice**
¼   **cup packed brown sugar**
1   **tablespoon cider vinegar**
1   **tablespoon soy sauce**
2   **teaspoons curry powder**
½   **teaspoon ground ginger**
½   **teaspoon red pepper flakes**
6   **(7-ounce) bone-in blade-cut pork chops, about ¾ inch thick, sides slit to prevent curling**
    Salt and pepper
1   **tablespoon water**
2   **teaspoons cornstarch**
2   **scallions, sliced thin**

1. Stir pineapple with juice, sugar, vinegar, soy sauce, curry powder, ginger, and red pepper flakes into slow cooker. Season pork chops with salt and pepper and nestle into slow cooker. Cover and cook until pork is tender, 6 to 8 hours on low or 3 to 5 hours on high.

2. Transfer pork chops to serving platter, tent loosely with aluminum foil, and let rest for 10 minutes. Let braising liquid settle for 5 minutes, then remove fat from surface using large spoon.

3. Whisk water and cornstarch together in bowl. Transfer braising liquid to saucepan, add cornstarch mixture, and simmer until reduced to 2 cups, about 12 minutes. Stir in scallions and season with salt and pepper to taste. Spoon 1 cup sauce over chops and serve with remaining sauce.

QUICK PREP TIP NO-CURL PORK CHOPS
To prevent your pork chops from curling, cut two slits, about 2 inches apart, into one side of each chop (this method works for both boneless and bone-in chops).

Pork Chops with Dried Fruit Compote

Serves 6   **Cooking Time** 6 to 8 hours on Low or 3 to 5 hours on High

✔ **WHY THIS RECIPE WORKS:** Pork and fruit are a natural combination but fresh fruit in a slow cooker is a dicey proposition unless you are using it just for flavor. So since we wanted the fruit to play a starring role alongside the pork, we turned to dried fruit, along with applesauce, to make a simple fruit compote for our slow-cooker pork chops. Balanced with shallots, brown sugar and vinegar, plus a cinnamon stick, this lively compote is packed with flavor. This recipe is a snap to make—the only prep work is cutting the apricots and mincing the shallots.

1   **cup applesauce**
1   **cup dried apricots, quartered**
½   **cup dried cherries**
2   **shallots, minced**
2   **tablespoons brown sugar**
1   **tablespoon cider vinegar, plus extra as needed**
2   **bay leaves**
1   **cinnamon stick**
6   **(7-ounce) bone-in blade-cut pork chops, about ¾ inch thick, sides slit to prevent curling (see page 110)**
    Salt and pepper
2   **tablespoons minced fresh parsley**

1. Stir applesauce, apricots, cherries, shallots, sugar, vinegar, bay leaves, and cinnamon stick into slow cooker. Season pork chops with salt and pepper and nestle into slow cooker. Cover and cook until pork is tender, 6 to 8 hours on low or 3 to 5 hours on high.

2. Transfer pork chops to serving platter, tent loosely with foil, and let rest for 10 minutes. Let braising liquid settle for 5 minutes, then remove fat from surface using large spoon. Discard bay leaves and cinnamon stick. Stir in parsley and season with salt, pepper, and vinegar to taste. Spoon 1 cup sauce over chops and serve with remaining sauce.

ON THE SIDE EASY BUTTERED GREEN BEANS
Cook 1½ pounds green beans, trimmed, in salted boiling water until crisp-tender, 3 to 5 minutes. Drain thoroughly, then toss with 2 tablespoons butter, season with salt and pepper, and serve hot. Serves 6.

Maple-Glazed Pork Loin

Serves 6   **Cooking Time** about 4 hours on Low

✔ **WHY THIS RECIPE WORKS:** Cooking a lean roast like a pork loin in a slow cooker is tricky because it can quickly turn overcooked and dry. So the key to this recipe is to monitor the temperature of the roast after a few hours and take it out of the slow cooker as soon as it reaches 145 degrees. Here our goal was to pair a tender pork loin with a spicy maple glaze. For flavor and color we browned the pork loin. Then we bloomed spices along with an onion and some garlic in the microwave. We stirred a cup of maple syrup and some chicken broth into the slow cooker along with the aromatics and spices. After cooking the loin, we reduced the braising liquid until it became a sticky, sweet glaze that paired perfectly with our juicy pork loin.

1	(4½- to 5-pound) boneless pork loin roast (see page 115), trimmed and tied at 1-inch intervals
	Salt and pepper
2	tablespoons vegetable oil
1	onion, minced
½	teaspoon ground cinnamon
¼	teaspoon ground cloves
⅛	teaspoon cayenne pepper
1	cup maple syrup
½	cup low-sodium chicken broth

1. Dry pork with paper towels and season with salt and pepper. Heat 1 tablespoon oil in 12-inch skillet over medium-high heat until just smoking. Brown pork well on all sides, 7 to 10 minutes; transfer to slow cooker.

2. Heat remaining tablespoon oil over medium-high heat until shimmering. Add onion, cinnamon, cloves, and cayenne and cook until the onion is softened and lightly browned, 8 to 10 minutes. Stir in maple syrup and broth, scraping up any browned bits; transfer to slow cooker.

3. Cover and cook until pork is tender and registers 140 to 145 degrees on instant-read thermometer, about 4 hours on low.

4. Transfer pork to cutting board, tent loosely with aluminum foil, and let rest for 10 minutes. Let braising liquid settle for 5 minutes, then remove fat from surface using large spoon. Transfer braising liquid to saucepan and simmer until reduced to 1¼ cups, about 15 minutes. Season with salt and pepper to taste.

5. Remove twine from pork, slice into ½-inch-thick slices, and arrange on serving platter. Spoon 1 cup sauce over meat and serve with remaining sauce.

SMART SHOPPING MAPLE SYRUP
The syrup options these days can be daunting. There are the imitation pancake—syrups like Mrs. Butterworth's and Log Cabin (basically high-fructose corn syrup laced with maple flavoring), and there's real maple syrup, which is sold as grade A (in light, medium, and dark amber), and darker grade B, often called "cooking syrup." Tasters unanimously panned the imitation stuff. Among the real syrups, they preferred dark with intense maple flavor to the delicate, pricey grade A light amber. The favorite was **Maple Grove Farms Pure Maple Syrup**, a grade A dark amber, but our runner-up, Highland Sugarworks, a grade B syrup, is great for those looking for even bolder maple flavor.

Pork Loin with Cranberries and Orange

Serves 6   **Cooking Time** about 4 hours on Low

WHY THIS RECIPE WORKS: Whether you're cooking a pork loin in the oven or the slow cooker, pairing the lean meat with a glaze or a sauce gives it a lot more appeal. Here we followed the cooking method we established with our Maple-Glazed Pork Loin (page 113), pairing it with both dried cranberries and whole canned cranberries. Cinnamon, orange juice, and orange zest livened up our easy-to-make sauce, which goes directly into the slow cooker. When choosing a pork loin, we prefer the blade-end—be sure to choose a fatter, shorter loin over the longer, skinnier ones.

1 (4½- to 5-pound) boneless pork loin roast, trimmed and tied at 1-inch intervals
Salt and pepper
1 tablespoon vegetable oil
1 (14-ounce) can whole berry cranberry sauce
½ cup dried cranberries
½ cup orange juice
3 (3-inch-long) strips orange zest, trimmed of white pith (see page 150)
⅛ teaspoon ground cinnamon

1. Dry pork with paper towels and season with salt and pepper. Heat oil in 12-inch skillet over medium-high heat until just smoking. Brown pork well on all sides, 7 to 10 minutes.

2. Stir cranberry sauce, cranberries, orange juice, orange zest, and cinnamon into slow cooker. Nestle browned pork into slow cooker. Cover and cook until pork is tender and registers 140 to 145 degrees on instant-read thermometer, about 4 hours on low.

3. Transfer pork to cutting board, tent loosely with aluminum foil, and let rest for 10 minutes. Let braising liquid settle for 5 minutes, then remove fat from surface using large spoon. Discard orange zest. Transfer braising liquid to saucepan and simmer until reduced to 2 cups, about 12 minutes. Season with salt and pepper to taste.

4. Remove twine from pork, slice into ½-inch-thick slices, and arrange on serving platter. Spoon 1 cup sauce over meat and serve with remaining sauce.

SMART SHOPPING **BUYING PORK LOIN ROASTS**
Buying the right pork loin will make all the difference in these slow-cooker recipes. Look for a 4½- to 5-pound pork loin roast that is wide and short and steer clear from those that are long and narrow. Narrow pork loins don't fit as easily into the slow cooker and are prone to overcooking because they cook through more quickly.

LONG AND NARROW

WIDE AND SHORT

ALL ABOUT Herbs

While slow cookers offer a hands-off approach to cooking, it can come at the cost of flavor, which is often dulled during the long cooking time. To keep the flavor of our slow-cooker recipes from turning washed out, we rely on a hefty amount of herbs, spices, and other aromatics when a building flavor base. Here are a few things we have discovered about herbs that will help you make the most of them in your slow-cooker dishes.

Keeping Herbs Fresh Longer

To get the most out of fresh herbs, we start by gently rinsing and drying them before loosely rolling them in a few sheets of paper towels. Then we put the roll of herbs in a zipper-lock bag and place it in the crisper drawer of our refrigerator. (Basil is an exception and should be rinsed just before using.) Stored in this manner, the herbs stay fresh and ready to use for a week.

Judging Freshness of Dried Herbs

If you are questioning the age and freshness of an already-opened jar of dried herbs, crumble a small amount between your fingers and take a whiff. If it releases a lively aroma, it's good to use. If the fragrance is present but relatively mild, consider using more than you normally would.

Is Fresh Always Best?

When we are ready to add herbs to our slow cooker, surprisingly, we don't always reach for fresh. That's because hearty dried herbs such as oregano and thyme are well suited for the moist environment of the slow cooker where their flavors can be extracted over a long period of time. (In general, we find we can add about a quarter as much dried herbs as fresh, and add them at the same time as we would add fresh.) Delicate leafy herbs, such as basil, parsley, and cilantro, are best used at the end of cooking, allowing their fresh flavors to stay intact and help brighten the final dish.

Steep Rosemary Last

Rosemary adds great flavor to many soups and stews, but after several hours in the slow cooker, it turns bitter and medicinal. Placing a sprig of rosemary in the slow cooker to steep for a few minutes at the end of cooking allows you to achieve just the right amount of fresh rosemary flavor.

Storing Bay Leaves

While dried bay leaves are often sold in large quantities, you rarely need more than one or two for a recipe. So to keep the remaining bay leaves fresh between recipes, we store them in a zipper-lock freezer bag in the freezer. This keeps them fresher much longer than if simply stored on the spice shelf.

Who Has the Thyme?

Picking minuscule leaves off fresh thyme can really pluck at your nerves. In the test kitchen, we rely on some tricks to make this job go faster. If the thyme has very thin, pliable stems, just chop the stems and leaves together, discarding the tough bottom portions as you go. If the stems are thicker and woodier, run your thumb and forefinger down the stem to release the leaves and smaller offshoots. The tender tips can be left intact and chopped along with the leaves once the woodier stems have been sheared clean and discarded.

Pork Pot Roast

Serves 8   **Cooking Time** 9 to 11 hours on Low or 5 to 7 hours on High

✔ **WHY THIS RECIPE WORKS:** The moist nature of the slow cooker and its slow, even heat provide a great environment for cooking a perfectly tender pork pot roast. We determined that the best cut of meat for this was a pork picnic shoulder roast: Because it is fatty and well marbled, it breaks down and becomes meltingly tender when cooked for a long time. We found that using two smaller roasts (2½ to 3 pounds each) yielded fork-tender meat more consistently than a single larger roast—plus it's easier to find smaller pork roasts and they are more manageable in the slow cooker. To get enough flavor into our dish without browning the meat, we browned the aromatics deeply, along with tomato paste, which gave the sauce a meaty foundation. And since we had our skillet out, we decided to make a roux to thicken the sauce rather than relying on tapioca. We paired the rich pork with sweet and hearty root vegetables (carrots and parsnips) and diced tomatoes.

2	tablespoons vegetable oil
2	onions, minced
6	garlic cloves, minced
1	tablespoon tomato paste
1	tablespoon minced fresh thyme or 1 teaspoon dried
¼	cup all-purpose flour
½	cup dry white wine
1	(28-ounce) can diced tomatoes, drained
1	pound carrots (about 6), peeled and cut into 1-inch chunks
1	pound parsnips, peeled and cut into 1-inch chunks
2	(2½- to 3-pound) boneless pork picnic shoulder roasts, trimmed and tied
	Salt and pepper
2	teaspoons white wine vinegar

1. Heat oil in 12-inch skillet over medium-high heat until shimmering. Add onions, garlic, tomato paste, and thyme and cook until onions are softened and lightly browned, 8 to 10 minutes. Stir in flour and cook for 1 minute. Slowly whisk in wine, scraping up any browned bits and smoothing out any lumps; transfer to slow cooker.

2. Stir tomatoes, carrots, and parsnips into slow cooker. Season roasts with salt and pepper and nestle into slow cooker. Cover and cook until pork is tender, 9 to 11 hours on low or 5 to 7 hours on high.

3. Transfer roasts to cutting board, tent loosely with aluminum foil, and let rest for 20 minutes. Let braising liquid settle for 5 minutes, then remove fat from surface using large spoon. Stir in vinegar and season with salt and pepper to taste.

4. Remove twine from roasts, slice into ½-inch-thick slices, and arrange on serving platter. Spoon 1 cup sauce over meat and serve with remaining sauce.

QUICK PREP TIP TYING A POT ROAST
We like to use two smaller roasts when making pot roast (both beef and pork pot roast) because the meat cooks more quickly and the small roasts are easier to manage in the slow cooker— and to find in the supermarket. To prepare the roasts for the slow cooker, first remove the elastic netting (if necessary), then open up the roast and trim away any excess fat. Then, tie each roast back together securely with butcher's twine.

MOROCCAN BEEF CHILI WITH CHICKPEAS AND RAISINS

Chilis

Weeknight Beef Chili

Serves 8 to 10   **Cooking Time** 6 to 8 hours on Low or 3 to 5 hours on High

✔ **WHY THIS RECIPE WORKS:** Gently simmered ground beef chili is certainly well suited for the slow cooker, but achieving the characteristic rich flavors and tender meat can be a challenge. To develop the all-American chili we were looking for, we started with the base, choosing a combination of diced and pureed tomatoes to create the proper consistency. Next, we incorporated a generous combination of chili powder, cumin, oregano, and red pepper flakes, bumping up the flavors even further with smoky chipotles. Browning the beef to develop flavor is standard in most traditional chilis, but produced overcooked, gritty meat in the slow cooker. To fix this, we found mixing the raw beef with a panade—a mixture of bread and milk often used in meatballs—before browning it worked wonders. We also stirred in a little soy sauce to help boost the meaty flavor; maybe a tad unconventional for chili, but it worked. Serve with your favorite chili garnishes.

2	slices high-quality white sandwich bread, torn into quarters
¼	cup whole milk
2	pounds 85 percent lean ground beef
	Salt and pepper
3	tablespoons vegetable oil
3	onions, minced
¼	cup chili powder
¼	cup tomato paste
6	garlic cloves, minced
1	tablespoon ground cumin
1	tablespoon minced fresh oregano or 1 teaspoon dried
½	teaspoon red pepper flakes
1	(28-ounce) can tomato puree
1	(28-ounce) can diced tomatoes
2	(15-ounce) cans dark red kidney beans, drained and rinsed
3	tablespoons soy sauce
1	tablespoon brown sugar
2	teaspoons minced canned chipotle chile in adobo sauce

1. Mash bread and milk into paste in large bowl using fork. Mix in ground beef, ½ teaspoon salt, and ½ teaspoon pepper using hands.

2. Heat oil in 12-inch skillet over medium-high heat until shimmering. Add onions, chili powder, tomato paste, garlic, cumin, oregano, and red pepper flakes and cook until vegetables are softened and lightly browned, 8 to 10 minutes.

3. Stir in beef mixture, 1 pound at a time, and cook, breaking up any large pieces with wooden spoon, until no longer pink, about 3 minutes per pound. Stir in 1 cup tomato puree, scraping up any browned bits; transfer to slow cooker.

4. Stir remaining tomato puree, diced tomatoes with juice, beans, soy sauce, sugar, and chipotles into slow cooker. Cover and cook until beef is tender, 6 to 8 hours on low or 3 to 5 hours on high.

5. Let chili settle for 5 minutes, then remove fat from surface using large spoon. Break up any remaining large pieces of beef with spoon. Season with salt and pepper to taste and serve.

SMART SHOPPING **CHILI POWDER**
While there are numerous applications for chili powder, its most common use is in chili. Considering that most chili recipes rely so heavily on chili powder (several of ours use a whopping ¼ cup), we thought it was necessary to gather up as many brands as possible to find the one that made the best chili. To focus on the flavor of the chili powder, we made a bare-bones version of our chili and rated each chili powder for aroma, depth of flavor, and level of spiciness. Tasters concluded that **Spice Islands Chili Powder** was the clear winner. This well-known supermarket brand was noted by one taster as having "a big flavor that stands out among the others."

Easy Taco Chili

Serves 4   **Cooking Time** 6 to 8 hours on Low or 3 to 5 hours on High

✔ **WHY THIS RECIPE WORKS:** When busy weeknights loom ahead, it's handy to have a seriously easy, family-friendly slow-cooker chili in your repertoire. Choosing frozen chopped onions and garlic powder kept us from needing our knife and cutting board while a packet of store-bought taco seasoning put an end to rummaging through the spice cabinet. Instead, we simply opened the packet and combined the spice mixture with the other aromatics before cooking. Canned tomatoes and black beans and frozen corn also helped this chili come together quickly. The onion and spice mixture will look soupy after microwaving. Serve with your favorite chili garnishes.

2	cups frozen chopped onions (or 2 onions, minced)
1	(1-ounce) packet taco seasoning
2	tablespoons tomato paste
2	tablespoons vegetable oil
1½	teaspoons garlic powder (or 6 garlic cloves, minced)
1	(15-ounce) can black beans, drained and rinsed
1	(15-ounce) can tomato sauce
1	(14.5-ounce) can diced tomatoes
1	tablespoon brown sugar
1	slice high-quality white sandwich bread, torn into quarters
2	tablespoons whole milk
1	pound 85 percent lean ground beef
	Salt and pepper
1	cup frozen corn

1. Microwave onions, taco seasoning, tomato paste, oil, and garlic powder in bowl, stirring occasionally, until onions are softened, about 5 minutes; transfer to slow cooker.

2. Stir beans, tomato sauce, tomatoes with juice, and sugar into slow cooker.

3. Mash bread and milk into paste in large bowl using fork. Mix in ground beef and ¼ teaspoon pepper using hands. Stir beef mixture into slow cooker, breaking up any large pieces. Cover and cook until beef is tender, 6 to 8 hours on low or 3 to 5 hours on high.

4. Let chili settle for 5 minutes, then remove fat from surface using large spoon. Break up any remaining large pieces of beef with spoon. Stir in corn and let sit until heated through, about 5 minutes. Season with salt and pepper to taste and serve.

SMART SHOPPING GARLIC SUBSTITUTE
For home cooks who don't use garlic on a regular basis, there are myriad garlic products available that seem like a convenient substitution for fresh: garlic powder, made from garlic cloves that are dehydrated and ground; dehydrated minced garlic, which is minced while fresh and then dehydrated; and garlic salt, which is typically 3 parts salt to 1 part garlic powder. When garlic is the predominant flavor in a recipe, we have found that nothing comes close to using fresh cloves, but in recipes where garlic is a background flavor and the recipe calls for only a clove or two, in a pinch you can use garlic powder. Substitute ¼ teaspoon of garlic powder for each clove of fresh garlic. We don't recommend dehydrated garlic (it takes a while to rehydrate and is quite mild) or garlic salt (our tasters disapproved of its "super-salty," "chemical" taste).

Three-Alarm Beef Chili

Serves 4   **Cooking Time** 6 to 8 hours on Low or 3 to 5 hours on High

✔ **WHY THIS RECIPE WORKS:** While most people enjoy moderately spiced chili, there are always those looking for more. For that reason, we turned up the heat to produce a spicy chili that is sure to cause a sweat. Focusing on great base flavor first, we started with a basic mixture of chili powder, cumin, oregano, and red pepper flakes cooked with onions and garlic. Ready for the heat, we then turned to minced habanero chiles and some hot sauce for a lasting, solid punch. Scotch bonnet chiles will work equally well. Dark red kidney beans added creaminess to this meaty chili while a bit of brown sugar helped balance the spiciness of the dish. Serve with shredded cheese, and chopped pickled banana peppers.

1	slice high-quality white sandwich bread, torn into quarters
2	tablespoons whole milk
1	pound 85 percent lean ground beef
	Salt and pepper
2	tablespoons vegetable oil
2	onions, minced
2	habanero or Scotch bonnet chiles, minced
2	tablespoons chili powder
2	tablespoons tomato paste
3	garlic cloves, minced
2	teaspoons ground cumin
2	teaspoons minced fresh oregano or ½ teaspoon dried
¼	teaspoon red pepper flakes
1	(15-ounce) can tomato sauce
1	(14.5-ounce) can diced tomatoes
1	(15-ounce) can dark red kidney beans, drained and rinsed
2	tablespoons soy sauce
1	tablespoon brown sugar
1	tablespoon minced canned chipotle chile in adobo sauce, plus extra as needed
	Hot sauce
	Sliced pickled banana peppers, chopped fine, for serving

1. Mash bread and milk into paste in large bowl using fork. Mix in ground beef, ¼ teaspoon salt, and ¼ teaspoon pepper using hands.

2. Heat oil in 12-inch skillet over medium-high heat until shimmering. Add onions, habaneros, chili powder, tomato paste, garlic, cumin, oregano, and red pepper flakes and cook until vegetables are softened and lightly browned, 8 to 10 minutes.

3. Stir in beef mixture and cook, breaking up any large pieces with wooden spoon, until no longer pink, about 3 minutes. Stir in tomato sauce, scraping up any browned bits; transfer to slow cooker.

4. Stir diced tomatoes with juice, beans, soy sauce, sugar, and chipotles into slow cooker. Cover and cook until beef is tender, 6 to 8 hours on low or 3 to 5 hours on high.

5. Let chili settle for 5 minutes, then remove fat from surface using large spoon. Break up any remaining large pieces of beef with spoon. Season with salt, hot sauce and additional chipotles to taste. Serve with banana peppers.

ON THE SIDE SWEET AND CAKEY CORNBREAD
Whisk 1½ cups all-purpose flour, 1 cup yellow cornmeal, 2 teaspoons baking powder, ¾ teaspoon salt, and ¼ teaspoon baking soda together in medium bowl. Process 1 cup buttermilk, ¾ cup thawed frozen corn kernels, and ¼ cup packed light brown sugar in food processor until combined, about 5 seconds. Add 2 large eggs and process until well combined (batter will be lumpy), about 5 seconds. Fold buttermilk mixture into flour mixture, then fold in 8 tablespoons melted unsalted butter. Scrape batter into greased 8-inch square pan. Bake in 400-degree oven until golden brown, 25 to 35 minutes. Let cool for 15 minutes before serving. Serves 6 to 8.

Moroccan Beef Chili with Chickpeas and Raisins

Serves 4   **Cooking Time** 6 to 8 hours on Low or 3 to 5 hours on High

✔ **WHY THIS RECIPE WORKS:** This interesting twist on beef chili gets its bold flavor from the use of traditional Moroccan spices—sweet paprika, cumin, ginger, cayenne, and cinnamon—which permeate the dish. To continue with the Moroccan flavors, we also included chickpeas (we chose canned for convenience) and some raisins in the chili. Added with the chickpeas, the raisins began to break down after hours in the slow cooker; stirring the raisins into the chili before serving ensured they had a more hardy texture. Finishing the chili with some fresh lemon zest and juice helped to brighten the flavors of the dish. Serve with plain yogurt, lime wedges, and scallions.

1	slice high-quality white sandwich bread, torn into quarters
2	tablespoons whole milk
1	pound 85 percent lean ground beef
	Salt and pepper
2	tablespoons vegetable oil
2	onions, minced
2	tablespoons tomato paste
3	garlic cloves, minced
2	teaspoons sweet paprika
2	teaspoons ground cumin
1½	teaspoons ground ginger
¼	teaspoon cayenne pepper
¼	teaspoon ground cinnamon
1	(15-ounce) can tomato sauce
1	(14.5-ounce) can diced tomatoes
1	(15-ounce) can chickpeas, drained and rinsed
2	tablespoons soy sauce
1	tablespoon brown sugar
½	cup raisins
½	teaspoon grated lemon zest
2	teaspoons fresh lemon juice

1. Mash bread and milk into paste in large bowl using fork. Mix in ground beef, ¼ teaspoon salt, and ¼ teaspoon pepper using hands.

2. Heat oil in 12-inch skillet over medium-high heat until shimmering. Add onions, tomato paste, garlic, paprika, cumin, ginger, cayenne, and cinnamon and cook until vegetables are softened and lightly browned, 8 to 10 minutes.

3. Stir in beef mixture and cook, breaking up any large pieces with wooden spoon, until no longer pink, about 3 minutes. Stir in tomato sauce, scraping up any browned bits; transfer to slow cooker.

4. Stir diced tomatoes with juice, chickpeas, soy sauce, and sugar into slow cooker. Cover and cook until beef is tender, 6 to 8 hours on low or 3 to 5 hours on high.

5. Let chili settle for 5 minutes, then remove fat from surface using large spoon. Break up any remaining large pieces of beef with spoon. Stir in raisins and let sit until heated through, about 10 minutes. Stir in lemon zest and juice, season with salt and pepper to taste, and serve.

ON THE SIDE COUSCOUS WITH FRESH MINT AND SCALLIONS
Toast 1½ cups couscous with 2 tablespoons olive oil in skillet over medium heat, stirring occasionally, until lightly browned, 3 to 5 minutes; transfer to medium bowl. Stir in ½ teaspoon salt and 2 cups boiling water, cover, and let sit until couscous is tender, about 12 minutes. Fluff with fork, stir in 2 tablespoons minced fresh mint and 2 minced scallions, and season with salt and pepper. Serves 4.

Texas Chili

Serves 8 to 10   **Cooking Time** 9 to 11 hours on Low or 5 to 7 hours on High

✔ **WHY THIS RECIPE WORKS:** Texans are famous for their style of chili featuring big chunks of beef slowly simmered in a chile-infused sauce. For our slow-cooker version we chose generous chunks of beef chuck, which remained moist while still turning impressively tender. To achieve the characteristic rich and smooth sauce, we used tomato puree and seasoned it with a hefty amount of onions and garlic mixed with an equally generous amount of aromatics and spices. Canned chipotle chiles and a little soy sauce added even more complexity of flavor. While beans are traditionally served alongside this chili, we liked the creaminess they provided when cooked with the meat so we included them in the mix. Serve with Easy White Rice (page 134) and your favorite chili garnishes.

3	onions, minced
¼	cup chili powder
¼	cup tomato paste
3	tablespoons vegetable oil
8	garlic cloves, minced
2	tablespoons ground cumin
1	tablespoon minced fresh oregano or 1 teaspoon dried
2	(15-ounce) cans dark red kidney beans, drained and rinsed
1	(28-ounce) can tomato puree
2	cups low-sodium chicken broth
¼	cup Minute tapioca
3	tablespoons soy sauce
2	tablespoons minced canned chipotle chile in adobo sauce
2	tablespoons brown sugar, plus extra as needed
2	bay leaves
1	(5-pound) boneless beef chuck roast, trimmed and cut into 1½-inch chunks (see page 59) Salt and pepper
3	scallions, sliced thin

1. Microwave onions, chili powder, tomato paste, oil, garlic, cumin, and oregano in bowl, stirring occasionally, until onions are softened, about 5 minutes; transfer to slow cooker.

2. Stir beans, tomato puree, broth, tapioca, soy sauce, chipotles, sugar, and bay leaves into slow cooker. Season beef with salt and pepper and nestle into slow cooker. Cover and cook until beef is tender, 9 to 11 hours on low or 5 to 7 hours on high.

3. Let chili settle for 5 minutes, then remove fat from surface using large spoon. Discard bay leaves. Season with salt, pepper, and sugar to taste, sprinkle with scallions, and serve.

ON THE SIDE GUACAMOLE
Using fork, mash 2 very ripe avocados until mostly smooth in medium bowl. Stir in 1 more avocado, cut into ½-inch pieces (see page 132), ¼ cup minced red onion, 1 small minced garlic clove, ¼ cup minced cilantro, and ½ teaspoon ground cumin. Season with salt, pepper, and lime juice to taste. Makes 3 cups.

Tomatillo Chili with Pork and Hominy

Serves 8 to 10   **Cooking Time** 9 to 11 hours on Low or 5 to 7 hours on High

✔ **WHY THIS RECIPE WORKS:** Green chili is a classic throughout Mexico and a perfect dish to create in the slow cooker. Chunks of pork slowly simmer in a bright, fresh sauce made from chiles and tomatillos (the tangy little tomatolike fruits common in Mexican cuisine) to create a dish with an appeal that is undeniable. The key to achieving the classic, bold flavors of this chili in a slow cooker was broiling the tomatillos along with the other aromatics and spices. Once charred, the vegetables and spices took on a rustic, smoky flavor, and we pureed them to create a flavorful base. The addition of hominy also contributed to the heartiness of the dish and helped to thicken the sauce. If you can't find fresh tomatillos, you can substitute three 11-ounce cans of tomatillos, drained, rinsed, and patted dry; broil as directed in step 1. Serve with your favorite chili garnishes.

1½	pounds tomatillos (16 to 20 medium), husks and stems removed, rinsed well, dried, and halved
1	onion, cut into 1-inch pieces
4	garlic cloves, minced
1	tablespoon minced fresh oregano or 1 teaspoon dried
1	teaspoon ground cumin
	Pinch ground cloves
	Pinch ground cinnamon
3	tablespoons vegetable oil
2	(15-ounce) cans white or yellow hominy, drained and rinsed
2½	cups low-sodium chicken broth
3	poblano chiles, stemmed, seeded, and minced
3	tablespoons Minute tapioca
2	teaspoons sugar
2	bay leaves
1	(4-pound) boneless pork butt roast, trimmed and cut into 1½-inch chunks (see page 59)
	Salt and pepper
¼	cup minced fresh cilantro

1. Position oven rack 6 inches from broiler element and heat broiler. Toss tomatillos, onion, garlic, oregano, cumin, cloves, and cinnamon with oil and spread onto aluminum foil–lined baking sheet. Broil until vegetables are blackened and begin to soften, 5 to 10 minutes, rotating pan halfway through broiling.

2. Let vegetables cool slightly. Pulse vegetables with accumulated juice in food processor until almost smooth, about 10 pulses; transfer to slow cooker.

3. Stir hominy, broth, poblanos, tapioca, sugar, and bay leaves into slow cooker. Season pork with salt and pepper and nestle into slow cooker. Cover and cook until pork is tender, 9 to 11 hours on low or 5 to 7 hours on high.

4. Let chili settle for 5 minutes, then remove fat from surface using large spoon. Discard bay leaves. Stir in cilantro, season with salt and pepper to taste, and serve.

SMART SHOPPING POBLANO CHILES
Poblano chiles are tapered, deep-green, medium-size Mexican chiles. They taste slightly bitter, similar to green bell peppers but with a spicier finish. Sold both fresh and dried (the dried are called anchos), they are used in many Mexican dishes, most famously in the United States in deep-fried, cheese-stuffed chiles rellenos. If you can't find poblanos, substitute one medium green bell pepper and 1 to 2 tablespoons of minced jalapeño (about ½ chile) per poblano.

New Mexican Red Pork Chili

Serves 6 to 8   **Cooking Time** 9 to 11 hours on Low or 5 to 7 hours on High

WHY THIS RECIPE WORKS: Inspired by the traditional New Mexican stew *carne adovada*, this chili features meltingly tender chunks of pork in an intense, richly flavored red chile sauce. For this long-simmered chili, we found that the considerable marbling of fat in pork butt (also known as Boston butt) produced supremely tender chunks of meat that didn't dry out. As for the sauce, traditional recipes called for toasting and grinding dried chiles—nearly two dozen—to achieve the recipe's distinct bitter, dried-fruit flavor, but we wanted a simpler, more pantry-friendly alternative. Chili powder, oregano, and chipotle chiles provided a solid baseline of warmth and depth, while fresh coffee brought a balance of robust, bittersweet flavors. And, since the flavor of dried chiles is sometimes described as raisiny, we went to the source, adding raisins before serving to achieve the desired fruity nuance. Stirring in fresh cilantro, lime zest, and lime juice at the end helped to brighten this earthy dish. Serve with your favorite chili garnishes.

2	onions, minced
¼	cup chili powder
2	tablespoons vegetable oil
6	garlic cloves, minced
2	tablespoons tomato paste
1	tablespoon minced fresh oregano or 1 teaspoon dried
2	cups low-sodium chicken broth
½	cup brewed coffee
¼	cup Minute tapioca
1	tablespoon minced canned chipotle chile in adobo sauce
1	tablespoon brown sugar, plus extra as needed
2	bay leaves
1	(4-pound) boneless pork butt roast, trimmed and cut into 1½-inch chunks (see page 59) Salt and pepper
½	cup raisins
¼	cup minced fresh cilantro
1	teaspoon grated lime zest
1	tablespoon fresh lime juice, plus extra as needed

1. Microwave onions, chili powder, oil, garlic, tomato paste, and oregano in bowl, stirring occasionally, until onions are softened, about 5 minutes; transfer to slow cooker.

2. Stir broth, coffee, tapioca, chipotles, sugar, and bay leaves into slow cooker. Season pork with salt and pepper and nestle into slow cooker. Cover and cook until pork is tender, 9 to 11 hours on low or 5 to 7 hours on high.

3. Let chili settle for 5 minutes, then remove fat from surface using large spoon. Discard bay leaves. Stir in raisins and let sit until heated through, about 10 minutes. Stir in cilantro, lime zest, and lime juice. Season with salt, pepper, sugar, and lime juice to taste and serve.

ON THE SIDE SCALLION-CHEDDAR MUFFINS
Whisk 3 cups all-purpose flour, 1 tablespoon baking powder, 1 teaspoon salt, and ⅛ teaspoon pepper together in large bowl. Stir in 1 cup shredded cheddar cheese and 2 thinly sliced scallions. In separate bowl, whisk 1¼ cups whole milk, ¾ cup sour cream, 3 tablespoons melted unsalted butter, and 1 lightly beaten large egg together. Gently fold milk mixture into flour mixture (batter will be very thick). Portion batter into greased 12-cup muffin tin and sprinkle with ½ cup grated Parmesan. Bake in 350-degree oven until golden brown, 25 to 30 minutes. Let cool for 15 minutes before serving. Makes 12.

Classic Turkey Chili

Serves 8 to 10   **Cooking Time** 4 to 6 hours on Low

✅ **WHY THIS RECIPE WORKS:** Turkey chili is a great alternative to classic beef chili, providing a leaner, but no less flavorful, meal for the dinner table. But because the meat is lean, it can quickly turn dry with a sandy consistency. To help protect our ground turkey from drying out, we enlisted the help of a panade—a paste of bread and milk—to provide added moisture. Mixed into the turkey before cooking, it ensured tender, moist pieces in our chili. We also found the addition of broth helped reinforce the meatiness of the leaner meat. Do not use ground turkey breast here (also labeled 99 percent fat free) or the turkey will still be very dry. Serve with your favorite chili garnishes.

2	slices high-quality white sandwich bread, torn into quarters
¼	cup whole milk
2	pounds ground turkey
	Salt and pepper
3	tablespoons vegetable oil
3	onions, minced
¼	cup chili powder
¼	cup tomato paste
6	garlic cloves, minced
1	tablespoon ground cumin
1	tablespoon minced fresh oregano or 1 teaspoon dried
½	teaspoon red pepper flakes
1	(15-ounce) can tomato sauce
2	(15-ounce) cans dark red kidney beans, drained and rinsed
1	(28-ounce) can diced tomatoes
1½	cups low-sodium chicken broth
3	tablespoons soy sauce
1	tablespoon brown sugar
2	teaspoons minced canned chipotle chile in adobo sauce

1. Mash bread and milk into paste in large bowl using fork. Mix in ground turkey, ½ teaspoon salt, and ½ teaspoon pepper using hands.

2. Heat oil in 12-inch skillet over medium-high heat until shimmering. Add onions, chili powder, tomato paste, garlic, cumin, oregano, and red pepper flakes and cook until vegetables are softened and lightly browned, 8 to 10 minutes.

3. Stir in turkey mixture, 1 pound at a time, and cook, breaking up any large pieces with wooden spoon, until no longer pink, about 3 minutes per pound. Stir in tomato sauce, scraping up any browned bits; transfer to slow cooker.

4. Stir beans, diced tomatoes with juice, broth, soy sauce, sugar, and chipotles into slow cooker. Cover and cook until turkey is tender, 4 to 6 hours on low.

5. Let chili settle for 5 minutes, then remove fat from surface using large spoon. Break up any remaining large pieces of turkey with spoon. Season with salt and pepper to taste and serve.

SMART SHOPPING CANNED KIDNEY BEANS
To see whether the brand of canned kidney beans you buy really matters when making chili, we put six brands of them through side-by-side taste tests. Tasting them straight from the can and in a simple chili recipe, we noticed substantial differences in both texture and flavor between the various brands. While some brands tasted mushy, chalky, and bland, **Goya Dark Red Kidney Beans** were "beautiful, plump red beans" with a "very sweet, strong bean flavor."

ALL ABOUT Tomato Products in the Slow Cooker

We put just about every canned tomato product available to work in our slow-cooker recipes, and often in unexpected ways (and combinations); the moist heat environment, which doesn't allow evaporation, and the long cooking time, which mutes flavor, posed challenges that required us to rethink when and how we used them. Here's what we learned about tomato products in the slow cooker along with the test kitchen's favorite brands (where we have one).

Whole Tomatoes

When big, bright chunks of tomato are what we are after, we reach for canned whole tomatoes and cut them ourselves. These tomatoes are pretty tender right out of the can, so we often reserve them for incorporating at the end of a recipe, such as our Vegetarian Black Bean Chili (page 139), to keep their fresh flavor intact. We found that whole tomatoes packed in juice rather than puree had a livelier, fresher flavor. Our top-rated brand is **Progresso Italian-Style Whole Peeled Tomatoes with Basil**.

Diced Tomatoes

Diced tomatoes stand up well against the steady heat of the slow cooker, making them ideal for providing a strong background of flavor as well as adding to the consistency of the final dish. We favor diced tomatoes packed in juice rather than puree because they have a fresher flavor. Our preferred brand is **Hunt's Diced Tomatoes**.

Crushed Tomatoes

The coarse consistency of crushed tomatoes provides great body and flavor for our Meatballs and Marinara (page 184) as well as many of our other tomato sauces, though we often combined it with other canned tomatoes to achieve the right consistency. We prefer chunky and fresh-tasting **Tuttorosso Crushed Tomatoes in Thick Puree with Basil**. Muir Glen Organic Crushed Tomatoes with Basil came in a close second in our testing.

Tomato Puree and Tomato Sauce

Tomato puree and tomato sauce are both cooked and strained to remove the tomato seeds, making them much smoother and thicker than other canned tomato products. They are a lifesaver for slow-cooker sauces where we wanted to achieve the same consistency of a stovetop sauce without the benefit of the reduction that comes with a long simmer in an uncovered pot or skillet. When it comes to hearty dishes like braised meat sauces, we found tomato puree worked best, though in sauces where the focus is more on the tomatoes, we turned to tomato sauce. We found **Hunt's Tomato Puree** to be the best with its thick consistency and tomatoey flavor.

Tomato Paste

Because it's naturally full of glutamates, which stimulate taste buds just like salt and pepper, tomato paste brings out subtle depths and savory notes. In our slow-cooker recipes, we made maximum use of tomato paste since the long cooking time tends to dull flavor. Cooked along with the aromatics, it provided body and richness to many of our soups and stews. You wouldn't expect to see tomato paste in the ingredient list for Homey Chicken Stew (page 44) or Chinese Chicken and Ramen Soup (page 21), but it adds a surprising amount of flavor and body without calling attention to itself. And, when we wanted a quicker alternative to browning meat, we learned that browning tomato paste serves as a faux fond allowing us to build the base of a sauce in a skillet without browning batches of meat. Our preferred brand is **Goya Tomato Paste**.

Tequila and Lime Turkey Chili

Serves 4   **Cooking Time** 4 to 6 hours on Low

✔ **WHY THIS RECIPE WORKS:** With our Classic Turkey Chili (page 129) mastered, we decided to get creative and incorporate two popular Tex-Mex flavors—tequila and lime—to produce a slow-cooker chili that was sure to grab attention. Added at the outset of cooking, the tequila provided a great base of flavor, but we still wanted a more vibrant presence. So we reserved a portion to stir in at the end with the lime juice. Some honey also helped bring out the tequila's sweetness while lime zest contributed to the bright citrus flavor. Do not use ground turkey breast here (also labeled 99 percent fat free) or the turkey will be very dry. Serve with your favorite chili garnishes.

1	**slice high-quality white sandwich bread, torn into quarters**
2	**tablespoons whole milk**
1	**pound ground turkey**
	Salt and pepper
2	**tablespoons vegetable oil**
2	**onions, minced**
2	**tablespoons chili powder**
2	**tablespoons tomato paste**
3	**garlic cloves, minced**
2	**teaspoons ground cumin**
2	**teaspoons minced fresh oregano or ½ teaspoon dried**
¼	**teaspoon red pepper flakes**
1	**(15-ounce) can tomato sauce**
1	**(14.5-ounce) can diced tomatoes**
1	**(15-ounce) can pinto beans, drained and rinsed**
¼	**cup tequila, plus extra as needed**
2	**tablespoons soy sauce**
1	**tablespoon honey**
1	**teaspoon minced canned chipotle chile in adobo sauce**
1	**teaspoon grated lime zest**
1	**tablespoon fresh lime juice, plus extra as needed**

1. Mash bread and milk into paste in large bowl using fork. Mix in ground turkey, ¼ teaspoon salt, and ¼ teaspoon pepper using hands.

2. Heat oil in 12-inch skillet over medium-high heat until shimmering. Add onions, chili powder, tomato paste, garlic, cumin, oregano, and red pepper flakes and cook until vegetables are softened and lightly browned, 8 to 10 minutes.

3. Stir in turkey mixture and cook, breaking up any large pieces with wooden spoon, until no longer pink, about 3 minutes. Stir in tomato sauce, scraping up any browned bits; transfer to slow cooker.

4. Stir diced tomatoes with juice, beans, 3 tablespoons tequila, soy sauce, honey, and chipotles into slow cooker. Cover and cook until turkey is tender, 4 to 6 hours on low.

5. Let chili settle for 5 minutes, then remove fat from surface using large spoon. Break up any remaining large pieces of turkey with spoon. Stir in remaining tablespoon tequila, lime zest, and lime juice. Season with salt, pepper, tequila, and lime juice to taste and serve.

QUICK PREP TIP EASIER ZESTING
Our favorite brand of rasp-style grater is **The Microplane 8½-Inch Grater/Zester** ($11.95), which has razor-sharp teeth and a design that's maneuverable over round or irregular shapes. When zesting citrus, we use the rasp grater upside down with fruit on the bottom and the inverted grater on the top. This way, you can see exactly how much zest you have and the zest won't scatter across your work surface.

White Chicken Chili

Serves 6 to 8   **Cooking Time** 4 to 6 hours on Low

✔ **WHY THIS RECIPE WORKS:** To achieve a great white chicken chili in the slow cooker, we needed to build flavor every step of the way. We started by choosing bone-in chicken thighs to ensure our chili had big chicken flavor. Sautéing the aromatics—including four jalapeño chiles—and spices together in the skillet also added a richer, deeper flavor, plus deglazing the pan ensured all the rich browned bits we developed ended up in the slow cooker. For convenience we used canned hominy and white beans, pureeing the hominy with broth to give the chili an appealing texture and a nice base of corn flavor. Serve with your favorite chili garnishes.

3 cups low-sodium chicken broth

1 (15-ounce) can white or yellow hominy, drained and rinsed

2 tablespoons vegetable oil

2 onions, minced

4 jalapeño chiles, stemmed, seeded, and minced

6 garlic cloves, minced

4 teaspoons ground cumin

2 teaspoons ground coriander

3 (15-ounce) cans cannellini beans, drained and rinsed

3 pounds bone-in chicken thighs, skin removed, trimmed
Salt and pepper

2 tablespoons minced jarred pickled jalapeño chiles

¼ cup minced fresh cilantro

2 avocados, pitted and cut into ½-inch pieces

1. Puree 2 cups broth and hominy in blender until smooth, about 1 minute; transfer to slow cooker.

2. Heat oil in 12-inch skillet over medium-high heat until shimmering. Add onions, jalapeños, garlic, cumin, and coriander and cook until vegetables are softened and lightly browned, 8 to 10 minutes. Stir in remaining 1 cup broth, scraping up any browned bits; transfer to slow cooker.

3. Stir beans into slow cooker. Season chicken with salt and pepper and nestle into slow cooker. Cover and cook until chicken is tender, 4 to 6 hours on low.

4. Transfer chicken to cutting board, let cool slightly, then shred into bite-size pieces (see page 21), discarding bones. Let chili settle for 5 minutes, then remove fat from surface using large spoon.

5. Stir in shredded chicken and pickled jalapeños and let sit until heated though, about 5 minutes. Stir in cilantro, season with salt and pepper to taste, and serve with avocado.

QUICK PREP TIP **CUTTING UP AN AVOCADO**
After cutting the avocado in half around the pit, lodge the edge of a knife blade into the pit and twist to remove, then use a wooden spoon to remove the pit from the blade. Make ½-inch crosshatch incisions in the flesh of each avocado half with a knife, cutting down to but not through the skin. Then separate the flesh from the skin with a soupspoon and gently scoop out the avocado cubes.

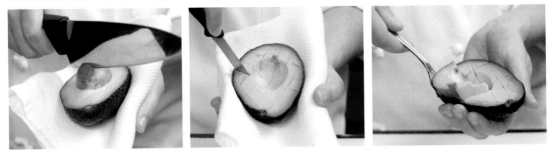

Mole Chicken Chili

Serves 6 to 8   **Cooking Time** 4 to 6 hours on Low

WHY THIS RECIPE WORKS: In Mexico, slowly simmered mole—a rich, complex sauce generally made with onions, garlic, dried chiles, chocolate, nuts, and spices—is often paired with mild-mannered chicken. We decided to take the flavors of chicken mole and create a delicious weeknight slow-cooker chili. Traditional moles contain an extensive list of ingredients, but we kept things simple, stopping at the pantry for staples like chili powder, cocoa powder, cinnamon, cloves, raisins, and peanut butter along with some aromatics. The mild acidity of diced tomatoes balanced the richness of the mole and a little tapioca ensured we achieved the perfect consistency. Stirring in a few fresh scallions at the end helped to brighten the dish. Serve with Easy White Rice.

2	onions, minced
2	tablespoons vegetable oil
2	tablespoons chili powder
2	tablespoons cocoa powder
3	garlic cloves, minced
½	teaspoon ground cinnamon
⅛	teaspoon ground cloves
2	cups low-sodium chicken broth
1	(14.5-ounce) can diced tomatoes
½	cup raisins
¼	cup peanut butter
3	tablespoons Minute tapioca
2	teaspoons minced canned chipotle chile in adobo sauce
2	pounds boneless, skinless chicken thighs, trimmed Salt and pepper
2	scallions, sliced thin
1	tablespoon sesame seeds, toasted (see page 87)

1. Microwave onions, oil, chili powder, cocoa powder, garlic, cinnamon, and cloves in bowl, stirring occasionally, until onions are softened, about 5 minutes; transfer to slow cooker.

2. Stir broth, tomatoes with juice, raisins, peanut butter, tapioca, and chipotles into slow cooker. Season chicken with salt and pepper and nestle into slow cooker. Cover and cook until chicken is tender, 4 to 6 hours on low.

3. Transfer chicken to cutting board, let cool slightly, then shred into bite-size pieces (see page 21). Let chili settle for 5 minutes, then remove fat from surface using large spoon.

4. Stir in shredded chicken and let sit until heated through, about 5 minutes. Stir in scallions, season with salt and pepper to taste, and serve with sesame seeds.

ON THE SIDE EASY WHITE RICE

Bring 4 quarts water to boil in large saucepan. Stir in long-grain white rice (see chart for rice amounts and serving sizes) and 2 teaspoons salt and return to boil. Reduce to simmer and cook gently until rice is tender, 12 to 17 minutes. Drain rice thoroughly and season with salt, pepper, and olive oil or unsalted butter to taste.

Servings	Amount of Rice
4	1½ cups
6	2¼ cups
8	3 cups
10	3¾ cups

Tempeh Chili

Serves 6 to 8   **Cooking Time** 4 to 6 hours on Low

✓ **WHY THIS RECIPE WORKS:** Creating a hearty, satisfying vegetarian version of classic ground beef chili can be difficult, especially in the slow cooker, where flavors are often muted. We were up for the challenge and began by creating a flavorful tomato base infused with a healthy amount of aromatics and spices. Using crumbled tempeh—a firm soybean cake often used in vegetarian cooking—gave our chili the hearty, meaty feel we were looking for and a can of kidney beans helped bulk things up even further. Any type of tempeh will work well in this chili. Fresh vegetable flavor was also key and we had the most success with carrots, red bell pepper, zucchini, and frozen corn. While the carrots and red bell pepper did well during the prolonged cooking, we found the zucchini and corn were best when added at the end. This ensured they stayed perfectly tender and fresh. Serve with your favorite chili garnishes.

2   **onions, minced**

2   **carrots, peeled and cut into ½-inch pieces**

1   **red bell pepper, stemmed, seeded, and chopped fine (see page 91)**

3   **tablespoons vegetable oil**

9   **garlic cloves, minced**

2   **tablespoons chili powder**

1   **tablespoon minced fresh oregano or 1 teaspoon dried**

2   **teaspoons ground cumin**

1   **(28-ounce) can crushed tomatoes**

1   **(15-ounce) can kidney beans, drained and rinsed**

1   **(8-ounce) package tempeh, crumbled into ¼-inch pieces**

1   **cup water**

1   **teaspoon minced canned chipotle chile in adobo sauce**

1   **zucchini (about 8 ounces), quartered lengthwise and sliced ½ inch thick**

1   **cup frozen corn**

½   **cup minced fresh cilantro**

   Salt and pepper

1. Microwave onions, carrots, bell pepper, oil, garlic, chili powder, oregano, and cumin in bowl, stirring occasionally, until vegetables are softened, 8 to 10 minutes; transfer to slow cooker.

2. Stir tomatoes, beans, tempeh, water, and chipotles into slow cooker. Cover and cook until chili flavors have melded and tempeh is tender, 4 to 6 hours on low.

3. Stir in zucchini, cover, and continue to cook on high until tender, 20 to 30 minutes. Stir in corn and let sit until heated through, about 5 minutes. Stir in cilantro, season with salt and pepper to taste, and serve.

SMART SHOPPING TEMPEH

Tempeh is made by fermenting cooked soybeans and adding other grains and flavorings, all of which is then formed into a firm, dense cake. Because it's better than tofu at holding its shape when cooked, it serves as a good meat substitute and is a mainstay of many vegetarian diets (and is particularly popular in Southeast Asia). Although it has a strong, almost nutty flavor, it tends to absorb the flavors of any foods or sauces to which it is added, making it a versatile choice for many sorts of dishes from chilis and stews to sandwiches and tacos. Tempeh is sold in most supermarkets and can be found with different grain combinations and flavorings.

Smoky Sausage and Bean Chili

Serves 6 to 8   **Cooking Time** 9 to 11 hours on Low or 5 to 7 hours on High

WHY THIS RECIPE WORKS: Similar to the classic cowboy chilis cooked over an open fire, this recipe is packed with tender chunks of sausage, creamy beans, and big smoky flavor. For a strong chili base, we relied on a hefty combination of chili powder, cumin, and oregano along with some onions, red bell peppers, and garlic. Since the small navy beans didn't require soaking, we then simply added them with the sausage and broth and allowed everything to cook until tender. Combining some andouille sausage with kielbasa gave our chili a pleasant spice and smokiness, but for really great campfire flavor, we found a little liquid smoke was key. Some brown sugar also enhanced the flavors of the dish. Serve with your favorite chili garnishes.

2	onions, minced
2	red bell peppers, stemmed, seeded, and minced (see page 91)
¼	cup chili powder
3	tablespoons vegetable oil
5	garlic cloves, minced
1	tablespoon ground cumin
1	tablespoon dried oregano
3	cups low-sodium chicken broth
2½	cups water
1	pound dried navy beans (2½ cups), picked over and rinsed
1	pound kielbasa sausage, sliced ½ inch thick
8	ounces andouille sausage, cut into ½-inch pieces
2	tablespoons soy sauce
1	tablespoon brown sugar
1	tablespoon minced canned chipotle chile in adobo sauce
1	teaspoon liquid smoke
2	bay leaves
	Salt and pepper
3	scallions, sliced thin

1. Microwave onions, bell peppers, chili powder, oil, garlic, cumin, and oregano in bowl, stirring occasionally, until vegetables are softened, about 5 minutes; transfer to slow cooker.

2. Stir broth, water, beans, kielbasa, andouille, soy sauce, sugar, chipotles, liquid smoke, and bay leaves into slow cooker. Cover and cook until beans are tender, 9 to 11 hours on low or 5 to 7 hours on high.

3. Let chili settle for 5 minutes, then remove fat from surface using large spoon. Discard bay leaves. Transfer 1 cup cooked beans to bowl and mash smooth with potato masher. Stir mashed beans into chili and let sit until heated through, about 5 minutes. Season with salt and pepper to taste, sprinkle with scallions, and serve.

SMART SHOPPING LIQUID SMOKE

We were among the many people who assume that there must be some kind of synthetic chemical chicanery going on in the making of "liquid smoke" flavoring, but that's not the case. Liquid smoke is made by channeling smoke from smoldering wood chips through a condenser, which quickly cools the vapors, causing them to liquefy (just like the drops that form when you breathe on a piece of cold glass). The water-soluble flavor compounds in the smoke are trapped within this liquid, while the nonsoluble, carcinogenic tars and resins are removed by a series of filters, resulting in a clean, smoke-flavored liquid. When buying liquid smoke, be sure to avoid brands with additives such as salt, vinegar, and molasses. Our top-rated brand, **Wright's Liquid Smoke**, contains nothing but smoke and water.

Vegetarian Black Bean Chili

Serves 6 to 8   **Cooking Time** 9 to 11 hours on Low or 5 to 7 hours on High

✔ **WHY THIS RECIPE WORKS:** Black bean chili is a hearty, satisfying dish and a great option for the slow cooker. But vegetarian versions are a bit trickier since there are no ham products, like meaty, smoky ham hocks, to build flavor over the long cooking time. To achieve the full flavors we expected from a traditional black bean chili, we started by browning a generous amount of aromatics and spices. This additional step was promising, but only got us so far—the chili still seemed pretty lean. Though a bit odd for a chili, a surprise ingredient, mustard seeds, added an appealing pungency and the level of complexity we were looking for. To bulk up the chili, we added bell peppers, white mushrooms, and canned tomatoes. We added the tomatoes at the end because when added at the beginning, their acidity prevented the beans from cooking through fully. And while canned diced tomatoes were convenient, they took more time to turn tender than hand-cut whole canned tomatoes, so we chose whole instead. Minced cilantro and a spritz of fresh lime provide welcome brightness and are a must. To make this dish spicier, add the chile seeds. Serve with your favorite chili garnishes.

2	tablespoons vegetable oil
2	onions, minced
2	red bell peppers, stemmed, seeded, and minced (see page 91)
2	jalapeño chiles, stemmed, seeded, and minced
9	garlic cloves, minced
3	tablespoons chili powder
4	teaspoons mustard seeds
1	tablespoon ground cumin
1	tablespoon dried oregano
2½	cups vegetable broth
2½	cups water
1	pound dried black beans (2½ cups), picked over and rinsed
10	ounces white mushrooms, trimmed and halved if small or quartered if large
1	tablespoon minced canned chipotle chile in adobo sauce
2	bay leaves
1	(28-ounce) can whole tomatoes, drained and cut into ½-inch pieces
2	tablespoons minced fresh cilantro
	Salt and pepper

1. Heat oil in 12-inch skillet over medium-high heat until shimmering. Add onions, bell peppers, jalapeños, garlic, chili powder, mustard seeds, cumin, and oregano and cook until vegetables are softened and lightly browned, 8 to 10 minutes. Stir in 1 cup broth, scraping up any browned bits; transfer to slow cooker.

2. Stir water, beans, mushrooms, remaining 1½ cups broth, chipotles, and bay leaves into slow cooker. Cover and cook until beans are tender, 9 to 11 hours on low or 5 to 7 hours on high.

3. Discard bay leaves. Transfer 1 cup cooked beans to bowl and mash smooth with potato masher. Stir mashed beans and tomatoes into chili and let sit until heated through, about 5 minutes. Stir in cilantro, season with salt and pepper to taste, and serve.

QUICK PREP TIP SEEDING JALAPEÑOS

Most of the heat in a chile pepper is in the ribs and seeds. An easy way to remove both is simply to cut the pepper in half lengthwise, then, starting at the end opposite the stem, use a melon baller to scoop down the inside of each half. (You can also use the sharp edge of the melon baller to cut off the stem.)

BARBECUED BEEF BRISKET

Barbecue Favorites and More

Barbecued Beef Brisket

Serves 8   **Cooking Time** 9 to 11 hours on Low or 5 to 7 hours on High

✔ **WHY THIS RECIPE WORKS:** To make a tender and moist barbecued brisket with robust spice and smoke flavor we started out with a simple spice rub, often the hallmark of great barbecue. Salt, pepper, brown sugar, cumin, and paprika provided the backbone of flavor, while chipotle chiles lent a smoky dimension. To allow the rub to penetrate the meat we pierced the brisket all over with a fork and then refrigerated it overnight. Though brisket releases flavorful juice during cooking (used for serving), we wanted to bump up the flavors even more. We microwaved onions, more chipotles, tomato paste, garlic, and chili powder and added them to the slow cooker, along with a little water. The resulting braising liquid was sweet, smoky, and spicy; all we needed to do to finish the sauce was stir in ketchup, vinegar, and liquid smoke.

½ **cup packed dark brown sugar**
3 **tablespoons minced canned chipotle chile in adobo sauce**
1 **tablespoon ground cumin**
1 **tablespoon sweet paprika**
   Salt and pepper
1 **(5-pound) flat-cut beef brisket, trimmed**
2 **onions, minced**
2 **tablespoons tomato paste**
4 **garlic cloves, minced**
1 **tablespoon vegetable oil**
1 **tablespoon chili powder**
½ **cup water**
¼ **cup ketchup**
1 **tablespoon cider vinegar**
¼ **teaspoon liquid smoke**

1. Combine sugar, 2 tablespoons chipotles, cumin, paprika, 1 teaspoon salt, and 2 teaspoons pepper in bowl. Using fork, prick brisket all over. Rub sugar mixture over brisket, wrap tightly in plastic wrap, and refrigerate for 8 to 24 hours. Unwrap brisket and place in slow cooker.

2. Microwave onions, tomato paste, garlic, oil, chili powder, and remaining tablespoon chipotles in bowl, stirring occasionally, until onions are softened, about 5 minutes; transfer to slow cooker. Add water to slow cooker. Cover and cook until beef is tender, 9 to 11 hours on low or 5 to 7 hours on high.

3. Transfer brisket to cutting board, tent loosely with aluminum foil, and let rest for 20 minutes. Let braising liquid settle for 5 minutes, then remove fat from surface using large spoon. Whisk in ketchup, vinegar, and liquid smoke and season with salt and pepper to taste.

4. Slice brisket ½ inch thick against grain (see page 101) and arrange on serving platter. Spoon 1 cup sauce over meat and serve with remaining sauce.

ON THE SIDE BUTTERMILK COLESLAW
Toss 1 medium head chopped green cabbage (12 cups) and 2 large shredded carrots with 1 teaspoon salt and let drain in colander until wilted, about 1 hour. Rinse cabbage and carrots with cold water, then dry thoroughly with paper towels and transfer to large bowl. Stir in ⅔ cup buttermilk, ½ cup mayonnaise, ¼ cup sour cream, 8 chopped scallions, 2 tablespoons sugar, and 1 teaspoon Dijon mustard. Season with salt and pepper to taste and refrigerate until chilled. Serves 8 to 10.

Shredded Barbecued Beef

Serves 8   **Cooking Time** 9 to 11 hours on Low or 5 to 7 hours on High

✔ **WHY THIS RECIPE WORKS:** Piled high on soft buns, saucy barbecued shredded beef is a real crowd pleaser. We chose a boneless chuck roast for the beef since we knew it would become tender and shreddable after hours in a slow cooker. For a richly flavored sauce, we got out our skillet, first browning bacon for smoky flavor and then sautéing onions and spices in the rendered bacon fat. We then added ketchup, mustard, and brown sugar plus a somewhat unusual ingredient—coffee—which when reduced down along with all the other sauce ingredients, lent just the complexity we were seeking.

4	ounces bacon (about 4 slices), minced
2	onions, minced
2	tablespoons chili powder
1	tablespoon sweet paprika
1½	cups ketchup
1½	cups brewed coffee
¼	cup packed dark brown sugar
2	tablespoons brown mustard
1	(5-pound) boneless beef chuck roast, trimmed and quartered
	Salt and pepper
1	tablespoon hot sauce
1	tablespoon cider vinegar
1	teaspoon liquid smoke

1. Cook bacon in 12-inch skillet over medium-high heat until crisp, about 5 minutes. Stir in onions, chili powder, and paprika and cook until onions are softened and lightly browned, 8 to 10 minutes.

2. Stir in ketchup, coffee, sugar, and 1 tablespoon mustard and simmer until mixture is thickened and measures 4 cups, about 10 minutes. Transfer 2 cups of mixture to slow cooker; reserve remaining mixture separately.

3. Season beef with salt and pepper and nestle into slow cooker. Cover and cook until beef is tender, 9 to 11 hours on low or 5 to 7 hours on high.

4. Transfer beef to large bowl, let cool slightly, then shred into bite-size pieces (see page 21) discarding excess fat; cover to keep warm. Let braising liquid settle for 5 minutes, then remove fat from surface using large spoon.

5. Strain liquid into medium saucepan and simmer until thickened and measures 1 cup, 20 to 30 minutes. Whisk in reserved ketchup mixture, hot sauce, vinegar, remaining tablespoon mustard, and liquid smoke and bring to simmer. Season with salt and pepper to taste.

6. Toss shredded beef with 1½ cups sauce; add more sauce as needed to keep meat moist. Serve with remaining sauce.

QUICK PREP TIP QUARTERING A ROAST
Compared to a single large roast, the four smaller pieces of meat will cook more evenly and soak up the flavors of the sauce better. Using a sharp chef's knife, cut the beef or pork roast into quarters, removing and discarding excess fat.

North Carolina Pulled Pork

Serves 8   **Cooking Time** 9 to 11 hours on Low or 5 to 7 hours on High

✔ **WHY THIS RECIPE WORKS:** To make authentic North Carolina pulled pork, with its succulent, smoky meat, and tangy vinegar-based sauce, we began by smothering a pork butt roast with a sweet and spicy dry rub made of brown sugar, paprika, chili powder, cumin, salt, and pepper. Refrigerating the meat overnight intensified the flavor, allowing the rub to penetrate the meat further. For authentic smokiness we cooked the pork with smoked ham hocks, which could be shredded later on. Reducing all of the defatted cooking liquid to a concentrated 1 cup on the stovetop, then stirring in cider vinegar, ketchup, more sugar, and liquid smoke, led to the perfect balance of tangy, sweet, and smoky flavors in the finished barbecue sauce. Note that this sauce is fairly thin compared to gooey molasses-based sauces. Don't shred the meat too fine in step 3; it will break up more as the meat is combined with the sauce. Serve on soft buns with pickle chips.

6	tablespoons dark brown sugar
¼	cup sweet paprika
2	tablespoons chili powder
1	tablespoon ground cumin
	Salt and pepper
1	(5-pound) boneless pork butt roast, trimmed and quartered (see page 143)
3	smoked ham hocks, rinsed
2	cups low-sodium chicken broth
1	cup cider vinegar
¾	cup ketchup
1½	teaspoons liquid smoke

1. Combine 3 tablespoons sugar, paprika, chili powder, cumin, 2 teaspoons salt, and 1 tablespoon pepper in bowl. Using fork, prick pork all over. Rub sugar mixture over pork, wrap tightly in plastic wrap, and refrigerate for 8 to 24 hours.

2. Place ham hocks in slow cooker. Unwrap pork and place on top of hocks. Pour broth over pork, cover, and cook until pork is tender, 9 to 11 hours on low or 5 to 7 hours on high.

3. Transfer pork and hocks to large bowl, let cool slightly, then shred into bite-size pieces (see page 21) discarding skin, bones, and excess fat; cover to keep warm. Let braising liquid settle for 5 minutes, then remove fat from surface using large spoon.

4. Strain liquid into medium saucepan and simmer until thickened and measures 1 cup, 20 to 30 minutes. Whisk in vinegar, ketchup, liquid smoke, and remaining 3 tablespoons sugar and bring to simmer. Season with salt and pepper to taste.

5. Toss shredded pork with 1½ cups sauce; add more sauce as needed to keep meat moist. Serve with remaining sauce.

ON THE SIDE SOUTHERN-STYLE COLLARD GREENS
Cook 4 slices chopped bacon in large Dutch oven over medium heat until fat begins to render, about 2 minutes. Stir in 1 minced onion and ¼ teaspoon salt and cook until softened, 5 to 7 minutes. Stir in 3 minced garlic cloves and cook for 30 seconds. Stir in 6 cups low-sodium chicken broth and bring to simmer. Stir in 2½ pounds collard greens, stemmed and chopped coarse, one handful at a time, until wilted. Cover, place pot in 350-degree oven, and cook until greens are tender and broth is flavorful, about 45 minutes. Season with salt and pepper to taste. Serves 8.

Beginner's Pulled Pork

Serves 8   **Cooking Time** 9 to 11 hours on Low or 5 to 7 hours on High

WHY THIS RECIPE WORKS: Pulled pork is a natural recipe for the slow cooker, and this super-easy recipe takes just minutes to prep; as a bonus, there is no sauce to reduce at the end of the cooking time—the defatted cooking liquid, seasoned with sugar and vinegar, makes a great dressing. We started by coating full-flavored pork butt (also called Boston butt) with a basic barbecue spice rub and refrigerated it overnight to allow the flavors to penetrate the meat. By cutting the meat into quarters, we exposed more surface area, which made the final dish even more flavorful. Just a cup of barbecue sauce—either homemade or store-bought—is all that is needed to create a tangy sauce during the long cooking time when the spices and juice from the meat are released. You can use either No-Cook Pantry Barbecue Sauce (page 154) or your favorite store-bought brand. Don't shred the meat too fine in step 3; it will break up more as the meat is combined with the sauce. Serve on white bread with pickle chips.

¼ **cup packed brown sugar, plus extra as needed**

¼ **cup sweet paprika**

1 **tablespoon garlic powder**

1 **tablespoon onion powder**

1 **tablespoon ground cumin**

1 **teaspoon cayenne pepper**

   Salt and pepper

1 **(5-pound) boneless pork butt roast, trimmed and quartered (see page 143)**

1 **cup barbecue sauce, plus extra for serving**

   Cider vinegar

1. Combine sugar, paprika, garlic powder, onion powder, cumin, cayenne, and ½ teaspoon salt in bowl. Using fork, prick pork all over. Rub sugar mixture over pork, wrap tightly in plastic wrap, and refrigerate for 8 to 24 hours. Unwrap pork and place in slow cooker.

2. Spread barbecue sauce evenly over pork, cover, and cook until pork is tender, 9 to 11 hours on low or 5 to 7 hours on high.

3. Transfer pork to large bowl, let cool slightly, then shred into bite-size pieces (see page 21) discarding excess fat; cover to keep warm. Let braising liquid settle for 5 minutes, then remove fat from surface using large spoon. Season with salt, pepper, sugar, and vinegar to taste.

4. Toss shredded pork with 1 cup braising liquid; add more liquid as needed to keep meat moist. Serve with barbecue sauce.

SMART SHOPPING BARBECUE SAUCE
Homemade barbecue sauce is pretty simple to make, but there may be times (such as when you need only a small amount) when you just want to open up a bottle of the store-bought variety. But which one? In just one local supermarket we found more than 30 varieties! To make sense of all these options, we conducted a blind taste test of leading national brands. We chose tomato-based sauces that were labeled "original" and tasted them as a dipping sauce for homemade chicken fingers. Although tasters' personal preferences varied, our winner was **Bull's-Eye Original Barbecue Sauce**, which was praised for being "well balanced" and gained points for its "great dark color" and "thick consistency."

Sweet and Sour Sticky Ribs

Serves 6 to 8 **Cooking Time** 6 to 8 hours on Low

✔ **WHY THIS RECIPE WORKS:** These ribs are the ultimate in sticky, succulent, bone-sucking goodness. To flavor the ribs we made a quick but deeply flavorful sweet and sour sauce using apricot jam, pineapple juice concentrate, soy sauce, and rice vinegar. To heat things up we added fresh ginger and red pepper flakes, then rounded out the flavors with dark brown sugar. After standing the racks of ribs upright around the perimeter and spiraling them in towards the center of the slow-cooker insert, we poured the sweet and tangy sauce over the top. This allowed the sauce to drip down, slowly basting and flavoring the ribs as they cooked. After cooking, we thickened the braising liquid with cornstarch and reduced it to a gooey, syrupy glaze that could be brushed over the ribs as they broiled to lacquered, sticky perfection. Avoid racks of ribs larger than 2 pounds as they will be difficult to maneuver into the slow cooker. We found that leaving the membrane coating the underside of the ribs attached helped hold the racks together.

2 tablespoons vegetable oil

1 onion, minced

1 red bell pepper, stemmed, seeded, and chopped fine (see page 91)

3 tablespoons minced or grated fresh ginger

6 garlic cloves, minced

2 tablespoons tomato paste

¼ teaspoon red pepper flakes

1 (12-ounce) jar apricot jam or preserves (1 cup)

6 ounces frozen pineapple juice concentrate (¾ cup)

⅓ cup soy sauce

5 tablespoons rice vinegar

¼ cup packed dark brown sugar

6 pounds pork baby back ribs
Salt and pepper
Vegetable oil spray

1 tablespoon cornstarch

1 tablespoon water

2 tablespoons minced fresh cilantro

1. Heat oil in 12-inch nonstick skillet over medium-high heat until shimmering. Add onion, bell pepper, ginger, garlic, tomato paste, and red pepper flakes and cook until vegetables are softened and lightly browned, 8 to 10 minutes. Stir in apricot jam, pineapple juice concentrate, soy sauce, ¼ cup vinegar, and sugar and simmer until thickened slightly, about 5 minutes.

2. Season ribs with salt and pepper and arrange upright in slow cooker, with meaty sides facing outward (see page 148). Pour sauce over ribs, cover, and cook until ribs are tender, 6 to 8 hours on low.

3. Position oven rack 10 inches from broiler element and heat broiler. Place wire rack in aluminum foil–lined rimmed baking sheet and coat with vegetable oil spray. Carefully transfer ribs, meaty side down, to prepared baking sheet and tent with foil. Let braising liquid settle for 5 minutes, then remove fat from surface using large spoon.

4. Strain braising liquid into medium saucepan. Whisk cornstarch and water together, then whisk into liquid. Bring to a simmer, whisking constantly, and simmer until thickened and measures 2 cups, 15 to 20 minutes. Stir in cilantro and remaining tablespoon vinegar and season with salt and pepper to taste.

5. Brush ribs with some sauce and broil until beginning to brown, 2 to 4 minutes. Flip ribs over, brush with more sauce, and continue to broil until ribs are well browned and sticky, 9 to 12 minutes longer, brushing with additional sauce every few minutes.

6. Transfer ribs to cutting board, tent with foil, and let rest for 10 minutes. Serve with remaining sauce.

Easy Barbecued Ribs

Serves 6 to 8   **Cooking Time** 6 to 8 hours on Low

WHY THIS RECIPE WORKS: We wanted to create a slow-cooker version of barbecued pork ribs with the same fall-off-the-bone texture as their authentic grill-roasted counterparts. We settled on baby back ribs for this recipe, which weigh about 1½ pounds per rack. To develop an authentic crispy, lightly charred exterior, we broiled the cooked ribs, brushing them with barbecue sauce every few minutes, until sticky and caramelized. You can use either No-Cook Pantry Barbecue Sauce (page 154) or your favorite store-bought brand (see the tasting on page 146). Avoid racks of ribs larger than 2 pounds as they will be difficult to maneuver into the slow cooker. We found that leaving the membrane coating the underside of the ribs attached helped hold the racks together.

3   tablespoons sweet paprika
2   tablespoons brown sugar
¼   teaspoon cayenne pepper
     Salt and pepper
6   pounds pork baby back ribs
3   cups barbecue sauce
     Vegetable oil spray

1. Mix paprika, sugar, cayenne, 1 tablespoon salt, and 1 tablespoon pepper together, then rub mixture evenly over ribs. Arrange ribs upright in slow cooker, with meaty sides facing outward. Pour barbecue sauce over ribs, cover, and cook until ribs are tender, 6 to 8 hours on low.

2. Position oven rack 10 inches from broiler element and heat broiler. Place wire rack in aluminum foil–lined rimmed baking sheet and coat with vegetable oil spray. Carefully transfer ribs, meaty side down, to prepared baking sheet and tent with foil. Let braising liquid settle for 5 minutes, then remove fat from surface using large spoon.

3. Strain braising liquid into medium saucepan and simmer until thickened and measures 2 cups, 15 to 20 minutes. Season with salt and pepper to taste.

4. Brush ribs with some sauce and broil until beginning to brown, 2 to 4 minutes. Flip ribs over, brush with more sauce, and continue to broil until ribs are well browned and sticky, 9 to 12 minutes longer, brushing with additional sauce every few minutes.

5. Transfer ribs to cutting board, tent with foil, and let rest for 10 minutes. Serve with remaining sauce.

QUICK PREP TIP ARRANGING RIBS IN SLOW COOKER
To ensure that the ribs cook evenly, stand the racks up along the perimeter of the slow cooker with the wide end down and the meatier side of the ribs facing the slow-cooker insert wall.

Asian Ribs

Serves 6 to 8   **Cooking Time** 6 to 8 hours on Low

WHY THIS RECIPE WORKS: Slow cooking the ribs in a sweet and gingery hoisin sauce ensured that the Asian flavors fully permeated the meat. We used the same mixture as a base for the glaze, reducing it with spicy red pepper jelly and tangy cider vinegar. The high sugar content in the glaze promoted caramelization and ensured sticky, sweet, slow-cooked ribs that left tasters scrambling for more.

1   **cup hoisin sauce**

1   **cup sugar**

½   **cup soy sauce**

½   **cup dry sherry**

½   **bunch fresh cilantro, stems and leaves separated, stems chopped coarse, leaves minced**

8   **scallions, white and green parts separated, whites chopped coarse, and greens sliced thin**

3   **tablespoons minced or grated fresh ginger**

6   **garlic cloves, minced**

4   **(3-inch-long) strips orange zest, trimmed of white pith**

1¾   **teaspoons cayenne pepper**

6   **pounds pork baby back ribs**
     Salt and pepper
     Vegetable oil spray

1   **(10-ounce) jar hot red pepper, red currant, or apple jelly (¾ cup)**

½   **cup cider vinegar**

1. Combine hoisin sauce, sugar, soy sauce, sherry, cilantro stems, scallion whites, ginger, garlic, orange zest, and 1½ teaspoons cayenne in bowl. Season ribs with salt and pepper and arrange upright in slow cooker, with meaty sides facing outward (see page 148). Pour sauce over ribs, cover, and cook until ribs are tender, 6 to 8 hours on low.

2. Position oven rack 10 inches from broiler element and heat broiler. Place wire rack in aluminum foil–lined rimmed baking sheet and coat with vegetable oil spray. Carefully transfer ribs, meaty side down, to prepared baking sheet and tent with foil. Let braising liquid settle for 5 minutes, then remove fat from surface using large spoon.

3. Strain 3 cups braising liquid into medium saucepan; discard extra braising liquid. Whisk in jelly, vinegar, remaining ¼ teaspoon cayenne, and cilantro leaves and simmer until thickened and measures 2 cups, 15 to 20 minutes. Season with salt and pepper to taste.

4. Brush ribs with some sauce and broil until beginning to brown, 2 to 4 minutes. Flip ribs over, brush with more sauce, and continue to broil until ribs are well browned and sticky, 9 to 12 minutes longer, brushing with additional sauce every few minutes.

5. Transfer ribs to cutting board, tent with foil, and let rest for 10 minutes. Sprinkle with scallion greens and serve with remaining sauce.

QUICK PREP TIP **MAKING ZEST STRIPS**
Use a vegetable peeler to remove long, wide strips of citrus zest from the fruit. Try not to remove any of the white pith beneath the zest, as it is bitter.

Huli Huli Chicken

Serves 4 to 6   **Cooking Time** 4 to 6 hours on Low

✓ WHY THIS RECIPE WORKS: We wanted to create a slow-cooker version of this Hawaiian chicken, with its tropical flavor and deep mahogany coating. Since traditional recipes are cooked over a live fire on a spit, we knew we had our work cut out for us. Fortunately the chicken's deep color gets a little help from a salty-sweet sauce (also called huli huli), which contains just a few basic pantry ingredients—brown sugar, ketchup, and soy sauce. Slow-cooker chicken emerges rather pale at the end of the cooking time, so we knew we'd have to finish ours in the oven in order to get the level of caramelization we were seeking. In addition, our sauce would have to be pretty thick and also fairly concentrated to be detected in the finished chicken. Precooking the sauce on the stovetop was ideal, as it thickened the mixture and concentrated the flavor. To balance the intensity of the soy sauce, we added pineapple juice and lime juice, which provided sweetness and acidity, while fresh garlic and ginger rounded things out. Basting the chicken frequently with the sauce in a hot oven before serving enabled us to achieve a traditional-looking mahogany huli huli lacquer (and great-tasting chicken).

⅔ **cup pineapple juice**
½ **cup packed brown sugar**
½ **cup ketchup**
¼ **cup fresh lime juice from 2 limes**
¼ **cup soy sauce**
6 **garlic cloves, minced**
2 **tablespoons minced or grated fresh ginger**
  Salt and pepper
  Vegetable oil spray
4 **pounds bone-in, skin-on chicken pieces (split breasts, thighs, and/or drumsticks), trimmed**

1. Simmer pineapple juice, sugar, ketchup, lime juice, soy sauce, garlic, and ginger in medium saucepan until thickened and measures 1½ cups, about 10 minutes. Season with salt and pepper to taste.

2. Coat slow cooker with vegetable oil spray. Transfer ½ cup sauce to slow cooker; reserve remaining sauce separately. Season chicken with salt and pepper, add to slow cooker, and coat evenly with sauce. Cover and cook until chicken is tender, 4 to 6 hours on low.

3. Adjust oven rack to middle position and heat oven to 450 degrees. Place wire rack in aluminum foil–lined rimmed baking sheet and coat with vegetable oil spray. Transfer chicken, skin side up, to prepared baking sheet; discard braising liquid.

4. Brush chicken with some reserved sauce and bake, brushing with more sauce every few minutes, until it has deep, mahogany lacquer, 20 to 30 minutes. Serve.

SMART SHOPPING SOY SAUCE
At its most basic, soy sauce is a fermented liquid made from soybeans and wheat. Soybeans contribute a strong, pungent taste, while wheat lends sweetness. Soy sauce should add flavor and complexity to your recipes, not just make them salty. We use it not only in numerous Asian-flavored dishes, but also to enhance meaty flavor in sauces, stews, soups, and braises. Our taste test winner is **Lee Kum Kee Tabletop Soy Sauce**, which has a robust flavor that holds up well throughout cooking.

Jerk Chicken

Serves 4 to 6   **Cooking Time** 4 to 6 hours on Low

WHY THIS RECIPE WORKS: Smoky, spicy Jamaican jerk chicken has become popular far beyond the small Caribbean island where it originated. We wanted to create an authentic-tasting jerk chicken recipe with fiery chiles, warm spices, and fragrant herbs in a slow cooker that tasted just as good as its more commonly grilled counterparts. First, we used a food processor to make a smooth paste of the traditional mix of aromatics—scallions, garlic, habanero chiles (also called Scotch bonnets), and ginger—along with sticky molasses, sweet-smelling dried thyme, allspice, salt, and oil to bind everything together. We coated the chicken with some of this paste before cooking and saved the rest for basting later on. After a slow braise in the slow cooker when the chicken was tender but still intact, we finished it under the broiler, basting it with more of the jerk rub, until it was lightly charred and crisp. With its nicely charred exterior and juicy interior, our jerk chicken was so appealing that tasters questioned whether we had a grill hidden somewhere outside the test kitchen. If you can't find habanero chiles, substitute 2 to 4 jalapeño chiles. To make this dish spicier, add the chile seeds.

8	**scallions, chopped coarse**
¼	**cup vegetable oil**
2	**habanero chiles, stemmed and seeded**
1	**(1-inch) piece fresh ginger, peeled and sliced ¼ inch thick**
2	**tablespoons molasses**
3	**garlic cloves, peeled**
1	**tablespoon dried thyme**
2	**teaspoons ground allspice**
1	**teaspoon salt**
4	**pounds bone-in, skin-on chicken pieces (split breasts, thighs, and/or drumsticks), trimmed**
	Vegetable oil spray
	Lime wedges, for serving

1. Puree scallions, oil, habaneros, ginger, molasses, garlic, thyme, allspice, and salt in food processor until smooth, about 30 seconds. Transfer ½ cup mixture to slow cooker; reserve remaining mixture separately.

2. Add chicken to slow cooker and coat evenly with scallion mixture. Cover and cook until chicken is tender, 4 to 6 hours on low.

3. Position oven rack 10 inches from broiler element and heat broiler. Place wire rack in aluminum foil–lined rimmed baking sheet and coat with vegetable oil spray. Transfer chicken, skin side down, to prepared baking sheet; discard braising liquid.

4. Brush chicken with half of reserved scallion mixture and broil until lightly charred and crisp, 10 to 15 minutes. Flip chicken over, brush with remaining scallion mixture, and continue to broil until lightly charred and crisp on second side, 5 to 10 minutes longer. Serve with lime wedges.

ON THE SIDE SWEET AND TART CUCUMBER SALAD

Toss 3 cucumbers, peeled, seeded, and sliced thin, and ½ cup sliced red onion with 1½ teaspoons salt in colander. Place water-filled gallon-sized zipper-lock bag on top and let cucumbers drain for 1 to 3 hours. Meanwhile, simmer ⅔ cup water, ½ cup rice vinegar, and 2½ tablespoons sugar in small saucepan until slightly thickened, about 15 minutes; transfer to bowl and let cool. Stir drained cucumber mixture and 2 finely chopped and seeded jalapeños into cooled dressing. Season with salt and pepper to taste and refrigerate until chilled. Serves 4 to 6.

Shredded Barbecued Chicken

Serves 6   **Cooking Time** 4 to 6 hours on Low

✔ **WHY THIS RECIPE WORKS:** A simple spice mixture and some barbecue sauce are all it takes to transform chicken thighs and breasts into tangy, silky, shredded chicken—perfect for a simple summer night's barbecue dinner for family or friends. Just cooking the chicken with sauce created lackluster, one-dimensional chicken, but when we coated the chicken with a simple blend of chili powder, paprika, cayenne, salt, and pepper we knew we had the ticket to a winning recipe. You can use either No-Cook Pantry Barbecue Sauce or your favorite store-bought brand (see the tasting on page 146). Warm the barbecue sauce before tossing it with the chicken; otherwise, it will cool the meat down too much. Don't shred the meat too fine in step 2; it will break up more as the meat is combined with the sauce. Feel free to use all white or dark meat if you prefer. Serve on white bread with pickle chips.

2	**teaspoons chili powder**
1	**teaspoon sweet paprika**
¼	**teaspoon cayenne pepper**
	Salt and pepper
1½	**pounds boneless, skinless chicken thighs, trimmed**
1½	**pounds boneless, skinless chicken breasts, trimmed**
1½	**cups barbecue sauce**

1. Mix chili powder, paprika, cayenne, ½ teaspoon salt, and ¼ teaspoon pepper together, then rub mixture evenly over chicken; transfer to slow cooker. Pour ½ cup barbecue sauce over chicken and toss to coat. Cover and cook until chicken is tender, 4 to 6 hours on low.

2. Transfer chicken to large bowl, let cool slightly, then shred into bite-size pieces (see page 21); cover to keep warm. Let braising liquid settle for 5 minutes, then remove fat from surface using large spoon.

3. Microwave remaining cup barbecue sauce in bowl until hot, about 3 minutes. Toss shredded chicken with hot barbecue sauce and 1 cup braising liquid; add more liquid as needed to keep meat moist. Serve.

ON THE SIDE NO-COOK PANTRY BARBECUE SAUCE
Whisk 2¼ cups ketchup, ¾ cup molasses, 3 tablespoons cider vinegar, 2 teaspoons hot sauce, and ¾ teaspoon liquid smoke together in bowl. Season with salt and pepper to taste. (For a spicier sauce, add 2 seeded and minced jalapeño chiles and 3 tablespoons minced canned chipotle chile in adobo sauce.) Makes 3 cups.

Fiery Hot Wings

Serves 4 to 6   **Cooking Time** about 4 hours on Low

WHY THIS RECIPE WORKS: Great hot wings should have juicy, tender meat and a crisp coating, both of which could be challenging (if not impossible) to achieve simultaneously in the slow cooker. To add serious flavor, we first tossed the wings with a fiery blend of spices. For the sauce we envisioned a tolerably spicy, slightly sweet, and faintly vinegary flavor profile so we combined melted butter with ample hot sauce, a little sugar, and a splash of cider vinegar to brighten things up—in essence creating Buffalo wing–style sauce. Broiling the wings after cooking, while basting with some of the sauce, created a crispy exterior and ensured our wings were fiery hot. This recipe can easily be doubled for a crowd, but you will need to broil the wings in two batches in the oven.

6 tablespoons (¾ stick) unsalted butter
1 cup hot sauce
2 tablespoons brown sugar
1 tablespoon cider vinegar
1 tablespoon sweet paprika
2 teaspoons chili powder
1 teaspoon cayenne pepper
Salt and pepper
4 pounds whole chicken wings, wingtips discarded and wings split (see page 157)
Vegetable oil spray

1. Melt butter in small saucepan over low heat. Whisk in hot sauce, 4 teaspoons sugar, and vinegar. Transfer ½ cup sauce to slow cooker; reserve remaining sauce separately.

2. Mix paprika, chili powder, remaining 2 teaspoons sugar, cayenne, 1 teaspoon salt, and 1 teaspoon pepper together, then rub mixture evenly over chicken; transfer to slow cooker. Cover and cook until chicken is tender, about 4 hours on low.

3. Position oven rack 10 inches from broiler element and heat broiler. Place wire rack in aluminum foil–lined rimmed baking sheet and coat with vegetable oil spray. Transfer chicken to prepared baking sheet; discard braising liquid.

4. Brush chicken with half of reserved sauce and broil until lightly charred and crisp, 10 to 15 minutes. Flip chicken over, brush with remaining sauce, and continue to broil until lightly charred and crisp on second side, 5 to 10 minutes longer. Serve.

SMART SHOPPING HOT SAUCE
Though usually added in small doses, hot sauce can add just the vinegary heat a dish might need. Over the years, we've found that while most hot sauces share the same core ingredients—chile peppers, vinegar, and salt—their heat levels can vary drastically. To avoid a searingly hot sauce, we recommend using the test kitchen's favorite brand, **Frank's RedHot**, which has mellow heat and deep flavor. Note that some brands of hot sauce, such as Tabasco and La Preferida, are nearly twice as hot as Frank's, so be careful!

Sticky Wings

Serves 4 to 6   **Cooking Time** about 4 hours on Low

✓ **WHY THIS RECIPE WORKS:** Perfect sticky wings are moist and lacquered with a slightly thick, sweet yet tangy sauce—the stickier and messier, the better. First, we coated the chicken with a pungent mix of dark brown sugar, soy sauce, and aromatics and let it cook for about 4 hours until tender. Meanwhile, we made an easy sauce with tomato paste, soy sauce, and more sugar and cayenne. We knew these wings would need some time under the broiler to become charred and crisp, and this sauce provided just the right finishing touch. This recipe can easily be doubled for a crowd, but you will need to broil the wings in two batches in the oven.

¾ **cup packed dark brown sugar**

¼ **cup soy sauce**

2 **tablespoons minced or grated fresh ginger**

4 **garlic cloves, minced**

½ **teaspoon cayenne pepper**

4 **pounds whole chicken wings, wingtips discarded and wings split**

   Salt and pepper

   Vegetable oil spray

¼ **cup water**

¼ **cup tomato paste**

1. Stir ¼ cup sugar, 1 tablespoon soy sauce, ginger, garlic, and ¼ teaspoon cayenne into slow cooker. Season chicken with salt and pepper, add to slow cooker, and toss to coat. Cover and cook until chicken is tender, about 4 hours on low.

2. Position oven rack 10 inches from broiler element and heat broiler. Place wire rack in aluminum foil–lined rimmed baking sheet and coat with vegetable oil spray. Transfer chicken to prepared baking sheet; discard braising liquid.

3. Combine remaining ½ cup sugar, water, tomato paste, remaining 3 tablespoons soy sauce, and remaining ¼ teaspoon cayenne in bowl. Brush chicken with half of mixture and broil until lightly charred and crisp, 10 to 15 minutes. Flip chicken over, brush with remaining mixture, and continue to broil until lightly charred and crisp on second side, 5 to 10 minutes longer. Serve.

QUICK PREP TIP CUTTING UP CHICKEN WINGS
Using kitchen shears or a sharp chef's knife, cut through the wing at the two joints and discard the wing tip.

Honey-Mustard Drumsticks

Serves 4 to 6   **Cooking Time** 4 to 6 hours on Low

WHY THIS RECIPE WORKS: This recipe is a real crowd pleaser, with its sweet and spicy glaze covering moist and tender chicken. We chose Dijon mustard for its bold, tangy, and sharp flavors, which balance the sweetness of the honey perfectly. In order to crisp the chicken skin, it was necessary to finish by baking the drumsticks in a hot oven until sticky and caramelized on both sides. Be sure to spray the slow cooker insert with vegetable oil spray to prevent sticking. Other types of mustard can be substituted for the Dijon.

	Vegetable oil spray
2	tablespoons brown sugar
1½	teaspoons garlic powder
1½	teaspoons onion powder
1	teaspoon dry mustard
	Salt and pepper
4	pounds bone-in, skin-on chicken drumsticks, trimmed
¾	cup Dijon mustard
½	cup honey

1. Coat inside of slow cooker with vegetable oil spray. Mix sugar, garlic powder, onion powder, dry mustard, 1 teaspoon salt, and ½ teaspoon pepper together, then rub mixture evenly over chicken; transfer to slow cooker.

2. Mix Dijon and honey in bowl. Pour ½ cup mixture over chicken and toss to coat; reserve remaining Dijon mixture separately. Cover and cook until chicken is tender, 4 to 6 hours on low.

3. Adjust oven rack to middle position and heat oven to 450 degrees. Place wire rack in aluminum foil–lined rimmed baking sheet and coat with vegetable oil spray. Transfer chicken to prepared baking sheet; discard braising liquid.

4. Brush chicken with half of reserved Dijon mixture and broil until lightly charred and crisp, 10 to 15 minutes. Flip chicken over, brush with remaining Dijon mixture, and continue to broil until lightly charred and crisp on second side, 10 to 15 minutes longer. Serve.

ON THE SIDE TANGY APPLE SLAW

Toss ½ head chopped green cabbage (6 cups) with 1½ teaspoons salt and let drain in colander until wilted, about 1 hour. Rinse cabbage with cold water, then dry thoroughly with paper towels and transfer to large bowl. Stir in 1 Granny Smith apple, cut into thin matchsticks, and 1 thinly sliced scallion. Bring ¼ cup cider vinegar, 3 tablespoons sugar, 3 tablespoon vegetable oil, ½ tablespoon Dijon mustard, and ⅛ teaspoon red pepper flakes to boil in saucepan, then toss with cabbage mixture. Season with salt and pepper to taste and refrigerate until chilled. Serves 6.

Barbecued Drumsticks

Serves 4 to 6   **Cooking Time** 4 to 6 hours on Low

✓ **WHY THIS RECIPE WORKS:** Although our slow-cooker barbecued drumsticks require some time under the broiler at the end to caramelize their skin until glossy brown, they are otherwise prep-free—it takes only a few minutes to measure out the spices and sauce and get them underway. You can use either No-Cook Pantry Barbecue Sauce (page 154), or your favorite store-bought brand (see the tasting on page 146).

1	tablespoon brown sugar
1	tablespoon sweet paprika
1	teaspoon dry mustard
1	teaspoon ground cumin
1	teaspoon garlic powder
1	teaspoon onion powder
¼	teaspoon cayenne pepper
	Salt and pepper
4	pounds bone-in, skin-on chicken drumsticks, trimmed
1½	cups barbecue sauce
	Vegetable oil spray

1. Mix sugar, paprika, mustard, cumin, garlic powder, onion powder, cayenne, 1 teaspoon salt, and 1 teaspoon pepper together, then rub mixture evenly over chicken; transfer to slow cooker. Pour ½ cup barbecue sauce over chicken and toss to coat. Cover and cook until chicken is tender, 4 to 6 hours on low.

2. Position oven rack 10 inches from broiler element and heat broiler. Place wire rack in aluminum foil–lined rimmed baking sheet and coat with vegetable oil spray. Transfer chicken to prepared baking sheet; discard braising liquid.

3. Brush chicken with ½ cup more barbecue sauce and broil until lightly charred and crisp, 10 to 15 minutes. Flip chicken over, brush with remaining ½ cup barbecue sauce, and continue to broil until lightly charred and crisp on second side, 5 to 10 minutes longer. Serve.

ON THE SIDE MACARONI SALAD
Boil ½ pound elbow macaroni in salted boiling water until tender. Drain macaroni, then rinse with cold water; leave pasta slightly wet. Combine pasta, ¼ cup minced red onion, 1 small minced celery rib, 2 tablespoons minced fresh parsley, 1 tablespoon lemon juice, ½ teaspoon Dijon mustard, pinch garlic powder, and pinch cayenne in large bowl, and let sit for 2 minutes. Stir in 1 cup mayonnaise, season with salt and pepper to taste, and refrigerate until chilled. Before serving, add cold water, 1 tablespoon at a time, to loosen dressing. Serves 6.

BIG-BATCH BOLOGNESE SAUCE

Pasta Sauces

Classic Marinara Sauce

Makes 9 cups   **Cooking Time** 9 to 11 hours on Low or 5 to 7 hours on High

✔ **WHY THIS RECIPE WORKS:** A rich and full-bodied marinara sauce usually takes a couple of hours of stovetop simmering so we wanted to develop a hands-off slow-cooker version—a bit of a challenge since the slow cooker doesn't provide any chance for evaporation and reduction. The biggest hurdle was choosing the right tomato products, as many of our tests produced sauces that were either too watery or too thick and overpowering. Our solution was a combination of four different tomato products (paste, crushed, diced, and sauce). The concentrated products (tomato paste and tomato sauce) provided lots of strong, complex flavor without unwanted water—no need for evaporation. For more layers of flavor, we sautéed a few anchovies with our aromatics and deglazed the pan with red wine before stirring everything together with 2 tablespoons of soy sauce—the anchovies and soy sauce added much-needed meaty flavor to the sauce. This recipe makes enough to sauce 3 pounds of pasta.

2   tablespoons extra-virgin olive oil
2   onions, minced
6   garlic cloves, minced
2   tablespoons tomato paste
2   tablespoons minced fresh
     oregano or 2 teaspoons dried
2   anchovy fillets, rinsed
     and minced
     Pinch red pepper flakes
1   cup dry red wine
1   (28-ounce) can crushed
     tomatoes
1   (28-ounce) can diced tomatoes,
     drained
1   (28-ounce) can tomato sauce
2   tablespoons soy sauce
½   cup minced fresh basil
2   teaspoons sugar, plus extra
     as needed
     Salt and pepper

1. Heat oil in 12-inch skillet over medium-high heat until shimmering. Add onions, garlic, tomato paste, oregano, anchovies, and red pepper flakes and cook until onions are softened and lightly browned, 8 to 10 minutes. Stir in wine, scraping up any browned bits, and simmer until thickened, about 5 minutes; transfer to slow cooker.

2. Stir crushed tomatoes, diced tomatoes, tomato sauce, and soy sauce into slow cooker. Cover and cook until sauce is deeply flavored, 9 to 11 hours on low or 5 to 7 hours on high.

3. Before serving, stir in basil and sugar and season with salt, pepper, and additional sugar to taste.

SMART SHOPPING ANCHOVY FILLETS VS. PASTE
Since most recipes call for only a small amount, we wondered whether a tube of anchovy paste might be a more convenient option. Made from pulverized anchovies, vinegar, salt, and water, anchovy paste promises all the flavor of oil-packed anchovies without the mess. When we tested the paste and jarred or canned anchovies side by side in recipes calling for an anchovy or two, we found little difference, though a few astute tasters felt that the paste had a "saltier" and "slightly more fishy" flavor. You can substitute ¼ teaspoon of the paste for each fillet. However, when a recipe calls for more than a couple of anchovies, stick with jarred or canned anchovies (**Ortiz Oil-Packed Anchovies** are our favorite), as the paste's more intense flavor will be overwhelming.

Fire-Roasted Tomato Sauce

Makes 9 cups   **Cooking Time** 9 to 11 hours on Low or 5 to 7 hours on High

WHY THIS RECIPE WORKS: Inspired by the cans of fire-roasted tomatoes on grocery store shelves, we set out to develop an easy tomato sauce with a kick. Working with our Classic Marinara Sauce as a starting point, we swapped two of our tomato products (diced and crushed tomatoes) for fire-roasted versions, giving our sauce a mild smokiness with no extra work. To further enhance the smoky flavor, after we sautéed our aromatics, we sautéed the drained diced tomatoes, browning them and intensifying and deepening their flavor. For a final dose of smoky flavor, we stirred in ¼ teaspoon of liquid smoke—which packs quite a smoky punch. This recipe makes enough to sauce 3 pounds of pasta.

2   tablespoons extra-virgin olive oil
2   onions, minced
8   garlic cloves, minced
2   tablespoons tomato paste
2   tablespoons minced fresh
     oregano or 2 teaspoons dried
     Pinch red pepper flakes
1   (28-ounce) can fire-roasted
     diced tomatoes, drained
1   cup dry red wine
1   (28-ounce) can fire-roasted
     crushed tomatoes
1   (28-ounce) can tomato sauce
¼   teaspoon liquid smoke
½   cup minced fresh parsley
     Salt and pepper

1. Heat oil in 12-inch skillet over medium-high heat until shimmering. Add onions, garlic, tomato paste, oregano, and red pepper flakes and cook until onions are softened and lightly browned, 8 to 10 minutes.

2. Stir in diced tomatoes and cook until dry and lightly browned, 8 to 10 minutes. Stir in wine, scraping up any browned bits, and simmer until thickened, about 5 minutes; transfer to slow cooker.

3. Stir crushed tomatoes, tomato sauce, and liquid smoke into slow cooker. Cover and cook until sauce is deeply flavored, 9 to 11 hours on low or 5 to 7 hours on high.

4. Before serving, stir in parsley and season with salt and pepper to taste.

ON THE SIDE EASY GARLIC ROLLS
Cut 2 pounds pizza dough into 12 pieces, roll pieces into balls, and arrange on parchment-lined baked sheet. Mix ¼ cup olive oil with 3 minced garlic cloves, ½ teaspoon salt, and ¼ teaspoon pepper. Brush half of garlic mixture over rolls. Bake in 350-degree oven until golden, 25 to 30 minutes, brushing rolls with remaining garlic mixture halfway through baking time. Makes 12.

Farm Stand Tomato Sauce

Makes 9 cups   **Cooking Time** 9 to 11 hours on Low or 5 to 7 hours on High

WHY THIS RECIPE WORKS: The beauty of this recipe is that you can put a bounty of peeled and cored fresh whole tomatoes into a slow cooker with a few other ingredients, walk away for up to 11 hours, and after a brief stovetop simmer to eliminate extra liquid, you end up with a brightly flavored tomato sauce—enough to serve a crowd (or plenty to freeze for later). This is the recipe to turn to when your local farmers' markets are overflowing with their late summer crop of field-grown tomatoes. The trick to making this fresh tomato sauce in a slow cooker is to add a hefty amount of tomato paste to deepen its flavor along with tapioca for thickening. A potato masher came in handy at the end to get the right chunky texture, while a quick stovetop simmer eliminated the liquid released by the tomatoes during the long cooking time. This recipe makes enough to sauce 3 pounds of pasta.

2	onions, minced
¼	cup tomato paste
2	tablespoons extra-virgin olive oil, plus extra as needed
6	garlic cloves, minced
1	tablespoon minced fresh oregano or 1 teaspoon dried
½	cup dry red wine
¼	cup Minute tapioca
2	bay leaves
7	pounds tomatoes (about 14 large)
¼	cup minced fresh basil
	Salt and pepper

1. Microwave onions, tomato paste, oil, garlic, and oregano in bowl, stirring occasionally, until onions are softened, about 5 minutes; transfer to slow cooker. Stir wine, tapioca, and bay leaves into slow cooker.

2. Core and peel tomatoes, then transfer to slow cooker. Cover and cook until tomatoes are very soft and beginning to disintegrate, 9 to 11 hours on low or 5 to 7 hours on high.

3. Discard bay leaves. Mash tomatoes until mostly smooth with potato masher. Transfer sauce mixture to large Dutch oven and simmer over medium-high heat until thickened, about 20 minutes.

4. Before serving, stir in basil and season with salt, pepper, and additional extra-virgin olive oil to taste.

QUICK PREP TIP **PEELING TOMATOES**
Cut out the stem and core of each tomato, then score a small X at the base. Lower the tomatoes into boiling water and simmer until the skins loosen, 30 to 60 seconds. Use a paring knife to remove strips of loosened skin starting at the X on the base of each tomato.

Weeknight Meat Sauce

Makes 12 cups   **Cooking Time** 9 to 11 hours on Low or 5 to 7 hours on High

WHY THIS RECIPE WORKS: Kid friendly and easy to make, our Weeknight Meat Sauce has all the flavor of the long-simmered traditional version without all the work. To ensure that our ground beef was still tender and flavorful after hours in the slow cooker, it was necessary to mix it with a panade (a paste of bread and milk). The panade bound with the meat, keeping it moist throughout the long cooking time. Instead of browning the meat, then the aromatics, we got enough flavor from simply browning our aromatics and deglazing the pan with wine, which saved us time in the kitchen. You can substitute ground turkey for the ground beef in this recipe. This recipe makes enough to sauce 3 pounds of pasta.

2	tablespoons extra-virgin olive oil
2	onions, minced
6	garlic cloves, minced
2	tablespoons tomato paste
2	tablespoons minced fresh oregano or 2 teaspoons dried
	Pinch red pepper flakes
1	cup dry red wine
1	(28-ounce) can crushed tomatoes
1	(28-ounce) can diced tomatoes, drained
1	(28-ounce) can tomato sauce
2	slices high-quality white sandwich bread, torn into quarters
¼	cup whole milk
2	pounds 85 percent lean ground beef
	Salt and pepper
½	cup minced fresh basil

1. Heat oil in 12-inch skillet over medium-high heat until shimmering. Add onions, garlic, tomato paste, oregano, and red pepper flakes and cook until onions are softened and lightly browned, 8 to 10 minutes. Stir in wine, scraping up any browned bits, and simmer until thickened, about 5 minutes; transfer to slow cooker. Stir crushed tomatoes, diced tomatoes, and tomato sauce into slow cooker.

2. Mash bread and milk into paste in large bowl using fork. Mix in ground beef, ½ teaspoon salt, and ½ teaspoon pepper using hands. Stir beef mixture into slow cooker, breaking up any large pieces. Cover and cook until beef is tender, 9 to 11 hours on low or 5 to 7 hours on high.

3. Let sauce settle for 5 minutes, then remove fat from surface using large spoon. Break up any remaining large pieces of beef with spoon. Before serving, stir in basil and season with salt and pepper to taste.

QUICK PREP TIP **KEEPING BASIL FRESH LONGER**
We usually end up with most of a large bunch of basil left over after preparing a single recipe, so we wondered how long we could keep the rest of the bunch and how best to store it. Since basil left out on the counter wilted within hours, we were stuck with refrigerator storage, which is about 15 degrees colder than the recommended temperature for basil. We tested storing basil, both plain and wrapped in damp paper towels (the latter being our preferred method for most leafy greens), in unsealed zipper-lock bags. After three days in the refrigerator, both samples were still green and perky. But after one week, only the towel-wrapped basil was still fresh-looking and fresh-tasting. Don't be tempted to rinse basil until just before you need to use it; when we performed the same tests after rinsing, the shelf life was decreased by half.

Meaty Tomato Sauce

Makes 12 cups   **Cooking Time** 9 to 11 hours on Low or 5 to 7 hours on High

✔ WHY THIS RECIPE WORKS: Nothing could be more welcoming on a cold night than coming home to a rustic, flavor-packed meat sauce ready to toss with some stick-to-your ribs pasta. For our slow-cooker version, we relied on country-style pork ribs, which turned meltingly tender during the long cooking. Once the pork was fully cooked, it was easy to break it into shreds using a spoon. To prevent the sauce from turning out watery, we relied on a trio of tomato products: tomato paste, diced tomatoes, and tomato puree. A dose of soy sauce further enhanced the sauce's meaty flavor. No one would ever guess that this rich-tasting and meaty sauce was so easy to make. This recipe makes enough to sauce 3 pounds of pasta.

2	onions, minced
12	garlic cloves, minced
¼	cup tomato paste
2	tablespoons extra-virgin olive oil
2	tablespoons minced fresh oregano or 2 teaspoons dried
¼	teaspoon red pepper flakes
1	(28-ounce) can diced tomatoes, drained
1	(28-ounce) can tomato puree
¾	cup dry red wine
⅓	cup soy sauce
2	bay leaves
3	pounds boneless country-style pork ribs, trimmed and cut into 1½-inch chunks
	Salt and pepper
¼	cup minced fresh parsley

1. Microwave onions, garlic, tomato paste, oil, oregano, and red pepper flakes in bowl, stirring occasionally, until onions are softened, about 5 minutes; transfer to slow cooker.

2. Stir tomatoes, tomato puree, wine, soy sauce, and bay leaves into slow cooker. Season pork with salt and pepper and nestle into slow cooker. Cover and cook until pork is tender, 9 to 11 hours on low or 5 to 7 hours on high.

3. Let sauce settle for 5 minutes, then remove fat from surface using large spoon. Discard bay leaves. Break up pieces of pork with spoon. Before serving, stir in parsley and season with salt and pepper to taste.

SMART SHOPPING SPAGHETTI
In the not-so-distant past, American pasta had a poor reputation, and rightly so. It cooked up gummy and starchy, and experts usually touted the superiority of Italian brands. To find out if this was still the case, we tasted eight leading brands of spaghetti—four American and four Italian. Ultimately, American-made **Ronzoni** was the top finisher, with tasters praising its nutty, buttery flavor and superb texture. De Cecco, an Italian brand, finished second in the tasting and was enjoyed for its wheaty flavor and pleasantly chewy texture. The more expensive brands, including Martelli at nearly $10 a pound, came in last, so save your money and don't bother with the expensive imported pastas—American-made is just fine.

Spicy Sausage Ragu with Red Peppers

Makes 12 cups   **Cooking Time** 9 to 11 hours on Low or 5 to 7 hours on High

✔ **WHY THIS RECIPE WORKS:** Spicy Italian sausages and sweet bell peppers are a classic pairing that we thought would translate perfectly into a bright, slightly sweet, and deeply flavored slow-cooker pasta sauce. We liked the flavorful heat that hot Italian sausages imparted, and a few minutes spent browning them and breaking them up in a skillet gave the sauce an even deeper and richer flavor. Since we had our skillet out, we sautéed our aromatics (onions, garlic, oregano, and red pepper flakes) and deglazed the pan with red wine. Tomato paste, crushed tomatoes, diced tomatoes, and tomato sauce were the perfect combination of tomato products with which to build our sauce—neither too watery nor too thick. As for the bell peppers, which rounded out the flavors and cut a little of the heat, we simply softened them in the microwave and stirred them into the sauce just before serving. This recipe makes enough to sauce 3 pounds of pasta.

2 tablespoons extra-virgin olive oil
2 pounds hot Italian sausage, removed from its casing
2 onions, minced
6 garlic cloves, minced
2 tablespoons tomato paste
2 tablespoons minced fresh oregano or 2 teaspoons dried
1 teaspoon red pepper flakes
1 cup dry red wine
1 (28-ounce) can crushed tomatoes
1 (28-ounce) can diced tomatoes, drained
1 (28-ounce) can tomato sauce
2 red bell peppers, stemmed, seeded, and cut into ½-inch pieces (see page 91)
½ cup minced fresh parsley
Salt and pepper

1. Heat 1 tablespoon oil in 12-inch skillet over medium-high heat until just smoking. Add sausage and brown well, breaking up large pieces with wooden spoon, about 5 minutes; transfer to slow cooker. Pour off all but 2 tablespoons fat left in skillet.

2. Add onions, garlic, tomato paste, oregano, and red pepper flakes to fat in skillet and cook over medium-high heat until onions are softened and lightly browned, 8 to 10 minutes. Stir in wine, scraping up any browned bits, and simmer until thickened, about 5 minutes; transfer to slow cooker.

3. Stir crushed tomatoes, diced tomatoes, and tomato sauce into slow cooker. Cover and cook until sauce is deeply flavored, 9 to 11 hours on low or 5 to 7 hours on high.

4. Let sauce settle for 5 minutes, then remove fat from surface using large spoon. Microwave bell peppers with remaining tablespoon oil in bowl, stirring occasionally, until tender, about 5 minutes. Stir softened bell peppers into sauce and let sit until heated through, about 5 minutes. Before serving, stir in parsley and season with salt and pepper to taste.

ON THE SIDE   SOFT AND CHEESY BREAD STICKS
Roll out 2 (1-pound) balls pizza dough separately on lightly floured counter into two 12 by 6-inch rectangles. Cut each rectangle crosswise into twelve 1-inch-wide strips and lay on well-oiled rimmed baking sheet (dough strips will touch each other). Brush breadsticks with 3 tablespoons olive oil, sprinkle with ½ cup grated Parmesan cheese, and season with salt and pepper to taste. Bake in 400-degree oven until golden brown, 20 to 25 minutes, rotating pan halfway through baking. Pull bread sticks apart and serve. Makes 24.

Short Ribs and Red Wine Sauce

Makes 12 cups   **Cooking Time** 9 to 11 hours on Low or 5 to 7 hours on High

✔ **WHY THIS RECIPE WORKS:** The classic pairing of short ribs and red wine sauce struck us as the perfect basis for a slow-cooker pasta sauce. Here boneless short ribs are cooked until tender and shreddable in a rich red wine–based sauce. To build our sauce we first sautéed aromatics (onions, carrots, celery, garlic, and tomato paste), then deglazed the pan with a healthy dose of red wine, reducing it down to concentrate its flavor and evaporate any unwanted liquid. To further complement the rich flavor of the meat and wine, we stirred diced tomatoes and tomato puree into the slow cooker, which gave our sauce just the right body and flavor. After cooking we simply shredded the meat and stirred in some parsley before serving the sauce over our favorite pasta. This recipe makes enough to sauce 3 pounds of pasta.

2	tablespoons extra-virgin olive oil
2	onions, minced
2	carrots, peeled and cut into ¼-inch pieces
1	celery rib, minced
¼	cup tomato paste
6	garlic cloves, minced
1½	cups dry red wine
1	(28-ounce) can diced tomatoes, drained
1	(28-ounce) can tomato puree
2	bay leaves
3	pounds boneless beef short ribs, trimmed and cut into 1½-inch chunks
	Salt and pepper
½	cup minced fresh parsley

1. Heat oil in 12-inch skillet over medium-high heat until shimmering. Add onions, carrots, celery, tomato paste, and garlic and cook until vegetables are softened and lightly browned, 8 to 10 minutes. Stir in wine, scraping up any browned bits, and simmer until thickened, about 6 minutes; transfer to slow cooker.

2. Stir diced tomatoes, tomato puree, and bay leaves into slow cooker. Season beef with salt and pepper and nestle into slow cooker. Cover and cook until beef is tender, 9 to 11 hours on low or 5 to 7 hours on high.

3. Let sauce settle for 5 minutes, then remove fat from surface using large spoon. Discard bay leaves. Break up pieces of beef with spoon. Before serving, stir in parsley and season with salt and pepper to taste.

ON THE SIDE ARUGULA SALAD WITH FIGS, PROSCIUTTO, AND WALNUTS
Fry 2 ounces thinly sliced prosciutto, cut into ¼-inch-wide ribbons, in 1 tablespoon olive oil in skillet over medium heat until crisp, about 7 minutes; drain on paper towels. Microwave ½ cup dried figs, stemmed and chopped, 3 tablespoons balsamic vinegar, and 1 tablespoon honey together in covered bowl until figs are plump, about 30 seconds. Stir in 3 tablespoons olive oil, 1 small minced shallot, ¼ teaspoon salt, and ⅛ teaspoon pepper and let cool. Toss fig dressing with 5 ounces arugula and sprinkle with crisp prosciutto, ½ cup toasted walnuts, and shaved Parmesan. Serves 6 to 8. (Recipe can be doubled to serve 12 to 14.)

Big-Batch Bolognese Sauce

Makes 14 cups   **Cooking Time** 9 to 11 hours on Low or 5 to 7 hours on High

✔ **WHY THIS RECIPE WORKS:** Unlike meat sauces in which tomatoes dominate, a Bolognese sauce is all about the meat, with the tomatoes in a supporting role. We wanted an easy big-batch recipe with all the flavor and rich meatiness of traditional versions, without all the work required to incorporate first the milk and then the wine into the meat, not to mention the long simmering time. To build a flavorful base, we sautéed the aromatics in butter and then deglazed the pan with white wine. As for the meat, meatloaf mix, with its mixture of ground beef, pork, and veal, was a simple solution. The problem was how to incorporate the dairy that gives Bolognese its hallmark richness and appeal. To tenderize the meat, we tried something unconventional: a panade, a mixture of bread and milk—but here we used cream instead for extra richness. This worked perfectly—we simply mixed the meat and the panade and added it raw to the slow cooker. At the end of hours of hands-off cooking, we had a rich Bolognese with concentrated flavor and a tender texture that rivaled that of our stovetop version. And better yet, this version could cook all day and gave us enough for a crowd or batches to freeze for busy nights. You can substitute 1½ pounds ground chuck and 1½ pounds ground pork for the meatloaf mix. This recipe makes enough to sauce 3 pounds of pasta.

3	tablespoons unsalted butter
1	onion, minced
1	carrot, peeled and minced
¼	cup minced celery
¼	cup tomato paste
3	garlic cloves, minced
1	teaspoon minced fresh thyme or ¼ teaspoon dried
½	cup dry white wine
2	(28-ounce) cans crushed tomatoes
3	slices high-quality white sandwich bread, torn into quarters
1	cup heavy cream
3	pounds meatloaf mix
	Salt and pepper

1. Melt butter in 12-inch skillet over medium-high heat. Add onion, carrot, celery, tomato paste, garlic, and thyme and cook until vegetables are softened and lightly browned, 8 to 10 minutes. Stir in wine, scraping up any browned bits; transfer to slow cooker. Stir tomatoes into slow cooker.

2. Mash bread and heavy cream into paste in large bowl using fork. Mix in meatloaf mix, ½ teaspoon salt, and ½ teaspoon pepper using hands. Stir meatloaf mixture into slow cooker, breaking up any large pieces. Cover and cook until beef is tender, 9 to 11 hours on low or 5 to 7 hours on high.

3. Let sauce settle for 5 minutes, then remove fat from surface using large spoon. Break up any remaining large pieces of meat with spoon. Season with salt and pepper to taste.

QUICK PREP TIP **FREEZING PASTA SAUCE**
One of the greatest things about making a large batch of pasta sauce is that you can freeze it in smaller batches for easy last-minute dinners in the future. We've found that the best way to freeze pasta sauce is to spoon it into zipper-lock freezer bags, then lay the bags flat in the freezer to save space. To reheat the sauce, simply cut away the bag, place the frozen block of sauce in a large pot with several tablespoons of water, and reheat gently over medium-low heat, stirring occasionally, until hot. Alternatively, you can microwave the frozen sauce in a covered bowl, stirring occasionally, until hot. Before serving, stir in any additional fresh herbs if desired, and season with salt and pepper and, if appropriate, olive oil or grated Parmesan.

Italian Sunday Gravy

Makes 16 cups   **Cooking Time** 9 to 11 hours on Low or 5 to 7 hours on High

✔ **WHY THIS RECIPE WORKS:** Traditional "Sunday Gravy" is more than just meat sauce—it's a labor of love, an all-day kitchen affair involving several types of meat and lots of work over the stove. We wanted to honor this meaty extravaganza but simplify it for the slow cooker and eliminate most of the work. Instead of browning six or seven types of meat, we found that we could cut the meat down to three different types, country-style pork ribs, Italian sausages, and flank steak; in more traditional versions the flank steak is stuffed and rolled into *braciole*, but for simplicity we left it whole and shredded it along with the pork ribs after cooking. Because of the juices released from all the meat, we opted to use concentrated tomato products—tomato paste, drained diced tomatoes, and tomato sauce—to prevent the sauce from turning out watery. This recipe makes enough to sauce 3 pounds of pasta.

2	onions, minced
1	(6-ounce) can tomato paste
12	garlic cloves, minced
2	tablespoons vegetable oil
2	tablespoons minced fresh oregano or 2 teaspoons dried
1	(28-ounce) can diced tomatoes, drained
1	(28-ounce) can tomato sauce
½	cup dry red wine
1½	pounds bone-in country-style pork ribs, trimmed
1½	pounds flank steak
	Salt and pepper
1	pound sweet Italian sausage
1	pound hot Italian sausage
3	tablespoons minced fresh basil

1. Microwave onions, tomato paste, garlic, oil, and oregano in bowl, stirring occasionally, until onions are softened, about 5 minutes; transfer to slow cooker

2. Stir tomatoes, tomato sauce, and wine into slow cooker. Season pork and flank steak with salt and pepper and nestle into slow cooker along with sausages. Cover and cook until meat is tender, 9 to 11 hours on low or 5 to 7 hours on high.

3. Transfer pork, flank steak, and sausages to cutting board, let cool slightly, then shred pork and flank steak into bite-size pieces (see page 21), discarding excess fat; slice sausages in half crosswise. Let sauce settle for 5 minutes, then remove fat from surface using large spoon.

4. Stir shredded pork, shredded flank steak, and sausages into sauce and let sit until heated through, about 5 minutes. Before serving, stir in basil and season with salt and pepper to taste.

ON THE SIDE CAESAR SALAD
Blend ¼ cup buttermilk, 3 tablespoons lemon juice, 2 teaspoons Worcestershire sauce, 2 teaspoons Dijon mustard, 2 minced garlic cloves, 6 rinsed anchovy fillets, ⅓ cup grated Parmesan cheese, ½ teaspoon salt, and ½ teaspoon pepper together in blender until combined. With blender running, gradually add ½ cup olive or canola oil until incorporated. Toss dressing with 6 chopped romaine hearts and sprinkle with shaved Parmesan. Serves 12 to 14.

Pasta 101

When you are cooking your favorite pasta to go with one of our slow-cooker pasta sauces, here is the test kitchen's method for the best results every time.

1. BRING PLENTY OF WATER TO A ROLLING BOIL

You'll need 4 quarts of water to cook 1 pound of dried pasta. Pasta leaches starch as it cooks; without plenty of water to dilute it, the starch will coat the noodles and they will stick. Use a pot with at least a 6-quart capacity.

2. SALT THE WATER, DON'T OIL IT

Adding oil to cooking water may prevent noodles from sticking, but it is problematic because it will also prevent sauce from coating the pasta. Adding salt to the water, however, is crucial, as it adds flavor. Add 1 tablespoon of salt per 4 quarts of water.

3. ADD PASTA, STIR IMMEDIATELY

Stirring the pasta for a minute or two immediately after you add it to the boiling water will prevent it from sticking. We like to use a metal or plastic pasta fork (the wood versions tend to be clunky and split after use).

4. CHECK OFTEN FOR DONENESS

The timing instructions given on the box are almost always too long and will result in mushy, overcooked pasta. Tasting is the best way to check for doneness. We typically prefer pasta cooked al dente, when it still has a little bite left in the center.

5. RESERVE SOME COOKING WATER, THEN DRAIN THE PASTA

Reserve about ½ cup cooking water before draining the pasta. The water is full of flavor and can help loosen a sauce that is too thick. Drain the pasta in a colander, but don't rinse the pasta or shake the colander vigorously, since some water helps the sauce coat the pasta.

6. SAUCE, SEASON, AND SERVE

Return the drained pasta to the empty pot and add your sauce. Toss the noodles with the pasta fork, or with tongs, to coat them, adding pasta water as needed to get your sauce to the right consistency.

Rustic Sausage, Lentil, and Swiss Chard Sauce

Makes 8 cups   **Cooking Time** 9 to 11 hours on Low or 5 to 7 hours on High

WHY THIS RECIPE WORKS: Pasta and lentils are a classic pairing—add sausage and Swiss chard and you have the ultimate cold-weather pasta dish: earthy, deeply flavored, and totally satisfying. To build flavor into this humble dish, we started by browning Italian sausage and then sautéing the aromatics in some of the fat left in the skillet. This gave us a chance to build a flour-thickened sauce, which formed the base of this dish. We used the small French green lentils known as *lentilles du Puy*, but ordinary brown lentils work fine as well. Added at the end, Swiss chard retains its earthy flavor and color. This recipe makes enough to sauce 1 pound of pasta.

1   tablespoon extra-virgin olive oil
1   pound Italian sausage, removed
    from its casing
2   onions, minced
2   carrots, peeled and cut into
    ¼-inch pieces
1   celery rib, minced
6   garlic cloves, minced
1   tablespoon minced fresh
    oregano or 1 teaspoon dried
⅓   cup all-purpose flour
½   cup dry white wine
5   cups low-sodium chicken broth
¾   cup lentilles du Puy or brown
    lentils (5¼ ounces), picked over
    and rinsed
2   bay leaves
1   pound Swiss chard, stemmed
    and leaves sliced ½ inch thick
    (see page 33)
    Salt and pepper

1. Heat oil in 12-inch skillet over medium-high heat until just smoking. Brown sausage well, breaking up large pieces with wooden spoon, about 5 minutes; transfer to slow cooker. Pour off all but 2 tablespoons fat left in skillet.

2. Add onions, carrots, celery, garlic, and oregano to fat in skillet and cook over medium-high heat until vegetables are softened and lightly browned, 8 to 10 minutes. Stir in flour and cook for 1 minute. Slowly whisk in wine, scraping up any browned bits and smoothing out any lumps; transfer to slow cooker.

3. Stir broth, lentils, and bay leaves into slow cooker. Cover and cook until lentils are tender, 9 to 11 hours on low or 5 to 7 hours on high.

4. Gently stir in chard, cover, and cook on high until tender, 20 to 30 minutes. Let sauce settle for 5 minutes, then remove fat from surface using large spoon. Discard bay leaves. Season with salt and pepper to taste.

ON THE SIDE CHEESE TOASTIES
Slice 1 large baguette on bias into ½-inch-thick slices and place on rimmed baking sheet. Sprinkle with 1 cup shredded Monterey Jack cheese (you can substitute Gruyère, Swiss, gouda, Colby, or Havarti). Bake in 400-degree oven until bread is crisp and golden at edges, and cheese is melted, 6 to 10 minutes. Serves 8 to 10.

Garden Vegetable Sauce with Chickpeas

Makes 6 cups   **Cooking Time** 9 to 11 hours on Low or 5 to 7 hours on High

✔ WHY THIS RECIPE WORKS: Drawing inspiration from pasta primavera, we set out to develop a vegetarian pasta dish for the slow cooker that was brightly flavored yet hearty. Since most of the vegetables we had in mind, with the exception of carrots, would go into the slow cooker at the end to ensure color and fresh flavor, the point of using a slow cooker was to build a flavorful base that would only taste better after hours of slow cooking. Since chickpeas and pasta are a classic pairing, we built our sauce around dried chickpeas, which have more nutty flavor than canned and which can withstand a full day's worth of cooking in the slow cooker and still emerge tender but intact. For our sauce, we used a skillet to brown the aromatics, a combination of onions, carrots, garlic, and red pepper flakes, and then we deglazed the pan with broth before we added everything to the slow cooker. To complement our chickpeas, we chose a mix of vegetables—zucchini, tomatoes, and spinach—and added them to the slow cooker at different times to cook them properly and ensure their fresh flavor. This recipe makes enough to sauce 1 pound of pasta.

2 tablespoons extra-virgin olive oil, plus extra as needed

3 onions, minced

2 carrots, peeled, halved lengthwise, and sliced ¼ inch thick

8 garlic cloves, minced

⅛ teaspoon red pepper flakes

¼ cup all-purpose flour

2 cups vegetable broth

2 cups water

1¼ cups dried chickpeas (8 ounces), picked over and rinsed

2 bay leaves

1 zucchini (8 ounces), quartered lengthwise and sliced ¼ inch thick

2 tomatoes (12 ounces), cored and cut into ½-inch pieces

6 ounces baby spinach (6 cups)

½ cup grated Parmesan cheese (1 ounce), plus extra for serving

Salt and pepper

1. Heat oil in 12-inch skillet over medium-high heat until shimmering. Add onions, carrots, garlic, and red pepper flakes and cook until vegetables are softened and lightly browned, 8 to 10 minutes. Stir in flour and cook for 1 minute. Slowly whisk in 1 cup broth, scraping up any browned bits and smoothing out any lumps; transfer to slow cooker.

2. Stir water, chickpeas, remaining cup broth, and bay leaves into slow cooker. Cover and cook until chickpeas are tender, 9 to 11 hours on low or 5 to 7 hours on high.

3. Stir in zucchini, cover, and cook on high until tender, 20 to 30 minutes. Discard bay leaves. Stir in tomatoes and spinach and let sit until heated through, about 5 minutes. Stir in Parmesan. Before serving, season with salt, pepper, additional extra-virgin olive oil, and additional Parmesan to taste.

SMART SHOPPING EXTRA-VIRGIN OLIVE OIL
Extra-virgin olive oil has a uniquely fruity flavor that makes it a great choice when making a vinaigrette or for drizzling over pasta, but the available options can be overwhelming. Many things can impact the quality and flavor of olive oil, but the type of olives, the harvest (earlier means greener, more bitter, and pungent; later, milder and more buttery), and processing are the most important factors. The best-quality oil comes from olives picked at their peak and processed as soon as possible, without heat (which can coax more oil from the olives but at the expense of flavor). Our favorite oils were produced from a blend of olives and, thus, were well rounded. Our favorite is **Columela Extra Virgin Olive Oil** from Spain.

Chicken, Tomato, and Olive Sauce

Makes 7 cups   **Cooking Time** 4 to 6 hours on Low

WHY THIS RECIPE WORKS: Mediterranean cuisines pair tomatoes with olives in many classic dishes and we thought they would be a great flavor profile for a simple, homey chicken pasta sauce. For simplicity's sake, we once again relied on the microwave to cook our aromatics, including red pepper flakes, which brought a mild spiciness to our sauce. For the tomatoes, we tried fresh tomatoes versus canned products, and we chose drained canned diced tomatoes and tomato sauce, which gave our sauce better body and more reliable flavor. Olives and parsley, which we stirred in during the final minutes of cooking, brought a bright zestiness to the final dish. This recipe makes enough to sauce 1 pound of pasta.

1   onion, minced
6   garlic cloves, minced
1   tablespoon extra-virgin olive oil, plus extra as needed
1   tablespoon minced fresh thyme or 1 teaspoon dried
¼   teaspoon red pepper flakes
1   cup low-sodium chicken broth
¼   cup dry white wine
1   (14.5-ounce) can diced tomatoes, drained
1   (15-ounce) can tomato sauce
2   tablespoons Minute tapioca
1½ pounds boneless, skinless chicken thighs, trimmed
     Salt and pepper
½   cup pitted kalamata olives, chopped coarse
¼   cup minced fresh parsley

1. Microwave onion, garlic, oil, thyme, and red pepper flakes in bowl, stirring occasionally, until onion is softened, about 5 minutes; transfer to slow cooker.

2. Stir broth, wine, tomatoes, tomato sauce, and tapioca into slow cooker. Season chicken with salt and pepper and nestle into slow cooker. Cover and cook until chicken is tender, 4 to 6 hours on low.

3. Transfer chicken to cutting board, let cool slightly, then shred into bite-size pieces (see page 21). Let sauce settle for 5 minutes, then remove fat from surface using large spoon.

4. Stir shredded chicken and olives into sauce and let sit until heated through, about 5 minutes. Before serving, stir in parsley and season with salt, pepper, and additional extra-virgin olive oil to taste.

SMART SHOPPING PARSLEY

You've probably noticed that your neighborhood grocer has two different varieties of this recognizable herb available (though there are actually more than 30 varieties out there): curly-leaf and flat-leaf (also called Italian). Curly-leaf parsley is more popular, but in the test kitchen flat-leaf is by far the favorite. We find flat-leaf to have a sweet, bright flavor that's much preferable to the bitter, grassy tones of curly-leaf. Flat-leaf parsley is also much more fragrant than its curly cousin. While curly parsley might look nice alongside your steak, don't count on it to improve flavor if you use it in cooking.

Chicken and Mushroom Sauce

Makes 5 cups   **Cooking Time** 4 to 6 hours on Low

✔ **WHY THIS RECIPE WORKS:** We wanted to transform store-bought mushrooms and boneless chicken thighs into something special—an earthy, full-flavored pasta dish with shredded chicken and an abundance of mushrooms. To keep things easy, we microwaved the aromatics and then added them, along with meaty boneless chicken thighs and sliced white mushrooms (no browning necessary), to the slow cooker. Our first tests were lacking deep mushroom flavor so we microwaved dried porcini mushrooms along with the aromatics, which added plenty of deep, earthy flavor and aroma. Chicken broth, white wine, and the liquid released by the mushrooms combined to create a flavorful sauce, into which we stirred cream and cheese at the end for added richness, along with a bit of parsley to liven it up a touch. This recipe makes enough to sauce 1 pound of pasta.

1	onion, minced
½	ounce dried porcini mushrooms, rinsed and minced
6	garlic cloves, minced
1	tablespoon extra-virgin olive oil
1	tablespoon tomato paste
1	tablespoon minced fresh thyme or 1 teaspoon dried
1	pound white mushrooms, trimmed and sliced thin
1½	cups low-sodium chicken broth
½	cup dry white wine
2	tablespoons Minute tapioca
1½	pounds boneless, skinless chicken thighs, trimmed
	Salt and pepper
¼	cup heavy cream
½	cup grated Parmesan cheese (1 ounce)
3	tablespoons minced fresh parsley

1. Microwave onion, porcini, garlic, oil, tomato paste, and thyme in bowl, stirring occasionally, until onion is softened, about 5 minutes; transfer to slow cooker.

2. Stir mushrooms, broth, wine, and tapioca into slow cooker. Season chicken with salt and pepper and nestle into slow cooker. Cover and cook until chicken is tender, 4 to 6 hours on low.

3. Transfer chicken to cutting board, let cool slightly, then shred into bite-size pieces (see page 21). Let sauce settle for 5 minutes, then remove fat from surface using large spoon.

4. Stir shredded chicken and cream into sauce and let sit until heated through, about 5 minutes. Stir in Parmesan. Before serving, stir in parsley and season with salt and pepper to taste.

SMART SHOPPING WHITE WINE FOR COOKING
When a recipe calls for dry white wine, it's tempting to grab whatever open bottle is in the fridge. Chardonnay and Pinot Grigio may taste different straight from the glass, but how much do those distinctive flavor profiles really come through in a cooked dish? To find out, we tried four varietals and a supermarket "cooking wine" in five different recipes. Only Sauvignon Blanc consistently boiled down to a "clean" yet sufficiently acidic flavor that played nicely with the rest of the ingredients. Vermouth can be an acceptable substitute in certain recipes, but because its flavor is stronger, we don't recommend using vermouth unless it is listed as an option in the recipe. Never buy supermarket "cooking wine," which has a significant amount of added sodium and an unappealing vinegary flavor.

Chicken and Broccoli Sauce

Makes 7 cups   **Cooking Time** 4 to 6 hours on Low

✔ **WHY THIS RECIPE WORKS:** Chicken, broccoli, and ziti is an American classic, boasting flavorful, meaty chicken and bright, tender broccoli in a cheesy, garlicky sauce. We wanted to translate this recipe into an easy, everyday slow-cooker dish. Right off the bat we decided to use boneless chicken thighs, which are meatier and have more flavor than breasts, and we stirred them right into the slow cooker—no browning required. Keeping with our easy approach, we microwaved the aromatics along with sun-dried tomatoes, which brought a lot of flavor to the dish without taking over. Overcooked broccoli was problematic, but our solution was to microwave the broccoli for a few minutes, then add it to the sauce with the shredded cooked chicken at the end to heat through. A healthy handful of grated Parmesan cheese and more sun-dried tomatoes stirred in just before serving added the final touches to this satisfying dish. This recipe makes enough to sauce 1 pound of pasta.

1	onion, minced
½	cup oil-packed sun-dried tomatoes, rinsed, patted dry, and sliced thin
6	garlic cloves, minced
2	tablespoons extra-virgin olive oil
1	tablespoon minced fresh thyme or 1 teaspoon dried
½	teaspoon red pepper flakes
2	cups low-sodium chicken broth
½	cup dry white wine
2	tablespoons Minute tapioca
1½	pounds boneless, skinless chicken thighs, trimmed
	Salt and pepper
12	ounces broccoli florets, cut into 1-inch pieces (4½ cups)
1	cup grated Parmesan cheese (2 ounces), plus extra as needed

1. Microwave onion, ¼ cup tomatoes, garlic, 1 tablespoon oil, thyme, and red pepper flakes in bowl, stirring occasionally, until onion is softened, about 5 minutes; transfer to slow cooker.

2. Stir broth, wine, and tapioca into slow cooker. Season chicken with salt and pepper and nestle into slow cooker. Cover and cook until chicken is tender, 4 to 6 hours on low.

3. Transfer chicken to cutting board, let cool slightly, then shred into bite-size pieces (see page 21). Let sauce settle for 5 minutes, then remove fat from surface using large spoon.

4. Microwave broccoli with remaining tablespoon oil in bowl, stirring occasionally, until tender, about 4 minutes. Stir shredded chicken and softened broccoli into sauce and let sit until heated through, about 5 minutes. Stir in Parmesan and remaining ¼ cup tomatoes. Before serving, season with salt, pepper, and additional Parmesan to taste.

SMART SHOPPING PARMESAN CHEESE
The buttery, nutty, slightly fruity taste and crystalline crunch of genuine Italian Parmigiano-Reggiano cheese are a one-of-a-kind experience, but supermarkets today offer many brands of shrink-wrapped, wedge-style American-made Parmesan at a fraction of the price, so you have to wonder how it compares. Simply put, it cannot. Our tasters effortlessly picked out the imports in our lineup of eight supermarket cheeses. The two genuine Parmigiano-Reggianos, sold by Boar's Head and Il Villaggio, were the clear favorites, and tasters deemed **Boar's Head Parmigiano-Reggiano** "best in show." The domestic cheeses, all made in Wisconsin, presented a wide range of flavors and textures, from quite good to rubbery, salty, and bland.

SWEET AND SOUR COCKTAIL MEATBALLS

Meatballs, Meatloaves, and More

Meatballs and Marinara

Serves 6   **Cooking Time** 4 to 6 hours on Low

✔ **WHY THIS RECIPE WORKS:** Our slow-cooker version of meatballs and marinara involves some advance work, but once everything is in the slow cooker, you've bought yourself hours of freedom with the promise of a great dinner waiting in the wings. To build a sauce with long-simmered flavor, we started by sautéing onions, tomato paste, and garlic and then we deglazed the pan with red wine. Crushed tomatoes, water, and a little soy sauce (for meaty depth of flavor) were all we needed to add to this base. And for the meatballs, a combination of ground beef and Italian sausage, along with some of the sautéed aromatics, Parmesan, and parsley, was a solid start for our meatballs, but they were still a bit dry. Adding a panade—a paste of bread and milk—provided the moisture they needed. Microwaving the meatballs before adding them to the slow cooker helped render just enough fat to ensure our sauce wasn't greasy. Serve with 1½ pounds cooked spaghetti.

2   tablespoons extra-virgin olive oil
2   onions, minced
¼   cup tomato paste
8   garlic cloves, minced
2   tablespoons minced fresh
      oregano or 2 teaspoons dried
¼   teaspoon red pepper flakes
½   cup dry red wine
2   (28-ounce) cans crushed
      tomatoes
½   cup water
2   tablespoons soy sauce
2   slices high-quality white
      sandwich bread, torn
      into quarters
⅓   cup whole milk
1¼   pounds 85 percent lean
      ground beef
4   ounces Italian sausage,
      removed from its casing
½   cup grated Parmesan cheese
      (1 ounce), plus extra for serving
¼   cup minced fresh parsley
2   large egg yolks
      Salt and pepper
2   tablespoons chopped fresh basil
1   teaspoon sugar, plus extra
      as needed

1. Heat oil in 12-inch skillet over medium-high heat until shimmering. Add onions, tomato paste, garlic, oregano, and red pepper flakes and cook until onions are softened and lightly browned, 8 to 10 minutes.

2. Transfer half of onion mixture to large bowl; set aside. Stir wine into skillet with remaining onion mixture and scrape up any browned bits; transfer to slow cooker. Stir tomatoes, water, and soy sauce into slow cooker.

3. Add bread and milk to bowl of onion mixture and mash to paste with fork. Mix in ground beef, sausage, Parmesan, parsley, egg yolks, ¾ teaspoon salt, and ½ teaspoon pepper using hands. Pinch off and roll mixture into 1½-inch meatballs (about 18 meatballs total).

4. Microwave meatballs on large plate until fat renders and meatballs are firm, 5 to 7 minutes. Nestle meatballs into slow cooker, discarding rendered fat. Cover and cook until meatballs are tender, 4 to 6 hours on low.

5. Let meatballs and sauce settle for 5 minutes, then remove fat from surface using large spoon. Gently stir in basil and sugar, season with salt, pepper, and sugar to taste, and serve.

ON THE SIDE GARLIC BREAD
Toast 10 unpeeled garlic cloves in small skillet over medium heat, shaking pan occasionally, until fragrant, about 8 minutes. Let garlic cool, then peel and mince. Using fork, mash garlic with 2 tablespoons unsalted butter, 2 tablespoons grated Parmesan cheese, and ½ teaspoon salt in small bowl. Cut 1 large loaf Italian bread in half lengthwise, spread both sides with butter mixture, then season with salt and pepper. Lay bread, buttered side up, on baking sheet. Bake in 500-degree oven until surface of bread is golden brown and toasted, 8 to 10 minutes. Slice and serve warm. Serves 6 to 8.

Easy Pesto Meatballs

Serves 4   **Cooking Time** 4 to 6 hours on Low

WHY THIS RECIPE WORKS: When time is at a premium, these flavorful but nearly no-prep meatballs will fit the bill. Here we rely on fresh pesto to give bright flavor to our meatballs, which are microwaved before going into the slow cooker to get rid of excess fat and firm them up. A couple jars of our favorite pasta sauce (Bertolli Tomato and Basil Sauce) simply cook along with them in the slow cooker, making this a great, family-friendly dinner. You can make your own pesto or use your favorite store-bought brand from the refrigerated section of the supermarket—they have a fresher flavor than the jarred pesto sold in the grocery aisles. Serve with 1 pound cooked spaghetti.

1   **pound 85 percent lean ground beef or ground turkey**
⅔   **cup plain bread crumbs**
⅔   **cup fresh basil pesto**
¼   **cup grated Parmesan cheese**
1   **large egg yolk**
2   **(24-ounce) jars tomato sauce (5 cups)**
½   **cup water**
    Salt and pepper

1. Mix ground meat, bread crumbs, pesto, Parmesan, and egg yolk in bowl using hands. Pinch off and roll mixture into 1½-inch meatballs (about 12 meatballs total). Microwave meatballs on large plate until fat renders and meatballs are firm, 5 to 7 minutes.

2. Stir tomato sauce and water into slow cooker. Nestle meatballs into slow cooker, discarding rendered fat. Cover and cook until meatballs are tender, 4 to 6 hours on low.

3. Let meatballs and sauce settle for 5 minutes, then remove fat from surface using large spoon. Season with salt and pepper and serve.

ON THE SIDE BASIC PESTO
Process 2 cups packed fresh basil leaves, 6 tablespoons extra-virgin olive oil, 2 tablespoons toasted pine nuts (see page 87), and 1 small, minced garlic clove in food processor until smooth, scraping down bowl as needed. Transfer pesto to bowl, stir in ¼ cup grated Parmesan cheese, and season with salt and pepper to taste. Makes about ⅔ cup.

Sweet and Sour Cocktail Meatballs

Serves 10 to 12   **Cooking Time** 4 to 6 hours on Low

✓ **WHY THIS RECIPE WORKS:** These cocktail meatballs are all about the sweet and sour sauce, which we were able to replicate in the slow cooker by microwaving the aromatics and adding a mixture of sweet and savory ingredients including tomato sauce and apricot jam. And as with our other cocktail meatballs, a quick blast of heat from a hot oven removed the excess fat from the raw meatballs, which we could then simply add to the insert along with our easy sauce. A 1¼-inch ice-cream scoop makes it easy to form these cocktail-size meatballs.

4	slices high-quality white sandwich bread, torn into quarters
1	cup whole milk
2	pounds 85 percent lean ground beef
¼	cup minced fresh parsley
2	large egg yolks
4	garlic cloves, minced
	Salt and pepper
1	onion, minced
1	tablespoon vegetable oil
⅛	teaspoon red pepper flakes
1	(15-ounce) can tomato sauce
1	(12-ounce) jar apricot jam or preserves (1 cup)
1	cup low-sodium chicken broth
2	tablespoons Worcestershire sauce
1	tablespoon Dijon mustard
3	scallions, sliced thin

1. Adjust oven rack to middle position and heat oven to 475 degrees. Place wire rack in aluminum foil–lined rimmed baking sheet.

2. Mash bread and milk into paste in large bowl using fork. Mix in ground beef, parsley, egg yolks, 2 garlic cloves, 1 teaspoon salt, and ½ teaspoon pepper using hands. Pinch off and roll mixture into tablespoon-size meatballs (about 60 meatballs total) and arrange on prepared baking sheet. Bake until lightly browned, about 15 minutes.

3. Microwave onion, oil, red pepper flakes, and remaining 2 garlic cloves in bowl, stirring occasionally, until onion is softened, about 5 minutes; transfer to slow cooker.

4. Stir tomato sauce, apricot jam, broth, Worcestershire, and mustard into slow cooker. Transfer meatballs to slow cooker, discarding rendered fat. Cover and cook until meatballs are tender, 4 to 6 hours on low.

5. Let meatballs and sauce settle for 5 minutes, then remove fat from surface using large spoon. Gently stir in scallions, season with salt and pepper to taste, and serve.

SMART SHOPPING PORTION SCOOPS

In the test kitchen, we like to use portion scoops—essentially spring-loaded ice-cream scoops made in specific sizes—to help us evenly and quickly portion out things like muffin batter, cookie dough, and cocktail meatballs. Scoop numbers stamped on the handle or spring-loaded trigger correspond to the number of level scoops it takes to fill 1 quart (or 32 fluid ounces). So for our cocktail meatballs, you'd need a #64 scoop, which is about 1 tablespoon. Handle colors often correspond to the numbers as well, but they vary from brand to brand. The test kitchen's preferred scoop is the **Fantes Stainless Steel Ice Cream Scoop** ($11.99), an industrial-type model that's easy to squeeze with either hand.

Spanish Cocktail Meatballs

Serves 10 to 12   **Cooking Time** 4 to 6 hours on Low

✔ **WHY THIS RECIPE WORKS:** Classic Spanish tapas often feature bite-size meatballs coated in a fragrant saffron-infused sauce. For our slow-cooker interpretation of this recipe, we simply microwaved the aromatics (including paprika and saffron) and added them along with broth, white wine, and tomatoes to the insert. This savory mixture became highly flavorful after several hours of cooking along with the meatballs. For the final, crowning touch, we looked to what in Spain is known as a *picada*, a mixture of ground toasted almonds, garlic, and herbs. We chose to keep things simple here and just added chopped nuts, parsley, and lemon directly to the slow cooker, which infused the sauce with vibrant flavor and an enticing aroma. A 1¼-inch ice-cream scoop makes it easy to form these cocktail-size meatballs.

4	slices high-quality white sandwich bread, torn into quarters
1	cup whole milk
2	pounds 85 percent lean ground beef
½	cup grated Parmesan cheese (1 ounce)
2	large egg yolks
¼	cup plus 2 tablespoons minced fresh parsley
6	garlic cloves, minced
	Salt and pepper
2	onions, minced
2	tablespoons extra-virgin olive oil
1	teaspoon sweet paprika
¼	teaspoon saffron threads, crumbled
2	cups low-sodium chicken broth
1	(14.5-ounce) can diced tomatoes, drained
¼	cup dry white wine
2	tablespoons Minute tapioca
2	bay leaves
2	tablespoons almonds, toasted (see page 87) and chopped fine
2	teaspoons fresh lemon juice

1. Adjust oven rack to middle position and heat oven to 475 degrees. Place wire rack in aluminum foil–lined rimmed baking sheet.

2. Mash bread and milk into paste in large bowl using fork. Mix in ground beef, Parmesan, egg yolks, ¼ cup parsley, 2 garlic cloves, 1 teaspoon salt, and ½ teaspoon pepper using hands. Pinch off and roll mixture into tablespoon-size meatballs (about 60 meatballs total) and arrange on prepared baking sheet. Bake until lightly browned, about 15 minutes.

3. Microwave onions, remaining 4 garlic cloves, oil, paprika, and saffron in bowl, stirring occasionally, until onions are softened, about 5 minutes; transfer to slow cooker.

4. Stir broth, tomatoes, wine, tapioca, and bay leaves into slow cooker. Transfer meatballs to slow cooker, discarding rendered fat. Cover and cook until meatballs are tender, 4 to 6 hours on low.

5. Let meatballs and sauce settle for 5 minutes, then remove fat from surface using large spoon. Discard bay leaves. Gently stir in almonds, remaining 2 tablespoons parsley, and lemon juice. Season with salt and pepper to taste and serve.

SMART SHOPPING SAFFRON
Cultivated from the crocus flower, saffron is a delicate red thread pulled from the stigma (the female part of the crocus) by hand at harvest each October. Because each flower yields only three stigmas, it can take the *mondadoras* (petal strippers) who perform the task of pulling the fragile filaments up to 200 hours to yield only 1 pound of saffron—thus explaining why it is the most expensive spice in the world. Saffron is available in two forms—threads and powder. While we generally prefer the flavor of saffron threads, we found powdered saffron can be a decent and more affordable option when substituted correctly. If substituting powdered saffron for threads, reduce the amount by a generous half.

Swedish Meatballs

Serves 10 to 12   **Cooking Time** 4 to 6 hours on Low

✓ **WHY THIS RECIPE WORKS:** Swedish meatballs are classic party fare and the perfect option for the slow cooker, where they can simmer away for hours before guests arrive. But when we tried adding our meatballs raw to the slow cooker, they released so much fat that our sauce was unappealingly greasy. Precooking the meatballs in the microwave, a trick we'd used with dinner-size meatballs to eliminate excess fat, proved cumbersome here since it required working with so many batches. Instead, arranging them on one sheet pan and baking them in a hot oven for 15 minutes solved the problem and was well worth the extra step. To boost the flavor of our meatballs and keep them moist while cooking, we combined the ground beef with a mixture of rye bread, sour cream, and broth. A little allspice and nutmeg rounded out the flavors. For the sauce, we started with a rich flour-and-butter roux, added beef broth, and then cooked the mixture down to the perfect consistency for clinging to the meatballs. A few tablespoons of soy sauce gave our sauce a rich, meaty backbone without overpowering the other ingredients. For the classic Swedish meatball flavor and creaminess, we stirred in some sour cream and dill at the end. A 1¼-inch ice-cream scoop makes it easy to form these cocktail-size meatballs.

4	slices seedless rye sandwich bread, torn into quarters
3	cups beef broth
1	cup sour cream
2	pounds 85 percent lean ground beef
2	large egg yolks
	Salt and pepper
½	teaspoon ground allspice
¼	teaspoon ground nutmeg
4	tablespoons (½ stick) unsalted butter
2	onions, minced
½	cup all-purpose flour
2	tablespoons soy sauce
1	tablespoon minced fresh dill

1. Adjust oven rack to middle position and heat oven to 475 degrees. Place wire rack in aluminum foil–lined rimmed baking sheet.

2. Mash bread, ½ cup broth, and ½ cup sour cream into paste in large bowl using fork. Mix in ground beef, egg yolks, 1 teaspoon salt, ½ teaspoon pepper, allspice, and nutmeg using hands. Pinch off and roll mixture into tablespoon-size meatballs (about 60 meatballs total) and arrange on prepared baking sheet. Bake until lightly browned, about 15 minutes. Transfer meatballs to slow cooker, discarding rendered fat.

3. Melt butter in 12-inch skillet over medium-high heat. Add onions and cook until softened and lightly browned, 8 to 10 minutes. Stir in flour and cook for 1 minute. Slowly whisk in remaining 2½ cups broth and soy sauce, scraping up any browned bits and smoothing out any lumps. Pour mixture over meatballs, cover, and cook until meatballs are tender, 4 to 6 hours on low.

4. Let meatballs and sauce settle for 5 minutes, then remove fat from surface using large spoon. In bowl, combine 1 cup hot cooking liquid with remaining ½ cup sour cream (to temper), then gently stir mixture into meatballs. Gently stir in dill, season with salt and pepper to taste, and serve.

ON THE SIDE EASY MULLED WINE
Toast 5 cinnamon sticks, 15 whole cloves, 10 black peppercorns, and 1 teaspoon whole allspice berries in large Dutch oven over medium-high heat until fragrant, about 2 minutes. Add 3 (750-ml) bottles red wine, 6 strips orange zest (see page 150), and 1 cup sugar, partially cover, and bring to simmer. Reduce heat to low and cook, stirring occasionally, until wine is infused with spice, 1 to 1½ hours. Strain wine, return to saucepan, and stir in 3 tablespoons brandy. Season with additional sugar and serve warm. Serves 10 to 12.

Classic Meatloaf

Serves 6 to 8   **Cooking Time** about 4 hours on Low

✔ **WHY THIS RECIPE WORKS:** While many cookbooks profess the ease of creating moist meatloaf in the slow cooker, we found it challenging to keep our loaves appealing. Our first tries were greasy and unattractive, and although we liked the ease of pressing the loaf directly into the cooker, we had to scoop the meat out of the slow cooker since the loaves fell apart. We tried using leaner beef and larger amounts of panade—a mixture of bread and milk—but our results were mushy and dry. Finally, in an attempt to solve both problems at once, we borrowed a technique from our slow-cooker casseroles: using an aluminum foil sling. The sling allowed us to use flavorful 85 percent lean beef and to remove the loaf easily, leaving the extra grease behind. Also, we were now able to place the meatloaf under the broiler to ensure an attractive, caramelized top. Because of its unique shape, this meatloaf looks best sliced into wedges, which also makes it easier to ensure equal-size portions. Serve with Easy Mashed Potatoes (page 96) and Roasted Maple-Butter Carrots.

Vegetable oil spray
1   onion, minced
6   garlic cloves, minced
1   tablespoon vegetable oil
2   teaspoons minced fresh thyme or ½ teaspoon dried
2   slices high-quality white sandwich bread, torn into quarters
½   cup whole milk
2   pounds 85 percent lean ground beef
2   large eggs
1   tablespoon Dijon mustard
1   tablespoon Worcestershire sauce
¼   teaspoon hot sauce
   Salt and pepper
½   cup ketchup
¼   cup packed light brown sugar
4   teaspoons cider vinegar

1. Line slow cooker with aluminum foil collar, then line with foil sling and coat with vegetable oil spray (see page 225). Microwave onion, garlic, oil, and thyme in bowl, stirring occasionally, until onion is softened, about 5 minutes.

2. Mash bread and milk into paste in large bowl using fork. Mix in onion mixture, ground beef, eggs, mustard, Worcestershire, hot sauce, 1½ teaspoons salt, and ½ teaspoon pepper using hands.

3. Transfer meat mixture to slow cooker and press into even layer. Combine ketchup, sugar, and vinegar in bowl. Brush meatloaf with half of mixture; reserve remaining ketchup mixture separately. Cover and cook until meatloaf is tender, about 4 hours on low.

4. Position oven rack 6 inches from broiler element and heat broiler. Using sling, transfer meatloaf with foil to rimmed baking sheet, allowing juice to drain back into slow cooker. Press edges of foil flat, brush meatloaf with remaining ketchup mixture, and broil until caramelized, about 5 minutes. Let cool for 15 minutes before serving.

ON THE SIDE ROASTED MAPLE-BUTTER CARROTS
Thoroughly pat 2 pounds baby carrots dry with paper towels, then toss with 1½ tablespoons olive oil and ½ teaspoon salt. Spread carrots in single layer on a rimmed baking sheet. Roast in 475-degree oven for 10 minutes. Meanwhile, melt 1 tablespoon unsalted butter in small saucepan over medium heat until deeply golden, about 1 minute, then stir in 1 tablespoon maple syrup. Pour butter mixture over carrots and continue to roast until carrots are browned and tender, about 8 minutes longer. Season with salt and pepper to taste. Serves 8.

Santa Fe Meatloaf

Serves 6 to 8   **Cooking Time** about 4 hours on Low

✓ **WHY THIS RECIPE WORKS:** Adding Southwest-inspired ingredients like corn, red bell pepper, and black beans to our standard meatloaf sounded like a great way to liven up our family-friendly classic. As we discovered, however, these additions led to a loose loaf that we could not begin to extract from the slow cooker in one piece. Not wanting to lose these flavorful add-ins, we experimented with methods for binding the loaf. Adding cheese helped, but the best solution was to mash the black beans in with the bread and milk, creating a more substantial binder for our meatloaf. A dash of chili powder, some cilantro, and a barbecue sauce glaze rounded out the flavors of this colorful recipe. Because of its unique shape, this meatloaf looks best sliced into wedges, which also makes it easier to ensure equal-size portions. Serve with Easy White Rice (page 134).

	Vegetable oil spray
1	onion, minced
1	red bell pepper, stemmed, seeded, and minced (see page 91)
2	tablespoons vegetable oil
4	garlic cloves, minced
1	tablespoon tomato paste
2	teaspoons minced fresh oregano or ½ teaspoon dried
2	teaspoons chili powder
1	(15-ounce) can black beans, drained and rinsed
2	slices high-quality white sandwich bread, torn into quarters
½	cup whole milk
2	pounds 85 percent lean ground beef
1	cup shredded cheddar cheese (4 ounces)
¾	cup frozen corn
2	large eggs
2	tablespoons minced fresh cilantro
	Salt and pepper
½	cup barbecue sauce

1. Line slow cooker with aluminum foil collar, then line with foil sling and coat with vegetable oil spray (see page 225). Microwave onion, bell pepper, oil, garlic, tomato paste, oregano, and chili powder in bowl, stirring occasionally, until vegetables are softened, about 5 minutes.

2. Mash black beans, bread, and milk into paste in large bowl using potato masher. Mix in onion mixture, ground beef, cheddar, corn, eggs, cilantro, 1 teaspoon salt, and ½ teaspoon pepper using hands.

3. Transfer meat mixture to slow cooker and press into even layer. Brush meatloaf with ¼ cup barbecue sauce. Cover and cook until meatloaf is tender, about 4 hours on low.

4. Position oven rack 6 inches from broiler element and heat broiler. Using sling, transfer meatloaf with foil to rimmed baking sheet, allowing juice to drain back into slow cooker. Press edges of foil flat, brush meatloaf with remaining ¼ cup barbecue sauce, and broil until caramelized, about 5 minutes. Let cool for 15 minutes before serving.

SMART SHOPPING BLACK BEANS
Most canned black beans have three main ingredients: beans, water, and salt. So how different could they taste? Plenty different, as we found out when we sampled six national brands—three of them organic—in a blind test. We tasted them plain (drained and rinsed), and also in a test kitchen recipe for black bean soup. The results neatly separated into three brands we like and three we don't. Predictably, our tasters had a strong preference for well-seasoned beans, but texture was important, too, as tasters disliked mushy beans. Tasters appreciated the "clean," "mild," and "slightly earthy" flavor of **Bush's Best Black Beans**, along with their "firm," "almost al dente" texture.

Sicilian Meatloaf

Serves 6 to 8   **Cooking Time** about 4 hours on Low

WHY THIS RECIPE WORKS: Sure to please ardent meat lovers, this Italian-inspired meatloaf offers ground meat enhanced with sausage, olives, and sun-dried tomatoes, and a filling of sliced deli meats and cheese. Traditionally, this meatloaf would be rolled up with swirls of the filling showing, but to keep things practical (we were using a slow cooker after all) we simply layered the filling on top of half of the ground meat mixture, topped it with the rest of the meat, then added a layer of tomato sauce as an easy topping. Serve with pasta or Buttered Egg Noodles (page 64).

	Vegetable oil spray
1	onion, minced
4	garlic cloves, minced
1	tablespoon vegetable oil
2	teaspoons minced fresh oregano or ½ teaspoon dried
2	slices high-quality white sandwich bread, torn into quarters
½	cup whole milk
1	pound 85 percent lean ground beef
8	ounces Italian sausage, removed from its casing
2	large eggs
⅓	cup minced fresh parsley
⅓	cup pitted green olives, chopped fine
⅓	cup oil-packed sun-dried tomatoes, rinsed, patted dry, and chopped fine
	Salt and pepper
4	ounces thinly sliced mortadella
4	ounces thinly sliced hard salami
4	ounces thinly sliced provolone cheese
¾	cup jarred tomato sauce

1. Line slow cooker with aluminum foil collar, then line with foil sling and coat with vegetable oil spray (see page 225). Microwave onion, garlic, oil, and oregano in bowl, stirring occasionally, until onion is softened, about 5 minutes.

2. Mash bread and milk into paste in large bowl using fork. Mix in onion mixture, ground beef, sausage, eggs, parsley, olives, sun-dried tomatoes, ¾ teaspoon salt, and ½ teaspoon pepper using hands.

3. Transfer half of meat mixture to slow cooker and press into even layer. Layer mortadella, salami, and provolone evenly over meat mixture. Press remaining meat mixture into even layer on top of provolone, covering it completely. Brush meatloaf with tomato sauce. Cover and cook until meatloaf is tender, about 4 hours on low.

4. Using sling, transfer meatloaf with foil to serving platter, allowing juice to drain back into cooker. Let cool for 15 minutes before serving.

SMART SHOPPER **SUN-DRIED TOMATOES**
Here in the test kitchen, we prefer oil-packed sun-dried tomatoes to their leatherlike counterparts; however, we have found that not all oil-packed sun-dried tomatoes taste the same, at least straight from the jar. Our favorite brand is **Trader Joe's Sun-Dried Tomatoes**, which are packed in olive oil, garlic, herbs, spices, and sulfur dioxide (to retain color), and have the right balance of flavors and sweetness. Many other brands have an overpowering musty, herbal flavor, though we found that we could improve their flavor by rinsing away excess herbs and spices. The rinsed tomatoes won't taste as good as our favorite brand, but they won't taste musty, either.

Tex-Mex Stuffed Bell Peppers

Serves 4   **Cooking Time** 4 to 6 hours on Low

✔ **WHY THIS RECIPE WORKS:** Creating an easy stuffed pepper recipe in the slow cooker required some tinkering since, in our experience, even good traditional versions can be problematic—bland fillings and tough or mushy peppers are the norm. We didn't want to spend time at the stove sautéing the beef, nor did we want to parcook the peppers; luckily, we found the long cooking time guaranteed that beef added raw would emerge fully cooked and the bell peppers would soften perfectly in the moist environment (as long as a little water was added at the outset). Getting perfectly cooked rice was more of a challenge. After trying many varieties of rice, both cooked and raw, we discovered that cooked white rice was truly the best option. Feel free to use leftover or precooked rice (sold as Ready Rice in supermarkets). As for flavoring, we wanted to up the ante by pairing the classic beef, rice, and cheese trio with strong Tex-Mex spices. We added a healthy dose of Monterey Jack cheese to help hold the filling together, frozen corn, and chili powder and chipotles for heat. A sprinkling of cilantro at the end added brightness. Try to choose peppers with flat bottoms so that they stay upright in the slow cooker.

1	onion, minced
6	garlic cloves, minced
2	tablespoons chili powder
1	tablespoon vegetable oil
4	(6-ounce) red, yellow, or orange bell peppers
1	slice high-quality white sandwich bread, torn into quarters
¼	cup whole milk
12	ounces 85 percent lean ground beef
1	cup frozen corn
1¼	cups shredded Monterey Jack cheese (5 ounces)
¾	cup cooked rice
2	teaspoons minced canned chipotle chile in adobo sauce
	Salt and pepper
2	tablespoons minced fresh cilantro

1. Microwave onion, garlic, chili powder, and oil in bowl, stirring occasionally, until onion is softened, about 5 minutes.

2. Cut top ½ inch off each pepper. Chop pepper tops fine, discarding stems. Remove core and seeds from peppers.

3. Mash bread and milk into paste in large bowl using fork. Mix in onion mixture, chopped pepper tops, ground beef, corn, 1 cup Monterey Jack, cooked rice, chipotles, 1½ teaspoons salt, and ½ teaspoon pepper using hands. Pack filling evenly into cored peppers.

4. Pour ⅓ cup water into slow cooker. Place stuffed peppers upright in slow cooker and sprinkle with remaining ¼ cup Monterey Jack. Cover and cook until peppers are tender, 4 to 6 hours on low.

5. Using tongs and slotted spoon, transfer peppers to serving platter, discarding liquid in slow cooker. Sprinkle with cilantro and serve.

QUICK PREP TIP MAKING STUFFED PEPPERS
When placing the stuffed peppers in the slow cooker, lean them against one another and the sides of the slow-cooker insert, so that they remain upright during cooking.

Italian Stuffed Bell Peppers

Serves 4   **Cooking Time** 4 to 6 hours on Low

WHY THIS RECIPE WORKS: Stuffed with Italian sausage and two kinds of cheese, these slow-cooker stuffed peppers are anything but boring. Keeping with our Italian theme and following the technique we established for making stuffed peppers in the slow cooker, we added tomato paste to the microwaved aromatics, as well as chopped zucchini to the filling, and a topping of Parmesan and minced fresh basil. Try to choose peppers with flat bottoms so that they stay upright in the slow cooker.

1	onion, minced
6	garlic cloves, minced
1	tablespoon extra-virgin olive oil
1	tablespoon tomato paste
¼	teaspoon red pepper flakes
4	(6-ounce) red, yellow, or orange bell peppers
1	slice high-quality white sandwich bread, torn into quarters
¼	cup whole milk
12	ounces Italian sausage, removed from its casing
1	small zucchini (6 ounces), cut into ¼-inch pieces
¾	cup shredded Monterey Jack cheese (3 ounces)
¾	cup cooked rice
¼	cup grated Parmesan cheese, plus extra for serving
	Salt and pepper
2	tablespoons minced fresh basil

1. Microwave onion, garlic, oil, tomato paste, and red pepper flakes in bowl, stirring occasionally, until onion is softened, about 5 minutes.

2. Cut top ½ inch off each pepper. Chop pepper tops fine, discarding stems. Remove core and seeds from peppers.

3. Mash bread and milk into paste in large bowl using fork. Mix in onion mixture, chopped pepper tops, sausage, zucchini, Monterey Jack, cooked rice, Parmesan, 1 teaspoon salt, and ½ teaspoon pepper using hands. Pack filling evenly into cored peppers.

4. Pour ⅓ cup water into slow cooker. Place stuffed peppers upright in slow cooker (see page 195). Cover and cook until peppers are tender, 4 to 6 hours on low.

5. Using tongs and slotted spoon, transfer peppers to serving platter, discarding liquid in slow cooker. Sprinkle with basil and additional Parmesan and serve.

SMART SHOPPING **READY RICE**

Various types of instant white rice have been around for years to help time-crunched home cooks avoid the process of cooking rice, or the need to have leftover rice handy for making recipes such as this one. In addition to boil-in-bag rice and instant rice, there is also fully cooked rice. This convenience product is coated with oil to keep the grains distinct and is packaged in microwavable pouches. While we don't love Uncle Ben's Ready Rice plain as a side dish, if time is tight we have found that it works as an acceptable substitute for home-cooked rice when used in combination with other ingredients.

Sloppy Joes

Serves 8   **Cooking Time** 6 to 8 hours on Low or 3 to 5 hours on High

✔ **WHY THIS RECIPE WORKS:** Since the texture of the meat is important when it comes to Sloppy Joes, we found it necessary to get out our skillet and brown the beef before adding it to the slow cooker; this simple step ensured small but consistent pieces of tender ground beef. We used a combination of ketchup and canned tomato sauce to give our sandwiches the right combination of gentle sweetness and strong tomato flavor, and a bit of brown sugar, chili powder, and hot sauce kept the sauce balanced. We limited the amount of ketchup and tomato sauce to only 3 cups, enough to keep the meat moist and saucy, but still able to fit on a bun. Another bonus: this recipe doubles easily if you're planning on feeding a crowd. Serve with Creamy Macaroni and Cheese.

2 **slices high-quality white sandwich bread, torn into quarters**
¼ **cup whole milk**
2 **pounds 85 percent lean ground beef**
   Salt and pepper
2 **tablespoons vegetable oil**
2 **onions, minced**
4 **garlic cloves, minced**
1 **teaspoon chili powder**
1 **(15-ounce) can tomato sauce**
1 **cup ketchup**
2 **teaspoons brown sugar**
½ **teaspoon hot sauce**
8 **hamburger buns**

1. Mash bread and milk into paste in large bowl using fork. Mix in ground beef, ½ teaspoon salt, and ½ teaspoon pepper using hands.

2. Heat oil in 12-inch skillet over medium-high heat until shimmering. Add onions, garlic, and chili powder and cook until onions are softened and lightly browned, 8 to 10 minutes.

3. Stir in beef mixture, 1 pound at a time, and cook, breaking up any large pieces with wooden spoon, until no longer pink, about 3 minutes per pound. Stir in 1 cup tomato sauce, scraping up any browned bits; transfer to slow cooker.

4. Stir remaining tomato sauce, ketchup, sugar, and hot sauce into slow cooker. Cover and cook until beef is tender, 6 to 8 hours on low or 3 to 5 hours on high.

5. Let meat mixture settle for 5 minutes, then remove fat from surface using large spoon. Break up any remaining large pieces of beef with spoon. Season with salt and pepper to taste. Spoon mixture onto buns and serve.

ON THE SIDE CREAMY MACARONI AND CHEESE
Cook 1 pound elbow macaroni in salted boiling water until tender; drain and set aside. Melt 5 tablespoons unsalted butter in Dutch oven over medium-high heat. Whisk in 6 tablespoons all-purpose flour, 1½ teaspoons powdered mustard, and ¼ teaspoon cayenne and cook for 1 minute. Whisk in 5 cups milk and bring to boil, whisking constantly. Reduce to simmer and cook, whisking often, until thickened, about 5 minutes. Off heat, stir in 2 cups shredded Monterey Jack cheese and 2 cups shredded cheddar cheese, one handful at a time, until smooth. Stir in cooked macaroni and season with salt and pepper to taste. Serves 8 to 10.

Spicy Smoky Joes

Serves 8   **Cooking Time** 6 to 8 hours on Low or 3 to 5 hours on High

✓ **WHY THIS RECIPE WORKS:** Even though we like our classic Sloppy Joes, we wanted to try our hand at a more grown-up version full of spice and smoke. To keep the consistency of the sandwiches similar, we kept our method and tomato products the same as the classic, instead switching up the spices. First we tried a simple variation. We subbed barbecue sauce for ketchup, and found the end result to taste like it came straight out of the bottle. Scratching that plan, we added chipotle peppers, a reliable source of both heat and smoke, but the flavor still fell flat. So we added a slow-cooker secret ingredient, liquid smoke, and then bumped up the chili powder. A splash of hot sauce was the final touch to these anything-but-boring and anything-but-neat sandwiches. Just like the classic Sloppy Joes, this recipe comes together quickly and doubles easily to feed a crowd.

2	slices high-quality white sandwich bread, torn into quarters
¼	cup whole milk
2	pounds 85 percent lean ground beef
	Salt and pepper
2	tablespoons vegetable oil
2	onions, minced
2	tablespoons chili powder
4	garlic cloves, minced
1	(15-ounce) can tomato sauce
1	cup ketchup
1	tablespoon minced canned chipotle chile in adobo sauce
2	teaspoons brown sugar
1	teaspoon liquid smoke
½	teaspoon hot sauce
8	hamburger buns

1. Mash bread and milk into paste in large bowl using fork. Mix in ground beef, ½ teaspoon salt, and ½ teaspoon pepper using hands.

2. Heat oil in 12-inch skillet over medium-high heat until shimmering. Add onions, chili powder, and garlic and cook until onions are softened and lightly browned, 8 to 10 minutes.

3. Stir in beef mixture, 1 pound at a time, and cook, breaking up any large pieces with wooden spoon, until no longer pink, about 3 minutes per pound. Stir in 1 cup tomato sauce, scraping up any browned bits; transfer to slow cooker.

4. Stir remaining tomato sauce, ketchup, chipotles, sugar, liquid smoke, and hot sauce into slow cooker. Cover and cook until beef is tender, 6 to 8 hours on low or 3 to 5 hours on high.

5. Let meat mixture settle for 5 minutes, then remove fat from surface using large spoon. Break up any remaining large pieces of beef with spoon. Season with salt and pepper to taste. Spoon mixture onto buns and serve.

ON THE SIDE SAUTÉED CORN WITH SCALLIONS
Melt 3 tablespoons unsalted butter in 12-inch nonstick skillet over medium-high heat. Add 4 minced scallions and 1 minced garlic clove and cook until softened, about 2 minutes. Stir in 1½ pounds frozen corn, increase heat to high, and cook, stirring often, until thawed and heated through but still crunchy, about 2 minutes. Season with salt and pepper to taste. Serves 8.

TACOS WITH SPICY GROUND BEEF TACO FILLING

Enchiladas, Tacos, and More

Everyday Shredded Chicken Filling

Makes about 4 cups   **Cooking Time** 4 to 6 hours on Low

✔ **WHY THIS RECIPE WORKS:** This filling features meaty chicken thighs and tender boneless chicken breasts cooked in a classic Mexican red sauce and shredded; it tastes great spooned on top of crisp tostadas, stuffed inside a cheesy burrito, or rolled up into corn tortillas for enchiladas. In our quest for a full-flavored red sauce we microwaved aromatics, chili powder, and a jalapeño, then stirred the mixture into canned plain tomato sauce. This sauce still lacked punch so we supplemented it with coriander and cumin, which lent just the complexity we were seeking. Although we like the mix of tender breast meat and meatier thigh meat, you can use all white meat or all dark meat in this recipe if desired. To make this dish spicier, add the jalapeño chile seeds. For recipes using this filling see pages 214–217.

1	onion, minced
3	tablespoons chili powder
2	tablespoons vegetable oil
1	jalapeño chile, stemmed, seeded, and minced
3	garlic cloves, minced
2	teaspoons ground coriander
2	teaspoons ground cumin
1	(8-ounce) can tomato sauce
1½	teaspoons sugar
1	pound boneless, skinless chicken breasts, trimmed
1	pound boneless, skinless chicken thighs, trimmed
	Salt and pepper
1	tablespoon fresh lime juice

1. Microwave onion, chili powder, oil, jalapeño, garlic, coriander, and cumin in bowl, stirring occasionally, until vegetables are softened, about 5 minutes; transfer to slow cooker.

2. Stir tomato sauce and sugar into slow cooker. Season chicken with salt and pepper, add to slow cooker, and coat evenly with sauce mixture. Cover and cook until chicken is tender, 4 to 6 hours on low.

3. Transfer chicken to large bowl, let cool slightly, then shred into bite-size pieces (see page 21); cover to keep warm. Let braising liquid settle for 5 minutes, then remove fat from surface using large spoon.

4. Toss shredded chicken with 1 cup braising liquid; add more liquid as needed to keep meat moist and flavorful. Stir in lime juice and season with salt and pepper to taste. (Filling can be refrigerated in airtight container for up to 3 days or frozen for up to 1 month. If frozen, let filling thaw completely before using.)

ON THE SIDE EASY MEXICAN RICE
Heat ⅓ cup vegetable oil in large Dutch oven over medium heat until shimmering. Add 2 cups rinsed long-grain white rice and cook, stirring often, until golden, about 10 minutes. Stir in 3 minced garlic cloves and 2 seeded and minced jalapeños and cook for 15 seconds. Stir in 1½ cups low-sodium chicken broth, 2 cups V8 juice, and 1 teaspoon salt. Bring to brief boil, then cover and bake in 350-degree oven until rice is tender and liquid is absorbed, 30 to 35 minutes, stirring well halfway through. Fluff rice with fork, fold in ½ cup minced fresh cilantro and 2 tablespoons lime juice, and season with salt, pepper, and hot sauce to taste. Serves 6.

ENCHILADAS WITH EVERYDAY SHREDDED CHICKEN FILLING

Shredded Tomatillo-Chicken Filling

Makes about 4 cups   **Cooking Time** 4 to 6 hours on Low

✓ **WHY THIS RECIPE WORKS:** We wanted to develop a recipe for shredded chicken infused with the tart essence of tomatillos. Since their flavor can be quite subtle, we knew we'd have to deepen it so they could withstand hours in the slow cooker. Broiling was the solution. It resulted in a nice char, which added smokiness and complexity to the dish. The flavor boost with this method was so significant that we ended up broiling the aromatics and spices along with them. After pulsing the broiled vegetables in a food processor we had a smoky, spicy, fresh-tasting green sauce that was perfect for braising boneless chicken breasts and thighs. To deepen the flavors even more we added minced poblanos and jalapeños to the slow cooker with the chicken. Feel free to use all white meat or all dark meat in this recipe if desired. To make this dish spicier, add the jalapeño chile seeds. If you can't find fresh tomatillos, you can substitute two 11-ounce cans of tomatillos, drained, rinsed, and patted dry; broil as directed in step 1. For recipes using this filling see pages 214–217.

12	ounces tomatillos (8 to 10 medium), husks and stems removed, rinsed well, dried, and halved
2	poblano chiles, halved lengthwise, stemmed, and seeded
2	jalapeño chiles, halved lengthwise, stemmed, and seeded
1	small onion, cut into 1-inch pieces
3	garlic cloves, minced
1½	teaspoons minced fresh oregano or ½ teaspoon dried
½	teaspoon ground cumin
	Pinch ground cloves
	Pinch ground cinnamon
2	tablespoons vegetable oil
1	pound boneless, skinless chicken breasts, trimmed
1	pound boneless, skinless chicken thighs, trimmed
	Salt and pepper

1. Position oven rack 6 inches from broiler element and heat broiler. Toss tomatillos, poblanos, jalapeños, onion, garlic, oregano, cumin, cloves, and cinnamon with oil and spread onto aluminum foil–lined rimmed baking sheet arranging poblanos and jalapeños skin side up. Broil until vegetables are blackened and begin to soften, 5 to 10 minutes, rotating pan halfway through broiling.

2. Let vegetables cool slightly, then transfer to food processor with accumulated juice and process until almost smooth, about 10 pulses; transfer to slow cooker. Season chicken with salt and pepper, add to slow cooker, and coat evenly with sauce mixture. Cover and cook until chicken is tender, 4 to 6 hours on low.

3. Transfer chicken to large bowl, let cool slightly, then shred into bite-size pieces (see page 21); cover to keep warm. Let braising liquid settle for 5 minutes, then remove fat from surface using large spoon.

4. Strain braising liquid and add strained solids to shredded chicken. Toss shredded chicken with ½ cup braising liquid; add more liquid as needed to keep meat moist and flavorful. Season with salt and pepper to taste. (Filling can be refrigerated in airtight container for up to 3 days or frozen for up to 1 month. If frozen, let filling thaw completely before using.)

SMART SHOPPING TOMATILLOS

Called *tomates verdes* (green tomatoes) in much of Mexico, tomatillos have a tangier, more citrusy flavor than true green tomatoes. When choosing tomatillos, look for pale-green orbs with firm flesh that fills and splits open the fruit's outer papery husk, which must be removed before cooking. The flavor of canned tomatillos is less bright but they make a fine substitute when fresh are not available.

Everyday Shredded Beef Filling

Makes about 4 cups   **Cooking Time** 9 to 11 hours on Low or 5 to 7 hours on High

WHY THIS RECIPE WORKS: Whether you're making quick burritos or enchiladas or have a hankering for comforting Mexican-style lasagna, this easy-to-make slow-cooker beef filling makes these normally involved recipes a snap to assemble. We turned to chuck roast, with its big beefy flavor, as the basis for the filling because it becomes meltingly tender and shreddable in the slow cooker—plus it's inexpensive and easy to find. Cutting the roast in half helped it cook faster and, as a result, become even more tender than when left whole. To make our red sauce we boosted the flavor of canned tomato sauce by cooking it with dried spices, sugar, and aromatics, finishing it with a dash of lime juice for brightness. Be sure to add a generous amount of the defatted braising liquid back to the meat at the end—it contains loads of rich, complex flavor. For recipes using this filling see pages 214–217.

2	onions, minced
⅓	cup chili powder
3	tablespoons vegetable oil
6	garlic cloves, minced
1	tablespoon ground coriander
1	tablespoon ground cumin
½	teaspoon cayenne pepper
1	(15-ounce) can tomato sauce
2	teaspoons sugar
1	(3-pound) boneless beef chuck roast, trimmed and halved
	Salt and pepper
1	tablespoon fresh lime juice

1. Microwave onions, chili powder, oil, garlic, coriander, cumin, and cayenne in bowl, stirring occasionally, until onions are softened, about 5 minutes; transfer to slow cooker.

2. Stir tomato sauce and sugar into slow cooker. Season beef with salt and pepper, add to slow cooker, and coat evenly with sauce mixture. Cover and cook until beef is tender, 9 to 11 hours on low or 5 to 7 hours on high.

3. Transfer beef to large bowl, let cool slightly, then shred into bite-size pieces (see page 21), discarding excess fat; cover to keep warm. Let braising liquid settle for 5 minutes, then remove fat from surface using large spoon.

4. Toss shredded beef with 1 cup braising liquid; add more liquid as needed to keep meat moist and flavorful. Stir in lime juice and season with salt and pepper to taste. (Filling can be refrigerated in airtight container for up to 3 days or frozen for up to 1 month. If frozen, let filling thaw completely before using.)

ON THE SIDE FENNEL-TANGERINE SLAW
Combine 2 thinly sliced fennel bulbs (see page 66), 2 peeled and coarsely chopped tangerines, 4 thinly sliced radishes, and ¼ cup minced cilantro in large bowl. In separate bowl, whisk ⅓ cup olive oil, 3 tablespoons lime juice, 2 thinly sliced scallions, 1 minced clove garlic, ½ teaspoon salt, and ¼ teaspoon pepper together. Toss dressing with fennel mixture and season with salt and pepper to taste. Serves 6.

BURRITOS WITH SMOKY SHREDDED CHIPOTLE BEEF FILLING

Smoky Shredded Chipotle Beef Filling

Makes about 4 cups   **Cooking Time** 9 to 11 hours on Low or 5 to 7 hours on High

✔ **WHY THIS RECIPE WORKS:** When you're looking for a shredded beef filling with a little more of a kick, this smoky chipotle beef is hard to beat. We braised boneless chuck roast in a tomato-based sauce along with aromatics, spices, canned chipotle chiles (dried and smoked jalapeños in piquant adobo sauce), and a fresh jalapeño. The chipotles imparted sweet and smoky notes and a warm, lingering heat to the finished dish, while the fresh jalapeño intensified the moderate, but not overwhelming, spiciness. This shredded beef filling was intensely flavorful but, since the essence of chipotles mellows during cooking, it lacked the distinct smokiness we were after. Adding a splash of liquid smoke with the sauce ensured a lasting smoky flavor. To make this dish spicier, add the jalapeño chile seeds. For recipes using this filling see pages 214–217.

2   **onions, minced**
⅓   **cup chili powder**
3   **tablespoons minced canned chipotle chile in adobo sauce**
2   **tablespoons vegetable oil**
6   **garlic cloves, minced**
1   **jalapeño chile, stemmed, seeded, and minced**
1   **tablespoon tomato paste**
1   **tablespoon ground cumin**
1   **(15-ounce) can tomato sauce**
2   **teaspoons light brown sugar**
½   **teaspoon liquid smoke**
1   **(3-pound) boneless beef chuck roast, trimmed and halved**
Salt and pepper

1. Microwave onions, chili powder, chipotles, oil, garlic, jalapeño, tomato paste, and cumin in bowl, stirring occasionally, until vegetables are softened, about 5 minutes; transfer to slow cooker.

2. Stir tomato sauce, sugar, and liquid smoke into slow cooker. Season beef with salt and pepper, add to slow cooker, and coat evenly with sauce mixture. Cover and cook until beef is tender, 9 to 11 hours on low or 5 to 7 hours on high.

3. Transfer beef to large bowl, let cool slightly, then shred into bite-size pieces (see page 21), discarding excess fat; cover to keep warm. Let braising liquid settle for 5 minutes, then remove fat from surface using large spoon.

4. Toss shredded beef with 1 cup braising liquid; add more liquid as needed to keep meat moist and flavorful. Season with salt and pepper to taste. (Filling can be refrigerated in airtight container for up to 3 days or frozen for up to 1 month. If frozen, let filling thaw completely before using.)

ON THE SIDE ONE-MINUTE SALSA
Pulse ¼ small red onion, 1 small garlic clove, 2 tablespoons fresh cilantro leaves, 2 teaspoons lime juice, ½ teaspoon minced canned chipotle in adobo sauce, ¼ teaspoon salt, and pinch pepper together in food processor until minced, about 5 pulses. Add 1 (14.5-ounce) can diced tomatoes, drained, and pulse until roughly chopped, about 2 pulses. Season with salt, pepper, additional lime juice, and additional chipotles to taste. Makes 1 cup.

Sweet and Spicy Shredded Pork Filling

Makes about 4 cups   **Cooking Time** 9 to 11 hours on Low or 5 to 7 hours on High

✔ **WHY THIS RECIPE WORKS:** To infuse sweet and smoky flavors into our shredded pork filling, we built a sauce using pineapple juice and ancho and chipotle chiles. (If you can't find whole chiles, you can substitute 3 tablespoons ancho chili powder and 1 tablespoon chipotle powder, skip step 1, and add the chili powders to the blender in step 2.) For recipes using this filling see pages 214–217.

3	dried ancho chiles
2	dried chipotle chiles
¾	cup pineapple juice, fresh or canned
4	garlic cloves, peeled
1	tablespoon light brown sugar
¼	teaspoon ground cumin
⅛	teaspoon ground cloves
1	(3-pound) boneless pork butt roast, trimmed and halved Salt and pepper
1	tablespoon fresh lime juice, plus extra as needed

1. Following photos, toast ancho and chipotle chilies in skillet over medium-high heat until dry and fragrant, 4 to 6 minutes (reduce heat if chiles begin to smoke). Let chiles cool slightly, then remove stem and seeds and tear into smaller pieces. Cover chiles with warm water and let soak until softened but not mushy, about 20 minutes; drain well.

2. Puree soaked chiles, pineapple juice, garlic, sugar, cumin, and cloves in blender until smooth, about 30 seconds; transfer to slow cooker. Season pork with salt and pepper, add to slow cooker, and coat evenly with sauce mixture. Cover and cook until pork is tender, 9 to 11 hours on low or 5 to 7 hours on high.

3. Transfer pork to large bowl, let cool slightly, then shred into bite-size pieces (see page 21) discarding excess fat; cover to keep warm. Let braising liquid settle for 5 minutes, then remove fat from surface using large spoon.

4. Toss shredded pork with 1 cup braising liquid; add more liquid as needed to keep meat moist and flavorful. Stir in lime juice and season with salt, pepper, and additional lime juice to taste. (Filling can be refrigerated in airtight container for up to 3 days or frozen for up to 1 month. If frozen, let filling thaw completely before using.)

QUICK PREP TIP USING DRIED CHILES
To deepen the flavor of dried chiles, they need to be toasted and rehydrated before using. Place whole chiles in a dry skillet and toast over medium-high heat until dry and fragrant, 4 to 6 minutes. Let the chiles cool slightly, then wearing gloves, remove the stems and seeds and tear the chiles into smaller pieces. Place the chile pieces in a bowl, cover with warm water, and let soak until softened but not mushy, about 20 minutes; drain well.

TOSTADAS WITH SWEET AND SPICY SHREDDED PORK FILLING

Everyday Shredded Pork Filling

Makes about 4 cups   **Cooking Time** 9 to 11 hours on Low or 5 to 7 hours on High

✔ WHY THIS RECIPE WORKS: This spicy, smoky shredded pork with Mexican flavors is a far cry from the bland burrito-joint fillings that are all too common north of the border. Boneless pork butt boasts an intense, sweet meatiness and a moist, tender texture after slow cooking, making it the ideal cut of pork for this recipe. We braised the pork in a rich chipotle-infused tomato sauce made by simply enhancing canned tomato sauce with aromatics and a handful of spices and a chipotle chile in adobo sauce, which added charred flavor and deep complexity. A squeeze of fresh lime juice enlivened the flavors at the end, leaving us with a pork filling that was smoky, spicy and complex. For recipes using this filling see pages 214–217.

2	**onions, minced**
¼	**cup chili powder**
3	**tablespoons vegetable oil**
6	**garlic cloves, minced**
1	**minced canned chipotle chile in adobo sauce**
1	**tablespoon ground coriander**
1	**tablespoon ground cumin**
1	**(15-ounce) can tomato sauce**
2	**teaspoons sugar**
1	**(3-pound) boneless pork butt roast, trimmed and halved**
	Salt and pepper
1	**tablespoon fresh lime juice**

1. Microwave onions, chili powder, oil, garlic, chipotles, coriander, and cumin in bowl, stirring occasionally, until onions are softened, about 5 minutes; transfer to slow cooker.

2. Stir tomato sauce and sugar into slow cooker. Season pork with salt and pepper, add to slow cooker, and coat evenly with sauce mixture. Cover and cook until pork is tender, 9 to 11 hours on low or 5 to 7 hours on high.

3. Transfer pork to large bowl, let cool slightly, then shred into bite-size pieces (see page 21), discarding excess fat; cover to keep warm. Let braising liquid settle for 5 minutes, then remove fat from surface using large spoon.

4. Toss shredded pork with 1 cup braising liquid; add more liquid as needed to keep meat moist and flavorful. Stir in lime juice and season with salt and pepper to taste. (Filling can be refrigerated in airtight container for up to 3 days or frozen for up to 1 month. If frozen, let filling thaw completely before using.)

ON THE SIDE MEXICAN STREET CORN
Brush 6 ears peeled corn with 1 tablespoon olive oil and place on aluminum foil-lined baking sheet. Broil corn until tender and well browned on both sides, 5 to 10 minutes per side. In large bowl, mix ½ cup mayonnaise, ¼ cup crumbled queso fresco or feta cheese, 2 tablespoons minced cilantro, 1 tablespoon lime juice, 1 minced garlic clove, 1 teaspoon chili powder, ¼ teaspoon salt, and pinch pepper together. Roll broiled corn in mayonnaise mixture to coat thoroughly and return to baking sheet. Spoon remaining mayonnaise mixture over corn, and continue to broil until lightly browned on top, about 1 minute longer. Serve with lime wedges. Serves 6.

Spicy Ground Beef Taco Filling

Makes about 6 cups   **Cooking Time** 6 to 8 hours on Low or 3 to 5 hours on High

WHY THIS RECIPE WORKS: When it comes to tacos, it's all about the filling. Fortunately, the road to taco filling perfection using a slow cooker requires minimal prep and mostly pantry ingredients. We started by microwaving plenty of aromatics, which we combined with a can of tomato sauce. The flavor was a little one-dimensional so we supplemented it with cumin, coriander, and oregano, in addition to a splash of cider vinegar and a touch of brown sugar. Now the sauce was an intensely flavorful complement to the beef. The meat, however, was a bit dry so we added a panade (a paste of milk and bread) to the raw meat before cooking to keep it moist. Spoon the filling into warmed taco shells and serve with your favorite toppings, or use in Mexican Lasagna (page 217).

2   **onions, minced**

¼   **cup chili powder**

3   **tablespoons vegetable oil**

6   **garlic cloves, minced**

2   **teaspoons ground cumin**

2   **teaspoons ground coriander**

1   **tablespoon minced fresh oregano or 1 teaspoon dried**

1   **(8-ounce) can tomato sauce**

2   **teaspoons cider vinegar**

2   **teaspoons light brown sugar**

2   **slices high-quality white sandwich bread, torn into quarters**

¼   **cup whole milk**

2   **pounds 90 percent lean ground beef**

     Salt and pepper

1. Microwave onions, chili powder, oil, garlic, cumin, coriander, and oregano in bowl, stirring occasionally, until onions are softened, about 5 minutes; transfer to slow cooker. Stir tomato sauce, vinegar, and sugar into slow cooker.

2. Mash bread and milk into paste in large bowl using fork. Mix in ground beef, ½ teaspoon salt, and ¼ teaspoon pepper using hands. Stir beef mixture into slow cooker, breaking up any large pieces (do not overmix). Cover and cook until beef is tender, 6 to 8 hours on low or 3 to 5 hours on high.

3. Let beef filling settle for 5 minutes, then remove fat from surface using large spoon. Break up any remaining large pieces of beef with spoon. Season with salt and pepper to taste. (Filling can be refrigerated in airtight container for up to 3 days or frozen for up to 1 month. If frozen, let filling thaw completely before using.)

ON THE SIDE HOMEMADE TACO SHELLS

For the ultimate tacos, try frying your own taco shells. In small skillet, heat ¾ cup vegetable oil over medium heat to 350 to 375 degrees; adjust heat as needed to maintain this oil temperature during frying. Using tongs and metal spatula, shape soft (6-inch) corn tortillas into taco shells while frying. Fry one side of tortilla until crisp, about 30 seconds, then flip tortilla over and fry second side until crisp, about 1½ minutes longer. Let shells drain upside down on paper towel–lined baking sheet before using.

Ground Turkey and Chipotle Taco Filling

Makes about 6 cups   **Cooking Time** 4 to 6 hours on Low

✔ WHY THIS RECIPE WORKS: It's nice to have a lighter alternative to a traditional beef taco filling so we set out to develop a recipe using ground turkey. To pump up the leaner flavor of ground turkey, we cooked it in a spicy, zesty chili-chipotle tomato sauce, the essence of which deepened during cooking. To boost the flavors even more we freshened up the filling at the end by adding fresh cilantro, minced scallions, and lime juice for brightness. The flavors were great now but the turkey was somewhat dry so we mixed it with a panade (a paste of milk and bread), which kept the meat moist and tender even after hours in the slow cooker. Unlike the ground beef taco filling, this ground turkey filling should only be cooked on low and for a shorter time to ensure that the meat remains tender. Do not use lean ground turkey breast here (also labeled 99 percent fat free) or the filling will be dry and grainy. Spoon the filling into warmed taco shells and serve with your favorite toppings, or use in Mexican Lasagna (page 217).

2	onions, minced
¼	cup chili powder
2	tablespoons vegetable oil
6	garlic cloves, minced
2	tablespoons minced canned chipotle chile in adobo sauce
1	tablespoon minced fresh oregano or 1 teaspoon dried
1	(8-ounce) can tomato sauce
2	teaspoons light brown sugar
2	slices high-quality white sandwich bread, torn into quarters
¼	cup whole milk
2	pounds ground turkey
	Salt and pepper
¼	cup minced fresh cilantro
3	scallions, sliced thin
1	tablespoon fresh lime juice

1. Microwave onions, chili powder, oil, garlic, chipotles, and oregano in bowl, stirring occasionally, until onions are softened, about 5 minutes; transfer to slow cooker. Stir tomato sauce and sugar into slow cooker.

2. Mash bread and milk into paste in large bowl using fork. Mix in ground turkey, ½ teaspoon salt, and ¼ teaspoon pepper using hands. Stir turkey mixture into slow cooker, breaking up any large pieces (do not overmix). Cover and cook until turkey is tender, 4 to 6 hours on low.

3. Let turkey filling settle for 5 minutes, then remove fat from surface using large spoon. Break up any remaining large pieces of turkey with spoon. Stir in cilantro, scallions, and lime juice and season with salt and pepper to taste before serving. (Filling can be refrigerated in airtight container for up to 3 days or frozen for up to 1 month. If frozen, let filling thaw completely before using.)

ON THE SIDE FOOLPROOF GREEN SALAD
Combine 1 tablespoon vinegar (red wine, white wine, or champagne), 1½ teaspoons minced shallot, ½ teaspoon mayonnaise, ½ teaspoon Dijon mustard, ⅛ teaspoon salt, and pinch pepper in small nonreactive bowl. Whisk until mixture is smooth and looks milky. Very slowly drizzle in 3 tablespoons extra-virgin olive oil while whisking constantly until emulsified. Toss with 8 to 10 cups lightly packed greens. Serves 4 to 6.

MEXICAN LASAGNA WITH GROUND TURKEY AND CHIPOTLE TACO FILLING

The array of Mexican fillings in this chapter puts a world of easy dinner options at your fingertips. The simplest options don't even require recipes! You can serve the filling over a bowl of rice or polenta or spoon it into a warmed soft tortilla. Burritos (below) and Tostadas (page 215) are also speedy dinners that you can make with any of the shredded meat fillings, and although they barely require a recipe, we do have a few tricks to share for each of them. For a real transformation, try making the Enchiladas (page 216) with any of the shredded meat fillings, or the Mexican Lasagna (page 217) with either a shredded or ground meat filling. Note that you will have enough filling to double all of these recipes if desired.

Burritos

Serves 4

Serve with salsa, guacamole, sour cream, and lime wedges.

Vegetable oil spray
2 **cups shredded chicken, beef, or pork filling (see pages 202–210)**
1 **(15-ounce) can pinto or black beans, drained and rinsed**
1 **cup cooked rice**
2 **cups shredded cheddar, Monterey Jack, Colby, or pepper Jack cheese (8 ounces)**
¼ **cup minced fresh cilantro**
Salt and pepper
4 **(10-inch) flour tortillas**

1. Adjust oven rack to middle position and heat oven to 450 degrees. Line rimmed baking sheet with aluminum foil and coat with vegetable oil spray. Microwave filling, beans, and rice together in large covered bowl until hot, stirring occasionally, 2 to 4 minutes. Stir in 1 cup cheese and cilantro and season with salt and pepper to taste.

2. Lay tortillas on clean counter and divide filling between tortillas. Following photos, mound filling into tidy pile over bottom half of tortillas, leaving 1- to 2-inch border around edges. Roll tortillas up tightly around filling into burrito, and lay, seam side down, on prepared baking sheet. Sprinkle with remaining cup cheese.

3. Cover burritos with foil that has been sprayed with vegetable oil spray (or use nonstick foil) and bake until heated through, about 10 minutes. Uncover and continue to bake until cheese is completely melted, about 5 minutes longer. Serve hot.

QUICK PREP TIP MAKING BURRITOS
To make a tidy burrito, mound the filling into a compact pile over the bottom half of the tortillas, leaving a 1- to 2-inch border around the edge. Fold the sides of the tortilla over the filling, then tightly roll the bottom edge of the tortilla up over the filling and continue to roll into a burrito.

Tostadas

Serves 4

If you're short on time, you can substitute one 16-ounce can of your favorite refried beans in this recipe and skip step 2. Similarly, feel free to use ready-made tostadas and skip step 1. Serve with sour cream and lime wedges.

10	**(6-inch) corn tortillas**
⅓	**cup vegetable oil**
2	**(15-ounce) cans pinto beans**
1	**tablespoon minced jarred pickled jalapeños plus 1 tablespoon pickled jalapeño juice**
	Salt and pepper
2	**cups shredded chicken, beef, or pork filling (see pages 202–210)**
½	**cup crumbled queso fresco or feta cheese (2 ounces)**
¼	**cup fresh cilantro leaves**

1. Adjust oven racks to upper-middle and lower-middle positions and heat oven to 450 degrees. Brush tortillas with 3 tablespoons oil and arrange on two rimmed baking sheets. Bake until lightly browned and crisp, about 10 minutes, rotating baking sheets halfway through baking.

2. Heat remaining oil in 12-inch skillet over medium heat until shimmering. Add beans with their canning liquid, jalapeños, and jalapeño juice and cook, mashing with potato masher, until mixture is thickened and hot, about 5 minutes. Season with salt and pepper to taste; cover to keep warm.

3. Microwave filling in covered bowl, stirring occasionally, until hot, 2 to 4 minutes. Spread bean mixture evenly over tostadas, then top with filling. Sprinkle with queso fresco and cilantro and serve.

SMART SHOPPING CORN TOSTADAS
In this recipe, we bake the tortillas rather than fry them to keep things simple. But another good option, if you can find them, is to buy already fried tostadas. Before using them you'll need to reheat them in a 450-degree oven until hot and crisp, about 5 minutes. Our favorite brand? We fried up our own to compare to five packaged brands, both plain and with refried beans. To our surprise, the winner, **Mission Tostadas Estilo Casero**, boasted such nutty corn flavor and such a pleasingly rustic texture that some tasters even preferred it to our home-made version.

Enchiladas

Serves 4 to 6

We prefer the flavor of our homemade enchilada sauce here; however, you can substitute 20 ounces (2½ cups) of canned enchilada sauce if desired. We like to garnish this casserole with chopped fresh tomatoes and cilantro.

SAUCE

- 1 **tablespoon vegetable oil**
- 1 **onion, minced**
- 3 **tablespoons chili powder**
- 2 **garlic cloves, minced**
- 2 **teaspoons ground cumin**
- 2 **teaspoons sugar**
- 1 **(15-ounce) can tomato sauce**
- ½ **cup water**
- **Salt and pepper**

ENCHILADAS

- 2 **cups shredded chicken, beef, or pork filling (see pages 202–210)**
- 2 **cups shredded cheddar, Monterey Jack, or pepper Jack cheese (8 ounces)**
- ½ **cup minced fresh cilantro**
- 1 **(4-ounce) can pickled jalapeños, drained and chopped (¼ cup)**
- **Salt and pepper**
- 12 **(6-inch) corn tortillas**
- **Vegetable oil spray**

1. FOR THE SAUCE: Heat oil in medium saucepan over medium heat until shimmering. Add onion and cook until softened, 5 to 7 minutes. Stir in chili powder, garlic, cumin, and sugar and cook until fragrant, about 30 seconds. Stir in tomato sauce and water and simmer until thickened slightly, about 5 minutes. Season with salt and pepper to taste.

2. FOR THE ENCHILADAS: Adjust oven rack to middle position and heat oven to 350 degrees. Microwave filling in large covered bowl until hot, stirring occasionally, 2 to 4 minutes. Stir in 1 cup cheese, cilantro, ½ cup enchilada sauce, and jalapeños and season with salt and pepper to taste; cover to keep warm.

3. Coat both sides of tortillas with vegetable oil spray. Arrange 6 tortillas on rimmed baking sheet and bake until tortillas are soft and pliable, 2 to 4 minutes.

4. Working quickly while tortillas are still warm and pliable, lay tortillas on clean counter. Place a scant ⅓ cup filling evenly down center of each tortilla. Tightly roll each tortilla around filling and arrange, seam side down, in 13 by 9-inch baking dish. Repeat with remaining tortillas and filling. (In order to fit 12 enchiladas into the baking dish, you will have to lay four of them on top of the others.)

5. Increase oven temperature to 450 degrees. Pour 1 cup more sauce over enchiladas and sprinkle with remaining cup cheese. Cover enchiladas tightly with aluminum foil that has been sprayed with vegetable oil spray (or use nonstick foil).

6. Bake until enchiladas are heated through, about 10 minutes. Remove foil and continue to bake until cheese is completely melted, about 5 minutes longer. Let enchiladas cool for 10 minutes, then serve with remaining sauce.

Mexican Lasagna

Serves 4 to 6

Quartering the tortillas that make up the top layer of this casserole makes it easier to cut and serve. You can substitute 3 ounces each of Colby and Monterey Jack cheeses for the Colby Jack. Serve with salsa, diced avocado, sour cream, and scallions.

2	cups shredded chicken, beef, or pork filling (see pages 202–210) or 3 cups ground meat taco filling (see pages 211–212)
1	(15-ounce) can pinto beans, drained and rinsed
1	(14.5-ounce) can diced tomatoes, drained
1	cup frozen corn
⅓	cup minced fresh cilantro
1	tablespoon fresh lime juice
	Salt and pepper
9	(6-inch) soft corn tortillas
	Vegetable oil spray
1½	cups shredded Colby Jack cheese (6 ounces)

1. Adjust oven rack to middle position and heat oven to 350 degrees. Microwave filling, beans, tomatoes, and corn in covered bowl until hot, stirring occasionally, 2 to 4 minutes. Stir in ¼ cup cilantro and lime juice and season with salt and pepper to taste.

2. Coat both sides of tortillas with vegetable oil spray, arrange on rimmed baking sheet (tortillas will overlap), and bake until tortillas are soft and pliable, 2 to 4 minutes.

3. Increase oven temperature to 450 degrees. Spread one-third of filling into 8-inch square baking dish. Layer 3 tortillas on top of filling, overlapping as needed, and sprinkle with ½ cup Colby Jack. Repeat with one-third more filling, 3 more tortillas, and ½ cup more Colby Jack. Spread remaining filling over top. Cut remaining 3 tortillas into quarters and scatter over filling. Sprinkle with remaining ½ cup Colby Jack.

4. Bake until bubbling and golden, about 15 minutes. Let cool for 5 minutes. Sprinkle with remaining cilantro and serve.

EASY PREP TIP **PREPPING TORTILLAS**
Spread the lightly oiled tortillas out over a baking sheet (they can overlap each other and overhang the edge of the baking sheet as needed) and bake in a 350-degree oven until they are warm, pliable, and refreshed. Cut three of the tortillas into quarters before scattering them over the top of the casserole. This will make the casserole much easier to serve.

CHICKEN DIVAN

Casseroles

Chicken Divan

Serves 6 to 8   **Cooking Time** 4 to 6 hours on Low

✔ **WHY THIS RECIPE WORKS:** For this cheesy chicken and broccoli casserole, we found it necessary to spend a few minutes at the stovetop with our skillet to create a flour-thickened sauce. Browning the aromatics first added a subtle roasted taste, while the addition of a little dried mustard helped to bring out the flavor of the cheese. Rice is often included in versions of this casserole and we decided to follow suit. Classic long-grain white rice remained undercooked even after 6 hours in the slow cooker, though instant rice, which is parcooked, turned perfectly tender in just 30 minutes (so we added it at the end after turning the slow cooker to high). Overcooked broccoli was also problematic, but our solution was to microwave the broccoli for a few minutes, then add it to the casserole at the end to heat through. Finished with a buttery crumb topping, our casserole was ready to serve. Don't shred the meat too fine in step 3; it will break up more as additional ingredients are included.

3	tablespoons vegetable oil
2	onions, minced
4	garlic cloves, minced
1	tablespoon minced fresh thyme or 1 teaspoon dried
3	tablespoons all-purpose flour
1	cup low-sodium chicken broth
½	cup heavy cream
1	teaspoon dry mustard
2	pounds boneless, skinless chicken thighs, trimmed Salt and pepper
2	cups instant rice (see page 221)
1	cup shredded cheddar cheese (4 ounces)
½	cup grated Parmesan cheese (1 ounce)
12	ounces broccoli florets, cut into 1-inch pieces (4½ cups)
1	recipe Toasted Bread-Crumb Topping (see page 241)

1. Heat 2 tablespoons oil in 12-inch skillet over medium-high heat until shimmering. Add onions, garlic, and thyme and cook until onions are softened and lightly browned, 8 to 10 minutes. Stir in flour and cook for 1 minute. Slowly whisk in broth, scraping up any browned bits and smoothing out any lumps; transfer to slow cooker.

2. Stir heavy cream and mustard into slow cooker. Season chicken with salt and pepper, add to slow cooker, and coat evenly with sauce. Cover and cook until chicken is tender, 4 to 6 hours on low.

3. Break up chicken into bite-size pieces with wooden spoon. Stir in rice, cheddar, Parmesan, and 1 teaspoon salt, cover, and cook on high until rice is tender, 20 to 30 minutes.

4. Microwave broccoli with remaining tablespoon oil in bowl, stirring occasionally, until tender, about 4 minutes. Stir softened broccoli into casserole and let sit until heated through, about 5 minutes. Sprinkle with Toasted Bread-Crumb Topping and serve.

QUICK PREP TIP PREPPING BROCCOLI
Even if you buy bagged precut broccoli florets, you will need to trim them down into evenly sized pieces before cooking. The best way to do this is to place the floret upside down on the cutting board and slice down through the stem. This way you'll have fewer small crumbly pieces.

Curried Chicken and Rice

Serves 6 to 8   **Cooking Time** 4 to 6 hours on Low

WHY THIS RECIPE WORKS: Curries are especially well suited for a slow cooker as their flavors benefit from the extended cooking time, melding together to gain depth and complexity. To pack the most flavor into our curried chicken and rice casserole, we started by blooming an aromatic mixture including a chile, onions, ginger, curry powder, and garam masala in our skillet before creating the sauce base. Coconut milk was a natural for this dish but the full-fat version caused the rice to turn gummy. We found the thinner consistency of light coconut milk helped the rice to maintain the proper texture. Cauliflower (which we microwaved), peas, and cilantro lent brightness as well as touches of color to the finished casserole. Sprinkling toasted almonds on at the end brought a nutty flavor that helped accent the flavors of the dish. Don't shred the meat too fine in step 3; it will break up more as additional ingredients are included.

3	tablespoons vegetable oil
2	onions, minced
1	jalapeño chile, stemmed, seeded, and minced
4	garlic cloves, minced
1	tablespoon minced or grated fresh ginger
1	tablespoon curry powder
1	teaspoon garam masala (see page 74)
3	tablespoons all-purpose flour
1	(14-ounce) can light coconut milk
2	pounds boneless, skinless chicken thighs, trimmed
	Salt and pepper
2	cups instant rice
½	head cauliflower (1 pound), cored and cut into 1-inch florets (3 cups) (see page 25)
1	cup frozen peas
3	tablespoons sliced almonds, toasted (see page 87)
2	tablespoons minced fresh cilantro

1. Heat 2 tablespoons oil in 12-inch skillet over medium-high heat until shimmering. Add onions, jalapeño, garlic, ginger, curry, and garam masala and cook until vegetables are softened and lightly browned, 8 to 10 minutes. Stir in flour and cook for 1 minute. Slowly whisk in coconut milk, scraping up any browned bits and smoothing out any lumps; transfer to slow cooker.

2. Season chicken with salt and pepper, add to slow cooker, and coat evenly with sauce. Cover and cook until chicken is tender, 4 to 6 hours on low.

3. Break up chicken into bite-size pieces with wooden spoon. Stir in rice and 1 teaspoon salt, cover, and cook on high until rice is tender, 20 to 30 minutes.

4. Microwave cauliflower with remaining tablespoon oil in bowl, stirring occasionally, until tender, about 4 minutes. Stir softened cauliflower and peas into casserole and let sit until heated through, about 5 minutes. Sprinkle with almonds and cilantro and serve.

SMART SHOPPING INSTANT RICE
Instant rice is simply white rice that is fully cooked then dried very fast, cooled, and packaged. While we aren't very impressed with how instant rice tastes on its own, we've found it to be the perfect choice for our slow-cooker rice-based casseroles. By comparison, raw long-grain white rice cooked very unevenly in this slow-cooker casserole, while fully cooked rice retained its distinct texture and didn't bind well. Instant not only cooked very evenly, but its slightly starchy texture helped the casserole bind together nicely.

Old-Fashioned Tamale Pie

Serves 6 to 8   **Cooking Time** about 4 hours on Low

✔ **WHY THIS RECIPE WORKS:** Popular Tex-Mex fare, tamale pie can be interpreted many ways but it always contains a juicy, spicy mixture of meat and vegetables with a cornmeal topping. We wanted to develop a really good slow-cooker tamale pie that could be assembled quickly and still boast great flavor. To create a simple filling we first microwaved onion and garlic along with some chili powder and cumin, then combined the mixture in the slow cooker with enchilada sauce and shredded cooked chicken (raw, cubed chicken had an unappealing texture). Canned black beans and creamed corn also helped the filling come together quickly. As for the topping, we further simplified things by making a quick polenta in the microwave using instant polenta. After about 10 minutes, the polenta was properly cooked and stirring in some butter and cheddar cheese helped to boost the flavor. Be sure to use dried, instant polenta in this recipe; do not substitute traditional polenta or precooked polenta in a tube. For the chicken, feel free to use a rotisserie chicken or any leftover chicken you may have; you can also use our recipe for Easy Poached Chicken, below.

2¼ **cups water**
¾   **cup instant polenta**
    Salt and pepper
1   **cup shredded cheddar cheese (4 ounces)**
1   **tablespoon unsalted butter**
1   **onion, minced**
1   **tablespoon vegetable oil**
3   **garlic cloves, minced**
1   **tablespoon chili powder**
1   **teaspoon ground cumin**
4   **cups shredded cooked chicken**
1   **(15-ounce) can black beans, drained and rinsed**
1   **(15-ounce) can creamed corn**
1   **(10-ounce) can enchilada sauce**
2   **tablespoons Minute tapioca**
2   **tablespoons minced fresh cilantro**
    Lime wedges, for serving

1. Combine water, polenta, and 1 teaspoon salt in bowl, cover, and microwave until most of water is absorbed, 6 to 8 minutes. Stir polenta thoroughly, then continue to microwave, uncovered, until polenta is creamy and fully cooked, 1 to 3 minutes longer. Stir in cheddar and butter and season with salt and pepper to taste. Cover to keep warm.

2. Microwave onion, oil, garlic, chili powder, and cumin in second bowl, stirring occasionally, until onion is softened, about 5 minutes; transfer to slow cooker.

3. Stir chicken, beans, corn, enchilada sauce, and tapioca into slow cooker. Spoon cooked polenta over chicken filling and smooth into even layer using spatula. Cover and cook until casserole is heated through, about 4 hours on low. Let casserole cool for 20 minutes, then sprinkle with cilantro and serve with lime wedges.

QUICK PREP TIP **EASY POACHED CHICKEN**
Pat dry 2 pounds boneless, skinless chicken breasts with paper towels and season with salt and pepper. Heat 1 tablespoon vegetable oil in 12-inch skillet over medium-high heat until just smoking. Carefully lay chicken in skillet and cook until well browned on first side, 6 to 8 minutes. Flip chicken, add ½ cup water, and cover. Reduce heat to medium-low and continue to cook until thickest part of chicken breasts registers 160 to 165 on instant-read thermometer, 5 to 7 minutes longer. Transfer chicken to cutting board, let cool slightly, then shred into bite-size pieces (see page 21). Makes about 4 cups. (This recipe can be halved to make 2 cups.)

Southern-Style Chicken and Dirty Rice

Serves 6 to 8   **Cooking Time** 4 to 6 hours on Low

✔ WHY THIS RECIPE WORKS: In the South, chicken is often paired with dirty rice—a side dish of cooked rice, cured meats, vegetables, and seasonings that give the rice a "dirty" appearance. We thought the flavors of chicken and dirty rice combined with the gentle heat of the slow cooker had the potential to create a delicious weeknight casserole. Browning kielbasa sausage was a must for developing an intense meaty background for the dish. With the skillet already out, we also browned a mix of onion, celery, bell pepper, and spices and deglazed the pan with chicken broth, seriously elevating the overall flavor. Adding the instant rice during the final 30 minutes of cooking enabled it to pick up the rich color and flavor of the braising liquid and turn perfectly tender. Sliced scallions added a touch of color and brightness to the finished dish. Don't shred the meat too fine in step 3; it will break up more as additional ingredients are included.

1   **tablespoon vegetable oil**
8   **ounces kielbasa sausage, cut into ½-inch pieces**
1   **onion, minced**
2   **celery ribs, minced**
1   **red bell pepper, stemmed, seeded, and cut into ½-inch pieces (see page 91)**
4   **garlic cloves, minced**
1   **tablespoon minced fresh thyme or 1 teaspoon dried**
2   **teaspoons chili powder**
⅛   **teaspoon cayenne pepper**
3   **tablespoons all-purpose flour**
1½   **cups low-sodium chicken broth**
2   **pounds boneless, skinless chicken thighs, trimmed Salt and pepper**
2   **cups instant rice (see page 221)**
2   **scallions, sliced thin**

1. Heat oil in 12-inch skillet over medium-high heat until just smoking. Brown sausage well, about 3 minutes. Add onion, celery, bell pepper, garlic, thyme, chili powder, and cayenne and cook until vegetables are softened and lightly browned, 8 to 10 minutes. Stir in flour and cook for 1 minute. Slowly whisk in broth, scraping up any browned bits and smoothing out any lumps; transfer to slow cooker.

2. Season chicken with salt and pepper, add to slow cooker, and coat evenly with sauce. Cover and cook until chicken is tender, 4 to 6 hours on low.

3. Break up chicken into bite-size pieces using wooden spoon. Stir in rice and 1 teaspoon salt, cover, and cook on high until rice is tender, 20 to 30 minutes. Sprinkle with scallions and serve.

SHOPPING KIELBASA

Kielbasa, or Polish sausage, is a smoked pork sausage that sometimes has beef added and is usually sold precooked. We tested five national supermarket brands, and **Smithfield Naturally Hickory Smoked Polska Kielbasa** slightly outranked Wellshire Farms Polska Kielbasa, but both had a smoky, complex flavor and a heartier texture compared to the springy, hot dog-like textures of the others. Smithfield can be found in national supermarket chains; Wellshire Farms at Whole Foods Markets.

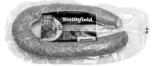

ALL ABOUT Casseroles

After slow cooking our way through several classic casseroles—and a couple of new ones of our own—we found that while not every successful casserole follows the same hard-and-fast rules, there are a few general guidelines to keep in mind. Here's what you should know.

Prepare Your Slow Cooker

Most slow cookers have a hotter side (typically the back side, opposite the side with the controls) that can cause casseroles and other dense dishes, like meatloaves, to burn. To solve this problem we lined the slow-cooker insert with an aluminum foil collar. For recipes that we wanted to lift out of the insert intact, we first lined the slow cooker with a foil collar, then lined it with a foil sling; this was very handy for our lasagnas and our breakfast casseroles.

To make a foil collar: Layer and fold sheets of heavy-duty foil until you have a six-layered foil rectangle that measures roughly 16 inches long by 4 inches wide. (Depending on the width of the foil, you will need either two or three sheets of foil.) Press the collar into the back side of the slow-cooker insert; the food will help hold the collar in place during cooking.

To make a foil sling: Line the slow-cooker insert with a foil collar. Then fit two large sheets of heavy-duty foil into the slow cooker, perpendicular to one another, with the extra hanging over the edges of the cooker insert. Before serving, these overhanging edges can be used as handles to pull the dish out of the slow cooker fully intact.

Make the Most of Convenience Products

For our lasagnas and macaroni and cheese, shelf-stabilized products like jarred alfredo sauce and condensed cheese soup were a lifesaver since they didn't curdle during the long cooking time. Other helpful products included jarred tomato sauce and prepared mashed potatoes (which top our Shepherd's Pie, page 231).

Don't Overcook Slow-Cooker Casseroles

None of our denser casseroles could withstand an entire day in the slow cooker; otherwise, we ended up with mushy pasta, bland vegetables, and dry meat. Moderate cooking times (from 2 to 3 hours on high to 4 to 6 hours on low) ensured vibrant flavors and properly cooked casseroles.

Drive Off Excess Moisture

In the moist environment of a slow cooker, there is no opportunity to drive off moisture as there is in an oven, so excess moisture in the form of sauce or liquid that has leached out of vegetables can cause havoc when it comes to casseroles that need cohesiveness. In addition to controlling the amount and thickness of our sauces, we also found it important to sauté (and in some cases microwave) all of the vegetables, like in our Lazy Man's Stuffed Cabbage (page 229). This both drives off excess moisture and builds additional flavor through browning.

Pasta: Raw or Cooked?

We found that, with the exception of lasagna noodles, we could add raw pasta to the slow cooker, provided that we cooked it on high and included plenty of sauce for the pasta to absorb and cook through. Cooked on low, the starches in the raw pasta were never able to set and resulted in casseroles full of blown-out pieces of pasta. As for our lasagnas, we attempted to incorporate raw noodles and cook on high—as we had with our other baked pastas—but found the denser casserole remained underdone in the middle. We found success when we precooked the noodles until al dente, then cooked the lasagna on low with a moderate amount of sauce. We also found that curly-edged noodles were a must—no-boil lasagna noodles disintegrated into mush.

Chicken Enchilada Casserole

Serves 6 to 8   **Cooking Time** about 4 hours on Low

✔ **WHY THIS RECIPE WORKS:** Chicken enchilada casserole turns the individual stuffed rolls into an easier, layered dish. We created a flavorful sauce base for the chicken filling by sautéing aromatics, tomato paste, chili powder, and cumin before we simmered them with chicken broth and tomato sauce. Using corn tortillas for the layers added rich flavor, but they dissolved in the slow cooker. Alternating toasted corn tortillas and toasted flour tortillas (which didn't dissolve) provided the perfect combination of flavor and texture. For a crispy topping, you can sprinkle the casserole with some torn tortillas and extra cheese during the last 10 minutes of cooking.

	Vegetable oil spray
10	(6-inch) corn tortillas
9	(6-inch) flour tortillas
3	tablespoons vegetable oil
2	onions, minced
⅓	cup tomato paste
3	tablespoons chili powder
8	garlic cloves, minced
2	teaspoons ground cumin
1	(15-ounce) can tomato sauce
1½	cups low-sodium chicken broth
4	cups shredded cooked chicken (see page 222)
2	cups shredded Monterey Jack cheese (8 ounces)
½	cup minced fresh cilantro
2	tablespoons minced jarred pickled jalapeños
½	teaspoon salt

1. Line slow cooker with aluminum foil collar, then line with foil sling and coat with vegetable oil spray (see page 225). Position oven rack 6 inches from broiler element and heat broiler. Arrange corn tortillas directly on oven rack and broil until spotty brown on both sides, 2 to 4 minutes per side. Transfer corn tortillas to plate and repeat with flour tortillas.

2. Heat oil in 12-inch skillet over medium-high heat until shimmering. Add onions, tomato paste, chili powder, garlic, and cumin and cook until onions are softened and lightly browned, 8 to 10 minutes. Stir in tomato sauce and chicken broth, scraping up any browned bits, and simmer until thickened slightly, about 5 minutes. Measure out and reserve 1 cup sauce for serving. Stir chicken, 1 cup Monterey Jack, cilantro, jalapeños, and salt into remaining sauce.

3. Place 3 flour tortillas in bottom of prepared slow cooker. Layer with 2 corn tortillas, one-third of chicken mixture, and 2 more corn tortillas. Repeat layering two more times, ending with chicken-mixture layer. Sprinkle with remaining 1 cup Monterey Jack. Cover and cook until casserole is heated through, about 4 hours on low.

4. Let casserole cool for 20 minutes. Using sling, transfer casserole to serving platter and serve with reserved sauce.

QUICK PREP TIP BROILING TORTILLAS
To get the most out of the tortillas for our Chicken Enchilada Casserole, we found it helpful to broil them first to both dry them out and give them a nice, toasty flavor. Rather than use a baking sheet or broiler pan, we found it best to lay the tortillas right on the oven rack and broil them for 4 to 8 minutes, flipping them over halfway through the broiling time.

Beef Pot Pie

Serves 6 to 8   **Cooking Time** 9 to 11 hours on Low or 5 to 7 hours on High

WHY THIS RECIPE WORKS: There is really no way to make a pot pie in the slow cooker from start to finish because you could never cook the pastry topping in the moist heat of a slow cooker. That said, you can make a great slow-cooker pot pie filling (this recipe makes enough for two pot pies), and then it's a snap to add a premade pie crust topping and bake it just before serving. For the filling, we browned our aromatics with tomato paste for a rich, complex base that allowed us to skip browning the beef—a big timesaver.

2	tablespoons vegetable oil
2	onions, minced
10	ounces white mushrooms, trimmed and halved if small or quartered if large
2	carrots, peeled and cut into ½-inch pieces
3	tablespoons tomato paste
2	tablespoons minced fresh thyme or 2 teaspoons dried
3	garlic cloves, minced
¼	cup all-purpose flour
1½	cups low-sodium chicken broth
¼	cup dry red wine
1	tablespoon soy sauce
1	(2-pound) boneless beef chuck roast, trimmed and cut into ¾-inch pieces (see page 59) Salt and pepper
1	cup frozen peas
1	(15-ounce) box Pillsbury Pie Crust (includes 2 crusts)

1. Heat oil in 12-inch skillet over medium-high heat until shimmering. Add onions, mushrooms, carrots, tomato paste, thyme, and garlic and cook until vegetables are softened and lightly browned, 8 to 10 minutes. Stir in flour and cook for 1 minute. Slowly whisk in broth and wine, scraping up any browned bits and smoothing out any lumps; transfer to slow cooker.

2. Stir soy sauce into slow cooker. Season beef with salt and pepper and nestle into slow cooker. Cover and cook until beef is tender, 9 to 11 hours on low or 5 to 7 hours on high. Let beef filling settle for 5 minutes, then remove fat from surface using large spoon. Stir in peas and season with salt and pepper to taste. (Filling can be refrigerated in airtight container for up to 2 days or frozen for up to 1 month. Reheat filling gently, adding additional broth as needed to loosen sauce consistency, before assembling pies.)

3. Adjust oven racks to upper-middle and lower-middle positions and heat oven to 425 degrees. Divide beef filling between two 9-inch pie plates. Gently lay 1 pie crust over top of each, then trim and crimp edges, and cut 4 vent holes.

4. Place pies on rimmed baking sheets and bake until crusts are deep golden brown, about 25 minutes, switching baking sheets halfway through baking time. Let cool for 10 minutes before serving.

QUICK PREP TIP TOPPING A POT PIE
Gently lay a pie crust over the filling in a 9-inch pie plate, then trim the edge of the dough so that it overhangs the plate by about ½ inch. Fold the edge of dough under and crimp the folded edge. Cut four oval-shaped vents, each about 2 inches long, in the top.

Lazy Man's Stuffed Cabbage

Serves 6 to 8   **Cooking Time** about 4 hours on Low

WHY THIS RECIPE WORKS: For this dish we envisioned a recipe with tender cabbage, moist meat filling, and robust sauce in a layered casserole form—no rolling and stuffing required. We also hoped to avoid sautéing the meat (ground beef and bratwurst) and blanching the cabbage. Luckily, we found the long cooking time guaranteed that meat added raw would emerge fully cooked; as for the cabbage, parcooking it in the microwave was the solution. Feel free to use leftover or precooked rice (see page 196).

Vegetable oil spray
1   head green cabbage (2 pounds), cored and cut into 1-inch pieces
3   tablespoons vegetable oil
    Salt and pepper
2   onions, minced
3   garlic cloves, minced
1   teaspoon ground ginger
½   teaspoon ground cinnamon
¼   teaspoon ground nutmeg
3   tablespoons all-purpose flour
1   (28-ounce) can tomato sauce
¼   cup packed brown sugar
3   tablespoons red wine vinegar
2   slices high-quality white sandwich bread, torn into quarters
¼   cup whole milk
1   pound 85 percent lean ground beef
1   pound bratwurst, removed from its casing
2   cups cooked rice

1. Line slow cooker with aluminum foil collar and coat with vegetable oil spray (see page 225). Microwave cabbage with 1 tablespoon oil and ½ teaspoon salt in bowl, stirring occasionally, until softened, 15 to 20 minutes. Drain cabbage and discard liquid.

2. Heat remaining 2 tablespoons oil in 12-inch skillet over medium-high heat until shimmering. Add onions, garlic, ginger, cinnamon, and nutmeg and cook until onions are softened and lightly browned, 8 to 10 minutes.

3. Transfer half of onion mixture to large bowl; set aside. Stir flour into skillet with remaining onion mixture and cook over medium-high heat for 1 minute. Stir in tomato sauce, sugar, and vinegar, scraping up any browned bits, and season with salt and pepper to taste.

4. Add bread and milk to bowl with onion mixture and mash to paste with fork. Mix in ground beef, bratwurst, rice, ½ teaspoon salt, and ¼ teaspoon pepper using hands.

5. Spread ½ cup sauce over bottom of prepared slow cooker. Pinch off one-third of meat mixture into tablespoon-sized pieces and drop over sauce. Spread one-third of cabbage over meat. Spoon one-third of remaining sauce mixture over cabbage. Repeat layering two more times. Cover and cook until beef is tender, about 4 hours on low. Remove foil collar and let casserole cool for 20 minutes before serving.

QUICK PREP TIP PREPPING CABBAGE
First, cut the cabbage into quarters, then trim and discard the hard core. Then separate the cabbage into small stacks of leaves that flatten when pressed and slice the cabbage into ¼-inch-thick strips. For chopped cabbage (as in the Lazy Man's Stuffed Cabbage recipe above), simply continue to chop the strips into 1-inch pieces.

Shepherd's Pie

Serves 6 to 8   **Cooking Time** 6 to 8 hours on Low or 3 to 5 hours on High

✔ **WHY THIS RECIPE WORKS:** Shepherd's pie is certainly a classic among hearty casseroles, but achieving the characteristic tender meat and rich flavors in the filling can be a challenge in the slow cooker. Browning the beef to develop flavor is standard in most traditional recipes, but produced overcooked, gritty meat in the slow cooker. To fix this, we found mixing the raw beef with a panade—a mixture of bread and milk often used in meatballs—before browning it worked wonders. A little tomato paste and soy sauce also helped to add meaty flavor and richness. As for the mashed potato topping, we simply whipped up a batch of our favorite spuds, spread it evenly on the top, and let it heat through at the end of the cooking time. You can use our Homemade Mashed Potato Topping recipe or any kind of prepared mashed potatoes found at the market (found often in the prepared food and/or refrigerated section). Be sure your mashed potatoes are warm and have a loose but not soupy texture; otherwise, they will be difficult to spread over the beef filling.

2	slices high-quality white sandwich bread, torn into quarters
¼	cup whole milk
2	pounds 85 percent lean ground beef
	Salt and pepper
¼	cup vegetable oil
10	ounces white mushrooms, trimmed and halved if small or quartered if large
2	onions, minced
2	carrots, peeled and cut into ½-inch pieces
3	tablespoons tomato paste
3	garlic cloves, minced
1	tablespoon minced fresh thyme or 1 teaspoon dried
⅓	cup all-purpose flour
1½	cups low-sodium chicken broth
¼	cup heavy cream
1	tablespoon soy sauce
1	cup frozen peas
3	cups mashed potatoes

1. Mash bread and milk into paste in large bowl using fork. Mix in ground beef, ½ teaspoon salt, and ½ teaspoon pepper using hands.

2. Heat 2 tablespoons oil in 12-inch skillet over medium-high heat until shimmering. Add beef mixture, 1 pound at a time, and cook while breaking up any large pieces with wooden spoon until no longer pink, about 3 minutes per pound; transfer to slow cooker.

3. Heat remaining 2 tablespoons oil in skillet over medium-high heat until shimmering. Add mushrooms, onions, carrots, tomato paste, garlic, and thyme and cook until vegetables are softened and lightly browned, 8 to 10 minutes. Stir in flour and cook for 1 minute. Slowly whisk in broth, scraping up any browned bits and smoothing out any lumps; transfer to slow cooker.

4. Stir heavy cream and soy sauce into slow cooker. Cover and cook until beef is tender, 6 to 8 hours on low or 3 to 5 hours on high.

5. Let beef filling settle for 5 minutes, then remove fat from surface using large spoon. Stir in peas and season with salt and pepper to taste. Spoon mashed potatoes over beef filling and smooth into even layer using spatula. Cover and cook on high until potatoes are heated through, 20 to 30 minutes. Let cool 20 minutes before serving.

QUICK PREP TIP HOMEMADE MASHED POTATO TOPPING

Cover 1½ pounds russet potatoes, peeled, sliced ¾ inch thick, and rinsed well, with water in large saucepan. Bring to boil, then reduce to simmer and cook until tender, 18 to 20 minutes. Drain potatoes, wipe pot dry, then return potatoes to pot. Mash potatoes thoroughly with potato masher. Fold in 3 tablespoons melted unsalted butter and ¾ cup hot half-and-half. Add additional hot half-and-half as needed until potatoes have a loose but not soupy texture. Season with salt and pepper to taste. Makes 3 cups.

Spinach and Mushroom Lasagna

Serves 6 to 8   **Cooking Time** about 4 hours on Low

✔ **WHY THIS RECIPE WORKS:** We think lasagna is the ultimate slow-cooker casserole, but our early attempts at slow-cooker lasagna yielded gummy noodles and washed-out flavors. With a few tricks, however, we were able to turn things around. First, we found that no-boil noodles simply didn't work in the slow cooker—they turned much too soft. Turning to regular lasagna noodles, we found that precooking the noodles was the solution to gummy, underdone noodles. Sautéing the mushrooms with some garlic helped to build a flavorful filling and also enabled us to remove excess moisture. As for the cream sauce, homemade sauces separated and curdled in the slow cooker, but store-bought alfredo sauce remained intact and kept things easy.

Vegetable oil spray

8 curly-edged lasagna noodles (7 ounces), broken in half

Salt and pepper

1 tablespoon extra-virgin olive oil

1½ pounds white mushrooms, trimmed and sliced thin

2 garlic cloves, minced

20 ounces frozen spinach, thawed, squeezed dry (see page 278), and chopped coarse

1 (15-ounce) jar alfredo sauce

1¾ cups ricotta cheese (15 ounces)

1¼ cups grated Parmesan cheese (2½ ounces)

½ cup minced fresh basil

1 large egg

4 cups shredded mozzarella cheese (1 pound)

1. Line slow cooker with aluminum foil collar, then line with foil sling and coat with vegetable oil spray (see page 225). Bring 4 quarts water to boil in large pot. Add broken lasagna noodles and 1 tablespoon salt and cook, stirring often, until al dente. Drain noodles, rinse under cold water until cool, then spread out in single layer over clean kitchen towels and let dry. (Do not use paper towels; they will stick to noodles.)

2. Heat oil in pot over medium-high heat until shimmering. Add mushrooms, garlic, and ¼ teaspoon salt, cover, and cook until mushrooms are softened, about 5 minutes. Uncover and continue to cook until mushrooms are dry and browned, 5 to 10 minutes longer. Stir in spinach and alfredo sauce, scraping up any browned bits, and season with salt and pepper to taste.

3. In bowl, mix ricotta, 1 cup Parmesan, basil, egg, ½ teaspoon salt, and ½ teaspoon pepper together. Spread ½ cup mushroom-spinach sauce into prepared slow cooker.

4. Arrange 4 lasagna noodle pieces in slow cooker (see page 234—they may overlap), then dollop 9 rounded tablespoons of ricotta mixture over noodles. Sprinkle with 1 cup mozzarella, then spoon 1 cup more mushroom-spinach sauce over top. Repeat layering of lasagna noodles, ricotta mixture, mozzarella, and mushroom-spinach sauce twice more.

5. For final layer, arrange remaining 4 noodles in slow cooker, then top with remaining mushroom-spinach sauce and sprinkle with remaining mozzarella and remaining Parmesan. Cover and cook until lasagna is heated through, about 4 hours on low.

6. Let lasagna cool for 20 minutes. Using sling, transfer lasagna to serving platter and serve.

Sausage Lasagna

Serves 6 to 8   **Cooking Time** about 4 hours on Low

✔ **WHY THIS RECIPE WORKS:** Following the success of our Spinach and Mushroom Lasagna (page 232), we decided to create a hearty sausage version. Boosting the flavors of the ricotta filling with a hefty amount of Parmesan and some fragrant basil certainly helped our cause, as did boldly flavored Italian sausage. To keep things simple, we found spooning dollops of ricotta over the noodles—instead of spreading it—and pinching off pieces of raw sausage helped to streamline assembly. As for the sauce, the test kitchen's favorite jarred sauce (Bertolli Tomato and Basil Sauce) worked perfectly.

Vegetable oil spray
8 curly-edged lasagna noodles (7 ounces), broken in half
Salt and pepper
1¾ cups ricotta cheese (15 ounces)
1¼ cups grated Parmesan cheese (2½ ounces)
½ cup minced fresh basil
1 large egg
1 (24-ounce) jar tomato sauce
1 pound Italian sausage, removed from its casing
4 cups shredded mozzarella cheese (1 pound)

1. Line slow cooker with aluminum foil collar, then line with foil sling and coat with vegetable oil spray (see page 225). Bring 4 quarts water to boil in large pot. Add broken lasagna noodles and 1 tablespoon salt and cook, stirring often, until al dente. Drain noodles, rinse under cold water until cool, then spread out in single layer over clean kitchen towels and let dry. (Do not use paper towels; they will stick to noodles.)

2. In bowl, mix ricotta, 1 cup Parmesan, basil, egg, ½ teaspoon salt, and ½ teaspoon pepper together. Spread ½ cup tomato sauce into prepared slow cooker

3. Arrange 4 lasagna noodle pieces in slow cooker (they may overlap), then dollop 9 rounded tablespoons of ricotta mixture over noodles. Pinch off one-third of sausage into tablespoon-sized pieces and drop over ricotta. Sprinkle with 1 cup mozzarella, then spoon ½ cup sauce over top. Repeat layering of lasagna noodles, ricotta mixture, mozzarella, and sauce twice more.

4. For final layer, arrange remaining 4 noodles in slow cooker, then top with remaining sauce and sprinkle with remaining mozzarella and remaining Parmesan. Cover and cook until lasagna is heated through, about 4 hours on low.

5. Let lasagna cool for 20 minutes. Using sling, transfer lasagna to serving platter and serve.

QUICK PREP TIP **ASSEMBLING LASAGNA IN A SLOW COOKER**
We tried several different methods for arranging the rectangular lasagna noodle pieces in the oval-shaped slow cooker and, though they all worked fine, we preferred to arrange them lengthwise. Lay the noodles as evenly as possible in each layer, overlapping them slightly, or leaving small bare spots, as needed.

Baked Ziti with Pepperoni, Mushrooms, and Ricotta

Serves 6   **Cooking Time** about 3 hours on High

✔ **WHY THIS RECIPE WORKS:** For a fresh and flavorful take on baked ziti, we came up with this rich and zesty version, which features pepperoni and, as a finishing touch, dollops of ricotta cheese and shredded mozzarella cheese. We cooked the aromatics and vegetables together both for flavor and to drive off the moisture released by the mushrooms. Crushed tomatoes and cream form the base of the sauce and the raw pasta cooks perfectly on high.

	Vegetable oil spray
2	tablespoons extra-virgin olive oil
2	onions, minced
10	ounces white mushrooms, trimmed and sliced thin
1	green bell pepper, stemmed, seeded, and cut into ½-inch pieces (see page 91)
4	garlic cloves, minced
1	tablespoon minced fresh oregano or 1 teaspoon dried
1	(28-ounce) can crushed tomatoes
½	cup heavy cream
8	ounces ziti (2½ cups)
6	ounces sliced pepperoni
½	teaspoon salt
¼	teaspoon pepper
1	(15-ounce) can tomato sauce
	Hot water, as needed
1	cup ricotta cheese (8 ounces)
1	cup shredded mozzarella cheese (4 ounces)
¼	cup chopped fresh basil

1. Line slow cooker with aluminum foil collar and coat with vegetable oil spray (see page 225). Heat oil in large pot over medium-high heat until shimmering. Add onions, mushrooms, bell pepper, garlic, and oregano and cook until vegetables are softened and lightly browned, 8 to 10 minutes.

2. Stir in tomatoes and heavy cream, scraping up any browned bits, and simmer until thickened slightly, about 5 minutes. Stir in ziti, pepperoni, salt, and pepper.

3. Transfer ziti mixture to prepared slow cooker and spread tomato sauce evenly over pasta. Cover and cook until pasta is tender, about 3 hours on high.

4. Remove foil collar. Gently stir pasta, adding hot water as needed to loosen sauce consistency. Dollop spoonfuls of ricotta over casserole, then sprinkle with mozzarella. Cover and let sit until cheese is melted, about 5 minutes. Sprinkle with basil before serving.

SMART SHOPPING PEPPERONI

Believe it or not, pepperoni dates back to ancient Rome where it was used as a convenient food for soldiers on the march. Yet it wasn't until the 20th century in New York City, when pepperoni was first put on top of a pizza, that it took off in terms of popularity. In fact, our recent tasting of sliced pepperoni turned up six national brands. Tasting them all straight from the package as well as baked on a pizza, we preferred those that tasted meaty, spicy, and chewy. The winning pepperoni, **Margherita Italian Style Pepperoni**, was praised for its balance of "meatiness and spice" as well as its "tangy and fresh" flavor. Some even picked up hints of "fruity licorice and peppery fennel."

Baked Ziti with Sausage and Peppers

Serves 6   **Cooking Time** about 3 hours on High

✔️ **WHY THIS RECIPE WORKS:** For this comfort food classic, we were determined to keep things easy and use raw, not cooked, pasta but when cooked on low, the pasta absorbed too much liquid and simply disintegrated into a soft, mushy mass—not very appealing. Cooking this dish on high, however, solved the problem since it brought the sauce to an actual simmer more quickly, thereby cooking and firming up the noodles. The sauce amount was crucial as well—too much caused bloated ziti and too little led to unevenly cooked ziti. A 28-ounce can of crushed tomatoes combined with ½ cup heavy cream formed the base of our sauce and a 15-ounce can of tomato sauce spread over the top of the casserole kept things moist. For flavor, browning Italian sausage with onions, peppers, and garlic was just the ticket. Serve with grated parmesan.

Vegetable oil spray
1 tablespoon extra-virgin olive oil
1 pound Italian sausage, removed from its casing
2 onions, minced
1 green bell pepper, stemmed, seeded, and cut into ½-inch pieces (see page 91)
1 red bell pepper, stemmed, seeded, and cut into ½-inch pieces (see page 91)
4 garlic cloves, minced
1 tablespoon minced fresh oregano or 1 teaspoon dried
1 (28-ounce) can crushed tomatoes
½ cup heavy cream
8 ounces ziti (2½ cups)
½ teaspoon salt
¼ teaspoon pepper
1 (15-ounce) can tomato sauce
Hot water, as needed
1 cup shredded mozzarella cheese (4 ounces)

1. Line slow cooker with aluminum foil collar and coat with vegetable oil spray (see page 225). Heat oil in large pot over medium-high heat until just smoking. Brown sausage well, breaking up large pieces with wooden spoon, about 5 minutes. Add onions, bell peppers, garlic, and oregano and cook until vegetables are softened and lightly browned, 8 to 10 minutes.

2. Stir in tomatoes and heavy cream, scraping up any browned bits, and simmer until thickened slightly, about 5 minutes. Stir in ziti, salt, and pepper.

3. Transfer ziti mixture to prepared slow cooker and spread tomato sauce evenly over pasta. Cover and cook until pasta is tender, about 3 hours on high.

4. Remove foil collar. Gently stir pasta, adding hot water as needed to loosen sauce consistency. Sprinkle with mozzarella, cover, and let sit until melted, about 5 minutes. Serve.

SMART SHOPPING FRESH VS. PRESHREDDED MOZZARELLA
Most supermarkets offer a variety of mozzarella choices that can be divided into two basic categories: high moisture (or fresh) and low moisture. Fresh mozzarella (left) comes in many sizes and is usually packed in brine. Its soft texture and milky flavor are best appreciated within a day or two of purchase, as it can quickly sour. Low-moisture mozzarella typically comes shrink-wrapped in a large block or preshredded in a resealable bag (right). This cheese, which was essentially developed for the U.S. pizza industry, is less perishable and melts into beautifully gooey strands. Because fresh mozzarella is more expensive, we tend to save it for eating raw and use low-moisture for cooking. Our favorite preshredded mozzarella is **Kraft Shredded Part-Skim Mozzarella**.

Chili Mac

Serves 8 to 10   **Cooking Time** about 2 hours on High

WHY THIS RECIPE WORKS: Chili mac is a classic American casserole in which a meaty, chili-flavored tomato sauce is blended with macaroni and cheese. Comfort food at its very best, this recipe, part chili, part pasta casserole, was definitely one we wanted to translate to the slow cooker. To develop the meaty chili sauce, we knew from past experience that we'd need to brown the meat (to which we added a panade for tenderness) for texture and flavor, so we used the skillet instead of the microwave to cook the onions and bell pepper along with a generous amount of garlic, chili powder, and cumin. A combination of crushed tomatoes and tomato sauce, added to the skillet after we browned the meat, created the proper consistency for our casserole. We added raw macaroni and water to this mixture and cooked it all on high, having learned from our baked ziti recipes (see pages 235 and 236) that this would deliver pasta that was properly cooked. We reserved a cup of the cheese for an appealingly cheesy topping.

Vegetable oil spray
1   slice high-quality white sandwich bread, torn into quarters
2   tablespoons whole milk
1   pound 85 percent lean ground beef
    Salt and pepper
3   tablespoons vegetable oil
2   onions, minced
1   red bell pepper, stemmed, seeded, and cut into ½-inch pieces (see page 91)
¼   cup chili powder
6   garlic cloves, minced
4   teaspoons ground cumin
1   (28-ounce) can crushed tomatoes
1   (15-ounce) can tomato sauce
1   tablespoon brown sugar
1   pound elbow macaroni
2½ cups water, plus extra hot water as needed
2   cups shredded Monterey Jack cheese (8 ounces)

1. Line slow cooker with aluminum foil collar and coat with vegetable oil spray (see page 225). Mash bread and milk into paste in large bowl using fork. Mix in ground beef, ¼ teaspoon salt, and ¼ teaspoon pepper using hands.

2. Heat oil in large pot over medium-high heat until shimmering. Add onions, bell pepper, chili powder, garlic, and cumin and cook until vegetables are softened and lightly browned, 8 to 10 minutes.

3. Stir in beef mixture and cook, breaking up any large pieces with wooden spoon, until no longer pink, about 3 minutes. Stir in tomatoes, tomato sauce, and brown sugar, scraping up any browned bits, and simmer until thickened slightly, about 5 minutes.

4. Stir in macaroni, water, 1 cup Monterey Jack, 1 teaspoon salt, and ¼ teaspoon pepper; transfer to prepared slow cooker. Sprinkle with remaining cup Monterey Jack. Cover and cook until pasta is tender, about 2 hours on high.

5. Remove foil collar. Gently stir pasta, adding additional hot water as needed to loosen sauce consistency. Season with salt and pepper to taste and serve.

SMART SHOPPING MACARONI
With so many brands of elbow macaroni on the market, which one should you buy? Are they all the same? To find out, we rounded up eight contenders and tasted them simply dressed with vegetable oil and in our recipe for classic macaroni and cheese. What we found is that an Italian brand (which makes pasta for the American market domestically) won our tasting by a large margin. Our tasters praised this brand, **Barilla Elbows**, for their "wheaty," "buttery" flavor and "firm texture," and they especially liked that these elbows have small ridges and a slight twist that "holds sauce well."

Macaroni and Cheese

Serves 6 to 8   **Cooking Time** about 2 hours on High

✔ **WHY THIS RECIPE WORKS:** Developing a creamy macaroni and cheese in the slow cooker is no small challenge. Cream sauces are notorious for breaking and curdling during extended cooking times, making macaroni and cheese a prime target for cooked noodles in a grainy, separated sauce. Developing a cheese sauce that stayed creamy in the slow cooker took some ingenuity, but in the end, we found that a combination of evaporated milk and condensed cheddar cheese soup, because of the stabilizers they contained, created a creamy base that didn't break. We also, much to our surprise, really liked the flavor of this recipe when made with them—it tasted rich and cheesy without even a hint that it had been made using canned soup. With the base sauce set we began adding the cheese. On its own, cheddar cheese provided excellent flavor, but brought back some of the grainy texture we had been trying to avoid. Mixing the cheddar with Monterey Jack cheese, which has a much creamier texture when melted, produced a sauce with excellent cheese flavor and a smooth consistency. To help boost the cheese flavor, we found that a little dry mustard and cayenne pepper did wonders. With our sauce assembled, we were ready to add the macaroni. As in some of our other slow-cooker pasta dishes, we found cooking raw macaroni on high and stirring additional water into the sauce produced pasta with the best texture. Placing a foil collar in the slow cooker before adding the macaroni mixture helped to prevent overbrowning.

Vegetable oil spray
2 **(12-ounce) cans evaporated milk**
2 **(11-ounce) cans condensed cheddar cheese soup**
2½ **cups water, plus extra hot water as needed**
Salt and pepper
1 **teaspoon dry mustard**
⅛ **teaspoon cayenne pepper**
2 **cups shredded sharp cheddar cheese (8 ounces)**
2 **cups shredded Monterey Jack cheese (8 ounces)**
1 **pound elbow macaroni**
1 **recipe Toasted Bread-Crumb Topping, optional (see page 241)**

1. Line slow cooker with aluminum foil collar and coat with vegetable oil spray (see page 225). Bring evaporated milk, condensed soup, water, 1 teaspoon salt, mustard, and cayenne to simmer in large pot. Slowly whisk in cheddar and Monterey Jack until completely melted, then stir in macaroni.

2. Transfer macaroni mixture to prepared slow cooker. Cover and cook until macaroni is tender, about 2 hours on high.

3. Remove foil collar. Gently stir pasta, adding hot water as needed to loosen sauce consistency. Season with salt and pepper to taste. Sprinkle with Toasted Bread-Crumb Topping, if using, and serve.

SMART SHOPPING SHARP CHEDDAR CHEESE
In a side-by-side taste test of sharp cheddars, we found three supermarket brands topped our list. We were surprised to find that modestly priced Cracker Barrel, which ended up in third place, outranked other cheddars that cost over twice as much. It was bested, however, by Vermont-made **Cabot Sharp Cheddar**, which sells for about $5 a pound, and Oregon-made Tillamook, which sells for about $10 a pound. All three possessed rich, tangy flavor and melted smoothly.

Tomato Macaroni and Cheese

Serves 6 to 8   **Cooking Time** about 2 hours on High

✔ **WHY THIS RECIPE WORKS:** Infused with big tomato flavor, this slow-cooker macaroni and cheese is certainly an eye opener. Following the method we developed for our Macaroni and Cheese (see page 239), we created a base with evaporated milk and condensed cheddar cheese soup, then boosted the cheese flavor with a combination of cheddar and Monterey Jack cheeses. When it came to incorporating tomatoes into the dish, we tried every type of tomato product we could think of, even ketchup and jarred tomato sauce. In the end, we found canned petite diced tomatoes provided the perfect balance of rich red color and bright tomato flavor. Backing down on the amount of water we incorporated with the raw pasta helped to account for the juice included with the tomatoes and ensured our pasta turned out properly cooked. A buttery crumb topping sprinkled on top just before serving provides the perfect finishing touch.

Vegetable oil spray

1 (28-ounce) can petite diced tomatoes

2 (12-ounce) cans evaporated milk

2 (11-ounce) cans condensed cheddar cheese soup

¾ cup water, plus extra hot water as needed

Salt and pepper

1 teaspoon dry mustard

⅛ teaspoon cayenne pepper

2 cups shredded sharp cheddar cheese (8 ounces)

2 cups shredded Monterey Jack cheese (8 ounces)

1 pound elbow macaroni

1 recipe Toasted Bread-Crumb Topping, optional

1. Line slow cooker with aluminum foil collar and coat with vegetable oil spray (see page 225). Bring tomatoes, evaporated milk, condensed soup, water, 1 teaspoon salt, mustard, and cayenne to simmer in large pot. Slowly whisk in cheddar and Monterey Jack until completely melted, then stir in macaroni.

2. Transfer macaroni mixture to prepared slow cooker. Cover and cook until macaroni is tender, about 2 hours on high.

3. Remove foil collar. Gently stir pasta, adding hot water as needed to loosen sauce consistency. Season with salt and pepper to taste. Sprinkle with Toasted Bread-Crumb Topping, if using, and serve.

QUICK PREP TIP   TOASTED BREAD-CRUMB TOPPING
Process 2 slices high-quality white sandwich bread, torn into pieces, to coarse crumbs in food processor, about 10 pulses. Melt 2 tablespoons butter in 12-inch skillet over medium heat. Add bread crumbs and toast, stirring often, until golden brown, 5 to 7 minutes. Transfer bread crumbs to bowl and season with salt and pepper to taste. Makes about 1 cup.

RATATOUILLE

On the Side

Orange-Glazed Carrots for a Crowd

Serves 8 to 10   **Cooking Time** 4 to 6 hours on Low

✔ **WHY THIS RECIPE WORKS:** Glazed carrots are one of those reliable side dishes we often turn to when hosting a holiday meal, and using the slow cooker eliminates all the last-minute fuss involved (and frees up the stovetop). Initially we tried cooking the carrots in broth but it detracted from their delicate sweet flavor. In the end, water that had been seasoned with a little sugar and salt was best for gently simmering the carrots. Once they were tender, we simply drained them and tossed them with tart orange marmalade, a pat of butter, and aromatic sage. The marmalade and butter melted to form a mock "glaze" that conveniently did not need to be reduced on the stovetop first. Simple, sweet, and delicious—nothing could be easier.

3	pounds carrots (about 18), peeled and sliced ¼ inch thick on bias
1½	cups water, plus extra hot water as needed
1	tablespoon sugar
	Salt and pepper
½	cup orange marmalade
2	tablespoons unsalted butter, softened
1½	teaspoons minced fresh sage

1. Combine carrots, water, sugar, and 1 teaspoon salt in slow cooker. Cover and cook until carrots are tender, 4 to 6 hours on low.

2. Drain carrots, then return to slow cooker. Stir in marmalade, butter, and sage. Season with salt and pepper to taste and serve. (This dish can be held on warm setting for 1 to 2 hours before serving; loosen with additional hot water as needed before serving.)

Honey-Glazed Carrots for a Crowd

Serves 8 to 10   **Cooking Time** 4 to 6 hours on Low

✔ **WHY THIS RECIPE WORKS:** Once we mastered the method for cooking carrots to perfection in the slow cooker, the possibilities for flavor variations seemed endless. In this version we traded the fruit preserves for a lesser amount of sweet honey and replaced the sage with bright parsley.

3	pounds carrots (about 18), peeled and sliced ¼ inch thick on bias
1½	cups water, plus extra hot water as needed
1	tablespoon sugar
	Salt and pepper
¼	cup honey
2	tablespoons unsalted butter, softened
1	tablespoon minced fresh parsley

1. Combine carrots, water, sugar, and 1 teaspoon salt in slow cooker. Cover and cook until carrots are tender, 4 to 6 hours on low.

2. Drain carrots then return to slow cooker. Stir in honey, butter, and parsley. Season with salt and pepper to taste and serve. (This dish can be held on warm setting for 1 to 2 hours before serving; loosen with additional hot water as needed before serving.)

Ratatouille

Serves 10 to 12   **Cooking Time** 4 to 6 hours on Low

WHY THIS RECIPE WORKS: This appealing French vegetable dish featuring eggplant, zucchini, and tomatoes hails from Provence and is great to have on hand because it can be eaten hot, cold, or at room temperature, tossed with pasta or couscous, served over polenta, or as an accompaniment to roasted meats. Traditionally, however, it is a labor of love, with many recipes demanding that each vegetable be cooked separately for the perfect texture. We found that the slow cooker eliminated much of this fussy preparation, though to ensure deep flavor after hours in the slow cooker we lightly browned the vegetables and aromatics in a skillet first. We added flour here as well so it would thicken the sauce, since the juices from the vegetables would not have a chance to evaporate in the slow cooker. Since the flavor of fresh tomatoes was muted after slow-cooking we opted to use canned diced instead, the flavor of which was lasting and sweet. A sprinkling of fresh Parmesan cheese and fresh basil help round out this simple dish.

6	tablespoons extra-virgin olive oil
2	eggplants (2 pounds), cut into 1-inch chunks
3	zucchini (1½ pounds), cut into 1-inch chunks
2	onions, halved and sliced ¼ inch thick
2	red bell peppers, stemmed, seeded, and cut into ½-inch pieces (see page 91)
2	garlic cloves, minced
2	teaspoons minced fresh thyme or ½ teaspoon dried
¼	cup all-purpose flour
1	(28-ounce) can diced tomatoes, drained, juice reserved
¼	cup chopped fresh basil or parsley
	Salt and pepper
	Grated Parmesan cheese, for serving

1. Heat 1 tablespoon oil in 12-inch skillet over medium-high heat until shimmering. Brown half of eggplant lightly on all sides, 5 to 7 minutes; transfer to slow cooker. Repeat with 1 tablespoon more oil and remaining eggplant; transfer to slow cooker. Working in two batches, repeat with 2 tablespoons more oil and zucchini; transfer each batch to slow cooker.

2. Heat remaining 2 tablespoons oil in skillet over medium-high heat until shimmering. Add onions, bell peppers, garlic, and thyme and cook until vegetables are softened and lightly browned, 8 to 10 minutes. Stir in flour and cook for 1 minute. Slowly whisk in reserved tomato juice, scraping up any browned bits and smoothing out any lumps; transfer to slow cooker.

3. Stir tomatoes into slow cooker. Cover and cook until vegetables are tender, 4 to 6 hours on low. Stir in basil, season with salt and pepper to taste, and serve with Parmesan. (This dish does not hold well on warm setting.)

QUICK PREP TIP CUTTING EGGPLANT
Cutting up an awkwardly shaped vegetable like eggplant can sometimes be a challenge. To cut an eggplant into even cubes for ratatouille, simply cut the eggplant crosswise into 1-inch-thick rounds, then cut the rounds into tidy 1-inch cubes.

Creamy Cauliflower with Bacon

Serves 8 to 10   **Cooking Time** 4 to 6 hours on Low

✔ **WHY THIS RECIPE WORKS:** Tender cauliflower smothered with a rich, velvety sauce and sprinkled with crisp bacon makes this a luxurious vegetable side dish few can resist. We used condensed cheddar cheese soup to make a super-easy, extra-creamy, and stable cheese sauce that wouldn't break after hours in the slow cooker. Since the cauliflower exudes liquid during cooking we knew the initial sauce mixture would have to be quite thick; otherwise, the resulting sauce would be too thin. We hydrated the melted condensed soup and cheese with a mere ¼ cup of water, which loosened the mixture just enough to easily coat the cauliflower. To give this dish a casserole feel, we coarsely chopped one of the cauliflower heads to act as a filler, much like rice or pasta, while the florets add texture.

Vegetable oil spray

4 **ounces bacon (about 4 slices), minced**

1 **(11-ounce) can condensed cheddar cheese soup**

¼ **cup water**
Salt and pepper

2 **cups shredded cheddar cheese (8 ounces)**

2 **heads cauliflower (4 pounds), cored, 1 head cut into 1-inch florets (6 cups) (see page 25), 1 head chopped coarse (6 cups)**

1 **tablespoon minced fresh parsley**

1. Line slow cooker with aluminum foil collar and coat with vegetable oil spray (see page 225). Cook bacon in large pot over medium heat until crisp, 5 to 7 minutes. Transfer bacon to paper towel–lined plate and refrigerate until serving. Pour off all bacon fat left in pot.

2. Bring condensed soup, water, ½ teaspoon pepper, and ⅛ teaspoon salt to simmer in pot. Slowly whisk in 1½ cups cheddar until completely melted; stir in cauliflower and coat evenly with sauce.

3. Transfer cauliflower mixture to prepared slow cooker and sprinkle with remaining ½ cup cheddar. Cover and cook until cauliflower is tender, 4 to 6 hours on low.

4. Remove foil collar, stir cauliflower well, and season with salt and pepper to taste. Microwave bacon on paper towel–lined plate until hot and crisp, about 30 seconds. Sprinkle cauliflower with crisp bacon and parsley before serving. (This dish does not hold well on warm setting.)

SMART SHOPPING CONDENSED CHEDDAR CHEESE SOUP
Though we are not huge fans of traditional casseroles made with condensed soup, we've found that it really was necessary in a few slow-cooker recipes such as our Macaroni and Cheese (page 239) and Creamy Cauliflower with Bacon side dish. Despite our best efforts to use a more traditional cheddar sauce in these recipes (a milk-based sauce with flour and cheese), we found it to be too unstable and it constantly curdled during the extended cooking times. Condensed cheese soup, on the other hand, which is stabilized for a long shelf life, is unbreakable and provides a stable, creamy platform on which we could easily build a flavorful cheese sauce. Throughout all of our months of recipe testing, we didn't encounter any brand of condensed cheese soup at the market other than Campbell's.

Green Bean Casserole

Serves 8 to 10   **Cooking Time** 4 to 6 hours on Low

WHY THIS RECIPE WORKS: We wanted to reinvent this classic to work in a slow cooker, freeing up valuable oven space and taking some of the last-minute stress out of entertaining. Many versions of this recipe call for using frozen—or, yikes, canned—green beans swimming in condensed cream of mushroom soup and topped with canned fried onions. (The best part being the tasty, crispy onions.) As you might guess, we wanted something more. Starting from scratch, we used fresh, raw beans and mushrooms. The beans were perfectly tender after cooking though the mushrooms had to be browned first for flavor and texture. Since we already had a skillet out it was easy to build a classic sauce of broth and cream, bound with flour, which we simmered briefly to reduce it and concentrate its flavor. The beans exuded moisture as they cooked, however, and the resulting sauce was far too thin. Increasing the flour made it thicker but also pasty. On impulse, we ground a handful of canned fried onions in the food processor then stirred them into the sauce with the flour. This not only thickened the sauce but also added a major boost of flavor. Topping the finished casserole with homemade buttery bread crumbs and more fried onions left tasters scrambling for seconds. Fresh green beans are essential here—frozen beans will turn to mush in the slow cooker.

3	**cups canned fried onions**
2	**slices high-quality white sandwich bread, torn into quarters**
5	**tablespoons unsalted butter**
10	**ounces white or cremini mushrooms, trimmed and sliced ¼ inch thick**
4	**garlic cloves, minced**
2	**teaspoons minced fresh thyme or ½ teaspoon dried**
¾	**teaspoon salt**
½	**teaspoon pepper**
¼	**cup all-purpose flour**
1¼	**cups low-sodium chicken broth**
1¼	**cups heavy cream**
2	**pounds green beans, trimmed and cut into 1-inch lengths**

1. Pulse 1 cup fried onions in food processor until finely ground, about 10 pulses; set aside. Pulse bread in food processor to coarse crumbs, about 10 pulses. Melt 2 tablespoons butter in 12-inch skillet over medium heat. Add bread crumbs and remaining 2 cups fried onions and toast, stirring often, until golden brown, 5 to 7 minutes; set aside for serving.

2. Wipe skillet clean with paper towels. Melt remaining 3 tablespoons butter in skillet over medium-high heat. Add mushrooms, garlic, thyme, salt, and pepper and cook until mushrooms are softened and lightly browned, 8 to 10 minutes.

3. Stir in processed fried onions and flour and cook for 1 minute. Slowly whisk in broth and cream, scraping up any browned bits and smoothing out any lumps. Bring to simmer and cook, stirring occasionally, until very thick and creamy, about 10 minutes; transfer to slow cooker.

4. Add beans to slow cooker and coat evenly with sauce. Cover and cook until beans are tender, 4 to 6 hours on low. Sprinkle with reserved bread-crumb mixture before serving. (This dish does not hold well on warm setting.)

SMART SHOPPING CANNED FRIED ONIONS
It wouldn't be green bean casserole without fried onions on top. We increased their impact by grinding some of the onions and using them to thicken and flavor the sauce.

Dixie Collard Greens

Serves 6   **Cooking Time** 9 to 11 hours on Low or 5 to 7 hours on High

WHY THIS RECIPE WORKS: Any Southerner will tell you that collard greens require long cooking and the smokiness of cured pork, and we tend to agree. Slow-cooking this hearty green in liquid tempers its assertive bitterness, and for that reason we thought it ideally suited to the slow cooker. After cooking the greens in varying amounts of liquid, we found that 6 cups total was ideal. This may sound like a lot, but in order for the collards to cook properly all of them must be in contact with the cooking liquid. A combination of seasoned broth and water made these greens palatable, and a ham hock imparted characteristic smokiness. We brightened up the liquid at the end of cooking with cider vinegar and hot pepper sauce—feel free to spoon a hefty amount of this liquid over your greens and sop it up with cornbread or biscuits.

1	onion, minced
6	garlic cloves, minced
1	tablespoon vegetable oil
½	teaspoon red pepper flakes
2	pounds collard greens, stemmed, and leaves cut into 1-inch pieces (see page 33)
4	cups low-sodium chicken broth
2	cups water
	Salt and pepper
1	smoked ham hock, rinsed
2	tablespoons cider vinegar, plus extra as needed
	Hot sauce

1. Microwave onion, garlic, oil, and red pepper flakes in bowl, stirring occasionally, until onion is softened, about 5 minutes; transfer to slow cooker.

2. Stir collard greens, broth, water, and 1 teaspoon salt into slow cooker. Nestle ham hock into slow cooker. Cover and cook until collard greens are tender, 9 to 11 hours on low or 5 to 7 on high.

3. Transfer ham hock to cutting board, let cool slightly, then shred into bite-size pieces (see page 21), discarding skin, bones, and excess fat. Stir shredded ham and vinegar into slow cooker. Season with salt, pepper, additional vinegar, and hot sauce to taste. (This dish can be held on warm setting for 1 to 2 hours before serving.)

SMART SHOPPING SALAD SPINNER
A salad spinner is an indispensable piece of kitchen equipment, especially when cleaning a large amount of greens, as in our Dixie Collard Greens recipe. Over the years, we've tested numerous brands and styles of salad spinners, but the same spinner always lands on top. The **OXO Good Grips Salad Spinner** has spun happily for years in the test kitchen; it boasts a large basket size, easy-to-use hand pump, and brake button to help stop the spin on a dime.

Sweet and Sour Braised Red Cabbage

Serves 6   **Cooking Time** 4 to 6 hours on Low

✔ **WHY THIS RECIPE WORKS:** The slow cooker, with its moist heat environment, is perfect for braising cabbage. However, adding the cabbage directly to the slow cooker left it too crunchy for our liking. To get the texture just right, we had to precook it in the microwave to soften it slightly. This step had the added benefit of getting rid of excess moisture that was otherwise detracting from the flavors of the dish. For the braising medium we selected sweet and fruity apple cider, enhancing it with traditional spices such as cinnamon, caraway seeds, and allspice. A bit of sugar rounded out the sweetness while vinegar perked up the flavors and added balance. Since tasters found the cabbage a little lean, we added bacon, which imparted a smoky depth and richness. This dish is a great accompaniment to roasted meats such as duck, pork, or beef. You can double this recipe if desired.

1	head red cabbage (2 pounds), cored and sliced thin (see page 229)
1	tablespoon vegetable oil
	Salt and pepper
4	ounces bacon (about 4 slices), minced
1	onion, minced
2	fresh thyme sprigs or ½ teaspoon dried
1	cinnamon stick or ¼ teaspoon ground cinnamon
½	teaspoon caraway seeds
¼	teaspoon ground allspice
1½	cups apple cider
2	tablespoons light brown sugar, plus extra as needed
3	bay leaves
2	tablespoons cider vinegar, plus extra as needed

1. Microwave cabbage with oil and ½ teaspoon salt in bowl, stirring occasionally, until softened, 15 to 20 minutes. Drain cabbage and discard liquid; transfer to slow cooker.

2. Cook bacon in 12-inch skillet over medium-high heat until crisp, about 5 minutes. Add onion, thyme sprigs, cinnamon stick, caraway seeds, and allspice and cook until onion is softened and lightly browned, 8 to 10 minutes. Stir in ½ cup cider, scraping up any browned bits; transfer to slow cooker.

3. Stir remaining cup cider, 1 tablespoon sugar, and bay leaves into slow cooker. Cover and cook until cabbage is tender, 4 to 6 hours on low.

4. Discard thyme sprigs, cinnamon stick, and bay leaves. Stir in vinegar and remaining tablespoon sugar. Season with salt, pepper, additional sugar, and additional vinegar to taste and serve. (This dish can be held on warm setting for 1 to 2 hours before serving.)

QUICK PREP TIP COOKING CABBAGE
For both our Lazy Man's Stuffed Cabbage casserole (page 229) and Sweet and Sour Braised Red Cabbage, we parcooked the cabbage in the microwave. Simply place the cabbage in a large bowl and microwave it, uncovered, on high power until it is wilted and has released some liquid, 15 to 20 minutes. Drain away the liquid before adding the cabbage to the slow cooker.

Cider-Braised Squash Puree

Serves 6   **Cooking Time** 4 to 6 hours on Low

✔ **WHY THIS RECIPE WORKS:** With its silky-smooth texture and earthy, slightly sweet flavor, pureed butternut squash is one of our favorite side dishes. Since the flavor of butternut squash is quite delicate, our goal was to bump up its flavor so it would taste great even after hours in the slow cooker. At first we tried cooking the squash in water to cover but this washed away some of the squash's subtle flavor, leaving us with a bland, watery puree. Since the squash exuded a lot of moisture during cooking we thought we could take down the amount of water dramatically. In the end it only took a bare minimum—½ cup—to properly braise the squash. Even this small amount of water, however, seemed to be diluting the squash flavor significantly. We considered alternative braising liquids and settled on apple cider, which accented the squash's innate sweetness and added a brightness tasters liked. A small amount of heavy cream and some butter rounded out the flavors and added complexity without overpowering the squash flavor. You can substitute delicata squash for the butternut squash if desired.

3	**pounds butternut squash, peeled, seeded, and cut into 1-inch chunks**
½	**cup apple cider, plus extra as needed**
	Salt and pepper
4	**tablespoons (½ stick) unsalted butter, melted**
2	**tablespoons heavy cream, warmed**
2	**tablespoons brown sugar, plus extra as needed**

1. Combine squash, cider, and ½ teaspoon salt in slow cooker. Cover and cook until squash is tender, 4 to 6 hours on low.

2. Mash squash thoroughly with potato masher. Stir in butter, cream, and sugar. Season with salt, pepper, and additional brown sugar to taste, and serve. (This dish can be held on warm setting for 1 to 2 hours before serving; loosen with additional hot cider as needed before serving.)

SMART SHOPPING BUTTERNUT SQUASH

It certainly saves prep time to buy precut, peeled butternut squash, but how does the flavor and texture of this timesaver squash stand up to a whole squash you cut up yourself? The test kitchen has found that whole squash that you peel and cube yourself can't be beat in terms of flavor or texture, but when you are trying to make the most of every minute, already peeled, halved squash is perfectly acceptable. Avoid the precut chunks; test kitchen tasters agree they are dry and stringy, with barely any squash flavor.

Mashed Potatoes

Serves 6   **Cooking Time** 4 to 6 hours on Low

✔ **WHY THIS RECIPE WORKS:** Creamy, velvety soft, and with a buttery finish, these slow-cooker mashed potatoes will keep you coming back for more. Instead of vigorously boiling potatoes in water, which can lead to a thin and watery mash, we used the slow cooker to gently simmer the potatoes in a moderate amount of seasoned water. We preferred Yukon Gold potatoes because their medium starch level and buttery richness translated to creamy potatoes in the slow cooker environment; you can use higher-starch russets but the potatoes will be more grainy.

3	pounds Yukon Gold potatoes (about 6 medium), peeled and cut into 1-inch chunks
1½	cups water
	Salt and pepper
6	tablespoons (¾ stick) unsalted butter, melted
1	cup half-and-half, warmed, plus extra as needed

1. Combine potatoes, water, and 1 teaspoon salt in slow cooker. Cover and cook until potatoes are tender, 4 to 6 hours on low.

2. Drain potatoes, then return to slow cooker. Mash potatoes thoroughly with potato masher. Fold in butter, then half-and-half. Add more half-and-half as needed to adjust consistency. Season with salt and pepper to taste and serve. (This dish can be held on warm setting for 1 to 2 hours before serving; loosen with additional warm half-and-half as needed before serving.)

Buttermilk and Scallion Mashed Potatoes

Serves 6   **Cooking Time** 4 to 6 hours on Low

✔ **WHY THIS RECIPE WORKS:** For a tangier, richer take on everyday mashed potatoes, we added a combination of buttermilk and sour cream instead of half-and-half and we folded in sliced scallions for bright flavor before serving.

3	pounds Yukon Gold potatoes (about 6 medium), peeled and cut into 1-inch chunks
1½	cups water
2	garlic cloves, peeled
1	bay leaf
	Salt and pepper
3	tablespoons unsalted butter, melted
½	cup buttermilk, warmed, plus extra as needed
½	cup sour cream, room temperature
3	scallions, sliced thin

1. Combine potatoes, water, garlic cloves, bay leaf, and 1 teaspoon salt in slow cooker. Cover and cook until potatoes are tender, 4 to 6 hours on low.

2. Drain potatoes, discarding garlic cloves and bay leaf, then return to slow cooker. Mash potatoes thoroughly with potato masher. Fold in butter, then buttermilk and sour cream. Add more buttermilk as needed to adjust consistency. Fold in scallions, season with salt and pepper to taste, and serve. (This dish can be held on warm setting for 1 to 2 hours before serving; loosen with additional warm buttermilk as needed before serving.)

Mashed Sweet Potatoes

Serves 6   **Cooking Time** 4 to 6 hours on Low

✔ **WHY THIS RECIPE WORKS:** Mashed sweet potatoes are often overdressed as a marshmallow-topped casserole at Thanksgiving. When it comes to flavor, however, this candied, overly sweet and spiced concoction doesn't hold a candle to an honest sweet potato mash. With a deep, natural sweetness that requires little assistance, the humble sweet potato, we think, tastes far better when prepared with a minimum of ingredients. It is a side dish, after all, not a dessert. After gently simmering the potatoes in seasoned water we mashed them with butter, a little heavy cream, and a mere 1½ teaspoons sugar, just enough to accentuate their natural sweetness. We left the spices in the spice rack and let the sweet potatoes' natural flavor shine through.

3   **pounds sweet potatoes (about 4 medium), peeled and cut into 1-inch chunks**
1½ **cups water**
    Salt and pepper
6   **tablespoons (¾ stick) unsalted butter, melted**
3   **tablespoons heavy cream, warmed, plus extra as needed**
1½ **teaspoons sugar**

1. Combine potatoes, water, and 1 teaspoon salt in slow cooker. Cover and cook until potatoes are tender, 4 to 6 hours on low.

2. Drain potatoes, then return to slow cooker. Mash potatoes thoroughly with potato masher. Fold in butter, cream, and sugar. Add more cream as needed to adjust consistency. Season with salt and pepper to taste and serve. (This dish can be held on warm setting for 1 to 2 hours before serving; loosen with additional warm heavy cream as needed before serving.)

Mashed Sweet Potatoes with Coconut Milk and Cilantro

Serves 6   **Cooking Time** 4 to 6 hours on Low

✔ **WHY THIS RECIPE WORKS:** There is nothing ordinary about these sweet potatoes which get their creamy richness from coconut milk and zesty flavor from garlic, red pepper flakes, and cilantro. We like to serve these potatoes with a simple roast pork loin or braised chicken.

3   **pounds sweet potatoes (about 4 medium), peeled and cut into 1-inch chunks**
1½ **cups water**
2   **garlic cloves, peeled**
¼   **teaspoon red pepper flakes**
    Salt and pepper
1   **cup light coconut milk, warmed, plus extra as needed**
1½ **teaspoons sugar**
2   **tablespoons minced fresh cilantro**

1. Combine potatoes, water, garlic cloves, red pepper flakes, and 1 teaspoon salt in slow cooker. Cover and cook until potatoes are tender, 4 to 6 hours on low.

2. Drain potatoes, discarding garlic cloves, then return to slow cooker. Mash potatoes thoroughly with potato masher. Fold in coconut milk and sugar. Add more coconut milk as needed to adjust consistency. Fold in cilantro, season with salt and pepper to taste, and serve. (This dish can be held on warm setting for 1 to 2 hours before serving; loosen with additional hot coconut milk as needed before serving.)

Scalloped Potatoes

Serves 6 to 8   **Cooking Time** 4 to 6 hours on Low

✔️ **WHY THIS RECIPE WORKS:** Tender potatoes and a smooth, creamy sauce with lots of cheese flavor are the hallmarks of well-made scalloped potatoes. All too frequently, however, the potatoes emerge over- or undercooked, the sauce separates, and the cheese burns. And this is in the oven, no less. Translating this recipe to the slow cooker would be no small feat. We had a hard time getting this creamy sauce to work with flour as it sometimes separated and also made the dish pasty. Ultimately, thickening the mixture with cornstarch, which remained consistently stable over the long cooking time, was best. Russet potatoes were selected for their fluffy texture; however, they were cooking unevenly: The bottom layer cooked through while the top remained crunchy. Giving the potatoes a head start in the microwave solved this problem and a little cream prevented them from sticking together. Monterey Jack and pungent sharp cheddar melted to produce a smooth, flavorful sauce. Extra-sharp cheddar, which becomes grainy during slow cooking, should not be substituted for the sharp cheddar. Don't soak the potatoes in water before using or the scalloped potatoes will be watery.

	Vegetable oil spray
3	pounds russet potatoes (about 6 medium), peeled and sliced ¼ inch thick
1¼	cups heavy cream
1	tablespoon unsalted butter
4	garlic cloves, minced
2	teaspoons minced fresh thyme or ½ teaspoon dried
1¼	cups low-sodium chicken broth
4½	tablespoons cornstarch
¼	teaspoon salt
½	teaspoon pepper
¾	cup shredded sharp cheddar cheese (3 ounces)
¾	cup shredded Monterey Jack cheese (3 ounces)

1. Line slow cooker with aluminum foil collar and coat with vegetable oil spray (see page 225). Microwave potatoes with 2 tablespoons cream in covered bowl, stirring occasionally, until nearly tender, 6 to 8 minutes; let cool slightly.

2. Melt butter in medium saucepan over medium heat. Add garlic and thyme and cook until fragrant, about 30 seconds. Whisk broth, remaining cream, cornstarch, salt, and pepper together, then whisk into saucepan. Bring to simmer, whisking constantly, and simmer until thickened, about 1 minute. Slowly whisk in cheddar and Monterey Jack until completely melted.

3. Spread half of sauce over bottom of prepared slow cooker. Shingle potatoes over sauce, then spread remaining sauce evenly over potatoes. Cover and cook until potatoes are tender, 4 to 6 hours on low.

4. Remove foil collar and let potatoes cool for 20 minutes before serving. (This dish does not hold well on warm setting.)

QUICK PREP TIP PREPPING POTATOES
Making scalloped potatoes in the slow cooker requires even ¼-inch-thick slices of potatoes and shingling the potatoes into even, tidy layers in the slow cooker. Feel free to use a mandoline or food processor to slice the potatoes as they can make the job easier.

Creamed Corn

Serves 6 **Cooking Time** about 4 hours on Low

WHY THIS RECIPE WORKS: Taste this homemade, slow-cooker version of creamed corn with its rich flavor and lush texture, and you'll never dream of reaching for the canned alternative. With loads of sweet corn flavor, this comforting side comes together with a minimum of prep and just a handful of pantry staples—shallot, garlic, thyme, and cayenne pepper. We knew fresh corn would be essential for flavor here. To get the best in both texture and flavor we used a combination of whole kernels cut away from the cobs and grated corn (the large holes of a box grater work best for this task). The kernels became tender yet maintained a slight bite owing to the gentle cooking environment of the slow cooker, while the grated corn contributed to a thicker body in the dish. Don't forget to scrape the cobs with the back of a knife to collect the flavorful corn pulp and "milk" before discarding them. This important step dramatically improves the corn flavor. Because heavy cream, unlike milk or half-and-half, can be simmered without curdling, it is essential here.

Vegetable oil spray
1 shallot, minced
2 tablespoons unsalted butter, melted
1 garlic clove, minced
½ teaspoon minced fresh thyme or ⅛ teaspoon dried
Pinch cayenne pepper
5 ears corn, husks and silk removed
1½ cups heavy cream, plus extra as needed
Salt and pepper

1. Line slow cooker with aluminum foil collar and coat with vegetable oil spray (see page 225). Microwave shallot, butter, garlic, thyme, and cayenne in bowl, stirring occasionally, until shallot is softened, about 2 minutes.

2. Cut kernels from 3 ears of corn into large bowl, reserving cobs. Grate remaining 2 ears of corn over large holes of box grater into bowl, reserving cobs. Firmly scrape all cobs with back of butter knife into bowl to collect pulp and milk.

3. Stir cream, shallot mixture, ¼ teaspoon salt, and ⅛ teaspoon pepper into bowl with corn; transfer to prepared slow cooker. Cover and cook until corn is tender, about 4 hours on low.

4. Remove foil collar and stir corn well. Season with salt and pepper to taste and serve. (This dish can be held on warm setting for 1 to 2 hours before serving; loosen with additional warm heavy cream as needed before serving.)

QUICK PREP TIP PREPARING FRESH CORN
First cut the kernels off three ears of corn using a paring knife, standing the cobs upright inside a large bowl to help catch any flying kernels. Second, grate two more ears of corn over the large holes of a box grater into the bowl. Third, use the back of a butter knife to scrape the corn milk from all of the spent cobs; this natural cornstarch helps thicken the sauce.

Easy Polenta

Serves 8 to 10   **Cooking Time** 4 to 6 hours on Low

✔ **WHY THIS RECIPE WORKS:** For the ultimate creamy texture and deep corn flavor, traditional polenta requires a fairly lengthy cooking time and lots of stirring. In translating this recipe to the slow cooker, we weren't concerned with the cooking time but did want this version to be essentially hands-free. (If we had to stir frequently we might as well stick to the stovetop.) Not wanting to sacrifice creaminess or texture, we focused on getting the polenta perfectly tender. Remarkably, thanks to the gentle heat of the slow cooker, our typical ratio of water to polenta worked just fine. We whisked together the polenta with the water and salt at the start and cooked it until tender, without stirring. It was done when most of the liquid had been absorbed and we finished the dish by stirring in nutty Parmesan, a pat of butter, and more seasoning. Use good-quality Parmesan cheese here and finely grate it yourself. Supermarket-grated cheese has a coarse, granular texture and doesn't melt as nicely. Be sure to use traditional polenta, not instant polenta.

	Vegetable oil spray
7½	**cups water, plus extra hot water as needed**
1½	**cups polenta**
	Salt and pepper
2	**cups grated Parmesan cheese (4 ounces)**
2	**tablespoons unsalted butter**

1. Coat slow cooker with vegetable oil spray. Whisk water, polenta, and 1½ teaspoons salt together in slow cooker. Cover and cook until polenta is tender, 4 to 6 hours on low.

2. Stir in Parmesan and butter, season with salt and pepper to taste, and serve. (This dish can be held on warm setting for 1 to 2 hours before serving; loosen with additional hot water as needed before serving.)

SMART SHOPPING POLENTA

Buying polenta can be confusing. Not only are there several different types of polenta widely available at the market—traditional, instant, and precooked—but they all simply label themselves as "polenta." Here's how to tell them apart. The real deal (left) is labeled as either "polenta" or "traditional polenta" and it is nothing more than a package of coarse-ground cornmeal with a very even grind and no small floury bits; it is often sold in clear bags so you can inspect it. Don't be tempted to buy coarse-grain cornmeal without the term "polenta" clearly listed on the package, as it often includes a portion of fine, floury bits that will make the polenta taste gluey. Instant polenta (center) and precooked tubes of polenta (right) are parcooked convenience products that have short cooking times (much like instant rice). Precooked polenta is easy to spot thanks to its tube-like packaging. Instant polenta, on the other hand, can look just like traditional polenta at the store and is only identifiable by the word "instant" in its title (which can be slightly hidden, in our experience).

Classic Thanksgiving Stuffing

Serves 10 to 12   **Cooking Time** about 4 hours on Low

✔ **WHY THIS RECIPE WORKS:** Cooking the Thanksgiving stuffing is always a thorny issue since the turkey takes over the oven for most of the day. To eliminate this issue, we wanted a slow-cooker recipe for stuffing, one that would serve a crowd and was just as flavorful and substantial. The first and most critical step was to dry out the bread in the oven (if you really plan ahead, you can skip the oven and simply leave the bread cubes out on the counter for a few days to become stale). We browned the sausage first to render its fat, which we used in combination with butter to soften the aromatics. Chicken broth and eggs moistened the stuffing, ensuring it didn't dry out after hours in the slow cooker.

	Vegetable oil spray
2	pounds high-quality white sandwich bread, cut into ½-inch cubes (16 cups)
12	ounces Italian sausage, removed from its casing
4	tablespoons (½ stick) unsalted butter
2	onions, minced
3	celery ribs, minced
2	tablespoons minced fresh thyme or 2 teaspoons dried
2	tablespoons minced fresh sage or 2 teaspoons dried
2½	cups low-sodium chicken broth
2	large eggs
1	teaspoon salt
1	teaspoon pepper

1. Line slow cooker with aluminum foil collar and coat with vegetable oil spray (see page 225). Adjust oven racks to upper-middle and lower-middle positions and heat oven to 250 degrees. Spread bread over two rimmed baking sheets and bake, shaking pans occasionally, until edges have dried but centers are slightly moist, about 45 minutes, switching baking sheets halfway through baking. Let bread cool for 10 minutes; transfer to very large bowl.

2. Brown sausage well in 12-inch skillet over medium-high heat, breaking up large pieces with wooden spoon, about 5 minutes; transfer to bowl with dried bread.

3. Add butter to sausage drippings left in pan and melt over medium-high heat. Add onions, celery, thyme, and sage and cook until vegetables are softened and lightly browned, 8 to 10 minutes. Stir in ½ cup broth, scraping up any browned bits; transfer to bowl with bread.

4. Whisk remaining 2 cups broth, eggs, salt, and pepper together, then pour over bread mixture and toss gently to incorporate; transfer to prepared slow cooker. Cover and cook until stuffing is heated through, about 4 hours on low.

5. Remove foil collar and let stuffing cool for 10 minutes before serving. (This dish can be held on warm setting for 1 to 2 hours before serving.)

SMART SHOPPING SANDWICH BREAD
Curious as to whether or not there was a difference between the various brands of white sandwich bread sold at the market, we gathered eight of the leading brands, in country styles with larger slices whenever possible, and held a blind tasting. Tasters sampled the bread plain, in grilled cheese sandwiches, and prepared as croutons seasoned only with olive oil and salt. They gave top marks to the hearty texture of **Arnold Country Classics Country White** (left) and **Pepperidge Farm Farmhouse Hearty White** (right), which has larger-than-usual slices and what tasters called "perfect structure" and "subtle sweetness."

Cajun Cornbread Dressing with Chorizo

Serves 10 to 12   **Cooking Time** about 4 hours on Low

✔ **WHY THIS RECIPE WORKS:** Since our method for making Classic Thanksgiving Stuffing (see page 261) in the slow cooker proved so successful, we were inspired to create another recipe, this time for cornbread dressing. We love the spicy, sweet flavors of Cajun cuisine and thought they would pair nicely with our cornbread stuffing. As with our classic stuffing, it was important to cube the cornbread and dry it out in the oven first. Our next step was replacing traditional pork sausage with something zestier. The obvious choice was spicy smoked Cajun andouille sausage; however, its texture was unappealing after hours in the slow cooker. Garlicky spiced chorizo fared much better and complemented the cornbread just as well. To give this stuffing a Cajun boost we added red bell peppers, garlic, and fiery cayenne pepper to our traditional mix of aromatics. And since cornbread needs a bit more moisture than white bread, we added more liquid here, along with an extra egg to bind it together. For the best in flavor and texture, make the cornbread from scratch (see the recipe below). Store-bought cornbread will work, but it tends to be sweeter and cakier than homemade cornbread, resulting in a slightly soggy and sweet-tasting dressing.

	Vegetable oil spray
2	pounds cornbread, cut into 1-inch cubes (12 cups)
2	onions, minced
2	red bell peppers, stemmed, seeded, and cut into ½-inch pieces (see page 91)
3	celery ribs, minced
4	tablespoons (½ stick) unsalted butter, melted
6	garlic cloves, minced
2	tablespoons minced fresh thyme or 2 teaspoons dried
2	tablespoons minced fresh sage or 2 teaspoons dried
⅛	teaspoon cayenne pepper
12	ounces chorizo sausage, cut into ½-inch pieces
2	cups low-sodium chicken broth
1	cup heavy cream
3	large eggs
1	teaspoon salt
1	teaspoon pepper

1. Line slow cooker with aluminum foil collar and coat with vegetable oil spray (see page 225). Adjust oven racks to upper-middle and lower-middle positions and heat oven to 250 degrees. Spread cornbread over two rimmed baking sheets and bake, shaking pans occasionally, until edges have dried but centers are slightly moist, about 45 minutes, switching baking sheets halfway through baking. Let cornbread cool for 10 minutes; transfer to very large bowl.

2. In separate bowl, microwave onions, bell peppers, celery, butter, garlic, thyme, sage, and cayenne, stirring occasionally, until vegetables are softened, about 5 minutes. Stir microwaved vegetables and chorizo into cooled cornbread.

3. Whisk broth, cream, eggs, salt, and pepper together, then pour over cornbread mixture and toss gently to incorporate. Let cornbread mixture sit until liquid has been completely absorbed, about 3 minutes; transfer to prepared slow cooker. Cover and cook until stuffing is heated through, about 4 hours on low.

4. Remove foil collar and let stuffing cool for 10 minutes before serving. (This dish can be held on warm setting for 1 to 2 hours before serving.)

QUICK PREP TIP CORNBREAD FOR DRESSING

Whisk together 3 large eggs, 1 cup buttermilk, and 1 cup milk in bowl. In separate bowl, whisk together 1½ cups yellow cornmeal, 1½ cups all-purpose flour, 1 tablespoon baking powder, ¾ teaspoon baking soda, 4 teaspoons sugar, and ¾ teaspoon salt. Make well in cornmeal mixture, add egg mixture, and stir together until just combined. Stir in 3 tablespoons melted unsalted butter. Transfer batter to greased 13 by 9-inch baking dish. Bake in 375-degree oven until golden, 30 to 40 minutes. Let cool completely, then cut into 1-inch cubes for dressing. Makes 12 cups.

No-Fuss Brown Rice

Serves 6   **Cooking Time** about 2 hours on High

✔ **WHY THIS RECIPE WORKS:** Many people shy away from cooking brown rice because it takes longer to cook and can be trickier than white rice to cook evenly. Since we enjoy the health benefits of brown rice, we wondered if the slow cooker might take the challenge out of cooking it. Could the steady, gentle heat of the slow cooker do the work for us? After some burnt rice and undercooked grains we found that brown rice needs a head start with boiling water in the slow cooker, but that it can indeed emerge with light and fluffy grains every time. Cooking on high was best. Brown rice cooked on low got mushy over time. For an accurate measurement of water bring a tea kettle to a boil then measure 3 cups.

Vegetable oil spray
2   cups long grain brown rice
1   tablespoon unsalted butter or vegetable oil
½   teaspoon salt
3   cups boiling water

1. Coat slow cooker with vegetable oil spray. Add rice, butter, and salt to prepared slow cooker, then stir in boiling water. Cover and cook until rice is tender, about 2 hours on high.

2. Fluff rice with fork and season with salt and pepper to taste. Drape towel over top of slow cooker, cover with lid, and let sit for 5 minutes before serving. (This dish does not hold well on warm setting.)

Mexican Brown Rice

Serves 6   **Cooking Time** about 2 hours on High

✔ **WHY THIS RECIPE WORKS:** This easy variation on plain brown rice is the perfect accompaniment to enchiladas and tacos as well as many simply prepared meat and fish dishes. Minced garlic, tomato paste, and cayenne infuse the rice with flavor as it cooks, while a few ingredients stirred in before serving—cilantro, scallions, and lime juice—provide bright, zesty flavor.

Vegetable oil spray
2   cups long grain brown rice
1   tablespoon unsalted butter or vegetable oil
½   teaspoon salt
¾   teaspoon chili powder
3   cups boiling water
3   tablespoons tomato paste
2   garlic cloves, minced
¼   cup minced fresh cilantro
2   scallions, sliced thin
Lime juice, as needed

1. Coat slow cooker with vegetable oil spray. Add rice, butter, salt, and chili powder to prepared slow cooker. Whisk together boiling water, tomato paste, and garlic, then pour into the slow cooker. Cover and cook until rice is tender, about 2 hours on high.

2. Fluff rice with fork and fold in cilantro, and scallions. Season with salt, pepper, and lime juice to taste. Drape towel over top of slow cooker, cover with lid, and let sit for 5 minutes before serving. (This dish does not hold well on warm setting.)

Parmesan Risotto

Serves 6   **Cooking Time** about 2 hours on High

✔ **WHY THIS RECIPE WORKS:** Risotto usually demands the cook's attention from start to finish which is why this hands-off slow-cooker version is so appealing. Here, we started the usual way by sautéing the aromatics in butter and then quickly cooking the rice until it turned translucent. After adding the wine and allowing the rice to absorb it, we poured the whole mixture into the slow cooker along with 3 cups of a hot broth–water mixture. We tried adding the all of the cooking liquid to the slow cooker at the outset but this resulted in blown-out grains and a porridgelike mush. We backed down slowly on liquid until we arrived at a moderate 3 cups. This was the right amount to achieve nicely tender grains, but the risotto was not yet creamy. Gently stirring in more of the hot cooking liquid at the end helped us obtain the creaminess we were after. It took 2 cups more liquid to get the consistency we liked and about 1 minute of stirring. The grains eagerly soaked up the additional liquid, becoming creamy, yet retaining their characteristic slight bite. (The consistency of risotto is largely a matter of personal taste; if you prefer a looser texture, add most of the extra broth mixture in step 3.) Finished with butter, nutty Parmesan, a dash of lemon juice, and fresh chives, this risotto is so creamy that no one would suspect you didn't spend time at the stovetop laboriously stirring it. Arborio rice, which is high in starch, gives risotto its characteristic creaminess; do not substitute other types of rice here.

Vegetable oil spray
4 tablespoons (½ stick) unsalted butter
1 onion, minced
1 garlic clove, minced
2 cups Arborio rice
½ cup dry white wine
5 cups low-sodium chicken broth
1½ cups water
1 cup grated Parmesan cheese (2 ounces)
2 tablespoons minced fresh chives
1 teaspoon fresh lemon juice
Salt and pepper

1. Coat slow cooker with vegetable oil spray. Melt 2 tablespoons butter in 12-inch skillet over medium heat. Add onion and cook until softened, about 5 minutes. Add garlic and cook until fragrant, about 30 seconds. Stir in rice and cook, stirring often, until ends of rice kernels are transparent, about 3 minutes. Stir in wine and cook until fully absorbed, about 1 minute; transfer to slow cooker.

2. Bring broth and water to boil in saucepan. Stir 3 cups hot broth mixture into slow cooker. Cover and cook until rice is tender, about 2 hours on high.

3. Return reserved broth mixture to boil. Slowly stream 2 cups more hot broth mixture into slow cooker, stirring gently, until liquid is absorbed and risotto is creamy, about 1 minute. Gently stir in Parmesan, chives, remaining 2 tablespoons butter, and lemon juice. (Adjust risotto consistency with additional hot broth mixture as needed.) Season with salt and pepper to taste and serve. (This dish does not hold well on warm setting.)

SMART SHOPPING ARBORIO RICE
To find the best brand of Arborio rice, we cooked up batches of Parmesan Risotto with two domestically grown brands of Arborio rice and four Italian imports; all brands are widely available in supermarkets. To our surprise, the winning rice hailed not from the boot, but from the Lone Star State. Texas-grown **RiceSelect Arborio Rice** was prized over all others with "creamy, smooth" grains and a "good bite."

Boston Baked Beans

Serves 6   **Cooking Time** 9 to 11 hours on Low or 5 to 7 hours on High

✔ **WHY THIS RECIPE WORKS:** The deep flavor and creamy texture of Boston baked beans is the product of simple, yet judiciously chosen ingredients and slow—very slow—cooking. It seemed a natural recipe to adapt to the slow cooker and, given our location, we were under pressure to get this recipe just right. We wanted our slow-cooker "baked" beans to have all the flavor and texture of the real deal and began by determining the correct ratio of water to beans. Once we had evenly tender beans throughout we focused on building flavor with traditional ingredients—salt pork, onion, molasses, brown sugar, and bay leaves went into the slow cooker. The flavor was decent but not deep enough and the texture of the salt pork was not appealing. We decided it was necessary to pull out a skillet to render the fat from the salt pork and soften the onion first, which made the salt pork palatable and greatly intensified the flavors of the dish. To brighten things up at the end of cooking, spicy mustard and a splash of cider vinegar went in, along with a touch more molasses to round out the acidity. Don't use dark or blackstrap molasses, which will become bitter tasting in the slow cooker. Be sure to let the beans sit and finish thickening for 10 minutes before serving.

4   **ounces salt pork, rind removed, cut into ½-inch pieces**
1   **onion, minced**
4½   **cups water, plus extra hot water as needed**
1   **pound dried navy beans (2½ cups), picked over and rinsed**
¼   **cup plus 1 tablespoon mild molasses**
¼   **cup packed dark brown sugar**
2   **bay leaves**
1   **tablespoon prepared brown mustard**
2   **teaspoons cider vinegar**
     Salt and pepper

1. Cook salt pork in 12-inch nonstick skillet over medium heat until most of fat has rendered, about 7 minutes. Add onion and cook until softened, about 5 minutes; transfer to slow cooker.

2. Stir water, beans, ¼ cup molasses, sugar, and bay leaves into slow cooker. Cover and cook until beans are tender, 9 to 11 hours on low or 5 to 7 hours on high.

3. Discard bay leaves. Stir in remaining tablespoon molasses, mustard, and vinegar and let sit until thickened slightly, about 10 minutes. Season with salt and pepper to taste and serve. (This dish can be held on warm setting for 1 to 2 hours before serving; loosen with additional hot water as needed before serving.)

SMART SHOPPING SALT PORK
Salt pork is cut from the belly of a pig, and has been cured or preserved in salt. Salt pork is marked by distinctive streaks of meat running through the fat, and for our Boston Baked Beans, we prefer to buy pieces of salt pork that are fattier, rather than leaner.

Barbecued Beans

Serves 6   **Cooking Time** 9 to 11 hours on Low or 5 to 7 hours on High

WHY THIS RECIPE WORKS: Following the success of our Boston Baked Beans (see page 266) we knew that beans were a side dish well suited for the slow cooker. After tasting different recipes we fell upon one for barbecued (also known as cowboy) beans and were instantly hooked. We knew how to cook the beans to perfection so we focused on building robust sweet, smoky, and spicy barbecue flavor. To keep things simple we turned to our preferred supermarket brand of barbecue sauce—Bull's Eye Original Barbecue Sauce. Barbecue sauce alone didn't add up to intense flavor so we incorporated smoky bacon; to keep things easy and avoid getting out our skillet to brown the bacon, we simply added whole slices to the slow cooker and removed them at the end. The dish was good and a little more barbecue sauce at the end freshened things up, but it still lacked complexity. For depth of flavor we replaced ½ cup of the water with brewed coffee here, which added just the complexity we were seeking. Serve these beans with hot sauce for heat.

1	onion, minced
4	garlic cloves, minced
1	tablespoon vegetable oil
4	cups water, plus extra hot water as needed
1	pound dried navy beans (2½ cups), picked over and rinsed
½	cup plus 2 tablespoons barbecue sauce
½	cup brewed coffee
⅓	cup packed dark brown sugar
4	ounces bacon (about 4 slices)
1	tablespoon prepared brown mustard
	Salt and pepper
	Hot sauce

1. Microwave onion, garlic, and oil in bowl, stirring occasionally, until onion is softened, about 5 minutes; transfer to slow cooker.

2. Stir water, beans, ½ cup barbecue sauce, coffee, sugar, and bacon slices into slow cooker. Cover and cook until beans are tender, 9 to 11 hours on low or 5 to 7 hours on high.

3. Discard bacon slices. Stir in remaining 2 tablespoons barbecue sauce and mustard and let sit until thickened slightly, about 10 minutes. Season with salt, pepper, and hot sauce to taste and serve. (This dish can be held on warm setting for 1 to 2 hours before serving; loosen with additional hot water as needed before serving.)

SMART SHOPPING DRIED BEANS
When shopping for beans, it is imperative to select "fresh" dried beans. Buy those that are uniform in size and have a smooth exterior. When dried beans are fully hydrated and cooked, they should be plump with a taut skin and have creamy insides; spent beans will have wrinkled skins and a dry, almost gritty texture. Uncooked beans should be stored in a cool, dry place in a sealed plastic or glass container. Though dried beans can be stored for up to one year, it is best to use them within a month or two of purchase.

Cuban-Style Black Beans

Serves 6   **Cooking Time** 9 to 11 hours on Low or 5 to 7 hours on High

WHY THIS RECIPE WORKS: Served as a side dish at almost every meal, black beans are at the heart of Cuban cuisine. Prior testing left us confident in our method for cooking the beans so we turned our attention to building layers of flavor. Pork is commonly added to the beans for much-needed depth so we began there. After trying bacon, ham, and a ham hock, we liked the smoky depth the ham hock added to the beans. Instead of adding aromatics to the beans at the start of cooking, we favored the custom of stirring a sofrito (typically sautéed onion, garlic, and green bell pepper) into the cooked beans instead. Microwaving the sofrito until the vegetables were tender saved us time and did not compromise flavor. This, along with chopped cilantro and lime juice, added a fresh layer of flavor to the beans without overwhelming them. Some recipes suggested pureeing the sofrito with some of the beans to thicken the sauce, but we preferred simply mashing the sofrito and beans in a bowl with a little of the cooking liquid. The texture of these beans is typically looser than that of other bean recipes. Serve with a dollop of sour cream and hot sauce to taste.

5	cups water, plus extra hot water as needed
1	pound dried black beans (2½ cups), picked over and rinsed
2	bay leaves
1	smoked ham hock, rinsed
1	onion, minced
1	green bell pepper, stemmed, seeded, and minced (see page 91)
6	garlic cloves, minced
2	tablespoons extra-virgin olive oil
2	tablespoons minced fresh oregano or 2 teaspoons dried
1½	teaspoons ground cumin
½	cup minced fresh cilantro
1	tablespoon fresh lime juice, plus extra as needed
	Salt and pepper

1. Stir water, beans, and bay leaves into slow cooker. Nestle ham hock into slow cooker. Cover and cook until beans are tender, 9 to 11 hours on low or 5 to 7 hours on high.

2. Discard bay leaves. Transfer ham hock to cutting board, let cool slightly, then shred into bite-size pieces (see page 21), discarding skin, bones, and excess fat.

3. Microwave onion, bell pepper, garlic, oil, oregano, and cumin in large bowl, stirring occasionally, until vegetables are tender, about 10 minutes.

4. Transfer 1 cup cooked beans and ½ cup cooking liquid to bowl with vegetables and mash smooth with potato masher. Stir vegetable mixture, shredded ham, cilantro, and lime juice into beans and let sit until thickened slightly, about 10 minutes. Season with salt, pepper, and additional lime juice to taste before serving. (This dish can be held on warm setting for 1 to 2 hours before serving; loosen with additional hot water as needed before serving.)

QUICK PREP TIP SORTING BEANS
Before cooking any dried beans, you should pick them over for any small stones or debris and then rinse them. The easiest way to check for small stones is to spread the beans out over a large plate or rimmed baking sheet.

Drunken Beans

Serves 6   **Cooking Time** 9 to 11 hours on Low or 5 to 7 hours on High

✔ **WHY THIS RECIPE WORKS:** Despite the presence of sausage, spices, and beer in this recipe, it was a bit of a challenge to achieve deep flavors in the slow cooker. We needed to sauté the aromatics in a skillet first, creating fond (flavorful browned bits on the pan bottom), which gave us a major boost in flavor. Adding beer directly to the slow cooker left an unappealing uncooked flavor that was too much, even for drunken beans. It was better to simmer it for a few minutes with the aromatics to get rid of its raw flavor. For heat, tasters preferred smoky chipotles, while chili powder, oregano, and garlic lent depth. Sugar rounded things out and kielbasa provided great meaty flavor. A hit of fresh lime juice and cilantro added brightness at the end. While the smaller navy and black beans in our other baked bean dishes did not require soaking prior to cooking, we found the extra step ensured that the large pinto beans in this dish turned perfectly tender.

1	tablespoon vegetable oil
1	onion, minced
4	garlic cloves, minced
1	tablespoon minced fresh oregano or 1 teaspoon dried
2	teaspoons minced canned chipotle chile in adobo sauce
1	teaspoon chili powder
¾	cup beer
2½	cups water, plus extra hot water as needed
1	pound dried pinto beans (2½ cups), picked over, salt-soaked (see page 35), and rinsed
8	ounces kielbasa sausage, cut into ½-inch pieces
1	tablespoon brown sugar
2	tablespoons minced fresh cilantro
1	tablespoon fresh lime juice
	Salt and pepper

1. Heat oil in 12-inch skillet over medium heat until shimmering. Add onion, garlic, oregano, chipotles, and chili powder and cook until softened and lightly browned, 8 to 10 minutes. Stir in beer, scraping up any browned bits, and simmer until thickened slightly, about 5 minutes; transfer to slow cooker.

2. Stir water, beans, sausage, and sugar into slow cooker. Cover and cook until beans are tender, 9 to 11 hours on low or 5 to 7 hours on high.

3. Stir cilantro and lime juice into beans and let sit until thickened slightly, about 10 minutes. Season with salt and pepper to taste before serving. (This dish can be held on warm setting for 1 to 2 hours before serving; loosen with additional hot water as needed before serving.)

SMART SHOPPING **BEER FOR COOKING**
Cooking intensifies the flavor of beer, so if you start with a dark or bitter brew, it will overwhelm the flavor of the final dish. We recommend using a light or medium beer, like a domestic lager, which will add just the right amount of depth of flavor without being all you taste in the finished dish.

FRENCH TOAST CASSEROLE

Eggs and Brunch

Spanish Egg and Potato Tortilla

Serves 8 to 10   **Cooking Time** about 4 hours on Low

WHY THIS RECIPE WORKS: Typically, a Spanish tortilla is made by slow-cooking potatoes and onions in olive oil and then adding beaten eggs to form a velvety cake somewhat like a frittata, with deep potato flavor. Served with a garlicky aïoli, it makes a great tapas dish when sliced into small squares or a hearty brunch or dinner when cut into wedges. Worried that the simplest version of a tortilla would be too bland emerging from a slow cooker, we chose to add chorizo and red bell pepper to the mix, along with a hefty dose of minced garlic and fresh oregano. To ensure that the potatoes were perfectly cooked, we sliced them thin then microwaved them before adding them to the slow cooker. And to deepen the flavor of this dish and render excess fat, we browned the chorizo in a skillet, adding the aromatics as well once it was cooked. Placing a foil collar and sling in the slow cooker before assembling the tortilla prevented overbrowning and made the tortilla easy to remove and serve. In a pinch, Yukon Gold potatoes can be substituted for the russets. Serve with hot sauce and Garlic Aïoli.

Vegetable oil spray
2   pounds russet potatoes (about 4 medium), peeled, quartered lengthwise, and sliced ⅛ inch thick (see page 274)
5   tablespoons extra-virgin olive oil
8   ounces chorizo sausage, cut into ½-inch pieces
2   onions, minced
1   red bell pepper, stemmed, seeded, and cut into ½-inch pieces (see page 91)
6   garlic cloves, minced
1   tablespoon minced fresh oregano or 1 teaspoon dried
¼   teaspoon red pepper flakes
12 large eggs
1   teaspoon salt
½   teaspoon pepper

1. Line slow cooker with aluminum foil collar, then line with foil sling and coat with vegetable oil spray (see page 225). Microwave potatoes and ¼ cup oil in large covered bowl, stirring occasionally, until nearly tender, about 7 minutes.

2. Heat remaining tablespoon oil in 12-inch skillet over medium-high heat until just smoking. Brown sausage well, about 3 minutes. Add onions, bell pepper, garlic, oregano, and red pepper flakes and cook until vegetables are softened and lightly browned, 8 to 10 minutes; transfer to bowl with potatoes and toss to combine.

3. Transfer potato mixture to prepared slow cooker and smooth into even layer. Whisk eggs, salt, and pepper together in bowl, then pour mixture evenly over potatoes. Gently press potatoes into egg mixture. Cover and cook until center of tortilla is set, about 4 hours on low.

4. Let tortilla cool for 20 minutes. Using sling, transfer tortilla to serving platter and serve.

ON THE SIDE GARLIC AÏOLI
Process 2 large egg yolks, 4 teaspoons fresh lemon juice, 1 minced garlic clove, ¼ teaspoon salt, ⅛ teaspoon sugar, and ⅛ teaspoon white pepper together in food processor until combined, about 10 seconds. With machine running, slowly drizzle in ¾ cup olive oil (or 6 tablespoons each extra-virgin olive oil and vegetable oil), about 30 seconds. Scrape down sides of bowl with rubber spatula and process for 5 seconds longer. Season with salt and pepper to taste. (Aïoli can be refrigerated in airtight container for up to 3 days.) Makes about 1 cup.

EGGS AND BRUNCH **273**

Sausage and Sun-Dried Tomato Tortilla

Serves 8 to 10   **Cooking Time** about 4 hours on Low

✓ **WHY THIS RECIPE WORKS:** Since our method for making a Spanish tortilla in the slow cooker proved so successful (see page 272), we were inspired to create another hearty version using Italian sausage instead of chorizo. Looking for an ingredient that would add both color and flavor to the tortilla, we settled on sun-dried tomatoes, which paired perfectly with the sausage and held up well in the slow-cooker environment. Browning the sausage on the stovetop proved essential to render excess fat and boost flavor and, following our established method, we also browned the aromatics before adding them to the slow cooker. In this version, we doubled the amount of garlic and red pepper flakes for a tortilla that is anything but mild. Placing a foil collar and sling in the slow cooker before assembling the tortilla prevented overbrowning and made the tortilla easy to remove and serve. In a pinch, Yukon Gold potatoes can be substituted for the russets. Serve with hot sauce and Garlic Aïoli (page 272).

	Vegetable oil spray
2	pounds russet potatoes (about 4 medium), peeled, quartered lengthwise, and sliced ⅛ inch thick
5	tablespoons extra-virgin olive oil
1	pound Italian sausage, removed from its casing
2	onions, minced
1	cup oil-packed sun-dried tomatoes, rinsed, patted dry, and chopped coarse
12	garlic cloves, minced
1	tablespoon minced fresh oregano or 1 teaspoon dried
½	teaspoon red pepper flakes
12	large eggs
1	teaspoon salt
½	teaspoon pepper

1. Line slow cooker with aluminum foil collar, then line with foil sling and coat with vegetable oil spray (see page 225). Microwave potatoes and ¼ cup oil in large covered bowl, stirring occasionally, until nearly tender, about 7 minutes.

2. Heat remaining tablespoon oil in 12-inch skillet over medium-high heat until just smoking. Brown sausage well, breaking up large pieces with wooden spoon, about 5 minutes; transfer to bowl with potatoes. Pour off all but 2 tablespoons fat left in skillet, add onions, tomatoes, garlic, oregano, and red pepper flakes and cook over medium-high heat until vegetables are softened and lightly browned, 8 to 10 minutes; transfer to bowl with potatoes and sausage and toss to combine.

3. Transfer potato mixture to prepared slow cooker and smooth into even layer. Whisk eggs, salt, and pepper together in bowl, then pour mixture evenly over potatoes. Gently press potatoes into egg mixture. Cover and cook until center of tortilla is set, about 4 hours on low.

4. Let tortilla cool for 20 minutes. Using sling, transfer tortilla to serving platter and serve.

QUICK PREP TIP **PREPPING POTATOES**
To cut the peeled potatoes into small pieces perfect for a potato tortilla, first quarter the potatoes lengthwise. Then slice the potato pieces crosswise into ⅛-inch-thick pieces. To be efficient, lay several potato pieces side by side on the cutting board and slice them simultaneously.

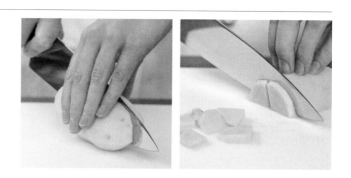

Classic Breakfast Strata with Sausage

Serves 8 to 10   **Cooking Time** about 4 hours on Low

✓ **WHY THIS RECIPE WORKS:** This rich-tasting strata makes an easy weekend breakfast for friends but it can also be the centerpiece of a holiday brunch. We found that pre-toasting the bread was key for producing a strata with a good texture, one that didn't turn to mush as it absorbed the eggy custard. And browning the sausage and aromatics gave the casserole deep flavor. To ensure flavor in every bite, we layered bread, sausage, and cheese before pouring on the egg mixture instead of simply stirring everything together. Placing a foil collar and sling in the slow cooker before assembling the strata prevented overbrowning and made the strata easy to remove and serve. Don't let this strata cook longer than 4 hours or it will become dried out and rubbery.

	Vegetable oil spray
¾	loaf supermarket French or Italian bread (12 ounces), cut into ½-inch pieces (12 cups)
1	tablespoon vegetable oil
8	ounces bulk breakfast sausage
1	onion, minced
2	garlic cloves, minced
2	teaspoons minced fresh thyme or ½ teaspoon dried
1½	cups shredded sharp cheddar cheese (6 ounces)
2½	cups half-and-half
9	large eggs
1	teaspoon salt
¼	teaspoon pepper

1. Line slow cooker with aluminum foil collar, then line with foil sling and coat with vegetable oil spray (see page 225). Adjust oven rack to middle position and heat oven to 225 degrees. Spread bread over rimmed baking sheet and bake, shaking pan occasionally, until dry and crisp, about 40 minutes.

2. Heat oil in 12-inch skillet over medium-high heat until just smoking. Brown sausage well, breaking up large pieces with wooden spoon, about 5 minutes; transfer to medium bowl. Pour off all but 2 tablespoons fat left in skillet, add onion, garlic, and thyme and cook over medium-high heat until onion is softened and lightly browned, 8 to 10 minutes; transfer to bowl with sausage and toss to combine.

3. Spread half of dried bread into prepared slow cooker and sprinkle with half of sausage mixture and ½ cup cheddar. Layer remaining dried bread, sausage mixture, and cheddar into slow cooker. Whisk half-and-half, eggs, salt, and pepper together in bowl, then pour mixture evenly over bread. Press gently on bread to submerge. Cover and cook until center of strata is set, about 4 hours on low.

4. Let strata cool for 20 minutes. To serve, either spoon strata onto individual plates or transfer strata to serving platter using sling.

QUICK PREP TIP **DRYING BREAD FOR CASSEROLES**
To ensure that the stratas (pages 275–278) and French Toast Casserole (page 282) have a lovely custardlike texture, rather than a wet and soggy one, it is important to dry the bread out in a 225-degree oven for about 40 minutes. Be sure to use a large baking sheet so that the bread cubes have plenty of room to dry out and shake the pan occasionally during baking.

Southwestern Breakfast Strata

Serves 8 to 10   **Cooking Time** about 4 hours on Low

✓ **WHY THIS RECIPE WORKS:** There is nothing ordinary about this spicy south-of-the border strata with its layers of bread and mixture of ham, peppers, chipotle chiles, cumin, and pepper Jack cheese. As with our other stratas, it was necessary to get our skillet out first—here we browned cut-up ham steak, the aromatics, and a red and green bell pepper to give the dish depth of flavor. A foil collar kept the custard mixture from burning and the sling made the strata easy to remove and serve. Don't let this strata cook longer than 4 hours or it will become dried out and rubbery.

	Vegetable oil spray
¾	loaf supermarket French or Italian bread (12 ounces), cut into ½-inch pieces (12 cups)
2	tablespoons vegetable oil
8	ounces ham steak, cut into ½-inch pieces
1	onion, minced
1	red bell pepper, stemmed, seeded, and cut into ½-inch pieces (see page 91)
1	green bell pepper, stemmed, seeded, and cut into ½-inch pieces (see page 91)
2	garlic cloves, minced
2	teaspoons minced canned chipotle chile in adobo sauce
2	teaspoons minced fresh thyme or ½ teaspoon dried
½	teaspoon ground cumin
1½	cups shredded pepper Jack cheese (6 ounces)
2½	cups half-and-half
9	large eggs
1	teaspoon salt
¼	teaspoon pepper

1. Line slow cooker with aluminum foil collar, then line with foil sling and coat with vegetable oil spray (see page 225). Adjust oven rack to middle position and heat oven to 225 degrees. Spread bread over rimmed baking sheet and bake, shaking pan occasionally, until dry and crisp, about 40 minutes (see page 275).

2. Heat oil in 12-inch skillet over medium-high heat until just smoking. Brown ham well, about 3 minutes. Add onion, bell peppers, garlic, chipotles, thyme, and cumin and cook until vegetables are softened and lightly browned, 8 to 10 minutes.

3. Spread half of dried bread into prepared slow cooker and sprinkle with half of ham mixture and ½ cup pepper Jack. Layer remaining dried bread, ham mixture, and pepper Jack into slow cooker. Whisk half-and-half, eggs, salt, and pepper together in bowl, then pour mixture evenly over bread. Press gently on bread to submerge. Cover and cook until center of strata is set, about 4 hours on low.

4. Let strata cool for 20 minutes. To serve, either spoon strata onto individual plates or transfer strata to serving platter using sling.

SMART SHOPPING EGGS

Theoretically, eggs come in three grades (AA, A, and B), six sizes (from peewee to jumbo), and a rainbow of colors. But the only grade we could find in the market was Grade A, the only colors were brown and white, and the only sizes were jumbo, extra-large, large, and medium. After extensive tasting, we could not discern any consistent flavor differences between egg sizes or colors. We only use large eggs in the test kitchen, but you can use this conversion chart to substitute other egg sizes.

Size	Weight
Medium	1.75 ounces
Large	2.00 ounces
Extra-Large	2.25 ounces
Jumbo	2.50 ounces

Mushroom and Spinach Breakfast Strata

Serves 8 to 10   **Cooking Time** about 4 hours on Low

✔ **WHY THIS RECIPE WORKS:** Once we mastered the method for our Classic Breakfast Strata with Sausage (see page 275), we wanted a recipe for a vegetarian version that would be equally satisfying. We turned to the classic pairing of mushrooms and spinach and swapped out the cheddar for nutty Gruyère, which served as a bold complement to the vegetables. To bring out the flavor of the mushrooms, we got out our skillet to brown them along with the aromatics and at the same time drive off any excess moisture, which would certainly ruin the texture of our strata. Stirring the spinach into the cooked mushroom mixture created a cohesive filling we could layer into the slow cooker along with dried bread and cheese before pouring in our eggy custard mixture. As with our other stratas, a foil collar kept the custard mixture from burning and the sling made the strata easy to remove and serve. Don't let this strata cook longer than 4 hours or it will become dried out and rubbery.

Vegetable oil spray

¾ loaf supermarket French or Italian bread (12 ounces), cut into ½-inch pieces (12 cups)

2 tablespoons vegetable oil

12 ounces white mushrooms, trimmed and sliced thin

1 onion, minced

2 garlic cloves, minced

2 teaspoons minced fresh thyme or ½ teaspoon dried

10 ounces frozen spinach, thawed, squeezed dry, and chopped coarse

1½ cups shredded Gruyère cheese (6 ounces)

2½ cups half-and-half

9 large eggs

1 teaspoon salt

¼ teaspoon pepper

1. Line slow cooker with aluminum foil collar, then line with foil sling and coat with vegetable oil spray (see page 225). Adjust oven rack to middle position and heat oven to 225 degrees. Spread bread over rimmed baking sheet and bake, shaking pan occasionally, until dry and crisp, about 40 minutes (see page 275).

2. Heat oil in 12-inch skillet over medium-high heat until shimmering. Add mushrooms, onion, garlic, and thyme and cook until vegetables are softened and lightly browned, 8 to 10 minutes; stir in spinach.

3. Spread half of dried bread into prepared slow cooker and sprinkle with half of mushroom mixture and ½ cup Gruyère. Layer remaining dried bread, mushroom mixture, and Gruyère into slow cooker. Whisk half-and-half, eggs, salt, and pepper together in bowl, then pour mixture evenly over bread. Press gently on bread to submerge. Cover and cook until center of strata is set, about 4 hours on low.

4. Let strata cool for 20 minutes. To serve, either spoon strata onto individual plates or transfer strata to serving platter using sling.

QUICK PREP TIP SQUEEZING FROZEN SPINACH
To rid the thawed spinach of excess water before adding it to strata or other recipes, simply wrap it in cheesecloth and squeeze it firmly.

Corned Beef Hash

Serves 6   **Cooking Time** about 4 hours on Low

✔ **WHY THIS RECIPE WORKS:** This slow-cooker version of corned beef hash captures what everyone loves about this diner classic with much less fuss. We turned to frozen diced or shredded potatoes to cut down on prep and we fried half of them to provide flavor and texture. Since we had our skillet out, we also sautéed the onions and aromatics. Adding cream to the potato mixture helped create a cohesive mixture. Once everything was in the slow cooker, including deli counter corned beef, we lightly packed it all down and let it cook for 4 hours. Serve with hot sauce.

Vegetable oil spray
¼ cup extra-virgin olive oil, plus extra as needed
2 pounds frozen diced or shredded potatoes, thawed and patted dry
2 onions, minced
6 garlic cloves, minced
1 tablespoon minced fresh thyme or 1 teaspoon dried
2 teaspoons sweet paprika
1 pound thinly sliced deli corned beef, cut into ½-inch pieces
½ cup heavy cream
Salt and pepper
¼ teaspoon hot sauce
6 large eggs (optional)

1. Line slow cooker with aluminum foil collar and coat with vegetable oil spray (see page 225). Heat oil in 12-inch nonstick skillet over medium-high heat until shimmering. Add 1 pound potatoes and cook until beginning to brown, about 5 minutes. (If pan becomes dry, add more oil, 1 tablespoon at a time.) Add onions, garlic, thyme, and paprika and cook until vegetables are softened and lightly browned, 8 to 10 minutes; transfer to large bowl.

2. Toss remaining pound potatoes, corned beef, cream, 1 teaspoon salt, ¼ teaspoon pepper, and hot sauce with fried potato mixture; transfer to prepared slow cooker and smooth into even layer. Cover and cook until hash is heated through, about 4 hours on low.

3A. FOR EXTRA-CRISP HASH: Heat 3 tablespoons oil in 12-inch nonstick skillet over medium-high heat until shimmering. Add hash, gently pack into skillet, and cook undisturbed for 2 minutes. Flip hash in sections, lightly repack into skillet, and continue to cook, flipping hash as needed, until well browned and crisp, about 6 minutes longer. Season with salt and pepper to taste and serve.

3B. FOR HASH WITH POACHED EGGS: Make six shallow holes (about 2½ inches wide) in hash using back of spoon. Crack 1 egg into each hole and sprinkle with salt and pepper. Cover and cook on low until eggs are just set, about 25 minutes. Serve immediately.

QUICK PREP TIP POACHING THE EGGS
Using the back of a large spoon, make six large holes in the surface of the hash, about 2½ inches wide and 1½ inches deep. Carefully crack an egg into each hole, season with salt and pepper, cover, and continue to cook on low until the eggs are just set, about 25 minutes.

Roast Beef Hash

Serves 6   **Cooking Time** about 4 hours on Low

✔ **WHY THIS RECIPE WORKS:** With our method for classic corned beef hash successfully nailed down (see page 279), we decided to give it a slightly Southwestern spin, with deli roast beef taking center stage. Green bell pepper, chili powder, and chipotle chiles, sautéed along with the onions, give this hash its character. Great as a lazy weekend breakfast or a weeknight dinner, this hearty hash is comfort food at its best. Feel free to substitute deli ham for the roast beef. Serve with hot sauce.

Vegetable oil spray

¼   cup extra-virgin olive oil, plus extra as needed

2   pounds frozen diced or shredded potatoes, thawed and patted dry

2   onions, minced

1   green bell pepper, stemmed, seeded, and cut into ½-inch pieces (see page 91)

6   garlic cloves, minced

2   tablespoons chili powder

1   tablespoon minced fresh thyme or 1 teaspoon dried

1   teaspoon minced canned chipotle chile in adobo sauce

1   pound thinly sliced deli roast beef, cut into ½-inch pieces

½   cup heavy cream
     Salt and pepper

¼   teaspoon hot sauce

6   large eggs (optional)

1. Line slow cooker with aluminum foil collar and coat with vegetable oil spray (see page 225). Heat oil in 12-inch nonstick skillet over medium-high heat until shimmering. Add 1 pound potatoes and cook until beginning to brown, about 5 minutes. (If pan becomes dry, add more oil, 1 tablespoon at a time.) Add onions, bell pepper, garlic, chili powder, thyme, and chipotles and cook until vegetables are softened and lightly browned, 8 to 10 minutes; transfer to large bowl.

2. Toss remaining pound potatoes, roast beef, cream, 1 teaspoon salt, ¼ teaspoon pepper, and hot sauce with fried potato mixture; transfer to prepared slow cooker and smooth into even layer. Cover and cook until hash is heated through, about 4 hours on low.

3A. FOR EXTRA-CRISP HASH: Heat 3 tablespoons oil in 12-inch nonstick skillet over medium-high heat until shimmering. Add hash, gently pack into skillet, and cook undisturbed for 2 minutes. Flip hash in sections, lightly repack into skillet, and continue to cook, flipping hash as needed, until well browned and crisp, about 6 minutes longer. Season with salt and pepper to taste and serve.

3B. FOR HASH WITH POACHED EGGS: Make six shallow holes (about 2½ inches wide) in hash (see page 279) using back of large spoon. Crack 1 egg into each hole and sprinkle with salt and pepper. Cover and cook on low until eggs are just set, about 25 minutes. Serve immediately.

SMART SHOPPING FROZEN POTATOES
To make our slow-cooker hash incredibly easy, we rely on the convenience of frozen potatoes. We've found that both frozen cubed potatoes and shredded potatoes are readily available, and both work well in the hash. The only trick to using them is to make sure they are thoroughly thawed and dried before using. To thaw frozen potatoes quickly, microwave them on high power for 5 to 8 minutes. Drain the thawed potatoes well, then spread them out over several towels, and pat dry thoroughly.

French Toast Casserole

Serves 8 to 10   **Cooking Time** about 4 hours on Low

✔ **WHY THIS RECIPE WORKS:** In the world of sweet breakfast casseroles, there is one that is king: the sweet, rich nut-topped casserole that mimics what everyone finds irresistible about French toast but without all the work. Translating this dish to the slow cooker proved tricky, but after dozens of mushy attempts, we found the right balance of custard to bread; seven eggs and a mixture of whole milk and heavy cream delivered just enough moisture to soften the bread and also create a rich, hearty texture. Drying the bread was key here, as it was with our stratas, because it ensured a stable texture. To make sure every mouthful of this casserole delivered sweet, warm flavors, we added a hefty dose of vanilla and cinnamon to our egg mixture along with a little nutmeg. As for the nuts, even when pretoasted, they became soft in the slow cooker when mixed into the casserole. To solve the problem, we turned to readily available candied nuts, mixing them with softened butter and brown sugar for a delicious topping that stayed crunchy over the 4-hour cooking time. Be sure to use supermarket-style loaf bread with a thin crust and fluffy crumb; artisan loaves with a thick crust and chewy crumb don't work well here. Serve with maple syrup.

Vegetable oil spray

1 loaf supermarket French or Italian bread (16 ounces), cut into 1-inch pieces (16 cups)

2½ cups whole milk

7 large eggs

1 cup heavy cream

⅓ cup granulated sugar

2 teaspoons vanilla extract

1 teaspoon ground cinnamon

¼ teaspoon ground nutmeg

½ cup packed light brown sugar

4 tablespoons (½ stick) unsalted butter, softened

2 cups candied walnuts or pecans, chopped coarse

1. Line slow cooker with aluminum foil collar, then line with foil sling and coat with vegetable oil spray (see page 225). Adjust oven rack to middle position and heat oven to 225 degrees. Spread bread over rimmed baking sheet and bake, shaking pan occasionally, until dry and crisp, about 40 minutes (see page 275).

2. Spread bread into prepared slow cooker. Whisk milk, eggs, cream, granulated sugar, vanilla, cinnamon, and nutmeg together in bowl, then pour mixture evenly over bread. Press gently on bread to submerge.

3. Mix brown sugar and butter in medium bowl until smooth, then stir in walnuts. Sprinkle walnut mixture over casserole. Cover and cook until center of casserole is set, about 4 hours on low.

4. Let casserole cool for 20 minutes. To serve, either spoon casserole onto individual plates or transfer casserole to serving platter using sling.

ON THE SIDE GINGERY FRUIT SALAD FOR COMPANY
Simmer ¼ cup sugar, ¼ cup finely chopped crystallized ginger, and 2 tablespoons water in small saucepan over medium heat until sugar dissolves, about 3 minutes; cool to room temperature. Layer 3 cups blueberries, 2 cups blackberries, 2 cups raspberries, and 2 thinly sliced star fruit in serving bowl. Just before serving, drizzle with ginger syrup and toss gently to combine. (The undressed salad can be refrigerated for several hours before serving.) Serves 8 to 10.

Irish Oatmeal

Serves 8   **Cooking Time** 4 to 6 hours on Low

✔ **WHY THIS RECIPE WORKS:** We love the chewy texture and fuller flavor of steel-cut oats (and also their health benefits). Although we set out to create an overnight version of these oats so they'd be ready to serve up the next morning, we found that the oats were mushy and blown out after the long cooking time. For perfectly cooked oats in the slow cooker, low heat and only 4 to 6 hours cooking time are key. Also, toasting the oats before putting them in the slow cooker brings out their nutty flavor. This oatmeal reheats well so it's well worth making these oats just to reheat them quickly a couple of mornings a week. Serve with your favorite toppings such as brown sugar, butter, maple syrup, cinnamon, raisins, dried fruit, or nuts.

2	tablespoons unsalted butter
2	cups steel-cut oats
8	cups water
1	teaspoon salt

1. Melt butter in 12-inch skillet over medium heat. Add oats and toast, stirring constantly, until golden and fragrant, about 2 minutes; transfer to slow cooker.

2. Stir water and salt in slow cooker. Cover and cook until oats are softened and thickened, 4 to 6 hours on low. Let oatmeal sit for 10 minutes; stir well and serve. (Oatmeal can be refrigerated in airtight container for up to 4 days. Reheat oatmeal either in microwave or in heavy-bottomed saucepan over medium-low heat; stir often and add hot water to adjust consistency.)

Irish Oatmeal with Cinnamon and Raisins

Serves 8   **Cooking Time** 4 to 6 hours on Low

✔ **WHY THIS RECIPE WORKS:** This simple variation on classic Irish oatmeal infuses the oats with sweet flavor. A full cup of raisins, which become plump during the hours in the slow cooker, gives this oatmeal its heartiness.

2	tablespoons unsalted butter
2	cups steel-cut oats
8	cups water
1	cup raisins
½	cup packed light brown sugar
1	teaspoon ground cinnamon
1	teaspoon salt

1. Melt butter in 12-inch skillet over medium heat. Add oats and toast, stirring constantly, until golden and fragrant, about 2 minutes; transfer to slow cooker.

2. Stir water, raisins, sugar, cinnamon, and salt into slow cooker. Cover and cook until oats are softened and thickened, 4 to 6 hours on low. Let oatmeal sit for 10 minutes; stir well and serve. (Oatmeal can be refrigerated in airtight container for up to 4 days. Reheat oatmeal either in microwave or in heavy-bottomed saucepan over medium-low heat; stir often and add hot water to adjust consistency.)

Irish Oatmeal with Bananas and Walnuts

Serves 8   **Cooking Time** 4 to 6 hours on Low

✔ **WHY THIS RECIPE WORKS:** This is the ultimate oatmeal if you love bananas or happen to have an excess of ripe bananas in your fruit basket. And since bananas and walnuts are a great combo, we added a cup of walnuts along with the mashed bananas to make this oatmeal especially hearty and flavorful. Serve with extra sliced bananas and toasted walnuts if desired.

2	tablespoons unsalted butter
2	cups steel-cut oats
7½	cups water
4	bananas, mashed
1	cup walnuts, toasted (see page 87) and chopped coarse
½	cup packed light brown sugar
1	teaspoon salt
¼	teaspoon ground cinnamon

1. Melt butter in 12-inch skillet over medium heat. Add oats and toast, stirring constantly, until golden and fragrant, about 2 minutes; transfer to slow cooker.

2. Stir water, bananas, walnuts, sugar, salt, and cinnamon into slow cooker. Cover and cook until oats are softened and thickened, 4 to 6 hours on low. Let oatmeal sit for 10 minutes; stir well and serve. (Oatmeal can be refrigerated in airtight container for up to 4 days. Reheat oatmeal either in microwave or in heavy-bottomed saucepan over medium-low heat; stir often and add hot water to adjust consistency.)

Irish Oatmeal with Apples and Raisins

Serves 8   **Cooking Time** 4 to 6 hours on Low

✔ **WHY THIS RECIPE WORKS:** For cold winter mornings, it's good to have a few options for jazzing up Irish oatmeal. One of our favorites is this one where the combination of shredded and dried apples gives the oatmeal a deep and fresh fruit flavor—apples alone didn't impart enough flavor, especially given that they were subjected to hours in a slow cooker. A handful of raisins, brown sugar, and cinnamon round out this sweet and fruity oatmeal. We recommend using sweet cooking apples here such as Fuji, Jonagold, Pink Lady, Jonathan, or Macoun.

2	tablespoons unsalted butter
2	cups steel-cut oats
8	cups water
1	pound apples (2 to 3), peeled, cored, and shredded
½	cup dried apples, cut into ½-inch pieces
½	cup raisins
½	cup packed light brown sugar
1	teaspoon ground cinnamon
1	teaspoon salt

1. Melt butter in 12-inch skillet over medium heat. Add oats and toast, stirring constantly, until golden and fragrant, about 2 minutes; transfer to slow cooker.

2. Stir water, apples, dried apples, raisins, sugar, cinnamon, and salt into slow cooker. Cover and cook until oats are softened and thickened, 4 to 6 hours on low. Let oatmeal sit for 10 minutes; stir well and serve. (Oatmeal can be refrigerated in airtight container for up to 4 days. Reheat oatmeal either in microwave or in heavy-bottomed saucepan over medium-low heat; stir often and add hot water to adjust consistency.)

CHERRY COBBLER

Desserts

Cherry Cobbler

Serves 6   **Cooking Time** about 4 hours on Low

✔ WHY THIS RECIPE WORKS: It doesn't get much easier or tastier than our slow-cooker cherry cobbler, full of sweet, saucy cherries, accented with almond, and topped with tender biscuits. But getting the filling just right took a little investigative work. We tested different types of cherries (including canned tart, canned sweet, frozen, and fresh cherries), and some turned out watery, while others completely disintegrated. Ultimately, we chose canned sweet cherries in syrup for this version. We discarded the syrup, which made the dish too sweet, then combined the cherries with sugar, Minute tapioca, almond extract, and red wine. The addition of almond and red wine added a nice counterpoint to the sweet cherries. Our biscuit topping (cooked separately in the oven) started out as a fairly standard drop biscuit, a mix of flour, butter, baking powder and soda, sugar, salt, and buttermilk. However, we added a dash of vanilla to the dough and sprinkled the biscuits with cinnamon sugar before baking them for crisp but tender biscuits with hints of vanilla and cinnamon, perfect for serving with our cherry-almond filling. Do not use tart cherries in water here. This recipe can easily be doubled to serve a crowd.

CHERRY FILLING
- 4 (15-ounce) cans sweet cherries in syrup, drained (5 cups)
- ¼ cup sugar
- ¼ cup dry red wine
- 1 tablespoon Minute tapioca
- ¼ teaspoon almond extract

BISCUITS
- 1 cup all-purpose flour
- ¼ cup plus 2 teaspoons sugar
- 2 teaspoons baking powder
- ¼ teaspoon baking soda
- ¼ teaspoon salt
- ⅓ cup buttermilk
- 4 tablespoons (½ stick) unsalted butter, melted and cooled
- ½ teaspoon vanilla extract
- ⅛ teaspoon ground cinnamon

1. FOR CHERRY FILLING: Combine all ingredients in slow cooker. Cover and cook until cherries are soft, about 4 hours on low.

2. FOR BISCUITS: Adjust oven rack to middle position and heat oven to 400 degrees. Line rimmed baking sheet with parchment.

3. Whisk flour, ¼ cup sugar, baking powder, baking soda, and salt together in large bowl. In separate bowl, whisk buttermilk, melted butter, and vanilla together. Gently stir buttermilk mixture into flour mixture until dough is just combined.

4. Divide dough into 6 equal pieces, round gently into biscuits, and place on prepared baking sheet, spaced about 1½ inches apart. Mix remaining 2 teaspoons sugar with cinnamon and sprinkle over top of biscuits. Bake until biscuits are golden and cooked through, 15 to 20 minutes. (The biscuits can be made 4 to 6 hours ahead and stored in an airtight container.)

5. To serve, spoon cherry filling into individual serving bowls and top with biscuits.

SMART SHOPPING CANNED CHERRIES
Fresh cherries simply can't compete with the convenience and year-round availability of canned cherries. When shopping for canned cherries, however, make sure to note the difference between tart cherries packed in water and sweet cherries packed in syrup. Cherries packed in water have a bland, washed-out flavor and color compared to sweet cherries packed in syrup, which look dark and glossy and have a deep, sweet taste. Be aware that these two types of canned cherries often have very similar looking labels.

Peach-Ginger Crisp

Serves 8 to 10   **Cooking Time** about 4 hours on Low

WHY THIS RECIPE WORKS: One of our all-time favorite fruit desserts is peach crisp, which should taste like summer, full of juicy peach flavor, with a buttery, nutty topping. We tried using fresh peaches, but we had trouble getting a consistent texture; some peaches turned out mushy while others refused to soften even after hours in our cooker. To get a consistent peach texture and flavor we opted to use frozen peaches, which are quickly frozen at the height of ripeness, ensuring their quality and flavor and making this dish possible any time of year. We decided to complement the sweet peach flavor with the spicy heat of ginger by using crystallized ginger in the filling and ground ginger in the topping. For the cookielike crisp topping, we made a simple dough, cooked it separately in the oven, and crumbled it over the top before serving.

PEACH FILLING

4	**pounds frozen peaches, thawed and drained (7 cups)**
¾	**cup granulated sugar**
3	**tablespoons crystallized ginger, chopped coarse**
4	**teaspoons Minute tapioca**
1	**teaspoon fresh lemon juice**
1	**teaspoon vanilla extract**

TOPPING

1	**cup all-purpose flour**
¼	**cup granulated sugar**
¼	**cup packed light brown sugar**
2	**teaspoons vanilla extract**
¾	**teaspoon ground ginger**
⅛	**teaspoon salt**
8	**tablespoons (1 stick) unsalted butter, cut into 6 pieces and softened**
½	**cup sliced almonds, toasted (see page 87)**

1. FOR PEACH FILLING: Combine all ingredients in slow cooker. Cover and cook until peaches are soft, about 4 hours on low.

2. FOR TOPPING: Adjust oven rack to lower-middle position and heat oven to 350 degrees. Line rimmed baking sheet with parchment.

3. Pulse flour, granulated sugar, brown sugar, vanilla, ginger, and salt together in food processor to combine, about 5 pulses. Sprinkle butter and ¼ cup almonds over top and process until mixture clumps together into large crumbly balls, about 30 seconds. Sprinkle remaining ¼ cup almonds over top and pulse to incorporate, about 2 pulses.

4. Spread topping evenly over prepared baking sheet, breaking it into ½-inch pieces. Bake until golden brown, about 18 minutes, rotating pan halfway through baking. Let cool slightly. Crumble topping over peach filling and serve. (The topping can be made up to a day ahead and stored in an airtight container.)

QUICK PREP TIP MAKING A CRISP TOPPING
The trick to making a topping that tastes crisp and toasted is to bake it in the oven before sprinkling it over the filling. Sprinkle the raw topping over a parchment-lined baking sheet and bake it in a 350-degree oven until well browned, about 18 minutes, then crumble it over the top of the filling before serving.

Rum-Raisin Bread Pudding

Serves 8 to 10   **Cooking Time** about 4 hours on Low

✓ **WHY THIS RECIPE WORKS:** Our slow-cooker version of bread pudding boasts tender bread cubes enveloped by a rich custard and accented with rum-soaked raisins. Getting the texture of this company-worthy dessert just right was the real challenge; early tests yielded mushy or dry puddings, not the creamy and moist texture we were after. After extensive testing of different types of bread, we settled on challah for its rich flavor. We cut it into cubes, which we toasted until dry before combining them with our custard (a combination of egg yolks, milk, heavy cream, sugar, and vanilla). Pressing the bread into the custard ensured every cube soaked up its share. We topped the bread pudding with a little cinnamon sugar and after 4 hours in the slow cooker, we had an easy-to-prepare bread pudding that rivaled our oven versions. If you cannot find challah, firm, high-quality sandwich bread may be substituted. Serve with Bourbon–Brown Sugar Sauce.

	Vegetable oil spray
1	**(14-ounce) loaf challah bread, cut into 1-inch pieces (12 cups) (see note)**
⅔	**cup golden raisins**
5	**teaspoons dark rum**
2½	**cups heavy cream**
2½	**cups whole milk**
9	**large egg yolks**
¾	**cup plus 1 tablespoon granulated sugar**
4	**teaspoons vanilla extract**
¾	**teaspoon salt**
2	**tablespoons light brown sugar**
⅛	**teaspoon ground cinnamon**

1. Line slow cooker with aluminum foil collar, then line with foil sling and coat with vegetable oil spray (see page 225). Adjust oven rack to middle position and heat oven to 225 degrees. Spread bread over rimmed baking sheet and bake, shaking pan occasionally, until dry and crisp, about 40 minutes. Let bread cool slightly, then transfer to very large bowl.

2. Microwave raisins and rum in small bowl until hot, about 20 seconds. Let mixture cool slightly, then toss with dried bread; transfer to prepared slow cooker.

3. Whisk cream, milk, egg yolks, ¾ cup granulated sugar, vanilla, and salt together in bowl, then pour mixture evenly over bread. Press gently on bread to submerge.

4. Mix remaining tablespoon granulated sugar, brown sugar, and cinnamon together, then sprinkle over top of casserole. Cover and cook until center is set, about 4 hours on low. Let cool for 30 minutes before serving.

ON THE SIDE BOURBON–BROWN SUGAR SAUCE
Whisk ½ cup packed light brown sugar and ½ cup heavy cream together in small saucepan. Bring to boil over medium heat, whisking frequently. Whisk in 2½ tablespoons unsalted butter and boil for 1 minute. Off the heat, whisk in 1½ tablespoons bourbon (or rum). Cool slightly before serving. Makes 1 cup.

Nutella Bread Pudding

Serves 8 to 10   **Cooking Time** about 4 hours on Low

WHY THIS RECIPE WORKS: The rich hazelnut and cocoa flavor of Nutella inspired this gooey, over-the-top variation of our Rum-Raisin Bread Pudding. Out went the rum, raisins, and cinnamon. In went chocolate chips and a large dose of Nutella—a common European breakfast spread of hazelnuts, skim milk, and cocoa, which is readily available in the United States. We simply whisked the Nutella spread into the custard (which we reduced by a cup to account for the Nutella) and poured the custard over the toasted bread cubes, once again pressing the cubes into the custard. We loved the addition of chocolate chips, which added a chocolaty boost that the Nutella couldn't without adding too much sweetness. Once cooked, the chocolate chips melted and added a decadent gooeyness that had tasters diving in for seconds. The perfect accompaniment for this bread pudding turned out to be softly whipped cream. If you cannot find challah, firm, high-quality sandwich bread may be substituted.

	Vegetable oil spray
1	(14-ounce) loaf challah bread, cut into 1-inch cubes (12 cups) (see note)
½	cup chocolate chips
2	cups heavy cream
2	cups whole milk
9	large egg yolks
1	cup Nutella
¾	cup plus 1 tablespoon granulated sugar
4	teaspoons vanilla extract
¾	teaspoon salt
2	tablespoons light brown sugar

1. Line slow cooker with aluminum foil collar, then line with foil sling and coat with vegetable oil spray (see page 225). Adjust oven rack to middle position and heat oven to 225 degrees. Spread bread over rimmed baking sheet and bake, shaking pan occasionally, until dry and crisp, about 40 minutes. Let bread cool slightly, then transfer to very large bowl.

2. Mix chocolate chips into dried bread; transfer to prepared slow cooker. Whisk cream, milk, egg yolks, Nutella, ¾ cup granulated sugar, vanilla, and salt together in bowl, then pour mixture evenly over bread. Press gently on bread to submerge.

3. Mix remaining tablespoon granulated sugar with brown sugar then sprinkle over top of casserole. Cover and cook until center is set, about 4 hours on low. Let cool for 30 minutes before serving.

SMART SHOPPING CHOCOLATE CHIPS

Nestlé first introduced chocolate chips to the public in 1939 in response to the chocolate chip cookie craze that swept the nation. Nowadays, you can find lots of different types and brands of chocolate chips on the market. We pitted eight widely available brands of semisweet and bitter-sweet chips against each another in a bake-off and, when the dust finally settled, there was a clear winner. **Ghirardelli 60% Cacao Bittersweet Chocolate Chips** handily beat out the competition with their distinct flavors of "wine," "fruit," and "smoke," and lower sugar content, which allowed the chocolate flavor to really shine.

Chocolate Pudding Cake

Serves 6 to 8   **Cooking Time** about 1½ hours on High

✓ **WHY THIS RECIPE WORKS:** The recipe for slow-cooker chocolate pudding cake may sound, well, like a recipe for disaster—combine dry ingredients with wet, pour into the slow cooker, sprinkle with sugar and cocoa powder, then pour boiling water over the whole thing—but trust us, all will be well and delicious. The cocoa and sugar on top of the batter bubble as they cook to form a pudding-style chocolate sauce on the bottom, while a chewy, brownielike cake rises to the top. The batter is a simple mixture of pantry staples—flour, sugar, cocoa powder, baking powder, and salt combined with milk, melted butter, egg yolk, and vanilla. We folded in a handful of chocolate chips to add another layer of flavor and ensure plenty of gooey pockets in the baked cake. Dutch-processed cocoa is less acidic than natural cocoa powder and produces a richer chocolate taste. This rich and fudgy chocolate pudding cake is excellent served with a scoop of vanilla ice cream or a dollop of whipped cream.

	Vegetable oil spray
1	cup all-purpose flour
1	cup sugar
½	cup Dutch-processed cocoa powder
2	teaspoons baking powder
¼	teaspoon salt
½	cup whole milk
4	tablespoons (½ stick) unsalted butter, melted
1	large egg yolk
2	teaspoons vanilla extract
½	cup chocolate chips
1	cup boiling water

1. Line slow cooker with aluminum foil collar and coat with vegetable oil spray (see page 225).

2. Whisk flour, ½ cup sugar, ¼ cup cocoa, baking powder, and salt together in large bowl. In separate bowl, whisk together milk, butter, egg yolk, and vanilla. Stir milk mixture into flour mixture until just combined. Fold in chocolate chips (batter will be stiff). Scrape batter into prepared slow cooker and spread to edges.

3. Mix remaining ½ cup sugar with remaining ¼ cup cocoa, then sprinkle over top. Slowly pour boiling water over top. Do not stir. Cover and cook until top of cake looks cracked, sauce is bubbling, and toothpick inserted into cakey area comes out with moist crumbs attached, about 1½ hours on high.

4. Remove foil collar and let sit for 10 minutes before serving.

SMART SHOPPING **DUTCH-PROCESSED COCOA**

Cocoa powder is produced by removing some of the cocoa butter from pure unsweetened chocolate. To counter the harsh, acidic flavor of natural cocoa, the powder is sometimes treated with an alkaline solution, or "Dutched." Cookbooks often claim that Dutching "mellows" chocolate flavor, but our tasters disagree. Without the distraction of natural cocoa's harsh acidity, the more subtle, complex chocolate flavors came to the fore. In testing brands of cocoa, we found widely available **Droste Cocoa** to be our favorite.

Rice Pudding

Serves 6 to 8   **Cooking Time** about 2 hours on High

✓ **WHY THIS RECIPE WORKS:** At its best, rice pudding boasts intact, tender grains bound loosely in a subtly sweet, milky sauce. For our slow-cooker version, we set out to determine how much and what types of liquid to use. Milk (often used in traditional recipes) did not fare well, leaving us with unappealing flecks of curdled milk throughout the pudding. Cream, on the other hand, was too rich and obscured the flavor of the rice. In the end, equal parts water and half-and-half worked best, providing a satisfying but not too rich consistency. We found that the rice was more evenly cooked when we boiled the liquids before adding them to the rice in the slow cooker and we also found that the rice cooked more evenly on high than on low. We prefer pudding made from medium-grain rice, though long-grain rice works too.

	Vegetable oil spray
1	cup medium-grain rice
¼	teaspoon salt
3	cups water, plus extra as needed
3	cups half-and-half
⅔	cup sugar
½	cup raisins
1½	teaspoons vanilla extract
1	teaspoon ground cinnamon

1. Coat slow cooker with vegetable oil spray, then add rice and salt.

2. Bring 3 cups water, half-and-half, and sugar to boil in saucepan; stir into slow cooker. Cover and cook until rice is tender, about 2 hours on high.

3. Stir in raisins, vanilla, and cinnamon and let sit until heated through, about 5 minutes. Adjust pudding consistency as desired before serving; if too loose, gently stir pudding until excess liquid is absorbed or, if too dry, stir in hot water as needed to loosen.

Coconut Rice Pudding

Serves 6 to 8   **Cooking Time** about 2 hours on High

✓ **WHY THIS RECIPE WORKS:** This variation on traditional rice pudding is popular in the Caribbean. We used light coconut milk as a substitute for the dairy here and finished with a little garam masala. Do not use regular coconut milk, which is too rich for this recipe and will result in a cloying pudding with a gluey consistency. Serve with toasted shredded coconut and chopped pistachios if desired.

	Vegetable oil spray
1	cup medium-grain rice
½	teaspoon salt
2½	cups water, plus extra as needed
2	(14-ounce) cans light coconut milk
⅔	cup sugar
1½	teaspoons vanilla extract
½	teaspoon garam masala (page 74)

1. Coat slow cooker with vegetable oil spray, then add rice and salt.

2. Bring 2½ cups water, coconut milk, and sugar to boil in saucepan; stir into slow cooker. Cover and cook until rice is tender, about 2 hours on high.

3. Stir in vanilla and garam masala. Adjust pudding consistency as desired before serving; if too loose, gently stir pudding until excess liquid is absorbed or, if too dry, stir in hot water as needed to loosen.

Chocolate Fondue

Serves 8 to 10   **Cooking Time** 1 to 1½ hours on Low

✔ **WHY THIS RECIPE WORKS:** Dipping an enormous red strawberry into a pot of warm melted chocolate is guaranteed to make just about anybody happy. For this version, we first chopped chocolate into small pieces before combining it with heavy cream and a pinch of salt. (We like more chocolate than cream as it results in a thick, velvety fondue.) The chocolate melted gently as the cream heated up and after about an hour all we needed to do was whisk the steaming mixture until smooth. At this point the fondue was rich and thick. A tablespoon of corn syrup made all the difference. The fondue became satiny—the perfect consistency for dipping—and retained a beautiful gloss. We found that semisweet chocolate produced both the most reliable consistency and the best flavor to pair with an array of accompaniments. We tested more than eight different brands of semisweet chocolate (including chips) and they all worked fine, though there were minor flavor differences between brands.(Be sure to taste the chocolate and make sure you like its flavor before making the fondue.) By comparison, white, milk, and bittersweet chocolates were neither consistent nor universally liked by all tasters; we don't recommend using them. For dipping, we like to use bite-size pieces of bread, pound cake, or fruit; make sure you have long skewers on hand to make things easy.

12	ounces semisweet chocolate, chopped medium
1⅓	cups heavy cream, plus extra as needed
1	tablespoon light corn syrup
	Pinch salt

1. Combine all ingredients in slow cooker. Cover and cook until chocolate melts and mixture is hot, 1 to 1½ hours on low.

2. Whisk chocolate mixture together until smooth and serve. (This dish can be held on warm setting for 1 to 2 hours; loosen with hot heavy cream as needed.)

Chocolate-Orange Fondue

Serves 8 to 10   **Cooking Time** 1 to 1½ hours on Low

✔ **WHY THIS RECIPE WORKS:** For this variation on classic chocolate fondue we steeped orange zest in the mixture as it heated up and finished with a splash of flavored liqueur for bright orange flavor.

12	ounces semisweet chocolate, chopped medium
1¼	cups heavy cream, plus extra as needed
4	(3-inch-long) strips orange zest, trimmed of white pith (see page 150)
1	tablespoon light corn syrup
	Pinch salt
2	tablespoons Grand Marnier or triple sec

1. Combine chocolate, heavy cream, orange zest, corn syrup, and salt in slow cooker. Cover and cook until chocolate melts and mixture is hot, 1 to 1½ hours on low.

2. Remove zest, whisk in Grand Marnier until smooth, and serve. (This dish can be held on warm setting for 1 to 2 hours; loosen with hot heavy cream as needed.)

EASY PREP

EASY PREP

Pears Poached in White Wine

Serves 6   **Cooking Time** about 2 hours on Low

✔ **WHY THIS RECIPE WORKS:** Here we poached pears in sugar-sweetened white wine with fresh herbs, lemon zest, vanilla, and cinnamon. But for a sauce thick enough to coat the pears, we needed to reduce it on the stovetop. Chilling the pears in the sauce allowed the fruit to absorb even more flavor, while taking on a lovely translucent appearance. Bosc or Bartlett pears are best in this recipe and should be moderately ripe but still firm. We recommend a medium-bodied dry white wine such as Sauvignon Blanc or Chardonnay.

1	**(750-milliliter) bottle dry white wine (3 cups)**
¾	**cup sugar**
6	**(3-inch-long) strips lemon zest, trimmed of white pith (see page 150)**
5	**fresh mint sprigs**
3	**fresh thyme sprigs**
1	**vanilla bean, halved lengthwise, seeds removed and reserved**
½	**cinnamon stick**
⅛	**teaspoon salt**
6	**Bosc or Bartlett pears**

1. Microwave wine, sugar, lemon zest, mint sprigs, thyme sprigs, vanilla seeds and pod, cinnamon stick, and salt in bowl, stirring occasionally, until sugar dissolves completely, about 3 minutes; transfer to slow cooker.

2. Peel, halve, and core pears; add to slow cooker. Cover and cook until pears are tender, about 2 hours on low.

3. Using slotted spoon, transfer pears to shallow casserole dish. Strain cooking liquid into large saucepan and simmer over medium heat until thickened and measures about 1⅓ cups, about 15 minutes. Pour over pears, cover, and refrigerate until well chilled, at least 2 hours or up to 3 days, before serving.

Pears Poached in Red Wine

Serves 6   **Cooking Time** about 2 hours on Low

✔ **WHY THIS RECIPE WORKS:** These poached pears are robust and spicy with the bold flavor of red wine, peppercorns, and pungent cloves. After cooking and chilling in the syrup, the pears take on a dramatic burgundy hue. We recommend a dry medium-bodied red wine, such as a Côtes du Rhône, Pinot Noir, or Merlot.

1	**(750-milliliter) bottle dry red wine (3 cups)**
¾	**cup sugar**
5	**fresh mint sprigs**
3	**fresh thyme sprigs**
1	**vanilla bean, halved lengthwise, seeds removed and reserved**
½	**cinnamon stick**
25	**black peppercorns**
3	**whole cloves**
⅛	**teaspoon salt**
6	**Bosc or Bartlett pears**

1. Microwave wine, sugar, mint sprigs, thyme sprigs, vanilla seeds and pod, cinnamon, peppercorns, cloves, and salt in bowl, stirring occasionally, until sugar dissolves completely, about 3 minutes; transfer to slow cooker.

2. Peel, halve, and core pears; add to slow cooker. Cover and cook until pears are tender, about 2 hours on low.

3. Using slotted spoon, transfer pears to shallow casserole dish. Strain cooking liquid into large saucepan and simmer over medium heat until thickened and measures about 1⅓ cups, about 15 minutes. Pour over pears, cover, and refrigerate until well chilled, at least 2 hours or up to 3 days, before serving.

TANGY ORANGE MARMALADE AND FRESH STRAWBERRY JAM

Basics

Fresh Strawberry Jam

Makes 10 cups   **Cooking Time** about 4 hours on Low

✔ **WHY THIS RECIPE WORKS:** Homemade strawberry jam is miles ahead of store-bought jams and, when strawberries are in season, is extremely economical. We figured we could use the slow cooker to really bring out the sweet jammy flavor of the berries, without much hands-on monitoring. Our biggest challenge was to find the appropriate ratios of pectin (a carbohydrate found in fruit responsible for thickening jams, jellies, and preserves) and sugar to fruit. We found that we needed to use a higher level of pectin than usually suggested since our jam, which couldn't really reduce down much in the slow cooker, had a higher amount of liquid than ordinary stovetop recipes. And since pectin needs to be heated until boiling in order to activate, we learned that we needed to transfer our cooked berry mixture to the stovetop, bring it to a boil, and add the pectin. Similarly, we also discovered that we needed to use a higher ratio of sugar than usual to set the pectin. In order to compensate for the sweetness, we stirred in a little lemon juice.

4 **pounds strawberries, hulled**
7 **cups sugar**
1 **tablespoon fresh lemon juice**
   Pinch salt
2 **(1.75-ounce) boxes fruit pectin**

1. Pulse 1 pound strawberries in food processor until almost smooth, about 12 pulses; transfer to slow cooker. Working in batches, pulse remaining 3 pounds strawberries in food processor until coarsely chopped, about 4 pulses; transfer to slow cooker.

2. Stir sugar, lemon juice, and salt into slow cooker. Cover and cook until berries are very soft and beginning to disintegrate, about 4 hours on low.

3. Place several small plates in freezer to chill, about 15 minutes. Transfer jam to large pot and bring to boil over medium-high heat. Stir in pectin, boil jam for 1 minute longer, then remove from heat.

4. Spoon ½ teaspoon jam onto frozen plate; jam should set up immediately and stay in place when plate is tipped slightly. If jam does not set up, continue to boil it in 1-minute increments and repeat frozen plate test until it does. (Jam can be canned following standard canning procedure—see directions that come with canning jars—and stored for up to 1 year; it can also be refrigerated for up to a month.)

QUICK PREP TIP SETTING UP JAM
We like to use the chilled plate test to check the consistency of a freshly cooked jam because it's easy and foolproof. To do this, simply spoon a small amount of the hot jam onto a well-chilled plate; if it sets up and doesn't run when the plate is tipped (left) then it's ready. If the jam runs (right), then it needs to be cooked a little longer.

Tangy Orange Marmalade

Makes 8 cups   **Cooking Time** 9 to 11 hours on Low or 5 to 7 hours on High

✔ **WHY THIS RECIPE WORKS:** Orange marmalade is an elegant addition to the breakfast table, but it can be a lot of work to make it yourself. We thought that a slow cooker would be the perfect vessel in which to easily turn the tart peels and pieces of everyday oranges into a sweet, jammy spread. The trickiest part of the testing process was figuring out how to slice our oranges. After trying a few batches with whole slices of oranges, we found that we got the most flavorful (and prettiest) results when we cooked thin strips of orange zest with finely chopped pieces of orange. Avoiding the pith—the bitter white membrane between the peel and orange pulp—prevented our marmalade from taking on any harsh flavors.

2	pounds navel oranges (4 medium)
5	cups sugar
2	cups water
1	cup orange juice
	Pinch salt
2	(1.75-ounce) boxes fruit pectin

1. Zest oranges into wide strips using vegetable peeler, then trim away any white pith using paring knife (see page 150). Cut zest into matchsticks; transfer to slow cooker.

2. Trim remaining peel from oranges using chef's knife, then cut oranges into coarse pieces, discarding any seeds. Working in batches, pulse orange pieces in food processor until finely chopped, about 8 pulses; transfer to slow cooker.

3. Stir sugar, water, orange juice, and salt into slow cooker. Cover and cook until oranges are very soft and beginning to disintegrate, 9 to 11 hours on low or 5 to 7 hours on high.

4. Place several small plates in freezer to chill, about 15 minutes. Transfer marmalade to large pot and bring to boil over medium-high heat. Stir in pectin, boil marmalade for 1 minute longer, then remove from heat.

5. Spoon ½ teaspoon marmalade onto frozen plate; marmalade should set up immediately and stay in place when plate is tipped slightly. If marmalade does not set up, continue to boil it in 1-minute increments and repeat frozen plate test until it does. (Marmalade can be canned following standard canning procedure—see directions that come with canning jars—and stored for up to 1 year; it can also be refrigerated for up to a month.)

SMART SHOPPING FRUIT PECTIN
Fruit pectin is a carbohydrate that occurs naturally in various fruits and vegetables (but is most commonly harvested from apples and citrus fruit) and is a standard thickener for jams, jellies, and preserves. Pectin must be used in conjunction with sugar and an acid (usually lemon juice) to reach its full thickening power. There are many different brands of pectin available at the market, and all will work well with our Fresh Strawberry Jam and Tangy Orange Marmalade.

Applesauce

Makes 4 cups   **Cooking Time** about 4 hours on Low

☑ **WHY THIS RECIPE WORKS:** Apples cook down beautifully in the slow cooker—the crisp fruit collapses into a sweet, creamy sauce. Since the apples cook down so much on their own, we found that we didn't need to lug out a food processor or food mill to puree the sauce at the end of cooking. A few quick swipes with a potato masher and our sauce was finished and needed little embellishment. We only needed to add a cup of liquid (we prefer to use apple juice or apple cider instead of water since they further amplify the flavor of the fruit) to reach the right consistency and a touch of sugar for flavor; however, you may need to adjust these amounts depending on the type of apples you use. We tested more than a dozen apple varieties for our applesauce recipe, and highly recommend using Jonagold, Pink Lady, Jonathan, or Macoun apples. Golden Delicious, Empire, Mcintosh, and Rome apples also worked fairly well. We don't recommend using Red Delicious, Granny Smith, Braeburn, Cortland, Baldwin, Northern Spy, or Honeycrisp apples.

3   **pounds apples (6 to 9), peeled, cored, and cut into 1½-inch chunks**

1   **cup apple juice or apple cider, plus extra as needed**

2   **tablespoons sugar, plus extra as needed**
    Pinch salt

1. Combine all ingredients in slow cooker. Cover and cook until apples are very soft and beginning to disintegrate, about 4 hours on low.

2. Mash apples thoroughly with potato masher. Season with additional sugar to taste and adjust consistency with additional hot apple juice as needed. Serve warm, at room temperature, or chilled. (Applesauce can be refrigerated in airtight container for up to 1 week.)

QUICK PREP TIP FLAVORING APPLESAUCE
Although our applesauce tastes great straight up, it takes well to a wide range of fun flavors. We tested dozens of options and here are our favorites:

Cinnamon Applesauce
Add 2 (3-inch) cinnamon sticks (or ¼ teaspoon ground cinnamon) to slow cooker with apples; remove sticks before mashing.

Buttery Applesauce
Stir 2 tablespoons unsalted butter into finished sauce.

Cranberry Applesauce
Add 1 cup fresh or frozen cranberries and 2 more tablespoons sugar to slow cooker with apples.

Gingery Applesauce
Add 3 (½-inch-thick) slices fresh ginger to slow cooker with apples; remove before mashing.

Red Hot Applesauce
Add ⅔ cup Red Hots candies to slow cooker with apples.

Holiday Cranberry Sauce

Makes 8 cups   **Cooking Time** 6 to 8 hours on Low or 3 to 5 hours on High

✔ **WHY THIS RECIPE WORKS:** A big batch of cranberry sauce comes together with virtually no hands-on time when using a slow cooker: perfect when you're busy cooking a large holiday meal. Looking to make a sauce with pure cranberry flavor and just enough sweetness to temper the tart fruit, we knew that we would need to make a few adjustments to the traditional back-of-the-bag recipe. First, since there is little evaporation in the slow cooker, we found that we only needed to add a little bit of water to keep the berries from burning before they began to break down and release their juice. We also discovered that the sugar easily stuck and burned on the bottom of the slow cooker. So instead of mixing it into the berries, we poured the sugar on top of the berries, where it slowly cooked down into the sauce. These changes in place, our big batch-cranberry sauce was fit to sit front and center at any holiday table. If using frozen cranberries, do not defrost.

4	**(12-ounce) bags fresh or frozen cranberries**
½	**cup water**
1	**teaspoon salt**
4	**cups sugar**

1. Combine cranberries, water, and salt in slow cooker, then pour sugar over berries (do not stir sugar into berry mixture). Cover and cook until berries are softened and beginning to pop, 6 to 8 hours on low or 3 to 5 hours on high.

2. Stir cranberry sauce well, then transfer to bowl. Let cool to room temperature before serving. (Cranberry sauce can be refrigerated in airtight container for up to 1 week or frozen for up to 3 months.)

Cranberry-Pear Sauce with Ginger

Makes 10 cups   **Cooking Time** 6 to 8 hours on Low or 3 to 5 hours on High

✔ **WHY THIS RECIPE WORKS:** The addition of sweet pears, spicy ginger, and cinnamon makes this sauce a uniquely satisfying version of classic cranberry sauce. Make sure to use the ripest pears you can find; we recommend using Bosc or Bartlett pears here. If using frozen cranberries, do not defrost.

4	**(12-ounce) bags fresh or frozen cranberries**
2½	**pounds pears (5 to 6), peeled, cored, and cut into ½-inch pieces**
½	**cup water**
¼	**cup minced or grated fresh ginger**
1	**teaspoon ground cinnamon**
1	**teaspoon salt**
4	**cups sugar**

1. Combine cranberries, pears, water, ginger, cinnamon, and salt in slow cooker, then pour sugar over berries (do not stir sugar into berry mixture). Cover and cook until berries are softened and beginning to pop, 6 to 8 hours on low or 3 to 5 hours on high.

2. Stir cranberry sauce well, then transfer to bowl. Let cool to room temperature before serving. (Cranberry sauce can be refrigerated in airtight container for up to 1 week or frozen for up to 3 months.)

Roasted Garlic

Makes 1 cup   **Cooking Time** 4 to 6 hours on Low

✔ **WHY THIS RECIPE WORKS:** Roasted garlic is a great ingredient to have around the house—its deep sweetness livens up everything from bland soups to mediocre crostini. A slow cooker is the perfect way to cook up a big batch since the slow heat gently caramelizes the cloves, and the closed lid keeps the garlic moist without needing to bother with foil packets. We found that the garlic needed nothing more than a bit of olive oil and salt to maximize its flavor, and that adding a small amount of water in the bottom of the cooker prevented burning. This recipe can be easily doubled. Roasted garlic will liven up lots of dishes, just puree it and add it to mashed potatoes, polenta, pasta sauces, soups and stews, gravies, and more. Roasted garlic cloves also taste great on pizza.

5 garlic heads
2½ teaspoons extra-virgin olive oil
    Salt

1. Slice top ½-inch from each garlic head to expose cloves. Pour ½ cup water into slow cooker. Place garlic heads, cut side up, in slow cooker. Drizzle each head with ½ teaspoon oil and sprinkle with pinch salt. Cover and cook until garlic is soft and golden, 4 to 6 hours on low.

2. Transfer garlic to cutting board, let cool slightly, then gently squeeze to remove cloves from skin. (Roasted garlic can be refrigerated in airtight container for up to 1 week.)

PUTTING ROASTED GARLIC TO WORK

Roasted Garlic Vinaigrette
Puree ⅓ cup roasted garlic, ¼ cup extra-virgin olive oil, ¼ cup hot water, 2 tablespoons balsamic vinegar, 2 teaspoons Dijon mustard, ½ teaspoon minced fresh thyme, ¼ teaspoon salt, ⅛ teaspoon pepper, and pinch sugar in blender until thick and smooth, about 1 minute. Add more hot water as needed to adjust vinaigrette consistency. Season with salt and pepper to taste. (The vinaigrette can be refrigerated in . container for up to 4 days.) Makes ½ cup.

Roasted Garlic Aïoli
Process 2 large egg yolks, 4 teaspoons fresh lemon juice, ⅛ teaspoon sugar, ¼ teaspoon salt, and ⅛ teaspoon pepper together in food processor until combined, about 10 seconds (do not use blender). With the machine running, gradually add ¾ cup olive oil (or 6 tablespoons each extra-virgin olive oil and vegetable oil) in slow, steady stream, scraping down bowl as needed. Continue to process until thick and creamy, about 5 seconds. Add ¼ cup roasted garlic and pulse to incorporate, about 5 pulses. Season with salt and pepper to taste. (The aïoli can be refrigerated in airtight container for up to 3 days.) Makes about 1 cup.

Big-Batch Caramelized Onions

Makes 2 cups   **Cooking Time** 8 to 10 hours on High

✓ **WHY THIS RECIPE WORKS:** From burger toppings to decadent dips, caramelized onions have many culinary uses. But making a big batch on the stovetop takes a good deal of attention. With their gentle heat, slow cookers are an ideal vessel to develop the deep sweetness characteristic of these caramelized onions. Wanting to keep our recipe as simple as possible, we began by filling our slow cooker with thickly sliced onions, butter, sugar, and salt and let them cook all day. Despite the long cooking time, this attempt yielded watery, crunchy, and anemic strips of onions. We knew we needed to find a way to cook the onions longer. Based on our success softening aromatics in the microwave, we decided to use this technique to give the onions a jumpstart. After 15 minutes, the onions had softened and, as a bonus, had let off a considerable amount of liquid, which we then drained. After microwaving, the onions needed only about 9 hours of cooking, and they were no longer swimming in their own watery juice. Instead, the onions were deeply browned, sweet, and juicy. These onions can be used in a variety of ways; use as a topping for steaks or pork chops, to add flavor to sandwiches, omelets, mashed potatoes, and rice, or to make a great-tasting dip like French Onion Dip below. We prefer using yellow onions for this recipe, not white onions or sweet Vidalia onions; yellow onions, when caramelized, strike a good balance between sweet and savory notes with mild onion flavor and beautiful color.

8   **onions, halved and sliced ¼ inch thick**
3   **tablespoons unsalted butter, melted**
    Salt and pepper
3   **tablespoons brown sugar**

1. Microwave onions with 1 tablespoon butter and 2 teaspoons salt in bowl, stirring occasionally, until softened, about 15 minutes. Drain onions, discarding liquid; transfer to slow cooker.

2. Stir sugar, remaining 2 tablespoons butter, and ½ teaspoon pepper into slow cooker. Cover and cook until onions are deep golden brown, 8 to 10 hours on high. Season with salt and pepper to taste. (Onions can be refrigerated in airtight container for up to 1 week.)

PUTTING CARAMELIZED ONIONS TO WORK

French Onion Dip
Cook 3 slices minced bacon in 12-inch skillet over medium heat until crisp, 5 to 7 minutes; transfer to paper towel–lined plate and let cool. Combine ¾ cup sour cream, ½ cup caramelized onions, 2 minced scallions, ½ teaspoon cider vinegar, and cooked bacon in serving bowl and season with salt and pepper to taste. Cover and refrigerate until flavors meld, at least 1 hour or up to 2 days. Makes 1½ cups.

Caramelized Onion Jam
Pulse 1 cup caramelized onions, 2 tablespoons dark rum, 1 tablespoon brown sugar, 1 teaspoon minced fresh thyme, and ½ teaspoon cider vinegar in food processor to jamlike consistency, about 5 pulses. Season with salt and pepper to taste. Makes 1 cup. Spread on sandwiches or serve with cheese. (The jam can be refrigerated in airtight container for up to 7 days.)

All-Purpose Gravy

Makes 4 cups   **Cooking Time** 9 to 11 hours on Low or 5 to 7 hours on High

✔ WHY THIS RECIPE WORKS: Meat gravies usually require a base of meat juice and pan drippings left over from cooking a roast. But what if you want a batch of gravy for mashed potatoes or a few roast chicken breasts? Enter the slow cooker. However, we faced two major challenges: finding a way to build long-roasted flavor without a roast, and figuring out how to thicken the gravy without reducing it on the stove. To build flavor, we browned the aromatics and meat. This way, we were able to develop a deep fond, mimicking the flavor of a long roasted piece of meat. We chose ground meat over whole pieces so that our recipe would remain easy and versatile (beef and turkey both work well). Finally, a combination of chicken and beef broth yielded well-rounded flavor, and bay leaves, thyme, and peppercorns lent classic balance. To get the right texture, the key was cooking a thick roux in the skillet on top of the meat and vegetable drippings, then smoothing it out with some broth before adding it to the slow cooker. After straining, our final gravy emerged velvety and rich, perfect for serving with all types of meat and sides.

8	tablespoons (1 stick) unsalted butter
1	onion, minced
2	carrots, peeled and chopped fine
2	celery ribs, chopped fine
1	pound 85 percent lean ground beef or 93 percent lean ground turkey
¾	cup all-purpose flour
3	cups low-sodium chicken broth
3	cups beef broth
1	teaspoon minced fresh thyme or ¼ teaspoon dried
5	black peppercorns
2	bay leaves
	Salt and pepper

1. Melt 1 tablespoon butter in 12-inch skillet over medium-high heat. Add onion, carrots, and celery and cook until well browned, about 10 minutes. Stir in ground beef and cook, breaking it up with wooden spoon, until no longer pink, about 3 minutes; transfer to slow cooker.

2. Melt remaining 7 tablespoons butter in skillet over medium-high heat. Stir in flour and cook, stirring constantly, until thoroughly browned and fragrant, about 5 minutes. Slowly whisk in chicken broth, scraping up any browned bits and smoothing out any lumps; transfer to slow cooker.

3. Stir beef broth, thyme, peppercorns, and bay leaves into slow cooker. Cover and cook until gravy is deeply flavored and rich, 9 to 11 hours on low or 5 to 7 hours on high.

4. Let gravy settle for 5 minutes, then remove fat from surface using large spoon. Strain gravy through fine-mesh strainer, pressing on solids to extract as much gravy as possible. Season with salt and pepper to taste. (Gravy can be refrigerated in airtight container for up to 4 days or frozen for up to 2 months. Gently reheat gravy in microwave or saucepan over low heat, adding hot water as needed to adjust consistency.)

SMART SHOPPING FINE-MESH STRAINER
Having a good fine-mesh strainer can make all the difference between silky and lumpy gravy. We put five strainers, all about 6 inches in diameter, to the test through a series of sauces and puddings. While all five of the strainers officially passed the straining portion of our test with only minor textural differences, two of the strainers broke during our durability test, which was designed to replicate years of kitchen use. In the end, we found the **CIA Masters Collection 6¾-Inch Fine Mesh Strainer** produced the smoothest sauces and puddings, has a wide bowl rest so it sits securely over medium and large bowls, and was as good as new after our durability test.

Chicken Broth

Makes 3 quarts   **Cooking Time** 6 to 8 hours on Low or 3 to 5 hours on High

✔ **WHY THIS RECIPE WORKS:** Chicken broth is one of the most versatile and often-used ingredients in any kitchen. But while making a successful broth on the stovetop can be a tedious task, an equally tasty slow-cooker version is a breeze. To make our broth, we wanted to be able to toss a few ingredients in the slow cooker, turn the device on for several hours, and end up with all of the depth and clarity of a long-attended broth. Searching for a broth with unadulterated chicken flavor, we tested many combinations of chicken parts, finding a whole cut-up chicken too fussy and chicken backs, legs, and necks too liver-y. Chicken wings were the surprise winner—the resulting broth was remarkably clear and refined and the long simmering time had eked out every last bit of flavor from the chicken bones. Additionally, we found that an onion, a little garlic, and some salt were all we needed to complement, and not distract from, the chicken. Finally, we found that a longer cooking time only yielded a better broth up to a point. After about 8 hours on low or 5 hours on high, we could no longer taste improvement—the meat and bones were spent.

3 **pounds whole chicken wings**
3 **quarts water**
1 **onion, chopped medium**
3 **garlic cloves, peeled and crushed**
1 **teaspoon salt**

1. Combine all ingredients in slow cooker. Cover and cook until broth is deeply flavored and rich, 6 to 8 hours on low or 3 to 5 hours on high.

2. Strain broth through fine-mesh strainer, then defat (see page 311). (Broth can be refrigerated in airtight container for up to 4 days or frozen for up to 2 months; see page 312 for information on freezing broth.)

Roasted Chicken Broth

Makes 3 quarts   **Cooking Time** 6 to 8 hours on Low or 3 to 5 hours on High

✔ **WHY THIS RECIPE WORKS:** If you have extra time, this easy variation on our Chicken Broth has a dark color and pleasantly deep caramelized flavor; it is well suited to stews, gravies, and sauces.

3 **pounds whole chicken wings**
1 **onion, chopped medium**
3 **quarts water**
3 **garlic cloves, peeled and crushed**
1 **teaspoon salt**

1. Adjust oven rack to lower-middle position and heat oven to 450 degrees. Roast chicken and onion in large nonstick roasting pan until golden, about 40 minutes; transfer to slow cooker.

2. Stir water, garlic, and salt into slow cooker. Cover and cook until broth is deeply flavored and rich, 6 to 8 hours on low or 3 to 5 hours on high.

3. Strain broth through fine-mesh strainer, then defat (see page 311). (Broth can be refrigerated in airtight container for up to 4 days or frozen for up to 2 months; see page 312 for information on freezing broth.

Rich Beef Broth

Makes 3 quarts   **Cooking Time** 4 to 6 hours on Low

✔ WHY THIS RECIPE WORKS: Rich, deep, beef broth is a must-have in any cook's kitchen, and with the help of the slow cooker, it can be whipped up with ease. Hoping to avoid the work involved in cutting up beef chuck or dealing with beef bones, we turned to ground beef since we had had success in the past using it as the foundation for a quicker beef broth—its increased surface area enables more beef flavor to be absorbed by the liquid. For additional meaty undertones, we included a full pound of white mushrooms, which we sautéed with onions and tomato paste before browning the beef and soy sauce (both tomato paste and soy sauce add depth of flavor without calling attention to themselves). Finally, we discovered that the broth needed to cook on low heat, and only for a relatively short period of time (4 to 6 hours on low). Any longer (or higher) and the mushroom flavor took over and the broth became cloudy. To round out our broth, we added red wine for color and acidity, and an onion, carrot, and celery rib for sweetness.

1	tablespoon vegetable oil
1	pound white mushrooms, trimmed and quartered
1	onion, chopped medium
3	tablespoons tomato paste
	Salt
1½	pounds 85 percent lean ground beef
¾	cup dry red wine
3	quarts water
1	carrot, peeled and chopped medium
1	celery rib, chopped medium
2	tablespoons soy sauce
3	bay leaves

1. Heat oil in 12-inch skillet over medium-high heat until shimmering. Add mushrooms, onion, tomato paste, and ¼ teaspoon salt, cover, and cook until mushrooms are softened, 5 to 10 minutes. Uncover and continue to cook until mushrooms are dry and browned, 5 to 10 minutes.

2. Stir in ground beef and cook, breaking up any large pieces with wooden spoon until no longer pink, about 3 minutes. Stir in red wine, scraping up any browned bits, and simmer until nearly evaporated, about 2 minutes; transfer to slow cooker.

3. Stir water, carrot, celery, soy sauce, bay leaves, and 1 teaspoon salt into slow cooker. Cover and cook until broth is deeply flavored and rich, 4 to 6 hours on low.

4. Strain broth through fine-mesh strainer, then defat. (Broth can be refrigerated in airtight container for up to 4 days or frozen for up to 2 months; see page 312 for information on freezing broth.)

QUICK PREP TIP DEFATTING BROTHS
Defatting a broth is important or else it will add unwelcome grease and fat to your finished dishes. If you do not own a fat separator, simply give the strained broth 10 minutes to settle, then use a large flat spoon to skim the fat off the top. Be sure to hold the spoon parallel to the surface of the soup; you want to collect as little broth as possible.

Vegetable Broth

Makes 3 quarts   **Cooking Time** 9 to 11 hours on Low or 5 to 7 hours on High

✔ WHY THIS RECIPE WORKS: Vegetable broth is essential to full-flavored vegetarian cooking, enhancing meat-free dishes with clean vegetal flavor. It needs gentle cooking and the slow cooker is the perfect medium in which to bring out the subtlety of many types of vegetables. We knew that in order to create a balanced intensely flavored broth we needed a precise mix of ingredients. First, we found that a base of onions, scallions, carrots, and celery along with a generous dose of garlic provided a strong background to the broth that was neither too vegetal nor too sweet. The addition of half a head of cauliflower, cut into florets and added with the water, gave our broth pleasant earthiness and nuttiness. Finally, a single tomato added acidic balance, and thyme, bay leaves, and peppercorns rounded out the flavors. To cook our broth, we initially wanted to be able to dump all the vegetables into the cooker raw, but we found that we needed the additional flavor developed from browning the aromatics. We chose a longer cooking time than our meat-based broths so that the flavor of all the different vegetables could shine through. To prevent the broth from looking cloudy, do not press on the solids when straining.

1	tablespoon extra-virgin olive oil
3	onions, chopped medium
4	scallions, chopped medium
2	carrots, peeled and chopped medium
2	celery ribs, chopped medium
15	garlic cloves, peeled and crushed
3	quarts water
½	head cauliflower (1 pound), cored and cut into 1-inch florets (3 cups) (see page 25)
1	plum tomato, cored and chopped medium
8	fresh thyme sprigs
1½	teaspoons salt
1	teaspoon black peppercorns
3	bay leaves

1. Heat oil in 12-inch skillet over medium-high heat until shimmering. Add onions, scallions, carrots, celery, and garlic and cook until vegetables are softened and lightly browned, 8 to 10 minutes. Stir in 1 cup water, scraping up any browned bits; transfer to slow cooker.

2. Stir remaining 11 cups water, cauliflower, tomato, thyme sprigs, salt, peppercorns, and bay leaves into slow cooker. Cover and cook until broth is deeply flavored and rich, 9 to 11 hours on low or 5 to 7 hours on high.

3. Strain broth through fine-mesh strainer without pressing on solids. (Broth can be refrigerated in airtight container for up to 4 days or frozen for up to 2 months.)

QUICK PREP TIP FREEZING BROTH
Broth can be refrigerated in an airtight container for up to 4 days or frozen for up to 2 months. When freezing broth, we like to portion it into either a nonstick muffin tin or freezer-safe zipper-lock bags. To release frozen broth from a muffin tin, simply twist the tin as you would an ice-cube tray; once frozen, the blocks of broth can be stored more efficiently in a zipper-lock bag. If portioning the broth directly into zipper-lock bags, use a 4-cup liquid measure (or a large yogurt container) to support the bag and hold it open while filling it; the bags of broth can be laid flat in the freezer to save space.

Index

NOTE: Page references in *italics* refer to photographs.